The Concordia Pulpit

for 1981

Publishing House
St. Louis

Concordia Publishing House, St. Louis, Missouri
Copyright © 1980 Concordia Publishing House
ISBN 0-570-06748-0

MANUFACTURED IN THE UNITED STATES OF AMERICA

CONTRIBUTORS

David M. Albertin
Troy, IL

Richard E. Bauerle
Sandusky, OH

Hubert F. Beck
College Station, TX

George H. Beiderweiden Jr.
Decatur, IL

Jack Breznen
Stamford, CT

Hans F. Bruss
Milwaukee, WI

Arthur H. Drevlow
St. James, MI

Paul J. Foust
Ypsilanti, MI

Ronald H. Goodsman
Des Moines, IA

Rudolph A. Haak
Anoka, MN

L. Dean Hempelmann
St. Louis, MO

William J. Hughes
Arlington Heights, IL

Richard G. Kapfer
Ames, IA

Arthur O. Kaul
Tell City, IN

Erwin J. Kolb
Troy, IL

Robert A. Kolb
St. Paul, MN

Robert R. Krueger
Platte Woods, MO

Arnold F. Krugler
Jacksonville, IL

Bruce J. Lieske
Fond du Lac, WI

Elmer W. Matthias
Chesterfield, MO

Norbert H. Mueller
Fort Wayne, IN

Richard P. Musser
Elm Grove, WI

Elmer A. Neitzel
Milwaukee, WI

Rudolph F. Norden
St. Louis, MO

Donald J. Poganski
San Luis Obispo, CA

Weldon L. Priebe
St. Paul, MI

Eldor W. Richter
Clinton, IA

John W. Saleska
Fort Wayne, IN

Martin H. Scharlemann
St. Louis, MO

Alfred T. Scheips
Ann Arbor, MI

Theodore W. Schroeder
Mehlville, MO

Henry A. Simon
Belleville, IL

Henry E. Simon
Wausau, WI

Rupert A. St. Pierre
Farmington Hills, MI

B. Dale Thomas
Utica, MI

Jaroslav J. Vajda
St. Louis, MO

Richard H. Warneck
Manchester, MO

Lester A. Wolf
Winston Salem, NC

TEXTS, THEMES, AND AUTHORS

Sermons for the Church Year
Based on the Epistle Lessons, Series A,
of the Three-Year Lectionary

First Sunday in Advent   Romans 13:11-14
Building an Advent Ark—Richard G. Kapfer 3

Second Sunday in Advent   Romans 15:4-13
Advent Hope Is Advent Power—Richard G. Kapfer 7

Third Sunday in Advent   James 5:7-10
Are You Expecting—or Just Waiting?—Hubert F. Beck 12

Fourth Sunday in Advent   Romans 1:1-7
The Gift of Life—Hubert F. Beck 17

The Nativity of Our Lord (Christmas Day)   Titus 2:11-14
The Grace of God Has Dawned—L. Dean Hempelmann 23

First Sunday After Christmas   Galatians 4:4-7
Adoption Accomplished—Martin H. Scharlemann 27

Second Sunday After Christmas   Ephesians 1:3-6, 15-18
You Are the Church—Rupert A. St. Pierre 32

The Epiphany of Our Lord   Ephesians 3:2-12
A World of Confidence—Rupert A. St. Pierre 37

First Sunday After the Epiphany   Acts 10:34-38
God Has No Favorites—William J. Hughes 41

Second Sunday After the Epiphany   1 Corinthians 1:1-9
Called to Be Saints—William J. Hughes 45

Third Sunday After the Epiphany   1 Corinthians 1:10-17
The Healing Power of the Gospel—Donald J. Poganski 49

Fourth Sunday After the Epiphany   1 Corinthians 1:26-31
Your Life in Christ—Donald J. Poganski 55

Fifth Sunday After the Epiphany   1 Corinthians 2:1-5
Wisdom of the Creator—Alfred T. Scheips 61

Sixth Sunday After the Epiphany   1 Corinthians 2:6-13
Wisdom of the Creature—Alfred T. Scheips 66

Seventh Sunday After the Epiphany   1 Corinthians 3:10-11, 16-23
The Continued Construction of Christ's Church—
    Rudolph F. Norden 71

The Transfiguration of Our Lord   2 Peter 1:16-21
Peter's Remembrance of the Transfiguration—Rudolph F. Norden . 77

Ash Wednesday   2 Corinthians 5:20b—6:2
From Enemies into Friends—Jaroslav J. Vajda 83

First Sunday in Lent   Romans 5:12, 17-19
The One and Only—Theodore W. Schroeder 88

Second Sunday in Lent   Romans 4:1-5, 13-17
The Ever-Recurring Question—Weldon L. Priebe 93

Third Sunday in Lent   Ephesians 5:8-14
The Call of the Cross—Richard P. Musser 97

Fourth Sunday in Lent   Romans 8:1-10
  The Dynamics of Salvation—Richard P. Musser 101

Fifth Sunday in Lent   Romans 8:11-19
  On the Way to Real Living—Elmer A. Neitzel 105

Sunday of the Passion   Philippians 2:5-11
  Palm Sunday and the Drama of Holy Week—Elmer A. Neitzel 110

Maundy Thursday   1 Corinthians 11:23-26
  It's Time to Remember—Erwin J. Kolb 115

Good Friday   Hebrews 4:14-16; 5:7-9
  Today in Gethsemane—Richard G. Kapfer 120

The Resurrection of Our Lord (Easter Day)   Colossians 3:1-4
  New Clothes for the Easter Parade—Jaroslav J. Vajda 123

Second Sunday of Easter   1 Peter 1:3-9
  The Christian's Hope a Living Hope—Hans F. Bruss 128

Third Sunday of Easter   1 Peter 1:17-21
  The Greatness of Our Redeemer's Work as Impelling Motive 133
     for Christian Living—Hans F. Bruss

Fourth Sunday of Easter   1 Peter 2:19-25
  The Straying Sheep Returned to the Shepherd—Norbert H. Mueller 137

Fifth Sunday of Easter   1 Peter 2:4-10
  God Calls Us His Church—Norbert H. Mueller 141

Sixth Sunday of Easter   1 Peter 3:15-22
  Where There's Hope, There's Life—Henry A. Simon 145

The Ascension of Our Lord   Ephesians 1:16-23
  Living Under Our Ascended Lord!—Henry E. Simon 150

Seventh Sunday of Easter   1 Peter 4:12-17; 5:6-11
  Come Down out of the Grandstand—George H. Beiderwieden Jr.... 153

The Day of Pentecost   Acts 2:1-21
  Words! Words! Words!—George H. Beiderwieden Jr. 157

The Holy Trinity   2 Corinthians 13:11-14
First Sunday After Pentecost
  What More Can You Ask?—Arthur O. Kaul 163

Second Sunday After Pentecost   Romans 3:21-25a, 27-28
  God's Plan Better than Man's Plan—Arthur O. Kaul 167

Third Sunday After Pentecost   Romans 4:18-25
  How Can I Be Right with God?—Eldor W. Richter 172

Fourth Sunday After Pentecost   Romans 5:6-11
  The Greatness of God's Love for Sinners—Eldor W. Richter 176

Fifth Sunday After Pentecost   Romans 5:12-15
  Possibility Living—Richard H. Warneck 180

Sixth Sunday After Pentecost   Romans 6:1-11
  Christians Alive—Richard H. Warneck 185

Seventh Sunday After Pentecost   Romans 7:15-25a
  Christ Will Deliver Me—Rudolph A. Haak 189

Eighth Sunday After Pentecost   Romans 8:18-25
  Groanings on Tiptoe—Rudolph A. Haak 193

Ninth Sunday After Pentecost   Romans 8:26-27
  When We Think We Can't Pray—Jack Breznen 198

Tenth Sunday After Pentecost   Romans 8:28-30
Those Who Love God—Jack Breznen 203

Eleventh Sunday After Pentecost   Romans 8:35-39
Your Loan Is Guaranteed! Go Ahead with the Building!—
Robert R. Krueger 208

Twelfth Sunday After Pentecost   Romans 9:1-5
Don't Think of Praying a "Crazy" Prayer—Robert R. Krueger 212

Thirteenth Sunday After Pentecost   Romans 11:13-15, 29-32
A Special Word to Gentiles About Jews—Bruce J. Lieske 217

Fourteenth Sunday After Pentecost   Romans 11:33-36
Let God Be God—Bruce J. Lieske 221

Fifteenth Sunday After Pentecost   Romans 12:1-8
Your Body Life Is in the Body of Christ—Elmer W. Matthias 226

Sixteenth Sunday After Pentecost   Romans 13:1-10
The Christian and the State—Elmer W. Matthias 231

Seventeenth Sunday After Pentecost   Romans 14:5-9
Through Death, Christ Is Owner and Lord of Everything—
John W. Saleska 237

Eighteenth Sunday After Pentecost   Philippians 1:1-5, 19-27
"Christ" Means to Be Alive, Free, and Together—John W. Saleska . 243

Nineteenth Sunday After Pentecost   Philippians 2:1-5 (6-11)
A Better Way—the Way of Humility—Paul J. Foust 248

Twentieth Sunday After Pentecost   Philippians 3:12-21
Citizens for Heaven—Paul J. Foust 253

Twenty-First Sunday After Pentecost   Philippians 4:4-13
A Life of Consistent Joy—Arnold F. Krugler 258

Twenty-Second Sunday After Pentecost   1 Thessalonians 1:1-5a
Loved by God—Arnold F. Krugler 261

Twenty-Third Sunday After Pentecost   1 Thessalonians 1:5b-10
A Sermon to the Faithful—Richard Bauerle 264

Last Sunday After Pentecost   1 Corinthians 15:20-28
Christ the King
That Last Enemy—Richard Bauerle 269

Sermons for Special Occasions

Reformation Sunday   Hebrews 2:14-15
In Flesh and Blood God Destroys Death—Robert Kolb 277

Thanksgiving Day   Philippians 4:6-20
Can November 26 Really Be Thanksgiving Day?—Lester A. Wolf.. 281

Confirmation Day   Luke 16:19-31
Faith—a Study in Contrast—Ronald H. Goodsman 286

One Hundredth Anniversary   Acts 20:32
Be to Him Commended—Arthur H. Drevlow 291

Wedding   Song of Solomon 8:7
The Finest Song Ever Sung—David M. Albertin 295

Funeral   Genesis 5:24
God Took Him—B. Dale Thomas 299

INDEX OF SCRIPTURE TEXTS

	Page
Gen. 5:24	299
Song of Sol. 8:7	295
Luke 16:19-31	286
Acts 2:1-21	157
Acts 10:34-38	41
Acts 20:32	291
Rom. 1:1-7	17
Rom. 3:21-25a, 27-28	167
Rom. 4:1-5, 13-17	93
Rom. 4:18-25	172
Rom. 5:6-11	176
Rom. 5:12-15	180
Rom. 5:12, 17-19	88
Rom. 6:1-11	185
Rom. 7:15-25a	189
Rom. 8:1-10	101
Rom. 8:11-19	105
Rom. 8:18-25	193
Rom. 8:26-27	198
Rom. 8:28-30	203
Rom. 8:35-39	208
Rom. 9:1-5	212
Rom. 11:13-15, 29-32	217
Rom. 11:33-36	221
Rom. 12:1-8	226
Rom. 13:1-10	231
Rom. 13:11-14	3
Rom. 14:5-9	237
Rom. 15:4-13	7
1 Cor. 1:1-9	45
1 Cor. 1:10-17	49
1 Cor. 1:26-31	55
1 Cor. 2:1-5	61

	Page
1 Cor. 2:6-13	66
1 Cor. 3:10-11, 16-23	71
1 Cor. 11:17-32 or	
1 Cor. 11:23-26	115
1 Cor. 15:20-28	269
2 Cor. 5:20b—6:2	83
2 Cor. 13:11-14	163
Gal. 4:4-7	27
Eph. 1:3-6, 15-18	32
Eph. 1:16-23	150
Eph. 3:2-12	37
Eph. 5:8-14	97
Phil. 1:1-5, 19-27	243
Phil. 2:1-5 (6-11)	248
Phil. 2:5-11	110
Phil. 3:12-21	253
Phil. 4.4-13	258
Phil. 4:6-20	281
Col. 3:1-4	123
1 Thess. 1:1-5a	261
1 Thess. 1:5b-10	264
Titus 2:11-14	23
Heb. 2:14-15	277
Heb. 4:14-16; 5:7-9	120
James 5:7-10	12
1 Peter 1:3-9	128
1 Peter 1:17-21	133
1 Peter 2:4-10	141
1 Peter 2:19-25	137
1 Peter 3:15-22	145
1 Peter 4:12-17; 5:6-11	153
2 Peter 1:16-21	77

Sermons on the Epistle Lessons, Series A
Three-Year Lectionary

Building an Advent Ark

FIRST SUNDAY IN ADVENT
ROMANS 13:11-14

Richard G. Kapfer

In any brief period of time the lives of people can change dramatically and deeply. The events causing these changes are often so great that people often ask, "What was it like before those events took place?" What was it like, for example, in early September of 1929, a few days before the stock market crashed and the great depression began? What was it like on December 6, 1941, the day before the bombing of Pearl Harbor and our nation's involvement in World War II? Our children are going to be asking us, I am sure, what it was like in early 1974 prior to the oil embargo and the chain of events that have brought us to where we are today. They'll be asking what it was like to have cheap energy and a seemingly unlimited supply.

Are we today heading for some history-making event that will be a reference point for generations to come? Are we heading for an event about which our children and grandchildren will ask, "What was it like in the days before that event took place?" We do not know the answer to that question, of course. Yet in a sense we are living in those days that precede an event we know is going to happen. That event is the second coming of Christ. The same Lord who made His advent into our world in the birth of our Savior and who made His advent into our hearts by faith is going to come again in judgment and bring this world to a close. In fact, the One who will bring this age to a close is the One who says in today's Gospel: "As were the days of Noah, so will be the coming of the Son of Man." We are living in those "Noah days."

"In those days before the flood," said Jesus, "they were eating and drinking, marrying and giving in marriage, until the day when Noah entered the ark" (Matt. 24:38). Life for the people in Noah's time went on in its usual way. The only difference was that there was a man out beyond the city limits who was building an ark. The blows from Noah's mallet sounded into the night, and people could hear those mallet blows. Then one day they ceased, the rains came, the world was faced with a deluge, and that age ended.

"So will be the coming of the Son of Man," said Jesus. That is the thrust of today's Gospel lesson. it calls us to be ready, because ready or not here God comes! The coming of Jesus is a matter of holy concern and genuine waiting. Or it is a matter of unholy unconcern and of ignoring the hammer blows in the night.

"Just as in the days of Noah." What were those days like? What is it like to be an ark-builder, building an ark and then waiting on God? Our text for today from St. Paul's Epistle to the Romans tells us of that.

Ark Building Calls for Vision

For the people of Noah's time life went on as usual. They were "eating and drinking, marrying and giving in marriage." The sweep of God's history and of His judgment and of His warnings were being ignored. The sounding blows were heard on their eardrums but not in their hearts. The raindrops that began to fall were not felt. They were too busy building their own kingdoms. What mattered was themselves. They were living in the sin of spiritual unconcern. God was excluded. The people lacked vision.

But not the ark-builder. God had called him and had spoken to him of rain and water, flood and destruction, of an end-time. The ark-builder lived with a sense of being *in* the world, but not *of* the world. The kingdoms that people build become meaningless when God's kingdom surges in and an ark must be built. An ark-builder must have a sense of detachment, of living in the tentative. Insurance policies, mortgages, layoffs from work, experiments bubbling in the laboratory, studies winding down toward final examinations, political elections, are all viewed from the perspective of the ark. All of these are important, but all of these are by no means of ultimate importance—not when you're building an ark!

The apostle Paul is telling us in today's Epistle that you and I are ark-builders. We are living in the "days before." Thus, St. Paul writes: "Besides this you know what hour it is, how it is full time now for you to wake from sleep. For salvation is nearer to us now than when we first believed; the night is far gone, the day is at hand" (Rom. 13:11-12a). Our text is telling us to wake up. St. Paul heard those blows in the night. He felt the world tensing for the final deluge. St. Paul was both wrong and right. He was wrong about its imminence, for the world has gone on for hundreds of years since Paul's time. Yet St. Paul was right about the nearness of the end. Each day brings us closer to the time when our Lord will be calling an end to all of human history. That day is closer to us now than it was at the time of St. Paul, and we do not know when it will come, but we are assured by our God that it will come. In terms of human history, we live in the day of the final day.

Because of this, God through our text calls us to have the vision of the ark-builder. The Lord is coming soon, and we are to live like people who know that. The vision of ark-building focuses on God's other, greater sign: "In the fullness of time, God sent forth His Son"

(Gal. 4:4). The vision of the Christian ark-builder is focused first at a manger in Bethlehem. God promised to come. He did! That is the first focus of our Advent preparation. God promises to come again. He will! That is the vision of the ark-builder. We as God's ark-builders are really "tween-agers." We live in between the coming of our Lord Jesus to Bethlehem and the coming of our Lord Jesus at the end of time.

Ark Building Calls for Practice

Did Noah and his family practice loading the ark? Did they determine ahead of time where they would stow the food and where they would place the animals and how they would live for days and months? Did Noah practice seamanship even though he had to practice it on dry land? Did people come to mock him? Probably he did all of these things, and probably the people did mock. An ark seems irrelevant and foolish on dry land. The worship of the God who commands the building of an ark on dry land seems even more foolish. Especially if it's not raining. Especially if you're building your own kingdom. Especially if you don't believe in the God who commands that arks be built.

What kind of life did Noah live? Did he have a job during the day and work on the ark at night? He must have been quite an employee! Was he trusted? Did Noah run for political office? Did he stand a chance of winning if he ran on a platform of ark building? Was Noah different because of the ark? I suspect so. Arks make people different, especially when it's God's ark they're working on.

Our text addresses us as New Testament ark-builders with the words: "Let us then cast off the works of darkness and put on the armor of light" (Rom. 13:12b). These words are calling God's ark-builders to be practicing constantly, to always be in readiness for the time of the ark. Our text is calling us not to put on the galoshes of timid religion, rubber boots that are easily slipped off when convenient. Our text is calling us not to put on waders that cover all but the head—an intellectual religion and moral neutrality that won't mix with ark building. Rather, our text calls us to "take the whole armor of God," the whole armor that St. Paul described in his letter to the Ephesians. Here he calls this armor the "armor of light." God is calling us to get dressed in light, which represents the full knowledge of our calling to be the people of God. To be dressed in light is to be dressed in the clothing of an ark-builder. We are called to be always practicing for the Big Day—"not in reveling and drunkenness, not in debauchery and licentiousness" (Rom. 13:13). To live that way is to live in darkness. That's dry-land living.

These sins of darkness that St. Paul has mentioned were especially Roman sins of the upper class that were often aped by the lower classes. A lot of Christians were apparently patterning themselves after this. There was a great need among the Christians at Rome for John the Baptizer's message from the wilderness: "Prepare! Prepare ye! Christ is coming soon!" There was a great deal of need for true repentance based on clear vision and the necessity to watch the signs of clouds and rain and water. The Roman Christians were in danger of getting out of practice as God's ark-builders.

In many ways the Sacrament of Holy Communion, in addition to the many other great blessings that it bestows upon us, is one way that we practice as God's ark-builders. Holy Communion is the way that we Christians get ready for that great banquet. It is practice for the heavenly praise and fellowship that we shall enjoy. It is practice for the prayers that we shall speak in heaven for all eternity. It is practice for the time when nothing else matters except to be at the banquet in the presence of our God.

There is a lot of need today among us to practice in the sunlight of the ark rather than in the gloom of this world's glittering but dead kingdoms. "As in the days of Noah," right?

Ark Building Calls for Commitment

Life must have been hard for Noah the ark-builder. Building an ark is hard work. It must have been hard emotionally on Noah's wife and children. They must have had to do without many things. They must have suffered intense ridicule. The other people around them were "getting ahead," while they were always falling behind financially. And spiritually, they had only the Word of God to go on. Was it enough? It ought to be. But it must have seemed so weird, so impossible, even so bizarre. But Noah persisted, and when the rains came, he was ready.

There are a lot of reasons for us not to be ark-builders. Intellectually, economically, socially it would be a lot easier not to be a follower of our Lord of Advent. But the ark-builder has the command of the Lord, His sure and certain Word: "But put on the Lord Jesus Christ, and make no provision for the flesh, to gratify its desires" (Rom. 13:14). The clear Word of God calls for a clear response—either yes or no, with no "Maybe" or "I will if...." "Make no provision for the flesh"—for sin—for it won't fit on the ark.

But faith will! That's the intended meaning of the words, "But put on Christ." Noah "put on" the promises of God, and everything else in life revolved around those promises. God was committed to him, so everything else in Noah's life flowed from that commitment. That's what compelled him to devote his energies to ark building.

Advent reminds us of God's loving commitment to us. He came in Jesus Christ to live among the this-world kingdom builders.

Eventually He mounted the wood of God's special ark—the cross—and was swept under by the waves fo sin. Now He comes to us as our risen and ascended Lord to place on us our Advent-Christmas wrapping of forgiveness. By faith we "put on Christ" and, like Noah, we find that everything else in life revolves around God's commitment of love. In response to that commitment, we receive the power to pick up the mallet of faith and to build the ark of the Christian life. Everything else in life flows from that. Then, as God's ark-builders, we are ready for the coming of the Son of Man. Each impressing blow of the growing Christian life is like the countdown toward the end of time and the beginning of eternity.

We Are His Ark-Builders

In this Advent season the God of all history calls us into His story and unites Himself with us to make of us His ark-buiders. This ark building calls for the vision to see the One who calls us to faithful ark building. This vision calls for us as God's ark-builders to be always in practice, always ready for His second coming. This vision calls us as God's ark-builders to that commitment that is focused on the One who was promised, who came, and who shall come again. As God renews in us that vision, that desire for practice, and that commitment, we become ark-builders every day, ready to bounce above the waters at any time. He makes us ready for the end-time that will usher in the time that has no end. And then we'll be ready for the Lord to take us to the new land under the permanent rainbow of God's peace that is secured by the Prince of Peace whose Advent we hail.

Advent Hope Is Advent Power

SECOND SUNDAY IN ADVENT
ROMANS 15:4-13

Richard G. Kapfer

On this Second Sunday in Advent we move one step closer to the threshold of the stable where our Savior will soon be born again in our hearts. This is a season of repentance. It is a time when we examine our lives in order to expose all of those sins and short-comings that stand between us and the manger where our Savior is to be laid. We would come to the manger with hearts that are thoroughly ready to sing His praises and to receive every blessing that He would pour out upon us.

It would indeed be wonderful if we could come to Christmas Eve this year with every sin that keeps nagging at us conquered, every problem that weighs us down totally resolved, and every difficulty that bogs down our hearts removed and taken away. It would be wonderful if Christmas could be that kind of new start wherein everything begins fresh and new and clean again, just like the birth of a baby. If we are realistic, though, we know that this is not necesarily going to happen. The problems, difficulties, sorrows, and nagging sins that may be with us this morning could still be with us after Christmas has passed.

Yet on Christmas Eve we'll all join in singing, "The hopes and fears of all the years *are met* in Thee tonight." In a powerful way, and in spite of our failings, our hopes and fears really *are* met in the Lord Jesus Christ at His birth. This is called Christian hope—the belief that things can become something new even though that hasn't happened yet.

This sounds strange. Do you mean, preacher, that even if my problems are not resolved, I can live as though they are because they will be? Precisely! What about the tensions in my relationship—in my home, marriage, family, work? Do you mean that I can live as though they have been overcome, that peace has come, love has come—even though neither one has, but they will? Precisely! What about the weaknesses and failures that still accompany me as I move toward the manger this morning? Do you mean I should live as though they have been overcome because they will be? Precisely!

That is what is called Christian hope. That is the Advent hope that is Advent power.

I. Advent Hope for a Hopeless Situation

It is about that kind of Christian hope that St. Paul is writing to the Roman Christians in our text for this morning. The Book of Romans is one of the most powerful messages in all of Scripture. It speaks about the utter sinfulness and helplessness of humankind. It makes emphatically clear God's answer for sin, that while we were *yet sinners* Christ died for us, the Righteous One for the unrighteous. The event at Bethlehem is the beginning of God's great action in coming to this earth *in person* in the person of Jesus Christ for sinners in order that we might have eternal life.

A Hopeless Situation?

The Christians at Rome, we can be sure, believed the Good News of God's love for them, just as we do this day. But things were not automatically perfect for them. In the preceding chapter St. Paul had addressed a problem that had separated these people from each other. They were believers, but they weren't getting along with each other. And the problem seems pretty petty to us today. They were arguing about diets and days!

The Jewish Christians observed one day as the proper day of worship, the Gentile Christians another. Still others said that every day ought to be a day of worship, and one can imagine that as they said this they had a very self-righteous smile on their faces. Further, some of the Christians at Rome were vegetarians and some were meat eaters, and this was tied in with eating foods that their heathen neighbors had sacrificed to idols.

Each group was right and wrong about days and diets, for they didn't understand Christian liberty. They didn't understand being sensitive to the conscience of weaker Christians. They didn't understand that God reads the heart of faith, not the religious diet or day.

St. Paul's Unusual Approach

St. Paul did an interesting thing about these arguing factions. He wrote to them about dropping their differences and "with one voice" (v. 6) praising God. Then he told them to "accept one another" (v. 7). Then he reminded them of God's faithfulness by citing various prophecies concerning Jews and Gentiles in verses 9 through 12. Now, that's not so unusual. It seems to fit St. Paul's concerns for their divisions. What *is* unusual is that he *framed* this plea for unity with Christian *hope* in verse 4 and verse 13, the opening and closing verses of our text. St. Paul wrote in verse 4: "For whatever was written in former days was written for our instruction, that by steadfastness and by the encouragement of the Scriptures we might have *hope*." He ended this section with the words: "May the God of *hope* fill you with all joy and peace in believing so that by the power of the Holy Spirit you may abound in *hope*."

The Roman Christians *weren't* praising God with one voice. They were arguing with each other. They *weren't* accepting each other. They were shunning and condemning each other. The situation seemed hopeless. Yet St. Paul spoke to them *as though* the problem *was resolved already* and they *could* praise God with one voice and *could* accept each other.

St. Paul, then, was writing about Christian hope, not the kind of hope expressed in the words, "I hope you Christians at Rome get along with each other," but rather, "Live like you *are* getting along right now!" That is Christian hope!

II. Advent Hope for Our "Hopeless" Situations

Have you ever had a problem so pressing that it was all that you thought about day and night? When you went to sleep, you slept not to get rest but from exhaustion. When you awoke in the morning, the problem returned with a rush to the pit of your stomach. You came to church, but you could not hear the sermon. You could not pray. You could only think about the problem, until you lost hope of it ever being resolved. Have you ever had problems with people that never seemed to get resolved and that made you want to give up on them or on yourself? To give up, to act and live as though things won't change, is to live without Christian hope. That is a form of unbelief, a lack of faith in the power and promises of God. It is not to believe the power of the Christmas event.

St. Paul's words seem to *ignore* your problems and to say emphatically: "May the God of steadfastness and encouragement grant you to live in such harmony with one another in accord with Christ Jesus, that together you may with one voice glorify the God and Father of our Lord Jesus Christ" (vs. 5, 6). How can *that* help you to resolve the problems *you* have and truly celebrate Christmas with a glad and joyful heart?

Have you ever gone to church angry? Have you ever come here bearing a hurt or a grudge and almost strangle on the words of worship? And did it seem to you that day that the sermon touched upon that one raw nerve, that one sin, grudge, or weakness, almost as though the preacher had read your mind or had inside information on your hidden life? To say that you can't forgive, to say that you can't be forgiven, to say that you are too weak or too sinful for God to work His mighty power in your life, is to live without Christian hope. And to live without Christian hope is a form of unbelief. It is not to believe the power of the Christmas event.

Again, St. Paul's words seem to *ignore* the problem and to say emphatically: "Welcome one another, therefore, as Christ has welcomed you, for the glory of God" (v. 7). How can *that* help you to resolve the problem *you* have before December 25th so that you can celebrate Christmas with a glad and joyful heart?

III. The Power of Christian Hope

The quotations from the Old Testament that St. Paul uses in our text go all the way back to Deuteronomy, the Psalms, and the prophets. All of these promises concerning the Gentiles joining the Jews in God's plan of salvation didn't happen until Christ came, hundreds of years later. God gave His promises, but that's all they had to go on. Looking back, the Roman Christians saw and we too can see how God carried out His plan through all those years; and we celebrate the fulfillment of His plan in the birth of Jesus Christ again this Christmas Eve. Yet the people who received these promises could not see what we see. All they could do was *hope*. To *hope* for them was to live *as though* the promises *would* come to pass. Those who believed and lived in those promises were the faithful people of Israel. Many of them did not believe and were not faithful. Yet that is what hope is, to believe the promises and live as though they have already come to pass even though they have not.

Perhaps you too can look back upon circumstances in your own lives when things were terribly dark and grim. Everything seemed to be hopeless. All that you could do was to cling to the promises of God. You could not read the future, but you could read the faithfulness of your God and hope on Him. Looking back, you can see the hand of God throughout those grim and dark circumstances, and you can praise God for having led you through that time into the present.

This week I received a letter from a young man who had been a member of my congregation a number of years ago. Cancer had taken his wife after just a few years of marriage, and he had been left with a two-year-old daughter. At that time things looked extremely grim and hopeless. All that we could do was to search the Scriptures and to trust in the promises of God. He was encouraged to live as though what was *not* happening *would* happen. He had to look beyond what his eyes saw and see his life through the eyes of faith. He had to hope in God, praise God, and accept the situation even though he couldn't and didn't want to. His letter this week told about a number of wonderful things that have happened to him recently. Looking back to that grim day years ago, he could express thanksgiving to God for all of His mercy and guidance and love. *Now* he can do this. *Then* he had to trust that today would eventually come. That is Christian hope.

For True Christmas Celebration

Your problems, sins, weaknesses, and sorrows may be with you yet this Christmas Eve when you stand at the manger, they may continue to plague you until next Christmas. That does not mean you are less of a Christian. That does not mean you cannot celebrate Christmas in all of its joy—not if you have Christian hope, hope in God's forgiveness which makes you clean every day, even if you don't always *feel* that way.

No Guarantees Except Hope

No one can pull down a movie screen, set up a projector, and tell you how your problems will be resolved. But the Bible does tell us to live *as though* the problems have been resolved, for through our faithful God they can and will be. That is Christian hope. To live *as though* the tensions in your life—in your family or marriage or work—will be overcome is to live in hope, trusting in God's power. To live *as though* the weaknesses and failures that still accompany you to the stable this Christmas Eve have been overcome is to live in hope, trusting in God's power.

To live in hope is to hope in God, who will not fail you and who will always come through on His promises. The event on Christmas Eve is evidence of God keeping His promises. The greater event on Good Friday when the Lord Jesus Christ died for all of your sins and cleansed you from everything that stands between you and your God and between you and other people is the guarantee of the hope in which you and I live. Christian hope focuses on that beautiful and wonderful love of God seen at the manger and at the cross. It is the guarantee when there are no other guarantees that can give us any hope at all.

Constant Hope and Life in Him

That is why we celebrate Christmas as an event for today and not merely as an event of long ago. The Christmas event tells us that the same Lord Jesus Christ who so faithfully loved us by becoming one of us and by being the One for us is still working His miracle of love. What *has* happened is that He has conquered sin and evil and spiritual death. What *is* happening is that He is *still* doing that. And that is our hope that makes no situation hopeless.

We can hope, even through tears, because the hopes and fears of all the years *are* met in Jesus Christ on that great Christmas night.

Therefore, "May the God of hope fill you with all joy and peace in believing, so that by the power of the Holy Spirit you may abound in hope."

Are You Expecting—or Just Waiting?

THIRD SUNDAY IN ADVENT
JAMES 5:7-10

Hubert F. Beck

Christmas is coming! Have you ever thought what a strange phrase this is? Christmas isn't really going anywhere! It is we who are going to Christmas. Christmas is not coming to us!

The phrase is appropriate because it describes the Christmas event so well. We did not come to God, but God came to us.

As a phrase describing the passage of time, however, it is typical of the way we speak. My birthday is coming. Her wedding is coming. The new year will soon be here. Much of our "time talk" goes like this.

There is a proper intuition at work in phrases like this, for much as we want to think of ourselves as the masters of time, it is time that ultimately masters us. Time comes and goes in spite of us, not because of us.

The question is not so much how we *master* time but how we *use* time—what we do as time comes to meet us and then rushes on by. How we deal with that depends on what we think time is bringing to us. For time brings forces to bear on us that we have no control over, whether we think we do or not.

The Nature of "Just Waiting"

Many people just wait out time. They have little expectation of time and harbor only a faint hope that time will not be too harsh on them. For them time is just something that happens, and the best one can do is to sort of fatalistically resign oneself to whatever time brings.

Time is hardly seen in terms of "preparation" by such a mind-set, for if one is not waiting for anything in particular, there is nothing to prepare for. How can one prepare for what you know nothing about? Time just passes.

This can raise considerable tension. There are many unknowns lying behind the future that can and will sweep in on mankind. To be sure, it is possible that something good may happen unexpectedly—"our ship may come in!" Good surprises are possible.

The possibilities of ill befalling us seem far better, though! There seems to be a sort of law about life, resembling the famous law of Murphy, that dictates something like this: "All things being equal, life will go downhill in a hurry." We can hardly bank our life on waiting for "our ship to come in." Better to keep fixing the leaks and hope it doesn't sink too soon! "Just waiting" is usually characterized more by anxiety than hope, for life has a way of getting out of hand all too easily.

In order to offset this threatening doom we set up myriads of minor goals and aims, hoping in this way to keep some order in our life, to maintain some direction, to exercise some semblance of control over matters that so often tend to spin dizzily out of control.

In the end, though, we know that all these short-term goals and anticipations are ultimately meaningless. They give us a measure of satisfaction in their coming and going, but when all is said and done, the only thing we are waiting for is death. Death rears its head over every project we undertake. It eventually claims us with our projects, and whatever meaning and direction they gave to our life is all washed out in the grave.

Whether we want to recognize it or not, then, to spend our life "just waiting" is eventually to be swallowed up in meaningless nothingness. The fabrication of our own little human devices to make us think otherwise is finally nothing more than a self-deceptive maneuver, for nothing withstands the onslaughts of that final time that comes to meet us.

In our text a word from the Lord changes everything that we have been talking about, though. "Establish your hearts, for the coming of the Lord is at hand."

The Nature of "Expecting"

One who knows the secret of the text is no longer "just waiting." Such a person is "expecting" someone in the future. Time is not just rushing senselessly by. It is bringing on its wings someone who can change all our restless waiting, all our anxious forebodings, all our fearful premonitions.

"Expecting" is very different from "just waiting."

Expecting is to wait with a definite anticipation of what is to come. It is more than just a hope or a wish dream. It is based on some realities rather than being grounded in illusionary idealism. Simple human examples illustrate what we mean:

Weddings, birthdays, Christmas and all such celebrations are days of expectation based on realities. They are not idealistic wishes that something would happen, but they are anticipations of or remembrances of very real events that are grounded in reality. To say that "Christmas is coming" is to set up "expectations" that are quite different from "just waiting."

Results of "Expecting"

A couple things that happen when we are expecting are quite different from what happens while we are just waiting.

One thing is that expecting keeps the anticipated event very clearly in mind. That one point of the oncoming future focuses all our attention and energy. To use the event around which the word "expecting" has taken on such meaning, we might say that expecting a child focuses all our attention and energy on the impending birth with all that implies. An upcoming wedding commands the whole direction of our life in planning and activity. Christmas, as we are all experiencing, does the same sort of thing. All attention is focused on what is coming, and all present activity is shaped by that event.

That is the frame of mind to which James calls us in this simple little phrase of the text, "Establish your hearts, for the coming of the Lord is at hand." Let your hearts and lives take their shape and form from this one overarching expectation, that Christ is imminently at hand.

The second thing that happens differently when we are expecting must be stated in paradoxical fashion: expecting takes things out of our hands at the same time that it puts everything into our hands.

When we expect something or someone, control over that event is removed from us. A mother who finds herself expecting a baby simply "lets nature take it course." She cannot hurry or slow up the development of the child. She can only moderately accommodate her discomfort as the child grows within her. Once the child is conceived, the expectation of the future is established.

So it is with all expectation. Christmas is like that, is it not? It will come on December 25 whether we are ready for it or not. We will get up one day in less than two weeks, and there it will be!

So it is with the coming of Christ referred to in the text. The only point of difference is that while we know the date of Christmas we do not know the date of Christ's return. Had we been in the shoes of those around Mary and Joseph, however, we would have known nothing more than that at a given date a child would be born. Little would we have dreamt of the earth-shaking nature of this birth. John the Baptizer speaks in something of these terms through his question in today's Gospel. Had the great thing really happened in Jesus, or were his expectations to look beyond this man to yet another? It was hard to tell!

Does this mean, then, that everything is taken out of our hands since certain events such as Christ's return are coming to us out of the future in such a way that we have no control over them? Hardly!

Paradoxically, it places everything into our hands! The fact that we cannot control death, for example, does not mean that we resort to "just waiting." Our expectation of death can put great meaning into life!

"Establish your hearts, for the coming of the Lord is at hand." Our expectation that Christ will return puts meaning into every moment leading up to that time.

Again Christmas can illustrate this. That Christmas is coming triggers great activity, does it not? You are not just waiting for Christmas. You are expecting Christmas, and that sets loose a great burst of baking and shopping and wrapping and preparations of all sort.

So it is with the expectation of Christ's return. We do not know just when he will return, so the focus of our activity is not on a time but an anticipated event. That makes our "preparation" a daily routine rather than a once-in-a-while kind of activity. Never knowing, we always prepare!

The Strain of "Expecting"

This puts something of a strain on life, of course. If ever you have expected friends who were on a trip and would drop in on you "sometime" in a given week and you were waiting on them day after day, you will know the strain this constant preparation accompanied by constant delay imposes.

It is so with Christ's return also! We must recognize that.

But this is the tension of not knowing *when* an event is to take place, which is far different from the tensions mentioned earlier of not knowing who or what was coming. We know who is coming, and we know that when he arrives all our waiting will have been worthwhile. So we wait expectantly.

Such "Expecting" Changes Everything

This expectation of Christ changes what we do and why we do it. We engage ourselves in doing what we would want Him to find us doing when He arrives. That is the one major guideline for Christian living! What do you think he wants to find yourself devoted to and busy with, given your situation, your gifts, your opportunities? Your answer to that question becomes the basic foundation of your life's values and actions.

This same expectation changes our reasons for doing things. If you expect Him to return in angry judgment over your works, your attitude and reasons for doing what you do will be quite different from what you will do if you expect Him to return in gracious forgiveness and acceptance of you as a person. It all depends on how you view His person, His suffering, His death, His resurrection. If the latter events were simply an act of human vengeance on a man who was envied for His popularity, then His return could be interpreted as a chance to "get even" with mankind. But if they were the way by which He mercifully gave Himself for our sins and opened for us the avenues to God's gracious heart of love, then we look forward to His return. For this is the fulfillment of a promise to come again to receive us into the new heavens and the new earth to which our first lesson for today so longingly looks with its visionary language. If that is our expectation, the reasons for what we do will be shaped and formed by the love that originated with God who has made His love flesh in the Christ of Bethlehem, the same who will return again.

Expecting with Patience

This expectation requires patience, as our text tells us. "Just waiting" leads to impatience and frustration; for it knows nothing of what it is waiting for, whether it has come or not; whether it is worth waiting for or not, whether it has meaning or not. "Expectations," however, while containing frustrations and tensions as we have spoken of, foster their own satisfactions and understand the meaning of "patience."

"Be patient, therefore, brethren, until the coming of the Lord." The farmer expecting rains ("the early and the late rain" refer to the two rainy seasons in Israel upon which the farmers depended) is held up as an example of this patience. Those rains could indeed be "expected" in the cycle of the seasons. One did not hurry them or call on them to come at will. One rather planted in anticipation of those times of rain. All life was geared to the expectations engendered by planting and harvesting, rain and sunshine.

The prophets are also held up as examples of such "patience." How they longed for the redeeming hand of the Lord to show itself. They suffered in the name of the Lord to show itself. They suffered in the name of the Lord as they attempted to clear the way for His coming through calls for repentance and renewal. We hear Jesus speak of John the Baptizer in just those terms in our Gospel for today. These men knew that God would reveal His merciful presence at some point, although they did not know just when. They were not men who "just waited," biding time in life with a hope against hope, wishful dreamers waiting for human idealism to be realized.

Quite the opposite, they were people of "expectation." They knew well that human idealism is only subject to futile frustration. The renewal of the world called for nothing short of divine intervention, and they knew that God would not fail in such intervention. *That* was their expectation, and their entire lives and hopes and activities were shaped by that.

"You also must be patient," we are admonished. That does not mean we should "just wait," nor does it direct us to human patience awaiting the realization of unrealistic human ideals.

It means that we are to be patient in our expectation, for we can be sure of this, "the coming of the Lord is at hand." He who has come is coming again. We can stake our lives on that—and expect Him to keep His promise.

This confidence, held in patience and with great intensity and certainty, will turn our lives inside out, for one who expects the coming of the Lord is no longer "just waiting," he is expecting something that calls for concentrated preparation!

The Gift of Life

FOURTH SUNDAY IN ADVENT
ROMANS 1:1-7

Hubert F. Beck

Is there a parent present with a child younger than ten who has not had to admonish the child to keep hands off the Christmas presents? The temptation is irresistible to feel presents under a

Christmas tree. Within fractions of an inch lie things wanted and hoped for, all hidden by a very thin layer of wrapping paper.

So near and yet so far. That's the way it is with presents wrapped and waiting for the moment of giving and receiving.

The Near Miss of Human Potential

That is how one might also describe the human scene. Wrapped in these layers of flesh we call our bodies there is so much potential for enriching the world. The possibilities of achieving love and harmony among mankind seem but a fraction of an inch away like a wrapped present.

This dream is the common theme of the Christmas cards we give and receive. This drive to actuate "peace on earth, good will to men" is spoken of and acted out in stories and commercials on radio and TV and written about in newspapers and magazines and Christmas classics.

This is, for that matter, a theme of the ages in every culture. Where does one find argument against the ideal of humans living together in harmony, for the mutual good of all? Every religion and culture and age of man has held this ideal. One need not celebrate Christmas in order to share these ideals of mankind.

The prophets of old used this as a constant theme of their message. Jesus was not the first to admonish God's people to "love your neighbor as yourself." Moses had said it long before Jesus (Lev. 19:18). Forms of such exhortations mark the message of the prophets of all the ages. The ideal held high for the chosen people of God was to love not only the lovable, but also the unlovable, the outcast, the needy, the oppressed.

The problem is how to move the ideal from theory into practice! How does one take what seems apparent to all and create reality out of it? The Scripture makes plain that our lives are to be patterned after our Creator who is described in terms of love. Humanity is described as having been "made in the image of God." The image portrayed in our public media, however, is an image of enmity, hatred, selfishness, lovelessness, fear—hardly akin to the image of our Creator or related to the intention He had for us.

Once in a while, like a warming sun, we catch a brief glimpse of the divine image through a news item about one who went out of the way for another. Then we are caught short wondering that this should be *news!* Should this not mark our daily life rather than make news? Although it is true that even a glimpse of the divine image is news—and *good* news, at that. It is equally true that this only accents how seldom we see the ideal even approached much less met.

On occasion we even sense that divine image through the many nice things done for us in daily routine which we frequently fail to notice. Then someone we trust betrays us. We discover that someone has taken advantage of us when we thought they were being kind. Our hopes are so easily shattered, and we so quickly retreat again from relationships that threaten to damage us beyond repair. Our dreams easily turn into cynical pessimism.

There are those times, for that matter, when we feel particularly inspired to do especially good things for people around us. We feel the surge of divine potential welling up within us when, of a sudden, someone does not appreciate what we do—or, worse yet, beset by a bad mood a person scolds us for doing our good things. Our good, to our horror, can even turn back on us on occasion, and we are crushed. It brings us up short to realize how much of our "good" is done to gain appreciation, to hear nice things about ourselves, to enhance our self-image. We do not want to admit that we do good for selfish reasons with more frequency than we realize, and it is startling to be brought face to face with such truth.

The point of all this is not to scold those who would do good or to run humanity into the ground or to make all good deeds appear poorly intentioned. The point, rather, is to be realistic both about how much potential lies within the grasp of the human family and how little we are able to capitalize on this very potential. We are much like a thirsty man within sight of water and yet separated from it by an impenetrable barrier. Why, after all the years of mankind's history with all the striving for and yearning after such purity of intentions and perfection of deeds are we no closer to achieving them today than ever? This is the age-old human dilemma.

The package of mankind looks beautiful. One is sure that when unwrapped something beautiful will be found inside. And we find nothing but dust!

The Near Brush of Divine Potential

Meanwhile, the one who wrapped this package has not been standing idly by! Paul describes himself in the text as "a servant of Jesus Christ, called to be an apostle, set apart for the gospel of God which He promised beforehand through His prophets in the Holy Scriptures." A promise from the God who wrapped the package of our body around us has gotten mixed into this near miss of our human potential, assuring us that the promise of the wrapping is not entirely misleading! When the breath of life was vacuumed out of this wrapping, leaving the wrapping relatively intact while depriving the dust inside of its life, the Father was deeply grieved. Nevertheless, if life could be vacuumed out of this wrapping, then life can also be put back into the dust contained in the wrapping again.

That was precisely the promise God made—that He would again breathe life into the dust of His creation. That is the promise of which Paul speaks as he refers to the prophetic word. As old as man's dilemma with sin and death is, so old also is the promise of God.

Paul almost sings a hymn about the way God has proceeded to keep that promise. His words seem so crafted in what follows that many think we may see reflected here a very early creedal statement, an early way by which the church confessed its faith in Jesus the Christ: "The gospel concerning His Son, who was descended from David according to the flesh and designated Son of God in power according to the Spirit of holiness by His resurrection from the dead, Jesus Christ our Lord." If it was not an early creed, it certianly is an exalted phrase by which Paul set before his Roman readers from the very beginning of the letter who Jesus was.

In Him the divine brushed against the human. The divine and the human were fused in the Christ in such a way that everything a human was meant to be was fulfilled in Him by the divine initiative. God's image, that image of creation in which mankind was to rule and subdue the earth, was renewed and presented again through the coming of God's Son in human flesh.

This is the essential thrust of today's Gospel—that God himself takes the initiative in doing what man cannot do alone. Being born of a virgin He is fully human. Being born by the overshadowing of the Holy Spirit He is fully divine. He does not come just as an overpowering God judging a sinful world. Nor does He come merely as a heroic and Promethean figure of a man. In Him is fused the promise of God into the flesh of humanity. When unwrapped, one finds in this flesh the figure of God's gift of life renewed once more!

This stands in a lesser way behind the promise of the First Lesson which forms the prophetic backdrop for the Gospel. Isaiah is urging the same truth on Ahaz—namely that the difficult situation in which Judah finds herself will never be resolved by human effort. Only the gracious power of the God of Israel can grant them relief. The sign seized on by today's Gospel is offered Ahaz—for him to trust in God's redeeming hand.

Paul's creedal words have been reworked to meet varying needs through the ages. We confess them in shorter form in the Apostles' Creed, "I believe in Jesus Christ, His only Son, our Lord; who was conceived by the Holy Ghost, born of the Virgin Mary." Truly man, born of woman; truly God, designated so "in power according to the Spirit of holiness by His resurrection from the dead, Jesus Christ our Lord." The Christmas package of Christ contains the life that first enlivened the dust that has now fallen back into the boxes of our own lives. John says it this way: "In the beginning was the Word, and the Word was with God, and the Word was God . . . all things were made through Him . . . in Him was life" (John 1:1-4).

Paul intends to write about what happens when this Christ touches down into the lives of mankind. It touched his life first, but through his life it was touching the lives of many others. "Through whom we have received grace and apostleship to bring about the obedience of faith for the sake of His name among all the nations, including yourselves who are called to belong to Jesus Christ . . . who are called to be saints."

Three things are suggested as resulting from this here and in the closing phrases of our text. We note them in closing:

The Fusion of God's Promise and God's Deed in Our Lives

First we note that this near brush of divine potential with the near miss of human potential, made available to us in the Christ, is received by us through "the obedience of faith." Paul's whole apostleship is focused on calling the nations to such an "obedience of faith," we are told.

Faith is the way by which we concede that our potential will never be realized. Faith is the way by which we surrender our potential, in spite of all the promise it has, to the Father's hands, asking that He would use it in a way that we ourselves can never use it. Faith is the way by which we entrust our humanity to God's promise of renewal in Christ. Faith is the way by which we entrust our whole self, body and soul, mind and spirit, to God's care and keeping, fully confident that He who kept Jesus through His life, suffering, death, and resurrection is able also to keep us from every harm, even when death itself wraps its cold shroud around us. Faith is to obediently trust God in everything, and obedience is faith made flesh.

Second, we note that such "obedience of faith" is more than just a passageway from the grave to heaven. It is the passageway from death to life already here and now. Paul does not speak of what will happen when we die. He says we have already now received His grace and His call to sainthood. "Grace to you and peace" right now! In these the new life is made possible beginning with this or any moment. It is a present tense that marks Christian faith, not just a future tense.

This gift of God in Christ works wonders on life! God's grace means that we can lay aside our anxieties; for one bigger than we and far bigger than the problems that burden us is in charge and promises to work in our behalf. God's grace means that we can lay aside our futile efforts at bending the world back into shape again, for it is He who will make the new heavens and the new earth, not we mortals.

This gift of God in Christ works wonders on life! God's peace means that we can lay aside our fears of what our sins will eventually lead to, for God covers them with His forgiveness and takes the sting out of their assaults on us. God's peace means that we can lay aside our restless uncertainties and insecurities, for our entire future, even in death, is held in the hand of and under the jurisdiction of one who has already dealt with all the enemies who want to jeopardize that future for us.

Lest that be taken to mean that we are now absolved of all responsibility, note carefully the third thing that Paul lays before us: In Christ we "are called to be saints," sharing the apostolic mission to which Paul had been called. That means we are called to responsibly exercise the grace and peace of God that have freed us from our enemies so that God's purposes might be served among us and throughout the whole earth. Our "obedience of faith" calls the whole person to discipleship. Privileged by grace and peace, we are now held responsible for extending the proclamation of their availability to the whole world, making them available through life as well as speech.

In these ways God's grace and peace penetrate the wrapping of our body and enliven the dust within it. That grace and peace has turned our near misses of human potential into the near brushes of divine providence! It has made us who are no different from others into "a letter from Christ . . . written not with ink but with the Spirit of the living God, not on tablets of stone but on tablets of human hears" (2 Cor. 3:1-3).

It is very difficult to recognize that we can become or actually are such "letters" from God to the world, for the dust still swirls around us. Living by "the obedience of faith" is not easy, for the dust of our sin gets into our eyes and nostrils, blinding us to the possibilities and threatening to stifle the very breath of life for a second time. It was not easy for Paul either, and he speaks later in this same letter of how his own mortal dust on occasion threatened to drag him back to the grave yet again.

That is why Paul's greeting to the Romans in our text is a key phrase for sending us into the world: "Grace to you and peace from God our Father and the Lord Jesus Christ." Without that, the boxes of our lives are not valuable gifts to anyone. They remain dust.

If people, however, can get even a peek into the wrappings of our life and discover there the "grace and peace from God our Father and the Lord Jesus Christ," they shall have discovered, as we have, that God can and does penetrate mortal wrappings with His breath of life, causing dust to live again! And thus God's gift of life to us makes us a gift of life to others!

The Grace of God Has Dawned

THE NATIVITY OF OUR LORD
CHRISTMAS DAY
TITUS 2:11-14

L. Dean Hempelmann

Listen to the modern cry of despair, "Look what the world has come to!" Now listen to the joyful shout of the early Christians, "See what has come to the world!" Look, God has made bare His great heart. Look at this Scripture text which sets before your eyes the radical nature of the Christmas event. His great favor toward us sinners is disclosed in the act of sending His Son; the Word of grace and truth becomes flesh. In this act of Jesus' birth, God reveals His determination to restore us again to Himself; to make us receivers of His life and His destiny. That is why we keep high feast. We need God for every moment and every day of our lives.

It is related of Michaelangelo that when he came down from the scaffolding from which he had for some weeks been painting the frescoes of a high ceiling, he had become so accustomed to looking upward that it was with real pain that he forced himself to turn his eyes to the ground. Would that we might evermore be so arrested and held by the confidence of God's love that we could never be satisfied to turn our eyes from His face.

Today, through St. Paul, we fix our eyes of faith upon Him who is the way to peace and joy and triumph; this life in Christ is the best preparation for the delights of the life to come when we shall see Him face to face. Now we fix our eyes on Him in His Son as he assures us that we can receive Him to ourselves, for this day the grace of God is dawning, calling us back to God, offering us new life with Him and encouraging us to hope.

I. Calling Us Back to God

Did you know that God invites you to turn to Him in a special way at Christmas time? Many people do not recognize this invitation of God, and for various reasons they do not always respond to God's call. Some are afraid of Him. Even as at the first fatal fall into sin Adam hid himself form his Maker, because he was afraid, so people are afraid today. Others may feel too small to be noticed. They feel nobody cares. They feel that God's good news is only for the strong and mighty and not for the despised and wretched. Many today have put God out of their lives, out of their thoughts and activities. The world lies in desperate wickedness. Man is estranged from God, in open rebellion against God, enslaved in his entire outlook and attitude and will under the prince of this world. The people of this world do not know how to come back to Him.

Today God's grace is revealed to us (v. 11). As we hear the familiar story from St. Luke (2:1 ff.), as we sing the traditional hymns and carols, we see God at work laboring and struggling to give Himself (v. 14) to a world which has rejected Him and turned away from Him. To people who don't even deserve Him, God willingly comes in love (v. 11). His unsolicited, wholly spontaneous goodness comes to us (Acts 15:11; Rom. 3:24). We cannot even go one step of the way, and He comes all the way to us.

God wants to return to our hearts and lives. He does not want to frighten anyone, so He comes as a tiny, helpless little Child. He offers Himself in a tender, simple way. His love and kindness appear as a revelation—as something new and wonderful and unheard of. How could He indicate His grace better than by sending His Son into our world? His grace appears in the Incarnation. His grace could be seen and handled and touched. It can be recognized and understood. The grace of God as a saving grace lies personified in Bethlehem's manger. It shines from the face of Him in whom dwells all the fullness of the Godhead bodily, of the Child born unto us, whose name is Wonderful, Counselor, the Mighty God, the Everlasting Father, the Prince of Peace. Yes, God's redeeming love shines on Bethlehem's field where the angel of the Lord appeared to the Shepherds and the glory of the Lord shone round about them and the majesty of God veiled itself in condescending grace, so that fear was turned to adoration by the message: "Unto you is born this day in the city of David a Savior, which is Christ, the Lord" (Luke 2:11; cf. Rom. 5:15; Luke 2:30). This is saving grace indeed, bringing "good tidings of great joy which shall be to all people" (Luke 2:10).

Through the Son, the Father calls us to become His children (v. 14). What greater joy can come to us this Christmas than to know that we are God's children! The story is told of a little girl who had a new baby brother born into her home. Everyday she went to school, and everyday she told her teacher something new about the baby. One day she told the teacher about the baby's hands and feet; then another day she told the teacher about the baby's lovely eyes! One day the teacher said to the little girl: "Mary, what is the best thing that you know about that little baby brother of yours?" Almost as quick as light the girl replied: "The best thing I know about him, teacher, is, 'he's all mine!' " Happy are we, when we come to Bethlehem, if we hear the Father say also to us: "he's all mine!" "She's all mine!"

This miracle of becoming God's children came through the gift of God's Son who brought us forgiveness of our sins. Christ is our Savior because He is our Substitute. He gave Himself for us and by His self-giving sacrifice in our stead, His perfect obedience, His innocence, suffering, and death, and the shedding of His holy precious blood, He accomplished His purpose: "that He might redeem us" (v. 14). His blood and death were the all-sufficient ransom. By the payment of the price our deliverance was effected. The manger and the cross cannot be separated (Gal. 1:4; Eph. 5:2; 1 Peter 3:18). We have complete deliverance!

We need to be the people on whom the grace of God dawns, because we need His power for life. And this is what the forgiveness of sins does—it brings God back into our lives. To be forgiven is to have God's life and God's power and God's Spirit restored to us. This is the gift He offers us in the manger bed of Bethlehem—the forgiveness of our sins.

II. Offering New Life in Him.

The power and efficaciousness of the grace of God can be seen in those who have become God's children. The end result of the revealing of the grace of God is the new life we now live before him. The forgiveness of sins brings life, as Luther says, "where there is forgiveness of sins, there is also life and salvation" (Luther's *Small Catechism*). This is a lifelong process of living the new life in the light of the full salvation brought us by the grace of God. In Luther's expressive phrase, "we have been liberated from the prison, but the stench and disease of the prison linger on in our bodies. Sin still clings to us, and so our whole life is to be a constant cleansing" (St. L. XII:123). The 12th verse of the text represents the necessary successive stages of the Christian life. A return to our baptism is suggested. There must be a death through sin, renouncing godless ways and worldly desires. This precedes the entry into new life. Having renounced the devil and all his works and all his ways and denied all connection with worldliness, we receive from God the power to live a life of service to Him and to our fellowmen.

We cannot see God's grace; we cannot grasp it. We can be sure of it, though, when men live their lives under God, using His power for life. The new life that St. Paul describes is something that is concrete and can be seen. When someone has the wisdom of self-control and a sense of responsibility that shows itself in a pure and honorable conduct, we know they walk in "Newness of life" (Rom. 6:4) or with "upright, godly lines" (v. 12). When we see someone actively engaged in promoting his neighbor's welfare and refraining from anything that would injure him, we know he is a just man (v. 12). When we see someone who fears, loves, and trusts in God above all things, who honors and worships Him, who communes with Him in prayer to hallow His name, lets His kingdom come and does His will, he knows he is a godly man (v. 12). This is the visible assurance that the invisible God is working in him. God's Christmas gift is a useful gift. It offers us new life, a new pattern for living, and a new power.

III. Encouraging Us to Hope

In the final verse of this text, St. Paul describes the glad expectancy which is the ruling and prevailing thought in the lives of men who are looking for their Lord's return. You see, our life is set in the frame established by two termini, the first appearance of Christ at His incarnation and the second appearance in glory at the end of days. The Christian's life reaches backward and forward. Its motivation lies in the revelation of God's saving grace in Christ; its goal is the return of Christ (1 Cor. 1:7; 1 Thess. 5:23).

From the world's viewpoint there may not be much for which to hope. But for the Christian there is reason for hope, "blessed hope" (v. 13). We can manage to live in this world with all its problems. We can remain unmoved in the midst of all the upheaval and turmoil around us because we look forward to the fulfillment of this happy hope. We know that each day brings us that much closer to the day when we finally will see our Savior as He really is.

Now we move by faith. God's grace transforms us, reshapes our thinking, redirects our will, restores our sense of values, so that, denying ungodliness and worldly lusts (Luke 21:34) "we may live soberly, righteously, and godly in this present world" (v. 12). And the power for all this? It is the crib and the cross and the empty cave. All the sublime facts of our holy faith—the saving grace of God, redemptive activity of Jesus Christ, and the expectation of the blessed object of our hope in the glorious second coming of our Lord—all these provide us overpowering stimuli for a life of eager devotion to God (Acts 18:25; 2 Cor. 9:2; Phil. 1:11; Titus 3:8).

The day is coming when Jesus Christ will be fully revealed with His Father as God from all eternity. Toward that day we strive; for that day we long and hope. Jesus heralds the dawn of that new day which is destined to end the rule of the night of death, hell, and sin. And that hope is in itself a special Christmas gift—the unshakable conviction that the grace God has appeared in Bethlehem and will appear again in glory. This is the miracle of Christmas!

Adoption Accomplished

FIRST SUNDAY AFTER CHRISTMAS
GALATIANS 4:4-7

Martin H. Scharlemann

"Going, going, gone!" That is about the way the ancient Romans sold their sons to be adopted by some one who might be rich and powerful. Twice the real father symbolically bought his son back, but the third time around he would not repeat the offer. After the sale the adopting father saw to the necesary legal details to make his new son really his own. That is how the great Augustus, the emperor named in the Christmas story, had become the son of Julius Caesar, even though he was, in fact, only a nephew.

By such adoption a son started a completely new chapter of his life. In every respect he gained all the family rights pertaining to his changed relationship and so became the heir of his new father's estate. His former connections were legally wiped out. All the possibilities inherent in his new situation were open to him to flaunt or to employ.

The Jews of Paul's day had no such practice of adoption. Instead, the term "adoption" was applied to the actions by which God had made them His very own people: by the waters of the Red Sea, the voice of revelation at Mount Sinai, and the sustenance provided by manna and water from the rock. The apostle had in mind both uses of the word "adoption," as we can see from his use of the plural "sons" in verse 6 and the marketplace word for "buying off," which is usually translated as "redeem" (v. 5). As a Roman citizen and at the same time a descendant of the tribe of Benjamin this double sense of the word came naturally to him.

For Paul the more precious element in the concept of adoption was his awareness that the God of his fathers by His mighty acts turned Israel into "a precious possession among all peoples" (Ex. 19:5). Paul never tired of praising God for the undeserved mercy of including even one born out of due time (1 Cor. 15:8) as the apostle to the Gentiles in divine actions designed to establish adoption as an accomplished fact. Paul had been baptized by water (Acts 9:18) after he was confronted with the voice of revelation and surrounded by celestial light on his way to Damascus. His new life was being sustained by Word and Sacrament, which moved him to respond with the childlike utterance, "Abba! Father!"

In today's text the apostle Paul sets before us both the moment and the method of the adoption accomplished in his own case. He does so to invite us to share with him the liberation achieved by God through His Son and appropriated to us individually by way of our baptism. God acted at a given juncture in history to set us free for a new life-style, our text assures us. Accordingly, we shall reflect on the two items of the *moment* and the *method* of our—

Adoption Accomplished

1. The Moment

World War II is long behind us. Yet it provides a telling analogy for understanding Paul's use of the phrase, "the fullness of time," at which point God sent forth that Son whose birth we celebrate during this Christmas season. When the Allied troops managed to land on the beaches of France in early June of 1945, one village in Norway was so sure of ultimate victory over Germany that its inhabitants drove their Nazi overlords out of town and re-established conditions of freedom. That is to say, these villagers saw the moment of landing as the day which gave full meaning to what General Eisenhower and his staff had been planning for many months. At the same time, the successful invasion of the Continent offered not only the hope but also the certainty of the restoration of freedom. These townsmen realized, of course, that there would be an interval of time between what was called D-day (debarkation day) and V-day, the moment of victory. In the certain expectation of freedom restored, the village in Norway set itself the challenge of adopting the life-style which characterizes the practices and habits of a free people.

It is in this sense that we are to understand the expression "when the time had fully come" (RSV) or, as the King James Version puts it, "when the fullness of the time was come." We are not to think of this moment in history as a high point in man's achieving. That is to say, God did not wait for mankind to reach a certain cultural level before sending forth His Son, "born of a woman, born under the law." On the contrary, He sent His Son to break into our history to set us free from the burden and curse of the law. We, therefore, celebrate Christmas to recall the measure of God's grace which was and is manifested in God's act of adopting us as His children.

Mankind was hopelessly trapped in the predicament of our fallen estate. In fact it was up in arms against God for insisting that His revealed Law be kept in thought, word, and deed. Yet at a time when men were enemies of God (Rom. 5:10), we were reconciled to God by actions from His side of this relationship: He sent His Son to where we were, alienated, in revolt against the will of our Creator. And that Son came quietly down the back stairs of Bethlehem to keep the Law for us and to die because of the fact that you and I could not and would not keep the Law.

One of our Lenten hymns eloquently describes the response of God's Son when the orders went out from the throne, so to speak, to go forth. Said the Son:

> Yes, Father, yea, most willingly
> I'll bear what Thou commandest;
> My will conforms to Thy decree,
> I do what Thou demandest.

The purpose of this joint-action Paul set forth in another place as follows: God sent His Son in the likeness of sinful flesh and for sin in order that the just requirements of the Law might be fulfilled *in us* (Rom. 8:4). Some one in our situation had to keep God's law. The old Israel failed to do so even under the kindest of God's care. So God sent Him whom we reckon as the true Israel to accomplish for God's ancient people and for us what is inherent in the relationship of adoption. Accordingly, we dare to think of the church as the new Israel. Our adoption has been fully accomplished by virtue of the fact that God sent forth His Son, born of the Virgin Mary, born under the law, to set us free from our servitude under Law.

Our text suggests that one other mighty act from God is part of what we have referred to, by way of analogy, as D-day; and that is Pentecost. We read that as part of God's way of adopting us, He sent the Spirit of His Son into our hearts so that we respond to what the Father has done for us by saying, "Abba! Father!" The moment of Pentecost, therefore, belongs to the series of God's acts by which our adoption was accomplished. It took the impulse of the Spirit "poured out" to turn a faithful remnant in Israel to become the worldwide church.

One of the major consequences of God acting in grace on our behalf is the awareness that our redemption rests on events in history which the Scriptures call His "wonderful deeds" (1 Peter 2:9 RSV). They have occurred. There is no way in which anything about such occurrences can be changed. It is simply not possible for us to turn back the clock of time and undo, let us say, the crucifixion or the resurrection of Jesus Christ. Our faith, therefore, rests on facts not speculation, whether philosophical or theological. The "fullness of time" is an expression that points to a moment in history which gives meaning to both what went before the life and death of Jesus Christ and also to what has happened since that item by way of our liberation. The new life-style we adopt as Christians, in other words, consists of our proper response to what God has done especially in that moment of history which, in the Christmas season, we celebrate as the "fullness of time."

With this consideration in mind we shall now turn to the second aspect of our adoption which we have alluded to by the word "method" in our subheading under the general theme of "adoption accomplished." We cannot, of course, make an absolutely clean distinction between "moment" and "method" as these are used in the organization of our reflections on today's text from Galatians. You may well have noticed, therefore, that we crossed over at several points from "moment" to "method." But with the section on the moment of our accomplished adoption behind us, we want to proceed to focus more sharply on what we have chosen to call the "method."

2. The Method

God's mighty moment in history is more than a subject for our reflection. It took place to move us to respond; and the method for our new life-style is depicted for us in today's text by way of a broad-brush treatment.

The main stroke in this picture is the reference to our "crying, Abba! Father!" Now, this kind of "crying" is not done with tears. It is, in its chief usage, a word about liturgical proclamation. It is so used, for example, at Judges 3:9, where Israel is described as crying to the Lord for deliverance. This was an occasion of public worship which included the acknowledgment of disobedience. It was attended, moreover, by the coming of the Spirit on Othniel, the new savior. Moreover, John the Baptist "cried" in this way when he pointed out Jesus as the one to whom he had testified with the words, "He who comes after me ranks before me" (John 1:15).

In that sense, we "cry" as adopted children, "Abba! Father!" This is both prayer and proclamation. As a prayer, some of us learned these two words when we were scarcely old enough to say more than "Mama" and "Papa." It says much for your parents if they set you out so soon on the kind of prayer life represented by these two words of the text. The first in this pair of synonyms is the most endearing term that a Jewish family dared to use within its own household circle. Its English equivalent is "Daddy!" as that word is used by a small child not only addressing its father but at the same time articulating a relationship of full confidence.

No Jew of Jesus' day, or before Him, would have thought of using such an intimate term. For him God was "the Holy One of Israel." To be sure, the Lord could be called the Father of the nation but only rarely was He prayed to as "Father" in terms of personal relationship. Even then the cozy Aramaic household "Abba" was not used.

However, Jesus used it regularly because of His special relationship to the Father who had sent Him forth. If parallels among the four gospels are counted, Jesus used this intimate term no less than 16 times. In fact, "My Father" is lacking in only one of Jesus' prayers; and that was during the awesome moment on Calvary when He cried out, "My God, My God, why hast Thou forsaken Me?" (Mark 15:34)

As His disciples, who have received God's Spirit by Baptism, we have been given the privilege, as Luther put it, of coming to our Father in heaven "with all boldness and confidence [to] ask Him as children ask their dear father" (Small Catechism). We have, therefore, been entrusted with the Lord's Prayer as a special gift to be used by such as are God's sons and daughters. In the early church, as a matter of fact, no one was permitted to say this "family prayer" of the church until he or she had been fully instructed and received into the fellowship of the church as a worthy communicant.

It is of special interest that in our text, as well as in Rom. 8:15, the familiar term used by Jesus Himself in His prayer life is retained by the apostle. This was his way of underlining the very heart of our new life-style as adopted children of God. We have Jesus Christ as our older brother (Rom. 8:29) offering us Himself as the model not only for our worship but also for our life. For what the use of "Abba! Father!" clearly implies is that we are no longer slaves but children. That is what these familiar words proclaim not only to us but to all who hear them.

A slave, by definition, has no particular future. He is at the mercy and under the full control of his master. He can not even think of being an heir. By way of contrast, a son or daughter enjoys the special privilege of inheriting whatever it is that the father may so designate.

To set us free to be sons, God sent forth His Son to be born under the Law. After all, Jesus was born not only as a man but as an Israelite. He subjected Himself totally and gladly to the laws that regulated Jewish life to the degree that they conformed to the revelation at Mount Sinai. In the Sermon on the Mount He even explained how His Father had originally intended for His law to be kept, including the thoughts of the heart. He Himself kept God's law in that total way in order to "condemn sin" (Rom. 8:3) right where it is at work, among us.

What is more, He went to the cross under the judgment of the Law pronounced on our sins. In that way Jesus Christ brought righteousness into this fallen world, offering it to us as a gift so that with this "foreign righteousness," as Luther called it, we might be able to stand in the presence of an holy God and enjoy His presence forever. That is our inheritance. The Father has so designated it and so made us fellow heirs with our older brother, born of the Virgin Mary.

Accoringly we live in hope. And this hope is not some vague expectation of something good that might come our way at some time in the future. It is faith looking forward in full confidence that He who has begun a good work in us will bring it to completion (Phil. 1:6). That kind of trust puts a spring into our walking in faith. Down with fears of frustration and futility! Up with the bright anticipation that attends the path which God's children travel as pilgrims on their way to their heavenly fatherland!

Toward the outset of today's homily we used the analogy of D-day and V-day. Christmas is a reminder that D-day is behind us as a fixed point in history: the moment of the crucifixion and resurrection. The day of full victory (V-day) lies ahead of us. Like those villagers in Norway we now live under conditions of spiritual liberation as adopted sons of God and therefore heirs of His kingdom.

What lies between D-day and V-day is the age of the church. In the terminology of World War II it is the period devoted to "mopping up operations" until the capitulation of the enemy that still surrounds us and besets us: the devil, the world, and our flesh!

As we engage in these activities that pertain to life in the church we can do so with the verve of Saint Augustine, who once observed that every moment of a Christian's life is filled with three presents: the present made possible by recollecting God's acts of the past; the present of living them out; and the present of the certain expectation of their consummation. Such is the moment and method of our adoption accomplished!

You Are the Church

SECOND SUNDAY AFTER CHRISTMAS
EPHESIANS 1:3-6, 15-18

Rupert A. St. Pierre

The birth of our Lord Jesus came "in the fullness of time" (Gal. 4:4) in order that the purposes of God might be fulfilled. From eternity God had determined to build His church through the merits of His only-begotten Son, the Babe of Bethlehem. At no other time in our secular calendar does the world so take note of God's activity—even though they may not understand the depths and heights of all that is happening.

We, too, have cause to wonder and worship as we behold the amazing working of our God as He fulfills His plan of salvation for us and for the world that He so loves. Here is both fulfillment and beginning! Here is culmination and initiation! Here is the basis of hope for the world! The Christ is born in order that through His life, death, and resurrection the one, holy, Christian church might be established. The church is that vehicle established by God to bring the salvation so dearly won by Jesus to the ends of the earth. It begins even as you and I began in the joy of a birth; it culminates in the fulness of eternal life. Between that birth and that crown of eternal life is the time of growth in praise and glory.

Does this description of the church sound a little familiar to you? It almost sounds like the composite summary of the life of a man, doesn't it? Just as the church began with a birth, so do we. Just as the church is blessed with the promise of fullness in eternity, so are we. Just as the church has that period of struggle and growth, so do we. And if there is validity in the parallel between the life of the church and the life of a man, it is for our learning. Because, you see, you are the church! The church is not brick and mortar—it is alive—with the life of God. The church is not a group of faceless people that are referred to as "they"—it is individual persons who get up each morning and struggle with the very real problems of the 20th century. The church is a living, breathing, loving, forgiving entity serving the Lord Jesus Christ according to His blessing and guidance. The church is never distant nor alien, because the church is *YOU!*

Satan attacks that church when he comes with his dulling and life-stealing innuendoes to make us into mere spectators. When we lose the awareness of God's claim upon us in our baptism and begin to observe as uninvolved, disinterested bystanders the life-death struggle of the church, then Satan has been at work. It is in the full meaning of the word "church" that you have your greatest identity and meaning, and it is here that Satan would blind you to the glorious realities of who you are and to what you are called. If he can dim that vision of God's glory; if he can point to the flaws and weaknesses of the church; if he can create envy, jealousy, anger, or selfishness in every heart against that which is called "church," then he rejoices in yet another victory!

But rather, the Word of our God before us this morning would point to what you truly are as church!

I. The Character of the Church
A. Blessed of God

St. Paul, inspired by the gracious Spirit, declares that the believer is blessed of God. This is more than a mere observation of fact. It is an empowering and enabling Word that provides even what it declares. The "characteristicum" of the Christian is that he dwells in a state of blessedness just because our God so chooses and determines that He will bless. "He destined us in love to be His sons through Jesus Christ" (v. 5). Nothing less than the blessings of

God's love for His creation is involved as we behold the birth of that Infant into our history. He was born as a man among men to make possible the fact of God's blessings upon mankind.

B. Chosen from Eternity

From eternity God has made the provision for the salvation He would accomplish. There is no hit or miss scattering of that amazing grace upon the face of the earth. It is a carefully determined and accomplished plan. Too often we tend to make the grace of God of none effect because we insist on the option of choosing for ourselves, as though we are able to assess either God's grace or our needs. There are not many plans of salvation nor are there various models of God between whom we leisurely make our selection. Nothing could be further from the truth! You are not just a biological accident! Rather, before you were formed in your mother's womb, the all-knowing Creator knew you and chose you to be His own. He is completely and fully aware of who, what, and where you are each moment of your life. There is nothing that is beyond His concern and involvement in your life. You are that chosen and precious one of God.

Don't allow Satan nor limited intellect to cause you to stumble at this Word of Promise. God has chosen you! Everything that God has worked throughout your lifetime is evidence of this choosing. The evidence of concerned and caring Christian parents who carried you in prayer to the throne of grace is clear. The reality of your baptism is proof positive of the activity of the Spirit claiming you as His own. Your presence today before the foot of the cross is indicative of the effective prompting and leading of that indwelling Spirit. Your life of prayer and service is witness of your spirit with His Spirit that you are God's child.

And He has not just chosen you and then left you on your own. Rather, He has blessed you with every spiritual blessing in Christ Jesus. Before God created man, He willed that man should be His child. It is just in being God's child that we foster the truly human in us. It is the essence of sin that we seek to deny our dependency upon God. Adam and Eve sought to declare themselves independent of God and built a wall of separation between humankind and God. In this separateness man has existed as a being less than he was made to be. True humanity is found only in that blessed relationship of creature and Creator. Without that relationship we actually are sub-human in our potential and in our essence. St. Augustine noted that "We are made for God, and our soul is restless until it rests in God." If we would be fully what God created us to be—if we would be fully human in all its meaning—then we must acknowledge the rich blessing that is ours in Jesus Christ. To claim to be a man and to deny the Christ is a complete contradiction. It is only in being Christian that we foster the truly human in us and begin to share again the image of our God who made us, sustains us, and blesses us. Anything less is to deny the essence of our humanity. Humanity becomes real only as it is cleansed, restored, and shaped by the Babe of Bethlehem. To acknowledge the lordship of Christ is to be a man—indeed, it is to be a blessed man!

C. Acceptable to God

To this end *God* has made us to be acceptable to Himself through the Babe of Bethlehem. In His blood we are washed and cleansed. By His atonement we are crowned with life abundant and eternal, "that we might show forth His praises" (1 Peter 2:9). It is to this that you have been called: to live life, in time and in eternity, holy and blameless before the God and Father of all. "The life we now live in the flesh, we live by the faith of the Son of God" (Gal. 2:20). It is this "living life" that is the blessing of the Father upon you through the unique distinction known as God's church. He has called you and empowered you to be His own. You are His church!

And it is just as "church" that we receive every spiritual blessing in heavenly places. You, uniquely and singularly you, are in fact that "holy priesthood" of the almighty God in your day. You are the one who has been called, cleansed, and set-aside for His special purposes; to declare His glory and to give unto Him the praise that is due His holy name. There is no other identity. There is no greater calling.

Thus it is that St. Paul, along with the saints of all the ages, had you in mind as he ceased not to give thanks—for you—in prayer and praise before the throne of grace. Throughout the ages God has called and kept His church—one person or several people—but in every age of history the Lord has kept His church—His man. And for this man, the church, the fervent prayer rises that the Father would give that Spirit of wisdom and understanding that you today might know what it is to be church. To truly know the hope of His calling and the riches of His kingdom is to be church. Can you imagine what God is doing within you? Do you behold the love in which He has called you to be His own and to serve Him in everlasting righteousness, inocence, and blessedness? You—uniquely and specifically you—are that adopted and chosen child of God for whom Jesus was born, lived, died, and rose again. You are indeed blessed of God in the heavenly places!

II. The Function of the Church

A. Show Forth His Glory

Because of this high and holy identity that has been given you in Christ Jesus, your role and function is apparent. You are a person, the highest of all of God's visible creation. You have been crowned with honor and dignity. You have been given a name that is above every name. All this and more, in order that you might show forth the glory of His grace. With the eyes of understanding opened and with the spirit of wisdom and revelation, you are now called upon to function in accord with the hope of your calling. To minister His grace to your fellowman; to exercise mercy and to do justice; to declare His glory among the nations: this is the fruit and fulfilling of your calling and election. God will be glorified! It is ever the function of "the church" to give Him that glory!

B. In the Darkness of the World

It is just here that you as "church" have the high and great privilege of service in the world. Because the world does not and cannot understand His grace, because men and women exist on levels below that which God intended for humankind, you have been chosen and called to show that world the wonder of His mercy and love. To have the eyes of the understanding opened by the Spirit is to behold things as they truly are. It is the gift of God to His church to be able to see clearly. The perspective of eternity clarifies values. Fiction is sorted from reality. Understanding is to recognize real truth and to set it forth gently and in understandable concepts. You, as church, are called upon to utilize that special gift on behalf of your fellowman. Indeed, "the things of the Spirit are foolishness" (1 Cor. 2:14) to the men of the world. They are discerned and understood only as the Spirit opens the eyes of understanding.

The world lives in avarice and greed. Man against man; parent against child; child against parent. Each one goes his own way and seeks to claim more and more things for himself. Love and mercy and justice are elien concepts. Forgiveness appears only as a sign of weakness. War, bloodshed, and vengeance are the way of humanity. The "wisdom" of this world is vanity and foolishness.

To be able to view the activity of God in the history of the Bethlehem event is to have an understanding that makes one wise unto eternity. "The fear of the Lord is the beginning of wisdom" (Ps. 111:10), and we behold that wisdom revealed in all His grace and truth in the Babe of Bethlehem. To proclaim peace and love between God and man is to show forth the glory of our great God and Savior. To separate trivia from truth is wisdom functioning in the understanding and compassion of Jesus. This is the design-function of the church. This is your purpose and calling—for you see, you are church! You are in Jesus' love and peace!

A World of Confidence

THE EPIPHANY OF OUR LORD
EPHESIANS 3:2-12

Rupert A. St. Pierre

Fear is a most powerful emotion. It is fear that can debilitate a man and can even freeze him into inaction in a moment of emergency. The manifestations of this emotion within us take on various forms from the subtle anxieties with which we are all so familiar to actual mental illnesses. Have you ever suffered from anxiety? That kind of groundless dread that won't let you relax and robs you of peace and rest? I assure you that you are not alone. This is not something new nor unusual to humankind but has been within the heart of man since the day of his rebellion in the Garden of Eden. At the root of all fear is the certain knowledge that he has displeased God by his stubborn and rebellious activity, and it is truly stated that "his soul is restless until it rests again in God."

It is to this that the text for this Epiphany Sunday speaks as it leads us to a confidence and assurance that is indeed real before the God of gods and Lord of lords.

I. The Mystery from Eternity

St. Paul speaks of this confidence as he lauds the "mystery" of God that has been revealed. This unique term for the love of God that overcomes all fear is both intriguing and meaningful. It is truly a "mysterion" in that it has existed in the heart of God from the eons of eternity and was made known to man only by the revelation of God.

The content of the mystery was ever present for the sons of men. But because of the blindness of men and the hardness of their hearts, they were unable to see or accept the uniqueness of what the eternal love of a gracious God would perform. It is an intrinsic part of the Fall into sin, that man recognizes his separation from God but does not recognize any way of effecting a reconciliation. We all feel that we must do something to placate an offended and angry Deity. Every manmade religious code has in it the requirement that surely I must—and can—do something to make God smile on me. In our day this thought shows itself with the idea of "doing the best that we can"—while recognizing, at least inwardly, that our "doing" leaves much to be desired. We know that it is really not enough—and thus anxiety and fear is ever with us.

Into this kind of world condition came the amazing activity of God. He chose a people to serve as the vehicle through which He would bless all of the sons of men. The nurture and tender-loving-care of God to Israel was a source of amazement, even to the Israelites. They were called, chosen, led, and nurtured. They were separated unto God from all other peoples and religious concepts. They were the holy ones of God. It was to this people that God sent His prophets with the message of His loving grace. The people of Israel were to be the "pipeline" of God's grace to all the generations of men upon the earth.

But, as in all areas with man, if there is a way to misconstrue or to do it wrong, man will do it. The Israelites began to look upon their calling as something special—not for the world, but for themselves alone. A Messiah that would be for the entire human race was beyond the ability of the children of Abraham to conceive. That God loved the entire creation was foreign to the thinking of a finite and self-centered creature marred by sin and death. And thus, the fullness of the divine purpose of God's plan lay hidden until the fullness of time. The darkness of sin veiled the eyes and closed the ears to the messages of the prophets of old. The selfishness set in motion in Eden by Satan clutched the hearts of men and would not allow them to hear or to receive the beauty of God's eternal love and grace for His creation.

The long-held promise of the Messiah was indeed precious to the people of God. It was in this that they placed their hopes and for which they prayed as they struggled with that debilitating fear that rampaged through their hearts. Surely, the God of the ages would hear and be merciful! And hear He did! Not only the prayers and entreaties of His particular people, but the sighings and supplications of those generations yet unborn. God was never far from His beloved creation. Rather, he was deliberately and persistently working out that unique and marvelous plan of salvation that would be revealed in the fullness of time through the Lord Jesus Christ.

II. Revealed in Christ Jesus

It is here that St. Paul speaks of the wonder and the depth of the grace and mercy of God. The mystery has now been revealed! Jesus Christ, the only-begotten Son of the Father from eternity, arrived at precisely that time known to God when all things were exactly right for His redemptive work. This mighty working of God was for the redemption of the entire world—Jew and Genitle alike. The whole of creation was to be restored to that state of blessedness which the holy God had created—a state in which man might live life in an open and free relationship with God Himself; a state in which the basis of relationship was not fear but love.

This is the marvel of the mystery that had been so veiled during the eons. It is not just the Jews ... it is the totality of the sons of men whom God has so loved and sought and purchased with the precious blood of Jesus Christ. All of humankind is cleansed through that washing. There is now a "Mediator between God and man, the man Christ Jesus" (1 Tim. 2:5). All of humankind—no distinction is made as to male or female, bond or free, Jew or Greek (Gal. 3:28), all are one in Christ by the declarative work of the almighty God through His only-begotten Son.

Even the angels themselves were not aware of the magnificent scope and majesty of this marvelous plan of universal salvation. They too wonder at the riches and depths of the graciousness of God. All of creation—caught up and bound in the slavery of sin and death—all is now released and restored in the merciful action of God. An action God had determined beforetime to bring about through His love for His creation. Sin, hell, death—these are all defeated along with Satan. The victory belongs to our God and to all those that are His!

This "good news" is the foundation and basis of the church. It is upon this Gospel message that God has chosen to reach the hearts of men with His saving grace. Wonder of wonders! "God has visited and redeemed His people" (Luke 1:68) and has restored paradise! Mystery of mysteries! "There is now no condemnation to them that are in Christ Jesus!" (Rom. 8:1). And it is the church, those "called-out ones," ever the agent of this marvelous mystery. "This Gospel shall be preached to the ends of the earth" (Matt. 24:14); "Ye shall be witnesses unto Me ... " (Acts 1:8); "Go ye, therefore, and make disciples of all nations ... " (Matt. 28:19); "Preach the Gospel to every creature..."(Mark 16:15). Why? Because the Lord our God has redeemed and restored His people. He has begotten us again as newborn creatures to a lively hope. We are indeed born again to life and reality in the Christ of God. The victory truly is accomplished. "And this is the victory that overcometh the world, even our faith" (1 John 5:4). God Himself has accomplished it for us.

III. Gives Confidence Before the Father

And if God has done it, then we need no longer cower in fear. Rather, we approach the mercy seat with all confidence and boldness. Our God is "for us" and has declared us to be sons and heirs of all of His mighty love and glory. "His Spirit bears witness with our spirit that we are the sons of God" (Rom. 8:16)—sons adopted and beloved by a gracious God and Lord. We are children who have not to fear nor dread. Guilt and condemnation are gone—fully and forever cleansed by that all-encompassing act of redemption in Christ Jesus. No one shall lay any charge against us;

no one can wrest the kingdom from us; Satan is judged and we are freed.

The highest earthly communion with God is ours just in that mystery of revelation which God has given into our care and stewardship. The message—to Jew and Gentile alike—is that God has indeed "so loved the world that whosoever believeth in Him should not perish, but have everlasting life" (John 3:16). Surely, we should exult and sing out with Luther of old in the battle hymn of the Reformation:

> Tho' devils all the world should fill,
> All eager to devour us,
> We tremble not, we fear no ill,
> They shall not overpow'r us.
> This world's prince may still
> Scowl fierce as he will,
> He can harm us none,
> He's judged; the deed is done;
> One little word can fell him.

That kingdom, the church, is the bastion of confidence in this world. To us and for all men the glad tidings go out. To us and for all of humanity, the note and call of peace with God and confidence for the souls of men is to be proclaimed.

But, "so what?" That "so what" must be answered with a twofold reply. First, we must recognize who we are and where we stand today in relationship to that revealed mystery. The Gospel of Jesus came by God's gracious revelation in the person of His Son. Through the life, death, and resurrection of Jesus Christ, the separation between God and man has been bridged. We—you and I—stand forgiven and redeemed—"chosen," if you will. We now have peace with God through our Lord Jesus Christ. Today, we Christians—we who are "church"—stand as God's new Israel. We have been called, chosen, led, and nurtured. God is our *God*! We rejoice and give thanks for His enduring and embracing love.

But we dare not become "another Israel" in that we receive God's love only for ourselves and turn our backs upon the bewildered and terrified sons of men. The import of the "so what" lies in the second-half of our response. We have a calling to fulfill—just as did Israel of old. The object of God's gracious revelation of the mystery of salvation is *for the world*. We have no choice in the matter of proclaiming God's peace. That is the very reason for our being chosen. God has made peace with the world! Fear is cast out in His eternal Love. Life is again available to man and the light of that life is Christ.

The very meaning of Epiphany is light—a light to shine into a dark and cowering world of anxious and fearful men. God's love is no longer a mystery! God's abundant forgiveness has been given to us and it is *for all*! It is our privilege and responsibility to share that love and light with the hearts that are in darkness. The mission imperative of the church is not just something "ever there." While we pray for both workers and harvest in the foreign fields, while we gladly give of our best to enable that proclamation to spread across the seas, while we encourage and train our sons and daughters to take up the calling and cause as laborers in God's world, we also must recognize that we have a tremendous privilege and responsibility here at home. We are in the spot and at the time where and when our God would have us—for His eternal purposes. We are charged with being His spokesmen to our generation in our locale. Fear and condemnation have been set aside in order that we may proclaim the wonder of His everlasting mercy and salvation. Life is now the destiny of men. Death has been swallowed up in the victory of our God.

This victory is ours—and for our neighbor also—that we might live and rejoice in the freedom with which we have been set free. "Stand fast, therefore, in the liberty wherewith Christ has made you free" (Gal. 5:1). Let us walk with our God and declare His name among the heathen—at home and abroad—in the assurance and confidence of His love and might! God *has* redeemed us! Life is now ours! We live and rejoice and serve with a world of confidence!

God Has No Favorites

THE BAPTISM OF OUR LORD
FIRST SUNDAY AFTER THE EPIPHANY
ACTS 10:34-38

William J. Hughes

Tom Sawyer told Huck Finn: "Huck, we can't let you into the gang if you ain't respectable."

There are church people who feel the same way. They don't want "undesirables" in the church. They want the fellowship to be pure. They want only to associate with deserving people—people like themselves. It's easy to push aside those who don't feed our egos, or strengthen our personal viewpoints, or meet our preconceived expectations. We easily form our own Christian ghettos.

There were some in the early church who practiced their Christianity this way. They were noisy. They were obstinate. They banned together, organized, and formed a circumcision party. They wielded immense influence. They wanted the church to remain Hebrew. They believed the Gospel, only they believed it wasn't for undesirables.

Their exclusivism raised serious questions: Does God have favorites? Is the Gospel for all people or only for some? Is church fellowship inclusive or exclusive? What are the requirements for church membership?

Church Fellowship—Inclusive or Exclusive

Peter began his career as a member of the "circumcision party" (Acts 11:2). His transformation came gradually. There were a series of experiences that slowly and painfully shifted his thinking.

It was while he was on a preaching mission that the Holy Spirit led Peter to do some unexpected things. First, he healed Aeneas, a paralytic and Greek-speaking former Jew at Lydda. Next, he went to Joppa where the congregation was in mourning for Dorcas, a woman. While there he forgot his Old Testament training and acted as the Spirit's instrument to raise her. The Spirit was pushing Peter past all religious boundaries. He even had him stay with Simon, a tanner, who handled dead animals. That was contrary to the law. Without being aware of it, the Holy Spirit was beginning to widen Peter's horizons.

It wasn't Peter's idea to go to the Gentiles. Perish the thought. That offended all he had ever been taught. He was of the "old school." He was strictly "kosher." He faithfully proclaimed the Gospel, but only to Jews.

One day while waiting to eat, Peter was meditating on the housetop. There he fell into a trance and saw a sheet coming down from heaven filled with various creatures. Then he heard a voice say, "Get up, Peter. Kill and eat." Peter's response was: "Surely not, Lord! I have never eaten anything impure or unclean." In reply the Lord said, "Do not call anything impure that God has made clean" (Acts 10:13-15 NIV). For emphasis this was repeated three times.

The threefold emphasis was not unique in Peter's experience. After he denied the Lord three times and was restored, the Lord, three times over, asked Peter if he loved him. Perhaps the apostle was so fixed in his convictions that he needed a repeated emphasis in order that he might not fail to understand what God was telling him.

What was the point of the sheet let down from heaven? It seems clear that it was that the Gospel was not to be limited to the Jews only. By supernatural illumination, God indicated that the Gospel of the grace of God was to be spread abroad among the Gentiles as well as the Jews. God was broadening the church's perspective. We should understand that in our time there is far less need for this illumination than in Peter's time. In his day the canon of Holy Scripture was not complete. He needed special instruction to impress upon his understanding just how universal the application of the Gospel was to be.

Peter was bewildered about the meaning of this strange vision. While he was trying to interpret it, he was interrupted by visitors. Have you noticed that God sometimes answers our doubts and perplexities by sending others to us for help? I have. God seldom gives us neat little answers, rather, He offers us opportunities for service and in these opportunities our questions resolve themselves. I guess interruptions become blessings. Peter's interruption made it possible for the Holy Spirit to break down the membership barrier in that early Christian community.

Peter's visitors came from Caesarea, a splendid city named in honor of Caesar Augustus. According to Josephus, the Jewish historian, there were five army cohorts and a squadron of cavalry stationed at Caesarea. One of these cohorts was known as "the Italian Regiment," and consisted of 1,000 men divided into 10 centuries. Cornelius was the centurion of one of these centuries (Acts 10:1). His name was that of a noble family of Rome, suggesting that he had a distinguished ancestry. He had come in conquest of Israel only to have Israel conquer him. "He and all his family were devout and God-fearing; he gave generously to those in need and prayed to God regularly" (Acts 10:2 NIV).

In ways not clear to us, God was preparing Cornelius' heart. Perhaps, someone had reported Philip's preaching to him, and he wanted to know who Jesus was. In any case, he prayed, and his prayer was answered. He was told to send for Peter in Joppa. With a fine sense of timing, the Spirit was preparing the stage for the first Gentile to be brought into the church. Cornelius' staff members arrived at the very moment Peter was puzzling over his dream.

Peter must have surprised himself. Because before he knew it, he "invited the men into the house to be his guests." The next day they would go to Caesarea.

Cornelius' interest in the Christian faith was not casual. He was serious. He had called together his family and close friends to hear the apostle. He told Peter that he was a humble and devout man who was trying as hard a she knew to please God.

There are those in the church today who would have said to Cornelius, "Keep it up, Cornelius. As long as you are praying sincerely, giving conscientiously, and acting decently, you'll get to heaven."

Church Fellowship—the Fellowship of Faith

But that's not what Peter told Cornelius. He confronted him with the person of Jesus Christ and concluded his sermon with a Gospel declaration: "Everyone who believes in Him receives forgiveness of sins through His name" (Acts 10:43 NIV). God gives what man can never earn: forgiveness. No matter how sincere and sweaty the effort, we can never work hard enough at giving or praying or anything else to get ourselves right with God. God does the impossible; he comes to us in the person of Jesus, establishing a new relationship. "Everyone," Peter emphasized, "who believes in Him receives forgiveness." It is completely unconditional. All who trust—Jew or Gentile, black, yellow, or white—receive new life through Jesus Christ.

Dr. Luke writes that "the Holy Spirit came on all who heard the message" (Acts 10:44 NIV). It was as though the Holy Spirit said "Amen" to Peter's observation: "I now realize how true it is that God does not show favoritism, but accepts men from every nation . . ." (Acts 10:34 NIV).

Those who accompanied Peter from Joppa were amazed. They agreed with Peter that there were no impediments to these Gentiles being baptized. Those six believers and Peter understood that the mission of the church was to be inclusive. The Holy Spirit had finally demolished the last barrier. As the first European or Westerner to be baptized into the Christian Faith, Cornelius is the spiritual ancestor of all of us.

It wasn't easy for Peter to return to Jerusalem. The "Hardliners" were waiting for him. "You went into the house of uncircumcised men and ate with them" (Acts 11:2 NIV). They tried to make him feel like he had sold out. Patiently—the old days were past—he recounted his vision in Joppa. "The Spirit told me to have no hesitation about going with them" (Acts 11:12 NIV), he said. How could he or they argue with the Holy Spirit?

Now Peter didn't arrogantly claim to have a hot line to the mind of Christ. He wasn't like some crackpots we encounter who claim to be "led by the Spirit" and then do senseless, even appalling, things. Peter tested the Spirit.

First, he did not act apart from the fellowship of other Christians. "These six brothers also went with men," Peter said, indicating that he refused to be a one-man church. Peter understood that the Holy Spirit works with believers within the context of the church.

Second, Peter insisted upon checking always with what Jesus had said: "I remembered what the Lord had said, 'John baptized with water, but you will be baptized with the Holy Spirit.' So if God gave them the same gift as He gave us when we believed in the Lord Jesus Christ, who was I to think that I could oppose God" (Acts 11:16-17 NIV). The Holy Spirit interpreted Jesus and His words to Peter, and they became the authority for his mission to Cornelius.

The Holy Scriptures are our "check" for the leading of the Spirit. We are not left to wonder whether God is prompting us on certain occasions—He gives us the Bible to test whether or not it is His leading.

God's church or man's? Each generation of Christians, each

congregation of believers is tempted to erect barriers. We want to be choosy about those with whom we will associate.

In spite of our inclination to say no to those who are not our types, the Lord Jesus keeps shouting Yes. "Everyone who believes in Him receives forgiveness. . . . " Forgiveness by Christ for every person who believes means fellowship by us with every person who believes! God shows no favorites, neither can we. In Christ none are "common" or "unclean." That's the way God has willed for men to be saved. The door of salvation is open to all. Praise and thank God, for if the door of salvation is open to all, this means that it is open to you and to me.

Called to Be Saints

SECOND SUNDAY AFTER THE EPIPHANY
1 CORINTHIANS 1:1-9

William J. Hughes

American preoccupation with sex sometimes makes us think that we live in history's most sex-saturated society. Of course, we don't. History has judged other societies worse than ours, for example, Sodom and Corinth.

For the Greeks and Romans in the first century, "to Corinthianize" was a naughty 13-letter word. Corinth boasted more than 1,000 religious prostitutes serving in the temple of Aphrodite alone. Devotees who worshiped the goddess enjoyed the pleasures of the "priestesses."

If the Corinthians practiced this kind of religion, it doesn't require much imagination to guess what the rest of their daily life was like. Sin of all kinds and descriptions had free rein among them.

Establishing the Relationships

The establishment of the Christian community in Corinth is recorded by Luke in Acts 18. The apostle Paul came to the city from Athens. His friends and co-workers, Silas and Timothy, were in Macedonia, northern Greece. Corinth is located in extreme southern Greece. Cut off from his friends and supporting churches, Paul worked at tentmaking, a craft he had learned as a youth, to meet his financial needs. He found both work and lodging with a Jewish couple, Priscilla and Aquilla, who practiced the same trade and who had been expelled from Rome because of the anti-Semitic decree of Emporer Claudius. This couple came to know Jesus Christ as their Messiah and Savior through Paul's ministry. Through the

outreach of this young couple and in his Sabbath preaching in the
synagog, the apostle—who was also a rabbi—pressed the claims of
Jesus Christ. His ministry was most effective among the proselytes
and God-fearers but had little impact on the orthodox Jews.
Nonetheless, the Holy Spirit blessed his ministry, and the church
was planted, and Paul remained in Corinth for a year and a half in
follow-up work. When he left for Ephesus, Corinth was probably the
largest of the younger churches.

There is a proverb we've all learned, "When the cat's away, the
mice will play." This dramatizes the situation in Corinth. Within
months of Paul's departure the congregation was engulfed in a
mass of thorny problems.

In letters to the struggling Christian community, Paul deals
with their difficulties: partisanship and divisions within the
congregation, open fornication, marriage problems, abuse of the
Lord's Table, and the use of spiritual gifts. While most of the
difficulties involve ethics rather than theology, the apostle, nevertheless, in each case develops a particular doctrine which under-
girds what he has to say about the issue. These eternal principles
are just as binding and appropriate today as they were in the first
century.

The root of the evil in the Corinthian church involved an
erroneous view of the relationship of the church to the world.
Instead of the church's winning the world as it should have been
doing, the world was rapidly winning the Corinthian church. The
devil was employing a subtle and effective technique to destroy all
that the apostle Paul had accomplished in Corinth. Paul, happily,
recognized the danger and wrote his letter in time to put a halt to the
trend.

Identification with the world Paul calls "carnality." Christians
today are faced with the same problem. The world will never be won
to Christ by worldly Christians—it will be won by Christians who
have made a break with the world, but who at the same time love
the world with an evangelistic passion. This truth underlies Paul's
writing. In today's text he tells the Corinthian Christians that they
have been "called to be saints." He speaks of their "relationship" to
him, to Christ, and to one another; and reminds them of God's
"resources" for living. Both are timely.

Paul speaks first of his relationship to Jesus Christ. He has been
"called to be an apostle of Christ Jesus by the will of God" (v. 1). He
establishes his authority in the church by making a threefold
claim. First, he is an *apostle*. Apostles were men who had seen the
resurrected Chirst and who had been commissioned directly by
Him to preach and to lay the foundation for the church. Throughout
his letters this ring of authority is sounded. Second, Paul is *called*
apostle. He did not assume the position, nor was he appointed by

human, apostolic vote, as was Matthias. Paul had seen Christ in a post-ascension appearance and was directly called by him into the office of apostle. Third, he claimed that his apostleship *came of the will of God.* It was God who decreed his salvation and apostleship.

Defining the Relationship

Having established his relationship to Christ and His church, the apostle then dentifies the Corinthians and defines their relationship to Christ and the church. He wants these believers to see who they are.

First, he calls them "the church of God." They are members of the one true church which Christ built and purchased through His death and resurrection. The word "church" translates a Greek word that literally means "called ones." The Corinthian believers were "called out" to be God's people. Their unity was not to be divided by warring, imperfect members. Second, he locates them at Corinth. Third, they were sanctified in Christ Jesus" (1:2). The Holy Spirit had brought them to faith in Jesus as Messiah and Savior, and his cleansing and edifying ministry through the Word was still operative among them. Fourth, he designated them "called saints." Just as Paul was an apostle by divine calling, they were saints by that same calling. Sainthood was not a part of their furture destiny; rather, it expressed their present standing. The big problem was that they were not saintly in their practice. Fifth, they shared the same position as believers in every place. How does one become a saint? By calling upon the name of Christ. The Corinthians had done this, and so had believers in other localities. In fact, this is the simplest definition of the procedure to secure personal salvation. Sixth, they had the same Lord as other believers throughout the world. There is one Lord and one faith. The unity of the church is hereby expressed. Paul emphasizes the Lordship of Jesus Christ in the lives of believers. The Corinthians needed to recognize that their divisive spirit was a sign of spiritual disobedience.

Here they were God's called out people in Corinth, and here we are also God's called out people. We have been given a flaming message to proclaim, the good news of redemption in Christ Jesus. Here is the Gospel for a city with all its corruption and sexual immorality—a Gospel that is completely adequate for every situation. So this letter is addressed not just to a few people in Corinth, a city that is now in ruins, but to the church of Jesus Christ in any city of the world, in any era of history, even the times in which we live. We are to know what we believe, to live it and proclaim it. That is the only way through which others can find the living Christ.

"Called out"—that is our relationship to God. We must never forget this. In this relationship God puts at our disposal resources that are adequate for anything and everything in life. Paul begins to list these resources in verse 3: "Grace and peace to you from God our Father and the Lord Jesus Christ."

If I asked you to define the word "grace," perhaps you would say, "It is the undeserved loving kindness of God in Jesus Christ." Yes, grace is that, but it is even more than that. It comes, as Paul says here, from God our Father through the Lord Jesus Christ: God the Father is the source, and Jesus Christ is the channel through whom it comes. Grace, therefore, is His life of purity and holiness; His death that was sufficient to pay the price for our sins; and His present ministry by which He imparts the Holy Spirit today, enabling us to live in His power.

It seems to me that "grace" in the New Testament is that which brings into our lives everything that delights the heart of God. There is grace to make me like Jesus, grace to make me patient where I would be impatient, grace to enable me to glorify Jesus in every situation. Are you concerned about pleasing God today? Let me remind you that He has already placed within your reach that possibility: His life, His character, His spirit.

The second word, "peace," does not imply laziness or inactivity. Peace is not simply the absence of strife, but the presence of positive blessings. It is spiritual prosperity. First, I have peace with God. That's a vertical relationship. Then I enjoy peace in my inter-personal relationships. That's a horizontal relationship, peace one with another. Lastly, I have peace within my own self. Peace reigns within—the peace of forgiveness, of reinstatement with God, of wholeness. All this because my feet are firm on the Rock which is Christ.

Not only have we been given grace and peace, but other wealth, as well. In verse 5 the apostle writes: "For in Him you have been enriched in every way—in all your speaking and in all your knowledge—because our testimony about Christ was confirmed in you." Whatever your abilities are, they were bestowed by God; you don't possess them by heredity or education. Jesus Christ has imparted to your life this spiritual wealth. "In all your speaking and in all your knowledge"—we have a message to proclaim, for God has given us His Gospel to preach, His Word to live by, His life to live out. God's most convincing argument to the world is the Christian who has been called and sanctified by the Holy Spirit and who lives accordingly. It is only through your life and mine that God does things in our homes, in our place of business, in our neighborhoods—things that would not be accomplished otherwise. God wants our lives to demonstrate that the One we believe in is alive and dwells within us. What a challenging thought: to know that God has a beachhead in us. And because of this, we "do not lack any spiritual gift." And because we do not lack anything, God "will keep you strong to the end, so that you will be blameless on the day of our Lord Jesus Christ" (v. 8). Remember what Luther taught in the explanation of the Third Article of The Apostles' Creed? "The Holy Spirit ... calls, gathers, enlightens, and sanctifies the whole Christian church on earth, and keeps it with Jesus Christ in the one true faith...." This is what Paul is talking about—the Holy Spirit's preserving power. Paul was thankful for God's faithfulness. God is not just true; He is also trustworthy. His Word is sure, and His promises are certain.

In addition, we are not alone in our Christian lives. We have each other—the communion of saints. The Greek word for fellowship is *koinonia,* which means having everything in common, a communing together, a mutual understanding. We have been made wealthy by the grace of God so that our lives may reveal Christ to others. We are in partnership with Christ and with one another.

A partnership is a business relationship, but it is also a family tie. A husband and wife may refer to the other one in their marriage as their "partner," because they have all things in common. At least, that is God's intention. We have the same thing in our Lord Jesus Christ. Your interests are His. Your mind, your body, your friends, your ambitions, your problems, your heartaches, your joys, your progress, your growth—these are His interests. All heaven's resources are yours and mine, because we have been given this great and precious privilege of partnership with Christ. His desire is to place these resources at your disposal. Paul challenged the Corinthians to live in this kind of vital, living relationship with Jesus. Today, I'm challenging you to live in this kind of vital, living relationship with Jesus. May I ask, will you?

The Healing Power of the Gospel

THIRD SUNDAY AFTER THE EPIPHANY
1 CORINTHIANS 1:10-17

Donald J. Poganski

There is a story in the form of a fable entitled "The Tools Quarrel." It seems that the carpenter's tools had a conference. Brother Hammer was in the chair. The conference informed him that he must leave the shop because he was too noisy. But he said, "If I am to leave, Brother Gimlet must go too, for he is so insignificant that he makes only a little impression." Little Brother Gimlet rose up and said, "All right, but then Brother Screw must go also, for he has to be turned around and around again and again to get him anywhere." Brother Screw said, "If you wish, I will go, but Brother Plane must also leave, for all the work he does is only on the surface.

There is no depth at all in it." So Brother Plane replied, "Brother Rule will have to withdraw from the shop, for he is always measuring things, as though he is the only one who is right." Brother Rule then complained against Brother Sandpaper and said, "I just don't care, but it must be said, that he is rougher than he ought to be. He is always rubbing others the wrong way. He must leave too." In the midst of these quarreling tools the Carpenter of Nazareth walked in. He came to perform his days's work. He put on His apron and went to work at His bench to make a pulpit from which to preach the Gospel to the poor. He used the hammer, the gimlet, the screw, the plane, the sandpaper, the rule, and other tools. After the day's work was done and the pulpit was finished, Brother Saw arose and said, "I perceive that all of us are laborers together with Him."

Just a fable, but with a clear point. Personalities and gifts which Christians have may vary, but they are to be employed together for the common good in a Christian congregation that the Gospel of Christ be preached by word and deed. The Christian life becomes a pulpit from which to herald the good news of God's redeeming love in Christ.

The text is part of the introduction to Paul's first letter to the Christians at Corinth. It focuses on one of the reasons for writing. That was to correct the spirit of factiousness and contention. Paul heard that there was quarreling among them, and he asked that there be no more dissensions. The members who acted like that had drifted away from the daily experience with the amazing grace of God and thought too much about human wisdom and things. Their egos and their old natures got in the way. So Paul points them again to the Gospel of Christ and shares with them and us.

The Healing Power of the Gospel
The Gospel Has Power to Heal Alienated Hearts

The apostle Paul would never forget his gospel experience on the Damascus Road that healed his heart, nor the commission he received to preach that Gospel. He said, "For Christ did not send me to baptize but to preach the Gospel." Prior to that experience his heart was torn by the hostility of sin, and he was alienated from God, He went blindly about his vain philosophy of life serving sin. All the while he thought he was doing God a service in fostering the murdering of Christians. But he met Christ (Acts 9) who became for him the "good news" in person. Then and there he experienced personal forgiveness. He found his heart believing in Christ. In the place of condemnation which he deserved because of his sins, he found himself "accepted in the beloved" through forgiveness. He found healing with God and healing within. That healing experience transferred him from darkness to light, from spiritual death to spiritual life. It turned his life around from sinner to saint and from persecutor to preacher. Thus Paul would never tire of preaching the Gospel to others. It meant everything to him as a daily experience of being right with God by faith in Christ.

He preached that Gospel at Corinth, and many believed by the power of the Spirit. It healed their hearts and lives too. In 1 Cor. 6:11 he writes, "such were some of you (idolaters, adulters, sexual perverts, thieves, greedy, drunkards, revilers, robbers), but you were washed, you were sanctified, you were justified in the name of the Lord Jesus Christ and in the Spirit of our God." To Paul the Gospel was always the "good news" that Christ was crucified for sinners, for when dealing with the factions at Corinth, he asks in v. 13, "Was Paul crucified for you?" In this question he directs the attention of the people to the centrality of the Gospel—that Christ was crucified for sinners, and in that suffering and death on Calvary He experienced everyone's eternal death penalty and paid it in full! When sinners believe that "good news," it results in personal healing of the heart through reconciliation with God. Then there is the healing peace with God and peace within.

Then Paul goes on to emphasize that the Gospel must be preached in simple terms in order to remain the healing Gospel. "For Christ did not send me to baptize but to preach the Gospel, and not with eloquent wisdom, lest the cross of Christ be emptied of its power." Paul is referring to two things here. One was the mixing of the Gospel with Old Testament ceremonial laws and human philosophy which fitted the proud Greek learning of the day. (See his letter to the Colossians.) The other was the fancy rhetoric and philosophical phraseology which the Greek mind so admired. The Greek Plutarah says of the silver-tongued rhetoricians of his day that they made their voices sweet with musical cadences and modulations of tone and echoed resonances. The emphasis was on how they were saying it, not on what they were saying. The apostle would not relent to such methodology and phraseology lest the people miss the message. After all, the Gospel is serious business. It was a real, live body that was nailed to the cross, the body of the Son of God. It was real blood that dripped from His wounds. And He really died to pay every sinner's death penalty. Think what that means! We would be condemned in hell if God let His wrath fall on us because of our many sins in thoughts, desires, words, and deeds. Instead, it fell on His Son, once for all, and He alone paid the penalty for all sins. Paul would never tire of preaching the Gospel in simple terms, like children hear it in:

Jesus loves me He who died, heaven's gates to open wide,
He will wash away my sin, let His little child come in.

Also, Paul makes a strong point, that the preaching of the Gospel is his first assignment as an apostle. "Christ did not send me to baptize but to preach the Gospel." When Paul was explaining why the parishioners at Corinth should not make a faction around him, he said in v. 14: "I am thankful that I baptized none of you except Crispus and Gaius [Acts 19:8; Rom. 16:23]; lest any one should say that you were baptized in my name. I did baptize also the household of Stephanas [first converts of Achaia, 1 Cor. 16:15]. Beyond that, I do not know whether I baptized any one else." Paul is not minimizing the power and importance of baptism for faith and life, but he is talking about the task of administering it. Baptism could well be performed by the hands of others. But for himself and other apostles the first assignment from the Lord was to preach and teach the Gospel. Administering Baptism required no immediate apostolic call, but preaching the Gospel was what the call was all about. The Gospel brought healing to alienated hearts.

Let us ponder what the Gospel message means for our hearts. Let us ponder it in simple terms and consider it the very "good news" which is central to our calling as Christians and from which our baptism and Holy Communion proceed as the "visual gospel." Consider, as you look to Christ who was nailed to the cross and say, "I am rich beyond measure, enriched in Christ with divine life, peace, and joy. For God sent His Son into flesh like mine, yet without sin, to take upon Himself my shame, my burden, and my alienation. He carried these for me and all people those 33 wonderful, yet terrible years—around His praying heart, on His holy soul, on His wounded back, and in His nail-scarred hands and feet and pierced side. He gave Himself, not just of Himself, when he endured "bonds and stripes, the cruel rod," when he was alienated from God to suffer the torments of hell in my place on calvary. He rose again to prove this certainly true. Now I am:

> Redeemed, restored, forgiven,
> Thro' Jesus' precious blood,
> Heirs of His home in heaven,
> Oh, praise our pardoning God! *TLH* 32:1

The Gospel Has Power to Heal Dissension in the Congregation

The healing which the Gospel brought to believers individually should now be the motivation and power to rise above party spirit and strife to a mature fellowship in response to such amazing grace. At Corinth many members were so busy philosophizing and intellectualizing that they failed to give attention to living in daily repentance by the power of the Gospel. The old nature took over the throne of their hearts, and they quareled as did the carpenter's tools. They created dissensions over gifts of the Spirit, over doctrines, and over personalities of members and pastors. Paul enlarges on the problem in this letter in 1 Cor. 3:3 saying, "For you are still of the flesh, for while there is jealousy and strife among you, are you not of the flesh?" In Gal. 5:19-20 these very sins are labeled works of the flesh along with fornication and idolatry. Sins to be repented of!

The apostle gets down to cases in point. "It is reported to me by Chloe's people that there is quarreling among you, my brethren. What I mean is that each one of you says, 'I belong to Paul,' or 'I belong to Apollos,' or 'I belong to Cephas,' or 'I belong to Christ' " (v. 11-12). Whether Chloe was a believer we do not know for sure, but it appears that her people, or servants, were Christians and members of the congregation at Corinth. They lovingly informed Paul about the seriousness of the factions. The factions were still internal. There was no outward separation as yet. But the factions created a lot of ill-will and cheap talk. The leaders preached the same Gospel and taught the same Christian way of life, but the members took occasion to exalt their leaders' personalities, methods, or gifts, and pitted one against the other.

Some said, "I belong to Paul." Paul was the first missionary and pastor at their church. He labored there eighteen months, teaching the word of God among them (Acts 18:1-18). Perhaps members of Gentile background gathered around his name because the Gospel he brought them made them see the light. They were so thankful. It is still true that Christians have a special love and regard for the pastor who first instructed them in the doctrines of God's Word.

Some said, "I belong to Apollos." There is a brief character sketch of Apollos in Acts 18:24—19:10 which includes his early labors at Corinth. He was a Jew from Alexandria, eloquent, and well versed in the Scriptures. Some members loved his Scriptural emphasis, his literary graces, his intellectualism, his innovations.

Some said, "I belong to Cephas." That name is the Jewish form of "Peter" which means "rock." We have no direct information from Scripture that Peter was ever at Corinth, but it is supposed from this statement. No doubt Christians from Jewish backgrounds were attracted to him for personal reasons (cf. Gal. 2:11-21). He seemed to conform to Jewish traditions more than the others. Besides, he had been the leader of The Twelve, so it was easy to be attracted to one of the great ones. A parishioner of mine happened to have her hand shook by our country's president and she said, "I was so proud, I didn't wash my hand for a week." There is that attraction to great leaders!

Others said, "I belong to Christ." This group was tired of the bickerings, and it seems they formed a group dedicated to Christ's name alone. Perhaps in doing so they left the impression that they were the only true Christians at Corinth, which made them rather intolerant and self-righteous.

The error was not in that these members exalted their leaders, but that they did it to an unwarranted degree as they pitted one against the other for self-aggrandizement. This created dissensions. The problem with the Christ party was not that they formed around His name, but that they placed Christ into competition with man as head of a party over against other parties. Paul asks, "Is Christ divided?" Has Christ been divided up like so many pieces of a pie, a piece for each group? Christ is One in His personal union, the God-Man, and the church which is His body is one, and therefore it must be one in action.

Paul asks, "Was Paul crucified for you?" The essence of salvation is the crucifixion of Christ. A Christian belongs to Him who died to redeem from eternal death! It is unthinkable that a person would get hooked on personalities of preachers when so great a saving act makes a person a Christian.

At Corinth they made a "Paul Christ," an "Apollos Christ," a "Cephas Christ," and a "Party Christ." It is so easy to make a Christ after our own image, whims, and ideas, isn't it? We might make a "stained-glass Christ" who is a model of moral virtue, attractive and all, but best left in the church window lest He change things around too much in daily life. We might make a "Divine bell-hop Christ" who is supposed to come running to carry out our earthly requests, quite divorced from His will and kingdom. We might invent a "Golden rule Christ" so fitting for our times when the crown of thorns and purple robe are replaced with the instructors cap and gown. This creates theological dissension and strife! But the real Christ of the Scriptures is the Christ of the cross. The only way those Christians at Corinth could rise above party spirit was to realize and experience the healing power of the Gospel. They would have to bring those sins of strife, jealousy, and quarreling to the cross and call them *sin*. They would have to ask forgiveness for them, as for any other sin, and in response to such matchless grace of God they would be led to say, "Thank you, Lord, for erasing sin's penalty. Now, Lord Jesus, take over the throne of my heart. Reign there supreme. Make a daily difference in my moral decisions, in my conversations, in my recreational choices, in my associations with others, including my brothers and sisters in the faith in my congregation."

The apostle makes his appeal that way in v. 10: "I appeal to you, brethren, by the name of our Lord Jesus Christ, that all of you agree and that there be no dissensions among you, but that you be united in the same mind and the same judgment." They were to use a right understanding and spiritual judgment in matters of faith and life. They were to express oneness in Bible doctrines, in use of spiritual gifts, and in conducting worship services. In general they were to express the fact that the ground is level at the cross, that they were all redeemed by one Redeemer, and all baptized into God's forever-family with His power to walk in newness of life. They were to further apply the healing power of the Gospel and say, "We are all accepted by the Father in Jesus Christ. We are given that blood-bought worthiness before God. We don't have to bolster our self-esteem by cutting down others and making ourselves look bigger by identification with big names. Rather we have a spiritual worth before God that makes us all one in His grace. We are "brethren" of the Lord together."

A group of Christians met for a retreat at a camp. The place where they held their daily worship had no altar. So they drew a circle on the floor in the center of the room. Every day it was someone's turn to find something to place in the circle to depict the Gospel. One day two boys were fighting and were covered with mud. Someone saw it and invited them to stand in the circle and make up. As they stood in the circle, they hugged each other and smiled. Everyone agreed that it was beautiful, and they understood the healing power of the Gospel. Thus, the Gospel that heals individual hearts heals congregational dissension.

> Blest be the tie that binds our hearts in Christian love,
> The fellowship of kindred minds is like to that above.
> *TLH* 464:1

Let us thank the Lord of the church for employing us in His kingdom-building program. Every congregation and every member of it who is healed by the Gospel becomes a pulpit from which the Carpenter of Nazareth preaches the Gospel to the poor in spirit. Let each of us show that healing Gospel-power in our daily lives and in our life together with members of our congregations as we labor together with Him.

Your Life in Christ

FOURTH SUNDAY AFTER THE EPIPHANY
1 CORINTHIANS 1:26-31

Donald J. Poganski

These words by an unknown author in "One Solitary Life" have inspired so many Christians: Nineteen wide centuries have come and gone, and today Christ is still the central figure of the human race and the leader of the column of progress. One is far within the mark when saying that all the armies that ever marched and all the navies that ever sailed and all the parliaments that ever sat and all the kings that ever reigned, put together, have not affected the life of man upon this earth as has that One Solitary Life: our Savior's.

At the church in Corinth there were many, it seemed, whose spiritual outlook and attitude was affected by worldly ideas. They were "washed, sanctified, and justified in the name of the Lord Jesus Christ" (1 Cor. 6:11), but somehow they began to think that the cross-method of salvation was unbecoming to a great and glorious God and that the greatness of man ought to figure in somewhere in their Christian calling. The apostle magnifies Jesus Christ in this letter and insists on the power of the cross in the first chapter as the power for their new spiritual life. In the text he invites them, and us, to consider:

Your Life in Christ

Your Life in Christ Is a New Life Lived by Faith-Relationship to Christ

The apostle says in v. 30, "He (God) is the source of your life in Christ Jesus." Yes, God is love! God did love the world so much that He gave His only-begotten Son. That makes God the source of our salvation. From our vantage point it means that all that we are and have as Christians is because of our relationship to Christ—"Your life in Christ." Christ is the very atmosphere in which we live. We are personally attached to the living Person, Jesus Christ, by faith. In connection with this Martin Luther once wrote:

> Faith must be taught correctly, namely, that by it you are so cemented to Christ that He and you are as one person, which cannot be separated but remains attached to Him forever and declares: "I am as Christ." And Christ in turn says: "I am as that sinner who is attached to Me, and I to him. For by faith we are joined together into one flesh and one bone." (Luther's Works, Vol 26. St. Louis: Concordia Publishing House, 1963 p. 168)

The Reformer spoke of this mystical union in another way saying, "If you were to knock at the door of my heart and ask, 'Who lives here?' I would answer, 'Martin Luther used to live here, but he moved out and Jesus Christ lives here now.' " So you see that to be in Christ is to have His mystical presence in you by faith. Then you are alive in Christ. He said, "I am the Life" (John 14:6) and "I came that they might have life" (John 10:10). It is true as the apostle Paul says, "Therefore, if any one is in Christ, he is a new creation" (2 Cor. 5:17).

Your Life in Christ Is a Life Lived in Connection with Christ's Gifts of Grace

Your life is changed by Christ's gift of wisdom: "Whom God made our wisdom." Wisdom is the very highest, gracious, heavenly series of thoughts of God in Christ which enlightens our souls with divine Life. When writing to Pastor Timothy, the apostle mentioned it, "From a child you have known the Holy Scriptures which are able to make thee wise unto salvation through faith which is in Christ Jesus" (2 Tim. 3:15 KJV). The Greek mind, which was so addicted to worldly wisdom, toyed with the idea that God certainly could have put the Gospel in a form which would appeal more to the intelligentsia. Could not God's Son be born in a wise philosopher's family, or be one with political clout? Shouldn't He have dwelt in the finest castle in the capital city? To that we might add, if we want to match the Gospel with our wisdom, why didn't He come with a super Caesar image, riding on some golden chariot, with archangels as His publicity agents to whip men into shape? Why, rather, a lowly virgin, a manger, Nazareth, and a cross? The answer to that is God's wisdom. God's methods were designed to meet God's purpose—to lift souls of spiritually dead people to eternal life with Him. That took a cross on which His Son died everyone's eternal death to bring them life. People who own up to their spiritual need in Christ and trust His grace have His wisdom and are changed from spiritual death to spiritual life. Christ is the "Word of God incarnate, the Wisdom from on high."

Your Life in Christ is a life credited with Christ's gift of righteousness: "Whom God made our ... righteousness." This is the righteousness which is credited to our account by faith in Christ. God the heavenly Judge has a right to "throw the book" at us for our many sins, but Christ our heavenly Attorney pleads our case and displays His nail-scarred hands in our behalf. Our faith trusts His blood and merit and God declares us "not guilty" as we are covered with Christ's righteousness. Christ's righteousness brings about a new relationship with God. He becomes our reconciled heavenly Father, for "God made Him (Jesus) to be sin who knew no sin, so that in Him we might become the righteousness of God" (2 Cor. 5:21). The Chinese character for "righteousness'" is a remarkable illustration of that. It consists of the character for a lamb which is above the character for the personal pronoun "me." As God looks upon me, a sinner, He sees His Lamb above me, and God sees not my sin but the righteousness of Christ covering me. Say in your heart with the prophet Isaiah, "I will greatly rejoice in the Lord, ... for He has clothed me with the garments of salvation, He has covered me with the robe of righteousness" (Isa. 61:10).

> Jesus, Thy blood and righteousness
> My beauty are, my glorious dress. *TLH* 371:1

Your Life in Christ is a life growing in Christ's gift of sanctification: "Whom God made our ... sanctification." When Christ dwells in us and we in Him, our thoughts, words, and deeds reflect

Christ. He is the inner power that transforms us by His Spirit. We cannot aspire to a godly life by our own strength. We have no power to perform truth or love according to the Commandments apart from Christ. But as we daily experience the height and depth and length and breadth of His forgiving love, we respond in love and thanksgiving, saying like Paul, "Lord, what do you want me to do?" Our sanctification will never be complete in this life, because the old nature clings to us, but this does not stop us from growing towards perfection.

A Sunday school teacher once taught a fine lesson on heaven, and some of the pupils disturbed the class a bit that day. When the teacher asked, "Who wants to go to heaven?" all raised their hands enthusiastically but one boy. When the teacher asked, "Why, don't you want to go to heaven?" He responded, "I really do, but not with this crowd." We can appreciate his remark because on this side of heaven "this crowd" is not perfect in living. "This crowd" of believers is under the construction of God's grace, living in repentance and reflecting faith in deeds of love. Motivated by His love, we seek His will, and thus we aim to let Jesus Christ make a daily difference. "This is the will of God, your sanctification" (1 Thess. 4:3). It's Christ's gift to bless our lives with good.

Your Life in Christ is a life focused upon final redemption: "Whom God made our . . . redemption." Because Christ has redeemed us from sin's penalty by His own precious blood, we enjoy new birth and new life by faith. We have peace with God, joy of salvation, and steadfast hope. But on that last great Day when Jesus comes in glory, we shall receive a glorious resurrection body like unto Christ's, our souls shall be renewed in God's perfect image, and we shall be done with the battle against sin. We shall be rid of tears, sorrow, and death forever. We shall enjoy God's pleasures forevermore. Besides, we shall inherit the many mansions prepared for us by Christ, and we shall be in the house of the Lord forever. Jesus Christ is our final redemption and all that it means.

> This is your life in Christ. You can say, "He means all this to me!"
> My Wisdom—No wisdom of my own have I, but humbly ask of Him,
>   Who gives to all men liberally Himself—The Light within.
> My Righteousness—My righteousness—but filthy rags; I shed them at His feet, And in His shining raiment clad, Made for His presence meet.
> My Sanctification—By His own loving sacrifice "For the Master's use made meet," I'm set apart to live for Him in lowly service sweet,
> My Redemption—A slave to all unrighteousness, Undone and lost in sin.
> He reaches out His pierced hand; Redeemed—I worship Him.
> (Lida E. Voight, "Still Waters, Green Pastures," Good Shepherd Home, Terra Bella, CA, p. 67)

Your Life in Christ Is a Life Lived in the Attitude of Christian Humility

The apostle insisted that God is the source of your life in Christ Jesus with all His gifts of grace. Then he goes on to point out in v. 29 "that no human being might boast in the presence of God." When man stands before the Maker, he cannot say, "Lord, let me into heaven because I was somebody and I lived such a good life." That way is not open to man! Rather, a person must be right with God now by receiving Christ and His righteousness. That act of faith brings human pride and boasting about man's goodness to nothing because experience with God's grace exludes human effort. "By grace you have been saved through faith . . . not because of works lest any man should boast" (Eph. 2:8-9).

The whole matter of God's gracious actions in the redemption plan and the Christian calling invites us to a life of humility. What Paul says in v. 26 is a call to humility. He expands the truth of God's actions in calling the Corinthians in three thoughts and shows that they have nothing to boast about. "For consider your call, brethren; not many of you were wise according to worldly standards." God chose to work His marvels through people who were, from the human point of view, most unpromising—lowly shepherds, uneducated fishermen, tax collectors—for the most part. And there at Corinth most of the members were very low on the social scale. Many were slaves and uneducated. But Paul says, "Not many of you were wise." He means that some were from the higher classes, like Stephanas, Crispus, and Erastus, the city treasurer (Rom. 16:23). These were humbled, too, by God's grace at the foot of the cross. "Not many were powerful." There were not many principal people in that congregation. "Not many were of noble birth." Not many came from famous families. The things which elevate man in the world—knowledge, influence, rank, are not the things which lead to God and salvation.

Then the apostle adds a list of things in vs. 27-28 which deflates human pride. "But God chose what is foolish in the world to shame the wise." Things like a manger, shepherds, a cross, shame the professional pride of those wise in their own conceits. "God chose what is weak in the world to shame the strong." Things like the lowly virgin, the little town of Bethlehem, God's Son dying a criminal's death penalty, certainly shame the strong. Oh, these who exalt self-importance in their lives, only to find it to be a sham in the end! "God chose what is low and despised in the world, even things that are not, to bring to nothing things that are." Let's reflect on the phrase, "Even things that are not." Here Paul flashes a light back on the three things just mentioned. "Things that are not" do not exist (until God creates them in the believer's heart).

—In foolish things, true wisdom does not yet exist.

—In weak things, true strength does not yet exist.

—In low and despised things, true dignity and value do not yet exist. These are often, "low and despised in the world." These "things that are not"—wisdom, strength, dignity, and value, are all gifts from God's grace. The secret of salvation is that God can enter with His grace only where the place is completely empty of self. Only where God can first sweep out what is "of the world" can He bring in what is "of the kingdom of heaven." This is expressed so well in "Treasures" by Martha Snell Nicholson:

> One by one He took them from me, all the things I valued most,
> Until I was empty-handed; every glittering toy was lost.
> And I walked earth's highways, grieving, in my rags and poverty,
> 'Till I heard His voice inviting, "Lift your empty hands to Me."
> So I held my hands toward heaven, and He filled them with a store
> Of His own transcendent riches, 'Till they could contain no more.
> And at last I comprehended with my stupid mind and dull,
> That God could not pour His riches into hands already full!
> (Cathedral press, Art Folder 7912, Long Prairie, MN)

While "things that are" do exist among men, like worldly wisdom, money-power, noble birth—they are opposites of "things that are not," like wisdom, strength, dignity, and value. Things that exist are transient. They are a vain show, nothing more. They get in the way of the kingdom, as Paul would testify in Phil. 3:4-11 and as we learn from John 3 in the life of Nicodemus. God is right and merciful in "bringing to nothing things that are" by exposing their vanity and non-value by "the things that are not" lest men go on relying on them to their everlasting disappointment. Humility is an attitude of heart and life which relies solely on the grace of God in Jesus Christ. Humility is so delicate a virtue which blooms only in the light of the cross, that to look upon itself it vanishes away. A lowly monk was once showing a prospective member around the monastery. He was rather apologetic about the lowly surroundings, so he said, "While other orders may have better sleeping accommodations and more modern commisaries and nicer chapels, when it comes to humility we are tops." To brag about humility is the height of pride. When people at Corinth bragged about themselves, they were acting in pride. What they needed to remember is that what they were as redeemed Christians was by the sheer grace of God. They were to express their gratitude in humility of heart and life. We need to join the apostle in declaring, "By the grace of God, I am what I am" (1 Cor. 15:10).

Paul concludes the discussion with a quote from Jer. 9:23-24, which he summarizes, saying, "Therefore, as it is written, 'Let him who boasts, boast of the Lord.'" As believers we sing, "Glory to God in the highest" as the theme of life. We extol God who has given us His all-sufficient grace, grace to cover every sin, grace to meet every hour of trial, and grace to bring us home. As a part of boasting of the Lord, we can afford to have a healthy self-esteem and self-image because that comes from gratefully knowing that in the eyes of God we are covered with the blood-bought worthiness of His Son. There are two extremes in our time. One is the promotion of success and greatness through exalted self-esteem and self-love. The other is the loneliness and poor self-image, hallmarks of our age, which cults and new religions take advantage of by offering instant worth through cheap acceptance. But the Bible teaches us that a healthy self-esteem and a true self-image and self-acceptance come from Christ. It is not self-worth, but Christ-worth! Thus, a Christian view of self is not so much a view of self, as it is a view of faith, and it is not so much a view of faith, as it is a view of Christ and His grace. To have and use these gifts to God's glory is a tribute to God's grace and "boasting of the Lord."

In a painting of the crucifixion by the famous Dutch artist Rembrandt, your attention is first drawn to the cross and to Christ who died there as your ransom. Then you notice the many people at Calvary and their various attitudes and actions. Then as your eyes drift off to the edge of the painting, you see a little figure of a man in the shadows. This is Rembrandt himself, He is saying, "My sins nailed the Savior there, but He died for me and I believe it." What humility of heart and what blessings of grace!

May you daily experience Your life in Christ and the abundant life that he promised! May you know the wonderful affect that One Solitary Life can have on you! Remember, apart from Christ there is only death. With Christ there is life.

Wisdom of the Creator

FIFTH SUNDAY AFTER THE EPIPHANY
1 CORINTHIANS 2:1-5

Alfred T. Scheips

> O Word of God Incarnate,
> O Wisdom from on high,
> O Truth unchanged, unchanging,
> O Light of our dark sky,—
> We praise Thee for the radiance
> That from the hallowed page,
> A lantern to our footsteps,
> Shines on from age to age. *(TLH* 294:1)

As we continue the rounds of another church year, we are approaching the end of the Epiphany season. These weeks began

January 6th with the account of the Wise Men from the East seeking and finding the Savior. Wise men and women still seek Him and find Him. We do this during these two months of the year and call the season Epiphany, which means manifestation—that Christ was manifested as the Savior of all, Gentiles as well as Jews. These weeks are very apropos for looking at wisdom's role in life.

God's Word and Wisdom

The Bible has much to say about wisdom. We're told in Proverbs that "wisdom is better than jewels, and all that you may desire cannot compare with her" (Prov. 8:11). In Psalm 90 (v. 12) there is the prayer of God, "so teach us to number our days that we may get a heart of wisdom." The King James Version suggests that we "apply our hearts unto wisdom." That sounds like a real goal for all Christians. Applying our hearts unto wisdom—that's what education is all about, regardless of age or race, sex or social status. It's significant that the earliest worshipers of the Christ included shepherds as well as Wise Men from the East. At separate times they paid tribute to the "Word of God Incarnate, the Wisdom from on high." They know this was the Word who "became flesh and dwelt among us, full of grace and truth"; and since then "we have beheld His glory, glory as of the only Son from the Father"(John 1:14—RSV).

Applying Our Hearts unto Wisdom

Bear in mind that the text is from 1 Corinthians. Ancient Corinth and Athens were great intellectual centers of the Mediterranean world. The ancient Greeks valued wisdom highly. Much of their philosphy dealt with the intellect and with metaphysical speculations about every conceivable subject. A Greek word that is often used in the New Testament, including the inspired words of today's Epistle, is the Greek word "sophia." Etymologically it's the one root of the word philosopher, a "lover of wisdom." The Greeks loved wisdom. They talked about it all of the time, as so many people do today. Little wonder that when the apostle Paul in his letter to the Corinthians went into detail about the Christian faith and about the power of God and the wisdom of God, he also spoke about the wisdom of the people. He spoke at great length about the wisdom and strength of the Creator; but he also writes about the strengths and the weaknesses of the creature.

Two Kinds of Wisdom

In these Sundays of the Epiphany season, when the epistles are from the first chapters of 1 Corinthians, we should say: "Let's apply our hearts unto wisdom." Today the emphasis is on the wisdom of the Creator, next Sunday on the wisdom of the creature. Both are so important. Paul in the first chapter of this epistle states that his message is not only to proclaim the testimony and the mysteries of God in lofty words of wisdom, but he also wants to emphasize the need for human wisdom. Both spiritual and secular wisdom are to be stressed. The duality applies to us.

Think of Paul's Message on Mars Hill

In the Book of Acts we're told about Paul's missionary journeys. When he came to ancient Athens, it disturbed him that he saw so many different gods worshiped but all were gods of man's creation. In his Mars Hill sermon he said he even saw one altar erected "to an unknown god." That sight prompted his words: "What therefore you worship as unknown, this I proclaim to you" (Acts 17:23). So when they cornered him in the market place and asked about this new wisdom, he used the natural knowledge of God ingrained in their hearts as a springboard to tell them about God Incarnate in the person of Jesus Christ. But when he came to the resurrection, they rather brusquely said to him: "Oh, we will hear you again about this matter." In other words, the wisdom of the creature was something they wanted to hear, but not the wisdom of the Creator, and not the wisdom of God in Christ.

Christ Our Wisdom

In the first chapter of this epistle Paul had spoken of Jesus Christ, "Whom God made our wisdom" (v. 30). This is our good news today too. We have the parallel situations today, with many people liking to hear about the wisdom of the creature. These new technical developments and discoveries are intriguing. But does this scientific progress with all of its gadgetry bring us a savior from sin? Do all of the isms and the cults and the movements redeem us? Do the philosophies and psychological sophistries answer the deep problems about the meaning of life, and the whence, the why, and the whither of life? Does wisdom of the creature answer the age—old problem about the abyss that exists between God and human beings by nature? We need a Savior from sin, and that is where the wisdom of the Creator comes in. Paul speaks to these worldly wise people at ancient Corinth and says he was not bringing "lofty words of wisdom" of a secular nature only. He was also telling them of the wisdom of the Creator, which paradoxically leads to the wisdom of the cross. Paul's message was Jesus Christ and Him crucified. This verse of the text is not the only place where we have the same emphasis of Christ-centered theology. Rom. 5:8 states: "God shows His love for us in that while we were yet sinners Christ died for us." How did He die? The crucified Christ witnesses to the wisdom of the Creator in contrast to the wisdom of the creature. There are several references to wisdom in this chapter: the wisdom of God and the wisdom of people. You can't separate these in us, since there is only one person involved.

Lessons from Corinth

Ancient Corinth was so full of human pride and sin, of materialism, of sophistry, and of secular wisdom. It knew so much in one way, and yet Paul knew it needed something more, the wisdom of the Creator. Anybody who has visited that site is intrigued by its archaeological accessibility. Jerusalem and many ancient cities saw generations come and go. As buildings were destroyed or crumbled, the new construction was built on the old ruins. Many strata must be excavated to discover what it was like in the first century. In ancient Corinth it was different. The new Corinth was built a couple of miles away. So you don't have layer upon layer of rubble to excavate—today visitors can see the streets and the market places and the temples of ancient Corinth. The guide books tell about life at the time when Paul wrote this letter. The life-style revolved around sensate pleasures, around things of the mind, and material things. But there was a haunting feeling that this was not enough. That's why the apostle Paul preached Christ crucified as the answer to a great need. This wasn't easy for him. It isn't easy for us when we approach people who are intrigued by intellectualism, by the wisdom of the creatures, and who at the moment are not concerned about the wisdom of the Creator.

Christ is the Answer

So the apostle says: "I came in weakness; I came in much fear and trembling." And again: "My message and my speech were not in plausible words of wisdom." He says, "I was no great orator." But he does go on, saying, "I have a message—Christ and Him crucified." That message is in demonstration of the spirit and power. This good news is not the wisdom of people, but the wisdom of God, the power and wisdom in Christ.

The Balanced Life

So when we hear the command of the Old Testament, repeated in the New, that we are to love God with all our heart and all our soul and all our mind, that gives us the balanced life. Those passages also add that we are to "love our neighbor as ourselves."

A Fourfold Fitness

When our Lord at the age of 12 amazed the people with His wisdom and went back to Nazareth, it is said in Luke 2: "He increased in wisdom and in stature, and in favor with God and man." There was a balanced growth, a fourfold fitness. This is so important for Christians today, when it is so easy to drift into obscurantism and anti-intellectualism. Religionists, in the Christian sense especially, should be intellectually respectable. But the reverse is true too, that intellectuals should be religiously respectable. Just as the Wise Men from the East came to find out more about religion and about God's promises in Christ, so also intellectuals should know about God and His plan of salvation and His inspired Word. How can one decide honestly whether he can follow the Christian faith and life unless he knows what it is?

Where True Wisdom Resides

The last verse of the text suggests the proper perspective so that "your faith might not rest in the wisdom of men, but in the power of God." The texts for today and next Sunday develop the Christian ideal by not negating the desirability of the wisdom of the creature. Faith rests according to this text in the wisdom of men as an incomplete foundation, but in the power of God as the true and complete foundation. That wisdom is Christ crucified.

What Do You Lack?

In ancient Athens and in Corinth on the streets and in the market places the vendors would go up and down peddling their wares, crying out: "What do you lack? What do you lack?" So all of us must ask: What do I lack? Am I sufficient, self-sufficient, materially and spiritually? Materially, many might say: "Yes, I can make it on my own." But spiritually there is the haunting feeling that we lack the bridge back to God. Of course, the good news is found in what Christ came to be. Simply stated, He is our Savior and Redeemer. The cross is the symbol of God's wisdom.

> In the cross of Christ I glory,
> Tow'ring o'er the wrecks of time,
> All the light of sacred story,
> Gathers round its head sublime. *(TLH* 354:1)

When Inquiry Ends

In Psalm 27 the inspired writer talks about beholding the beauty of the Lord. Then he goes on and suggests that we are to inquire in His temple, to bring the mind, to bring human wisdom to bear in our life's plan. We aren't to trade God for gadgets. We aren't to disparage human reason. We aren't to disdain the wisdom of people. There should be no one-sided, but a balanced view of wisdom, the wisdom of the Creator and the wisdom of the creature.

Love Builds Up

Christ said the greatest word is love. Paul wrote to these same Corinthians later in chapter 8: "Knowledge puffs up, but love builds up." Knowledge and love together give us the power. Thus Phillips' *New Testament in Modern English* heads our text:

> "I came to you in God's strength, not my own," and renders today's epistle in these picturesque words: "I did not come equipped with any brilliance of speech or intellect. You may as well know now that it was my secret determination to concentrate entirely on Jesus Christ Himself and the fact of His death upon the cross. As a matter of fact, in myself I was feeling far from strong; I was nervous and rather shaky. What I said and preached had none of the attractiveness of the clever mind, but it was a demonstration of the power of the Spirit of God! Plainly God's purpose was that your faith should rest not upon man's cleverness but upon the power of God."

We pray that God might ever open our hearts to the wisdom of the Creator and to the wisdom of the creature. A hymn has a beautiful closing thought:

> Immortal, invisible, God only wise
> In light inaccessible, hid from our eyes
> Most blessed, most glorious, the ancient of days
> Almighty, victorious, Thy great name we praise. (*WS* 769:1)

Wisdom of the Creature

SIXTH SUNDAY AFTER THE EPIPHANY
1 CORINTHIANS 2:6-13

Alfred T. Scheips

Dozens of Bible passages suggest the desirability of applying our hearts unto wisdom. Some of the key verses are found in Paul's writings to the Corinthians. The two-pronged nature of wisdom is illustrated in the second lessons for last Sunday and today, with the emphasis on both "The Wisdom of the Creator" and "The Wisdom of the Creature." Last Sunday when the former was the theme, there was an undertone about the wisdom of the creature. Today when the overtone is the wisdom of the creature, there is an undertone about the wisdom of the Creator.

The Light of Epiphany

The hymns of the Epiphany season remind us of Jesus, who is "God of God and Light of Light" (*TLH:* 132:1). We sing of Him: "Thy Light is drawing near" (*TLH* 126:1). Of the Wise Men we sing: "As with joy they hailed its light", (*TLH* 127:1). In the natural world light is so important, so basic for plant and animal life. Spiritually there is also darkness. This text says the natural eye doesn't see these spiritual truths. But God has revealed them to us through the Spirit. So we know the Epiphany King, the Light to lighten the Gentiles, as well as the glory of His people Israel. The wisdom of the creature has brought to our generation the LASER beam discovery. This is an acronym for *Light Amplification by Stimulated Emission of Radiation.* Research in the LASER field holds a great future in such areas as photography, medicine, and energy. But the wisdom of the creature doesn't bring "the emission of the radiation" of Epiphany. While LASER research is tricky and powerful and frightening, it is not so with God's "light amplification" in Christ. Christ came as the Light of the world. John the Baptist said: "There is the Light; I am not the light."

Spreading the Light

When Matthew, Mark, Luke, and John were putting together the fourfold biographical account of our Lord, what were they doing but amplifying this Light of Christ? This emission of the Good News continued in the Book of Acts. Here we see too the early church putting it into action. We don't know what the wisdom of the creature will discover in the LASER field with its hopeful and yet frightening possibilities, but we do know the good that comes from "God's LASER beams" in Christ, the power of God and the wisdom of God.

When Paul Saw the Light

Acts 9 tells how a "light from heaven" streamed on Paul as he approached Damascus, with the result that Saul the persecutor became Paul the preacher. Later on in his missionary journeys he who had seen the Light came to Corinth, a city of intellectual light and materialistic light, a few miles from Athens, another intellectual center. Paul saw a life-style structured with two great emphases—material goods and the intellectual pursuits. When he looked at their mystical religions, with these Hellenistic rites, he saw a reflection of these areas of life. He saw nothing about God revealing Himself in His incarnate Son, the Son who lived and suffered and died and rose again for mankind.

Paul Spreads the Light

Little wonder that the apostle saw fit to write two epistles to the Corinthians, both rather lengthy, but filled with hope and love and concern. In these two letters he isn't trying to put down secular wisdom. There is no downplaying of the mind and its achievements. All he is telling them is that there is more wisdom than the wisdom of the creature. So in chapter two, from which this text is taken, we find this discussion of total wisdom.

Both Wisdoms are Needed

For the Corinthians and for us it is both the wisdom of the

Creator and the wisdom of the creature. It's not an "either-or" but a "both-and" situation. Paul's span of ministry at Corinth was long enough to know the people and to know the city. In one verse in his second letter to these believers he writes something that is really the whole heart and core of interpersonal relationships: "I am not seeking what is yours, but I'm seeking you." He wanted to help them as persons. This should be our goal too. The first verses of this lesson refer to the wisdom of this age and the rulers of this age, doomed to pass away. So with human philosophers, we have popularized this word to mean somebody who is dealing in speculative thought, in something that is metaphysical, in something that is theoretical. That all has its place. But there has to be more than theory; there must be practical results. The wisdom of this age, also for the Corinthians, promised things material. Many of our philosophies do that today too. Some are so grandiose in the theory that they offer Utopia as a starter! Then comes the disillusionment, when people realize there is more to life than that. There is a passage in the Book of Proverbs which says: "Happy is the person who gets wisdom and who with all his getting gets understanding." In other words, here is wisdom in theory, but also in its practical application.

The Wisdom of Love

The first part of this epistle sets the theory but goes on to sections like 1 Corinthians 13, one of the great chapters in the Bible. Little wonder this chapter is selected by so many couples for inclusion in their wedding service. We begin with the thought in the text about "what God has prepared for those who love Him." Then that love is reflected toward those whom we love. This is how we apply these theories to practice.

God's Wisdom Revealed

This chapter speaks about the secret and hidden wisdom of God revealed in us. "None of the rulers of this age understood this; for if they had, they would not have crucified the Lord of glory. But, as it is written, 'What no eye has seen, nor ear heard, nor the heart of man conceived, what God has prepared for those who love him' " (vs. 8, 9) God has revealed. Secular wisdom thus is supplemented by "the things of God that have been revealed to us by the Spirit." There are many sensate pleasures that are very legitimate, and we thank God for them. Other sensate pleasures are illegitimate, as you heard outlined in the first lesson and in the Gospel for today. God's commandments are clear. God has given us His inspired Word, so that when secular wisdom falls short, spiritual wisdom fills in the gaps. God *has* revealed these things to us by His Spirit. The perfect tense, the tense of completed action, is used. Something that has been revealed now stands. In His sixth statement on the cross Jesus used this same tense when He cried out with a loud voice: "It is finished." It's been accomplished. Redemption is completed, and that's why we treasure the Word of God so—not in the sense of worshiping a book, but in the sense of worshiping the Almighty God who as a personal being has inspired these writers, the holy men of God who spoke as they were moved by the Holy Ghost. All Scripture is given us by inspiration of God. This is exactly what the text says when it explains that God has revealed these things to us by His Spirit.

The Superior Wisdom of the Creator

In one of his epistles, 1 John 3:18, John says: "Little children, let us not love in word or speech but in deed and in truth." The creature doesn't see this wisdom applied to life, but the Creator does and reveals it to us as the practical side of God's love. The wisdom that is here revealed is not against nature; it isn't contra-natural. It is supernatural. "Super" simply means above, on a higher level. We often talk about humans as being finite. That word comes form the Latin word "finis" which means end. There is a definite limit there. God is not finite; He is infinite. These things then become super-natural. V. 11 in this text speaks again of wisdom, but it refers to spiritual truths comprehended by the Spirit of God. The text infers that we are not to use human wisdom and oratorical ability as the determinate factor in God's plan of salvation. The epistle tells of a certain Apollos who labored in Corinth. He was a great preacher, a great speaker. Acts 18:28 says of him: "He powerfully confuted the Jews in public, showing by the Scriptures that the Christ was Jesus." Yet, even though he had oratorical abilities, this was not his forte. His message was Christ and Christ crucified.

No Partyism in Christ

We find reference in the epistle to the Corinthians to factions in the church. Because of the fact that he was such a great orator, some people said: "I'm for Apollos." Others said: "I'm for Paul." Other: "I'm for Peter." In his message the apostle denounces them for this partyism. In effect he said: "I wasn't crucified for you. Peter wasn't crucified for you. Apollos wasn't crucified for you. Jesus Christ was." That is our message. In the previous chapter Paul warned against "letting the cross of Christ be emptied of its power" (v. 17).

Wisdom Taught by the Spirit

Verse 12 says: "Now we have received not the spirit of the world, but the Spirit which is from God, that we might understand the gifts bestowed on us by God." One of the synonymous terms for the

Spirit in the Bible is Comforter. Our Lord said: "The Holy Comforter will come to you." That's a beautiful word and thought: Comforter. This third Person of God, who through the Gospel, calls, gathers, enlightens, and sanctifies us is not to be a sedative to ease the pains of life that all of us have but the Comforter who strengthens us! If you look up the derivation of this word, you will find that "comforter" has the same root as "fort" in fortify or fortification. The prefix "com" means "with," and so a comforter is one with strengthening, with fortifications. This role is suggested in the last verse of the text: "We impart this in words not taught by human wisdom but taught by the Spirit, interpreting spiritual truths to those who possess the Spirit."

Wisdom Taught by the Creature

As then we think about human wisdom, spiritual wisdom, the wisdom of the Creator, the wisdom of the creature, we review our total educational growth. The "wisdom of the creature" has developed the field of television, which has such an impact on the education of children and adults. An average high school graduate, according to one study, has watched 440,000 television commercials. For weal or woe, there is an educational process involved—from the Christian perspective it is distorted. A great educational tool like television must not bring a one-sided wisdom. There is a passage in Is. 11 about the future Messiah being the Spirit of God; the spirit of wisdom shall rest upon Him. It's a bit ironic that the more the wisdom of the creature enables people to manipulate the natural world to their seeming advantage, the less meaningful they find it. There is a haunting menace of directionlessness, of meaninglessness. Our Lord said: "What will it profit a man if he gains the whole world and forfeits his life?" (Matt. 16:26)

Two-Sidedness Needed for a Balanced Life

So the wisdom of the creature needs the balance of the wisdom of the Creator. We need both for a balanced life. A one-sidedness, with a person obsessed with the wisdom of the creature, leads to frustration, because the wisdom of the Creator is neglected. On the other hand, if you simply try to be a mystic and talk only about the wisdom of the Creator that too is an imbalance in life. A patient once said to a psychologist: "If I only knew that my life had some meaning and some purpose, I don't think I would have any silly problem about my nerves."

These Corinthians Greeks, with their Hellenistic mystery cults and their philosophy buffs, were equipped for an intellectual life but not for a total life.

The Source of True Wisdom

We today have modern counterparts of these ancient isms, life-styles, and cults. But, as in ancient Corinth, they don't unravel the deepest mysteries and secrets of God, and that's why we need sacred truths that God has revealed to us by His Spirit. Paul notes that if the people of the time had known the truth they would not have crucified the Lord of glory. That's why he witnessed to God's truth in Christ—as do we! Matt. 13 is a great chapter. It has a number of parables. At the end of the chapter we find the people asking the question: "Where did this Man get this wisdom?" And the answer in effect simply is: He was true God, the Divine Teacher of secular and sacred wisdom. That is why He could take those life situations of the parables and teach with human wisdom the sacred wisdom, telling the people about the kingdom of God. The word of Christ on the cross is the word of wisdom, and it's the only word with a true answer to all of the problems facing us. Our Lord once said: "We don't live by bread alone—by material things alone." Similarly we don't live by spiritual things alone. There must be both. Our prayer is that of a couplet in a hymn that closes each stanza: "Grant us wisdom, Grant us courage, for the facing of this hour" (WS 778:1).

O Lord, give us light to see you steadily and see You whole in all Your world; give us wisdom to fear and to obey and trust the God unseen whom we can see, O God made visible by Your own illumining, to trust You round all corners, down all streets, in all shadows, across all puddles, through all mud, in Your world, ruled by Your almighty and all-giving hand, through Jesus Christ our Lord. Amen. (Pray for Joy, by Martin H. Franzmann. St. Louis: Concordia Publishing House, 1970. "A Prayer for Wisdom," pp. 47-48)

The Continued Construction of Christ's Church

SEVENTH SUNDAY AFTER THE EPIPHANY
1 CORINTHIANS 3:10-11, 16-23

Rudolph F. Norden

How long does it take to put up a church? Unlike European cathedrals that were centuries in the making, most modern church structures are completed in record time. The cornerstone is laid, and gradually but steadily the building is reared. There comes a day when the last nail has been driven, the last stone put into place. The contractor removes the scaffolding and takes his construction crew elsewhere. The church is finished, awaiting occupancy by the congregation.

It is different with the holy Christian church, the communion of saints. It is never finished. As long as it abides in this world, the church of Jesus Christ continues to grow, to mature, to reach out to new territory, to gain converts. To this end, as per Christ's instruction, the church proclaims the Gospel and makes disciples of all nations by baptizing them. The same work that Paul and the other apostles began we carry forward until the Lord Himself will bid our building efforts cease. Whether we think of ancient Corinth or of any of our modern cities or communities, Christ's disciples are engaged in the upbuilding of the church.

I. The Basis of the Church

We can speak of the upbuilding of Christ's church as a continuing process because the basis on which is it constructed is not material, mundane, or human but spiritual, heavenly, and divine.

A. The Foundation of the Church Is Jesus Christ

Paul tells the troubled Corinthians, "No other foundation can anyone lay than that which is laid, which is Jesus Christ" (v. 16). This needed to be said, for the church in Corinth was badly fractured, due largely to the belief that the church was to be founded on men—on Paul, Apollos, or Cephas. The Corinthians could "be united in the same mind and the same judgment" (1:10) only if they turned from the cult of human leadership and acknowledged Jesus Christ as the church's one foundation.

This foundation is a "given," for the apostle refers to it as "that which is laid." Who gave it? God Himself, for it was He who, in Isaiah's words, "laid in Zion for a foundation a Stone, a tested stone, a precious Cornerstone, of a sure foundation" (Is. 28:16). In his First Epistle (2:6) Peter establishes that this Cornerstone is Jesus Christ. In eternity God appointed Him and in due time anointed Him with the Holy Spirit and with power to be the foundation of the church.

The church's promised foundation became a reality when Jesus Christ so loved the church that He gave Himself for it. The love that impelled the Son of God to give His life in atonement for man's sin and to rise again in certification of the fullment of His redeeming work is declared to us in the Gospel, and all who believe it are added to the saving church. The truth that makes Jesus Christ the foundation of the church—the truth on which the church stands or falls—is this: "Jesus our Lord . . . was put to death for our trespasses and raised for our justification" (Rom. 4:25).

All who accept Jesus Christ as their Savior are members of the church that is continually being built on the foundation God Himself has laid.

B. Proper Use of the Foundation

Human teachings are an improper basis for the church. They can be very deceiving. In Corinth people not only said that they followed Paul, Apollos, and Cephas but also claimed, "We belong to Christ." And they, too, were sectarians. You can hear them say, "Sure, we accept Jesus Christ as the foundation of the church," but then they sought to build little shacks or huts of human speculation on it. Therefore Paul goes on to say about the foundation that is Christ, "Let each man take care how he builds upon it" (v. 10).

Human teachings may vary in value, ranging from "gold, silver, precious stones" to the less durable "wood, hay, stubble," but in the end they must pass the test of God's Word, and whatever is at variance with it does not deserve to be built on the foundation God Himself has laid.

As Himself the foundation, our Lord made provision for the church to be built on Him. He gave the church His Word, and He instituted the sacraments. When the church continues in Christ's teaching of Law and Gospel and faithfully administers the sacraments of Holy Baptism and Holy Communion, it truly honors Jesus Christ as the foundation God has laid for the internal and external upbuilding of the church.

Here we think not only of what God does through the means of grace in the sanctuary but also of the interaction of Christians at home and in other places where Christ becomes a reality in their lives, and this always by the use of His Word. Whatever the setting, this is how all who constitute the holy Christian church build themselves up on Jesus Christ as the foundation. "Let the Word of Christ dwell in you richly, as you teach and admonish one another in all wisdom, and as you sing psalms and hymns and spiritual songs with thankfulness in your hearts to God" (Col. 3:16). Christ's Word is at work, as Martin Luther put it, "through the mutual conversation and consolation of the brethren." And when this is so, Christ is honored as the true foundation of the church.

II. The Builders of the Church

Sometimes congregations, perhaps because of factors beyond their control, never get out of their basement churches. The foundation is there, but the superstructure never materializes. As far as His holy Christian church is concerned, God is not satisfied to have merely the foundation, good as it is; He wants the church to be built on it. But who is to do the building?

A. The True Builder Is the Holy Spirit

Paul speaks of the church as the place where "God's Spirit dwells" (v. 16), a place He Himself has created. Whenever we confess the Third Article of the Apostles' Creed, we are reminded that our "I believe in the Holy Ghost" is immediately followed by a reference to His work: "the holy Christian church, the communion of saints." Martin Luther explains the Spirit's workmanship by saying, "He calls, gathers, enlightens, and sanctifies the whole Christian church on earth."

So frequently in the Bible, especially in the Book of Acts, do we read that the Holy Spirit, poured out on the disciples on Pentecost, directed the upbuilding of Christianity. Almost as a refrain, as various episodes are related in Acts, come the words: "The Lord added to the church."

B. We, Too, Are Builders

The apostles and their assistants were given leading roles as builders of the church. This emerges from the text, with Paul saying in due modesty: "According to the commission of God given to me, like a skilled master builder. . . . " The Greek word for "master builder" is the easily recognized *architekton.* Not for a minute does Paul regard himself a novice or amateur. He was a master; he knew what he was doing and how to do it. He had deeply searched the Scriptures in preparation for his work. And, as elsewhere, he insists that his apostleship is authentic, for Christ Himself had commissioned him.

Besides Paul and the other apostles, also Apollos and other helpers preached the Gospel and were thus the agents of the Holy Spirit for the growth of the church. Earlier in the chapter the point is made that the work of these spiritual leaders is not competitive but complementary: "I planted, Apollos watered . . . He who plants and he who waters are equal . . . For we are fellow workers for God" (Vs. 6, 8-9).

Christian pastors today, as successors to the apostles, are divinely called to be the builders of Christ's church. Although frail human beings, "earthen vessels" (2 Cor. 4:7)—and often in the world's eyes "cracked pots"—pastors become effective builders of Christ's church through proclaiming the Gospel, which is God's dynamic power for the salvation of souls. Their ministry has to be seen in the larger perspective. The pastor in Blantyre, Scotland, for example, was criticized because the church didn't grow. But he did give pastoral guidance to one of the members, David Livingstone, through whom the church of Christ was built in Africa.

Through pastors God equips all His saints to be builders. Paul speaks of the members of the church as workers together with God, as partners with him in the Gospel. His epistles reflect the instruction he gave them to be kingdom builders. He holds that apostles, prophets, evangelists, pastors, and teachers are God's gifts to the church "for the equipment of the saints, for the work of ministry, for building up the body of Christ" (Eph. 4:12).

It is not enough when only the pastor is a builder; that would be a one-man church with corresponding results. In St. Louis and other cities people greatly appreciated the performance of actor Alec McCowen, who as a one-person cast put on the play, "St. Mark's Gospel." While in drama one can admire such a *tour de force,* one cannot approve a church performance in which the pastor is the only actor while the members are the spectators. St. Peter urges, "As living stones be yourselves built into a spiritual house ... You are a chosen race, a royal priesthood, a holy nation, God's own people, that you may declare the wonderful deeds of Him who called you out of darkness into His marvelous light" (1 Peter 2:5, 9).

III. The Church as God's Building

When, having Christ as the foundation, pastors and people believe, live, teach, and confess the Gospel, there comes about a beautiful edifice: the church, the community of believers. How is this edifice described?

A. The Church Is God's Temple

"Do you not know that you are God's temple and that God's Spirit dwells in you?" the apostle asks (v. 16). In Jesus Christ, the Cornerstone, "the whole structure is joined together and grows into an holy temple in the Lord" (Eph. 2:21). Meant here, of course, is not the structure in which we are now worshiping, with its bricks and mortar and glass, but the communion of believers. "That temple you are," writes Paul (v. 17).

This temple, Paul declares, "is holy." It is set aside for and consecrated to the service of God. It is there for worship, for hearing the Word, for administering the sacraments, for instruction, for fellowship. God's temple is kept holy when Christians continue in apostolic teaching and fellowship, in the breaking of bread and prayers.

This temple is also the Spirit's dwelling place. It is where the Holy Spirit makes His home. Whenever and wherever the Word of God is in use, there the Holy Spirit is present. What a beautiful dwelling place for us is the church because God dwells there! In his book *My Parents: A Differing View,* James Roosevelt recalls that he, his sister, and brothers were grown-ups when his father and mother lived in the White House and really never lived there themselves. But he adds, "Home was where he [father] was." Because the church is God's temple, the home of the heavenly Father, it is also home to us.

B. The Church's Responsibilities

As God's temple the church has the responsibility of fostering spiritual growth in young and old, for only in that way are Christians "God's field, God's building" (v. 9). What a joyful sight it is when God's people "grow up in every way into Him who is the Head" (Eph. 4:15), "grow in the grace and knowledge of our Lord and Savior Jesus Christ" (2 Peter 3:18) through sharing Christ in Bible study and in other situations of Christian fellowship!

As God's temple the church has the responsibility to guard its purity of Christian teaching and living. Paul takes a very dim view about the efforts of some to destroy and desecrate this temple. In Corpus Christi, Tex. it happened that a man, enraged because he was refused Holy Communion, entered the cathedral and did $50,000 worth of damage by tearing up books, shattering statues, and ripping up the vestments. As bad as this was, the temple of God suffers much greater damage when, as in Corinth, people prefer the wisdom of man to the Word of God.

Again, the temple of God is polluted when instead of the incense of prayer people introduce the smog of human opinions. It is said that sulphur dioxide issuing from foundries is corroding the more than 340-year-old, beautiful, white-marble Taj Mahal at Agra, India, which an emperor built to show His love for the queen. The church is the temple of God, the heavenly bride, that Christ loved and died for. Shall it be corroded by false doctrine? What Paul writes in vs. 18-20 about the dangers of worldly wisdom is plain enough.

C. The Church's Privilege and Power

The church as God's temple is the recipient of many blessings, of privileges of the highest order. Those who were once a non-people are now the people of God. Indeed, "blessed be the God and Father of our Lord Jesus Christ, who has blessed us in Christ with every spiritual blessing in the heavenly places" (Eph. 1:3). To privilege is added power.

The church, specifically the local congregation, has been endowed with unique power, with the Office of the Keys. This is a strong point in Paul's presentation here: "All things are yours" (v. 21). Through the church God calls His servants of the Word, who with and through the members fulfill the church's ministry and mission. Paul goes on, "Whether Paul or Apollos or Cephas or the world or life or death or the present or the future, all are yours." No higher power, whether of state or church, can supersede the "all things are yours" promise to Christ's church in a given place. And, lest this privilege and power be abused, the apostle bids the church remember whose it is: "You are Christ's; and Christ is God's" (v. 23).

Our Commitment

The epistle for this Sunday brings home to us that the construction of Christ's church on earth will continue in the measure that Christians accept Jesus Christ as the church's sole foundation; through the Word and the Spirit's power Christians function as builders of the church, and more and more become what they already are: God's holy temple.

Someone has said, "Most of us are singing about standing on the promises, and we are just sitting on the premises." Paul's words in the text give each one of us occasion to ask: Is this true of me? Let each take care that he builds on the only foundation in Christ.

Peter's Remembrance of the Transfiguration

THE TRANSFIGURATION OF OUR LORD
LAST SUNDAY AFTER THE EPIPHANY
2 PETER 1:16-21

Rudolph F. Norden

Remembrances, especially memories that bless, help us bring the past into the present for a good purpose. Thanks to memory, we can relive joyful moments. The power to recall good days when evil days overtake us is also of value, as Michael W. Balfe declares in his song "The Heart Bowed Down": "Memory is the only friend That grief can call its own."

Memory is a wonderful gift of God for our spiritual well-being as well. In our personal lives we can to our benefit recall Biblical truths we once learned or meaningful experiences that deepened faith and understanding. As a congregation we can on various occasions, such as church anniversaries, recount God's deeds among us in past years, always with the assurance that these same mercies of God will attend us in years to come. So with the psalmist we say, "I remember the days of old, I meditate on all that Thou hast done" (Ps. 143:5).

In our text Peter shares with us his recollection of a most memorable occasion: the transfiguration of our Lord. How often in his life and apostolate must he not have pondered the meaning of this event and drawn strength from it! Now in his older years, as he contemplates his departure in the not-too-distant future, he reminds us once more of the great truths of the Gospel he proclaimed at Christ's direction.

I. Peter's Remembrance Is the Testimony of an Eyewitness

If someone were to ask, "Peter, were you there when Jesus was transfigured?" he would say, "I certainly was, together with two other eyewitnesses." Consequently what the apostle shares with us in the text is not hearsay, or rumor, or a cleverly devised myth, but a report of what he himself saw. As one present he gives us a firsthand account of what took place on that holy mountain.

A. An Eyewitness Who Was There

What, precisely, did Peter see? He calls himself and the other two apostles "eyewitnesses of His majesty" (v. 16). He saw the outward manifestation of Christ's divine majesty—light, splendor, a whiteness beyond that of clothes washed with the best soap powder—as his Lord "received honor and glory from God the Father" (v. 17).

Thus with his own eyes Simon Peter beheld the glory that was Christ's as the Son of God. He saw a glorious change in Him as "His face shone like the sun and His garments became white as light" (Matt. 17:2). The transfiguration of Jesus was God's own seal on the truthfulness of the confession Peter had made but six days before: "You are the Christ, the Son of the living God" (Matt. 16:16). What magnificent splendor, what sublime radiance! This is the light of holiness in which God Himself dwells (1 Tim. 6:16) and of which the hymn writer says, "No angel in the sky can fully bear that sight." Little wonder that Peter and the others had to shield their eyes.

Peter had seen manifestations of Christ's glory on previous occasions. He was present when Jesus revealed His glory in the performance of His first miracle in Cana. He was on the scene when the Master healed the sick, including his own mother-in-law. He was on hand when Jesus recalled pallid corpses to life. The same eyewitness now reaches back in his memory to recount a special revelation of Christ's glory which had made an indelible impression on him: the transfiguration of Jesus on the holy mount.

B. As an Earwitness Who Was There

On the occasion of Jesus' transfiguration Peter, together with James and John, were also earwitnesses, for they heard the Father's voice that said, "This is My beloved Son, with whom I am well pleased" (v. 17). This voice "was borne to Him [Jesus] by the Majestic Glory," that is, by the Father of Lights. It is significant that Peter includes James and John as also earwitnesses, saying, "We heard." The presence of two other witnesses rules out the possibility that Peter was just imagining or dreaming all this. Two other men saw and heard the same things, and in the prolog of his First Epistle John puts his concurring testimony on record: "We have heard," "we have seen with our eyes," "we have looked upon and touched with our hands, concerning the Word of Life."

The remembrance that Peter here relates was the kind of

testimony the apostles were to render, for Christ has appointed them to be His witnesses (Acts 1:8)—witnesses of His resurrection (Acts 1:22) and the events preceding it.

What does this remembrance mean to us here and now? It strikes a sure keynote in our hearts and minds, for we know it to be the testimony of an eye- and earwitness. It always means more in everyday life when the persons to whom we go for advice know from firsthand experience what they are talking about. If it is a product they suggest, it helps if they can say, "We ourselves have tried it and seen its good results." If it is a doctor or lawyer they recommend, it bears weight when they say, "This is the man we know and to whom we ourselves go." Peter speaks to us as one who had been with Jesus, and what he tells us is trustworthy. This is not a blind man describing beautiful colors. His words carry special force, for they are the testimony of an eye- and earwitness.

II. Peter's Remembrance Is a Testimony of the Fullness of Salvation in Christ

Our writer is painstaking in recalling the transfiguration events because they are related to and support the great truth behind Christ's glorification: "the power and coming of our Lord Jesus Christ" (v. 16). He mentions "power." On the holy mountain, as on the occasion of His many miracles, Jesus revealed Himself as the Son of God with power, in fact, with all power in heaven and on earth. The transfiguration confirms Jesus to be God's Son, the very truth that Peter confessed and proclaimed.

A. God's Plan of Salvation

But Peter is concerned not only with the Father-attested Sonship and deity of Christ with power, but also with His "coming," that is, with the whole compass of the Gospel that declares why He came. Like Paul, also this apostle is committed to declaring "the whole counsel of God" (Acts 20:27) for the fulfillment of which God's Son came into the world.

That counsel or plan of salvation for fallen mankind was conceived in eternity. The hymn writer Paul Gerhardt has put this heavenly consultation into the form of a dialog or conversation between the Father and the Son:

"Go forth, My Son," the Father saith, "And free men from the fear of death from guilt and condemnation. The wrath and stripes are hard to bear, but by Thy Passion men shall share the fruit of Thy salvation."

And how does the Son reply? Like this:

Yea, Father, yea, most willingly I'll bear what Thou commandest; My will conforms to Thy decree, I do what Thou demandest."

This is indeed the saving truth "into which angels long to look" (1 Peter 1:12).

At the fullness of the time this counsel of salvation was due to go into effect. He who was to come did come—come not primarily as a teacher or a moral exemplar but, in Christ's own words, "to seek and to save the lost" (Luke 19:11) by laying down His life to save all sinners.

So beginning with our Lord's physical coming into the world as the Babe of Bethlehem, God's eternal plan for our redemption went into a step-by-step fulfillment. Included in Christ's coming as per God's plan are the incarnation, His obedience to the Law in our stead, His vicarious atonement, resurrection, ascension, session at God's right hand, sending of the Spirit, and His promised Second Coming.

B. Peter's Witness to Christ's Salvation

Advanced in years and about to honor his Lord with a martyr's death, Peter remembers the transfiguration as an event most closely connected with "the power and coming of our Lord Jesus Christ." This salvation in Christ, Peter and the other apostles "made known to you" (v. 16). It is what he witnessed to, what he preached.

Let us recall some of his testimonies of the fullness of salvation in Jesus. Soon after Pentecost we hear him testify in behalf of the crucified and risen Christ: "There is salvation in no one else, for there is no other name under heaven given among men by which we must be saved" (Acts 4:12).

In Peter's First Epistle we have the testimony on which Martin Luther based his explanation of the Second Article of the Apostles' Creed: "You know that you were ransomed from the futile ways inherited from your fathers, not with perishable things such as silver or gold, but with the precious blood of Christ, like that of a lamb without blemish or spot" (1 Peter 1:18-19). And who can forget that great introduction to this First Epistle, showing the power of Christ's resurrection in our lives: "Blessed be the God and Father of our Lord Jesus Christ! By His great mercy we have been born anew to a living hope through the resurrection of Jesus Christ from the dead" (1:3).

Our salvation is fully in Christ—that is the truth we need to fix firmly in our hearts and minds. What blessed assurance! Let us imagine for a moment what life would be like—and how nonexistent the prospects of eternal life would be—if "the power and coming of our Lord Jesus Christ" were a cleverly devised myth and we were thrown on our own resources to gain peace with God! When the treasures of King Tut's tomb were shown in this country, there was quoted what the ancient Egyptians' *Book of the Dead* told people to say to the divine judges as they sought to pass into the next life: "I have always shunned evil; I have given bread to the hungry, water to the thirsty, clothes to the naked, a ship to the stranded; to the orphan I was a father, to the widow a husband, to the roofless I gave a home." This is good-words religion. Now Jesus in Matt. 25:31-46 enumerates similar good works the righteous have done, but these works they did not in order to be saved but *because* they were saved. Our full salvation is in Christ, and it is ours by faith, not by works.

In *Anna Karenina,* Leo Tolstoy says this of one of the men in the story: "Levin felt suddenly like a man who had changed his warm fur cloak for a muslim garment and, going for the first time into the frost, is immediately convinced . . . that he is as good as naked." Can this happen to us spiritually? Not if by faith we accept Christ's salvation. In the robe of His righteousness we are well dressed and warmly clothed.

III. Peter's Remembrance is a Testimony Bidding Us to Heed God's Word

In his reminiscing mood the apostle recalls the testimony he has rendered—and renders here anew—about the Word of God concerning Christ. At the transfiguration the Father spoke this Word: "This is My beloved Son." This same Word of God concerning Jesus as the Christ was spoken in the Old Testament Scirpture, and this truth, too, Peter and the others have "made known."

A. Peter's Use of the Word

In his Pentecost sermon Peter preached the Word as the Holy Spirit gave him utterance. All that he said about Jesus—the Spirit's descent as per Christ's promise, His crucifixion to redeem all people, His burial, resurrection, and ascension—was declared to be in fulfillment of the Scripture, specifically of the prophecies of Isaiah, Joel, and David in the Psalter.

Further, to the "house church" assembled in the home of Cornelius, Peter said, "You know the Word which God sent to Israel, preaching good news of peace by Jesus Christ" (Acts 10:36). This "good news of peace" is the Gospel as proclaimed in the Old Testament, especially by Isaiah, who wrote (52:7): "How beautiful upon the mountains are the feet of him who brings good tidings, who publishes peace!"

In his First Epistle the apostle records his testimony concerning the Word of God—how we have been born anew "through the living and abiding Word of God" (1:23), then quoting from Isaiah 40; how we should long for the pure spiritual milk of the Word that we "may grow up to salvation" (2:2). All this, Peter recalls, he had "made known," asserting that the Word concerning Christ is true, for He had been an eyewitness of His majesty at the transfiguration.

B. The Word Sure and Clear

It seems likely that the writer had anticipated this question from a reader or hearer: "Peter, we don't want to dispute your recollection of the transfiguration and what it means, although it did happen many years ago. But put yourself in our shoes. We weren't there on the mount to see Christ glorified and declared to be God's dear Son. How can we be sure of the truth concerning 'the power and coming of our Lord Jesus Christ'?"

The reply is this: "We have [and you have] the prophetic Word made more sure" (v. 19). This "prophetic Word he identifies as the "prophecy of Scripture" (v. 20). The reference is to the writings of Moses and the prophets, of which Jesus said, "They bear witness to Me" (John 5:39). This prophetic Word is "made more sure." The prophetic Word in the Old Testament Scripture is independently true; it is not made more *true* but made more *sure* by the fulfillment of the Messianic prophecies in Jesus as demonstrated in the New Testament.

This sure prophetic Word did not come "by the impulse of man, but men moved by the Holy Spirit spoke from God" (v. 21). Since this is so, it follows that we cannot interpret it in keeping with our own personal impulse, will, wisdom, interest, or convenience, for "no prophecy of Scripture is a matter of one's own interpretation" (v. 20). So we put aside our own preconceived notions and let the Word speak for itself—let clear Scripture interpret Scripture.

The prophetic Word, so Peter further testifies, is not only sure but also clear, for it is "a lamp shining in a dark place" (v. 19). With great clarity does it direct people to the Savior of whom the prophets spoke. When, for example, the Wise Men of the East inquired where Christ was to be born, the birthplace could be pinpointed on the basis of Micah 5:2. Because the Old Testament Scripture is clear, the psalmist likens it to a "lamp" and a "light" (Ps. 119:105). The Bible is especially a light, for we have also "the other Scriptures" of which Peter speaks in this epistle (3:16), by which he means the New Testament writings which so clearly focus on Jesus as the promised Christ.

The writer of our text makes a pointed application when he urges us to "pay attention" to this shining lamp. As long as we are "in a dark place" (v. 19), which we certainly are as long as we are in this world, we need the guidance of God's Word. That's why we give heed to the Word not only here in church but also at home when we conduct family devotions.

In possession of this light, we are able to be light-bearers in this world. We pass on the light to others. Centuries ago relay races were run in Greek stadia. Runners bearing torches would cover a certain distance and then pass the torches on to their partners. The Greek spectators, very fond of this light race, would shout as the exchange took place: "Let those who have the light pass it on." That is what we Christians do when we share the Gospel with our fellow human beings at home and abroad.

All Glory and Honor to Christ

Peter's remembrance as (I) the testimony of an eyewitness of Christ's transfiguration, (II) as the testimony of full salvation in Christ, and (III) as a testimony to the certainty of God's written Word, is intended to give all honor and glory to Jesus Christ. About to enter His Passion and the valley of the shadow of death, the transfigured Christ is revealed in His divine majesty. Although in the state of humiliation He did not always and not fully use His majesty, the transfiguration reveals that He did possess it. He is God's true Son.

The story is told that Alfred, king of England in the ninth century, had to flee for his life when the invading Danes had taken over much of the land. Laying aside the tokens of his royalty, he sought refuge in a peasant's cottage. The wife gave him the job of watching the oatmeal cakes baking on the hearth. Preoccupied with the problems of his realm, Alfred let the cakes burn and for that had to endure the indignity of a tongue-lashing from a peasant woman.

Jesus our heavenly King, too, was deeply humiliated, despised, and rejected by many people. Soon he would enter the deep degradation of a slave's death, even death on a cross. During His Passion He had "no form or comeliness," and some would say that He has no divine majesty at all. But the transfiguration assures us that Jesus is indeed our heavenly King, the promised Christ, the Son of God, the Lord of glory. To this King, humiliated but soon to be exalted, we give our hearts.

From Enemies into Friends

ASH WEDNESDAY
2 CORINTHIANS 5:20b—6:2

Jaroslav J. Vajda

In London on May 24, 1738, John Wesley, who later became the founder of Methodism, was invited by a friend to attend an evening meeting with Moravian Brethren. He was reluctant to go, but went to please his friend. About 8:45, while listening to a reading of Martin Luther's Preface to Romans, he felt his heart "strangely warmed"; in fact, he considered that moment the turning point of his life and career. Remarkably it left an indelible mark not only on the Church of England but on social conditions in the factory towns.

I hope it is more than an annual habit that has moved us to keep this Ash Wednesday appointment with our Lord. I hope we feel the need for healing so strongly that nothing could have kept us away from hearing once again how God—yes, God!—desired our friendship from eternity and how He made it possible for us to be restored to that relationship which we have broken by our unfaithfulness and indifference.

I hope, for your sake, that when you hear how much God loves you that you become convinced of that love so profoundly that it will enable you to live a new life and, living a new life, to be moved with compassion to tell others: "Let God change you from enemies into friends."

From Enemies into Friends
I. Recognize Your Need for Reconciliation

Someone observed that a person is lucky to develop one true friendship in a lifetime. How do you rate in that kind of poll? How many people can you consider to be true and loyal friends: people who accept you as you are, who are not envious of you, who are happy when something good happens to you, who can be trusted to keep your secrets and confidences, who will forgive you when you let them down or unknowingly hurt them, who will go out of their way to help you with no expectation of reward, who will not desert you when you get sick or become invalid or lose your job or your savings, who would be willing to give you one of their kidneys, and who would pray for you without your asking? Most people are lucky to have one such other person in the world who meets these requirements of a friend. Sometimes that one person is one's spouse or a parent or a child. But the number is small—and so such friendships are rare, and anything so rare has got to be almost priceless.

Can you imagine anyone, having found such a rare friend, who would treat such a relationship casually or neglect it or take it for granted or do anything that would break it? And yet such tragedies take place in great numbers daily. People who have spent years dreaming of and searching for just the right mate, who have vowed lifelong loyalty to that cherished person, who have spent aching days and hours away from each other until they could be together always, who have spent hundreds of dollars on phone calls and dates, who have even perhaps flaunted customs and social disapproval to live with that person without getting married—that many such people, including those who have made their vows to each other before witnesses and before God, have lived to see that closest of friendships become dull and weak and finally die. And they face the rest of their lives without any assurance that they can ever replace what they have lost. Those who were once the closest of friends, the truest of friends, the rarest of friends, become enemies who no longer pray for each other, gradually try to forget each other, and eventually either lose all their feelings for each other or become enemies who look for ways to hurt each other.

Not all broken friendships are the result of broken marriages. There are friendships that have been achieved at great cost and investment of time and attention that are allowed to wither and die because of disinterest or other momentary affections that prove to be empty, or simply and perhaps most commonly, because the friendship was not valued for the precious thing that it is.

Ah, and when it is broken and the loss is realized, hardly, if ever, can it be restored or mended or recaptured in its original beauty and strength. It is gone, and there is nothing to do but weep and envy those who did not neglect their rare friendships.

What is marriage but the search and hope for the closest and most lasting of friendships? And what is remarriage but the desperate wish to recapture what one once had? And this is what keeps pastors and marriage counselors and psychiatrists busy: trying to restore broken relationships or helping people to establish such relationships. On a national scale, leaders in government, labor and industry wear themselves out trying to reconcile opposing factions, to get people to work together, to overcome their differences, and to be friends instead of enemies.

I hope that you and I are here tonight because we have two friendships that need mending, two relationships that need restoration to that lovely and inspiring state we remember when the friendship was just a dream and a promise. For we do need reconciliation with our loved ones who need us and whom we need, and with our God, who loved us and whom we have so lightly abandoned and whom we have hurt by our neglect, ingratitude, indifference, and willful disobedience. These relationships are in daily need of repair and nurture, and here in Lent is where we find the means to not only restore these relationships but to make them more rewarding than ever.

II. Recognize God's Achievement of Peace

To be honest, we must admit that we have become estranged from each other by sin. We have offended the holy God by our ingratitude and rebellion. For this rebellion God has every right to turn His back on us, to destroy us for trampling His goodness and mercy, and to banish us forever from His holy presence. We are no longer worthy to be called His sons and daughters. We have willfully deserted Him. We have disregarded His wishes by disobeying His commandments, something one should never do to a friend, we have denied that He is our God and Father, deserving of our total loyalty and trust. We have preferred to serve our own interests above His. We have in fact become His enemies, doing the will of His sworn enemy, the devil.

But God is not happy about this estrangement from His creatures, whom He placed in a special world created for their enjoyment, and upon whom He lavished His goodness and mercy, and whom He chose to call His children. No parent can help but be heartbroken when his child leaves home and will have nothing to do with them. Some parents finally give up on their children and will even agree to have them punished by the state for their crimes. But God is not like that. God is love. His creatures are someone special to Him. He made them to enjoy eternal life with Him. There can be no doubt about God's feelings toward His creatures when we hear of His plan to save them from the death their sins earned them, and when we see Him taking what is the dearest and most precious possession even He has, His only Son, placing all our sins and the sins of all the world on that sinless Son, and then offering Him up on the cross for His rebellious creatures! Listen to St. Paul telling the Corinthians in the second letter and us how God arranged our reconciliation: "Christ was without sin, but God made Him share our sin in order that in union with Him we might share the righteousness of God" (5:21 TEV).

Restoration of a broken relationship costs dearly in terms of time and effort and sacrifice. Look what it takes to try to bring Israel and Egypt to an agreement! Look what patience and determination are required to bring about peace between two warring nations, like the United States and Vietnam, between North and South Korea, between Russia and China, between Irish factions, between the Arabs and Jews! Try getting an estranged husband and wife together after they've been separated for a year—then try after 5 years! You could wear yourself out trying to accomplish that kind of reconciliation.

Reconciliation is costly. In a Pennsylvania congregation there were two brothers and their families who were once very close but who fell out over a dispute over an inheritance, as so many children do. They stopped talking to each other, stopped visiting each other, and when one continued to go to church, the other quit going in order to avoid having to meet. The pastor tried in vain to bring the two brothers together. Nothing worked, no appeals to their former closeness, no warnings about God's judgment over grudges, no invitations to accept an arbitrator for their disagreement. Nothing worked. One day the younger son's lovely six-year-old daughter was taken to the hospital. A tumor was found in her stomach. Within a month the child died. But at the funeral of that child the brothers met again for the first time in years, sobbed on each others' shoulders, shook hands, and were reconciled. But look what it cost to achieve that reconciliation!

Friends, look what it cost God to achieve our reconciliation not only to Himself but between us and those from whom we have become estranged—and that includes anyone who should be the recipient of our love: our spouse, our parents, our children, our brothers or sisters, our neighbors, our fellow Christians, and even those whom we never mention in our prayers. It is that cost that we gather during Lent to consider and marvel over and thank God for and apply to our broken relationships. It is that cost that alone can make us into God's friends.

Paul says something that is easily overlooked in this touching and fervent appeal for reconciliation. He says: "In our work together with God, then, we beg of you: you have received God's grace, and you must not let it be wasted," (6:1). Did you hear that? "You must not let it be wasted." Friends, dear, dear, friends, this grace of God which restored us to friendship with God by the sacrifice of Jesus on the cross—this grace of God is priceless, it's the one and only cure for our deadly sickness, it is the only balm for our wounds, it is like the only cure for cancer. Don't waste it. Don't treat it lightly. Don't neglect it. Everything we review in Lent becomes the motivation for a Christian regenerated life. It is pure Gospel, the power of God unto salvation to everyone who believes, to everyone who does not waste it. It will be the subject of every sermon—or had better be—if our faith is to remain alive and if our relationship with God through Christ is going to bear fruit, if our faith is going to result in noble thoughts, sincere love, deeds of mercy, and the hope of everlasting life. Don't waste it, says Paul. And he says it because God says: "I heard you in the hour of my favor; I helped you in the day of salvation" (6:2). God has heard our unspoken cry; He has answered long before we called or even thought of calling; He knew our need and filled it. He made the first move toward reconciliation. He paid the price of our renewal. This is what changes us from enemies to friends. Nothing else. Absolutely nothing else!

"Listen!" says Paul. "This is the hour to receive God's favor; today is the day to be saved" (6:2)! Opportunities for reconciliation are rare. You have to grab them when they come. There have been couples who failed to restore their marriage because one or the other of them missed the golden opportunity when it came, perhaps unexpectedly. Well, here we are tonight. How lucky we are that just what we need most for our peace and happiness is being offered here tonight! Who knows if we'll have another chance like this again?

What we deal with during Lent is as vital to our spiritual life as the sun is to our survival. Drink it in deeply, dwell on it, review it, revel in it, praise God for it, and show it to others. You know how much it is needed all around you, at work, in your home, in the world that is breaking into fragments of humanity, in a world where peace is an endangered species.

Is it the blessed life you want for yourself and for others, the life that has God's smile and approval? Then remember what Jesus said: "Blessed are the peacemakers, for they shall be called sons of God" (Matt. 5:9). Jesus was God's peacemaker between God and us and us and God. He was the Son of God, the Prince of Peace. God's children are seekers of peace and makers of peace, reconcilers of enemies. There are not too many of us in a world whose greatest shortage is peace and love. Millions are dying who have never really lived, who have never known peace. God doesn't want this for His creatures. Do we?

Once we have found this peace for ourselves and are once again secure in the family of God, knowing Him as our friend, we can and should be ambassadors for Christ, saying with Paul: "Here we are, then, speaking for Christ, as though God Himself were appealing to you through us: on Christ's behalf we beg you, let God change you from enemies into friends." You'll never do anyone a greater favor as long as you live.

The One and Only

FIRST SUNDAY IN LENT
ROMANS 5:12, 17-19

Theodore W. Schroeder

Suppose

Right now, I told you that a feature of our worship service this morning would be an opportunity to have the figure of a cross permanently tattooed on your forehead! Assuming we could get used to the idea of being tattooed, which of us would go ahead with it—be permanently marked with a cross in a prominent place like our forehead?

And if I announced it, what thoughts would go through your mind as you considered it? How would others react to your mark? How would others treat you? Do you think some would be hostile? What kind of reaction would you get from those you work with or go to school with or those in your own family?

As we consider some of these reactions, we see how firmly we are caught in the constant tension between our inner desire to be unique and the external pressure from others to be alike—to conform.

The illustration with the tattoo points out how strong the pressure is to

Be Like Other People.

Society—people are really very intolerant of anyone who is different. Think of children in a play-yard. What do they say to the child who is too fat, too short, or handicapped? Among adults what attitudes and feelings are shown by one group toward another in which others are different in some way? And for all of their rebellion, those of us who have teens in our house know that they live in a cult of conformity so severe that it prescribes not only what clothes are "right" to wear but also how they are to be worn and when. We are all under constant spoken and unspoken pressure to dress, act, do, buy, own, live, and work like others around us. If we do not, we will be considered "different"—and more, may be considered strange, odd, and an object of ridicule. For most of us, most of the time, keeping up with the Joneses means imitating them.

But, on the other hand, we sense in ourselves a strong

Need to Be Different.

We don't simply want to be a rubber stamp model like everyone else, so conformed to the society in which we live that we blend into the crowd and kind of disappear. We need to be different, to be unique, to be outstanding and to be noticed.

A wise man once said that every person has a sign painted on the inside of his forehead. It says "Notice me. I am important." Those who are most successful in dealing with others treat each person as though that sign could be seen and responded to.

And for all our attempts at conformity we are indeed unique. We sometimes run into a person who says, "You know, you look just like . . ." And when we see the person we are supposed to resemble, we may even see the similarity; but in close comparison the differences become obvious. We are different. No one has our face, our appearance, our fingerprints—and certainly no one shares that unique set of memories, thoughts, attitudes, and feelings that make up our character and personality.

But our very uniqueness, though we need and desire it on the one hand, often, especially when we are troubled, becomes

A Prison.

No matter how well we know another person, we really don't know what is going on inside of him. We can only know a portion of his thoughts and feelings at any given time. And we often feel quite

different from him, at least from the appearance that he permits us
to see.

Often others around us seem so capable, so well adjusted. They
seem quite at home with themselves and quite able to deal with
day-to-day pressures. They seem to "have it all together," as the
saying goes. Surely we run across those who are troubled and
distressed, but often we find ourselves envying others because they
seem to be able to do and to be all the things we would like to do and
to be.

From that position of envy we find our problems rather unique.
We feel we might be the only one to ever feel as lonely as we do
sometimes, to feel as depressed as we do. We feel we might be the
only one who faces an uncaring spouse and the pain of that
situation—the only one to be rejected by a child and involved in
that kind of heartbreak. We often feel that the pits of our own
despair must be deeper than anyone else's and the problems we are
called upon to solve must be the toughest in the world.

But, remarkable, when we have the time to hear others, we will
find that the inner conflicts and hurts that we face are not at all
unique—but are common to many. For all of our struggling to
affirm our uniqueness, the pain inside is not much different from
one person to another.

Who has not felt the desperate gloom of the knowledge that we
have failed ourselves or someone else again? Which of us has not
felt the helplessness of having done exactly what we had intended
not to do. Who has not felt the desperation of facing a problem that
we seem unable to deal with, no matter what we do?

Which of us has not said with St. Paul:

"For I do not do the good I want, but the evil I do not want is
what I do. Wretched man that I am" (Rom. 7:19, 24a)!

We Are Not Unique

And some would have us believe that there is no sin, that
somehow all of the desperation, separation, alienation, and conflict
in us, in each of us, is a manifestation of bad thinking or bad
environment. Somehow, these people believe, that if we get good
parents doing good things to their children in a good environment
we will be able to heal the human pain that continues in every one
of us.

But It Will Not Happen

The text said it, "Therefore as sin came into the world through one
man and death through sin, so death spread to all men because all
men sinned..." (Rom. 5:12). We can feel it. We know it is true. When
Adam took that step away from God, he did not jaunt into an
experiment in individualized living, nor did he pioneer a new life-

style free from the confining rules laid down by God. He became sin—and we live in a posture of

Sinful Rebellion

because of it.

And whether we like the word or not; whether we think it fashionable or not to talk about the sin-sickness of ourselves; whether we would rather join in the crowd of educators and social scientists who insist on talking about alienation, the inclination toward self-destruction, and internal conflict—the fact remains that we are all, every one of us, at war with ourselves and others, cut off from God, and trapped in the process of the painful realization that we are dying. We are neither capable of putting our lives together in some kind of a whole, nor of healing the rifts, breaks, and breeches in the attempts we make to structure our day-to-day living.

And if this were a little lecture on the internal workings of the human spirit; if we were talking here about the prospect of creating a person and a society in which all good would happen and all evil be overcome, there would be little more to say. We could simply state the fact that it will not happen. The one truth that has remained constant through the centuries, the one invariable variable in the process of history is that whatever changes in externals there may have been, the soul of man is desperately evil and absolutely unable to do anything about it.

But Now the Good News:

good news better than the bad is bad. Our text says:

"If, because of one man's trespasses, death reigned through that one man, much more will those who receive the abundance of grace and the free gift of righteousness reign in life through the one man Jesus Christ" (Rom. 5:17).

We are so much alike that our dying becomes the very fabric of our human life, and yet we are so unique and special that God Himself sent His Son to die for each of us that we might "reign in life."

Sometimes we think of the work of Christ as a kind of modified

Insurance Policy.

Christianity is for dying, it is said. Faith is the insurance against death—as if we were left on our own devices to muddle through the days and hours until we find it necessary to cash in on our eternal insurance—when our "number is up."

But what a terrible loss. The truth is that we have already died, and we are now made alive as a free gift by Jesus Christ. The victory is already ours. As surely as the hurt and pain are there from the one man Adam, so is the healing, health, and life there from Jesus Christ—there in us, now as a gift.

Unique?

Certainly we are unique. In a dying world, so confused by inner hurt that the people of the world can't even realize that the pain of being in the process of dying is the same for all. In a world where people desperately try to find cures for the deadly conflict that rages in them they turn to fashions and fads and cults and cures. We have the answer. We have the healing and life. We have the unique gift.

Surely it would not be much help to get a cross tattooed on our forehead to mark ourselves as Christian. The tattoo would probably only gain us attention and scorn. But the mark of God in our life through Jesus Christ is more encompassing and important, more vital and noticeable than a tattoo could ever be.

We have been changed from death to life. We have been transformed from victim to victor. We have been made from a slave to ourselves and the evil in us to a ruler of life now and eternally. And all because of Jesus Christ.

It is all done. "The death He died He died to sin, once for all, but the life He lives He lives to God. So you must consider yourselves dead to sin and alive to God in Christ Jesus" (Rom. 6:10-11).

Unique among the slaves of sin, only we are free to live as though marked by the cross of Christ. "But now that you have been set free from sin and have become slaves of God, the return you get is sanctification and its end, eternal life" (Rom. 6:22).

Now in this

Season of Lent

Let us take time to come to the cross and see our sinfulness. Let us take time to reflect on the sin-sickness in ourselves that continues to assault us and drag us into slavery. Let us be aware once more of the inner pain and conflict which is so often a part of our lives. But more, let us take the time to celebrate the victory which is our gift now in Jesus Christ.

And let us seek the power to live as slaves of God, so different from our dying fellow men that we might as well be marked on the forehead with a tattoo of the cross of Christ.

The Ever-Recurring Question

SECOND SUNDAY IN LENT
ROMANS 4:1-5, 13-17

Weldon L. Priebe

Down through the centuries many questions have agitated the minds of people. However, the one question that looms like Mt. Everest over all questions is, "How can I get right with God?" The reason why people have always been asking this question is that deep down in their hearts they know that something is wrong in their relationship to God. Because of his repeated sinning against God, a person is going to wonder from time to time how he will make out on the Day of Judgment. How can his life, which has been full of wrong, ever be made "right" and win the approval of the Supreme Judge?

Most people have come to conclude that the answer to the ever-recurring question, "How can I get right with God?" is, "I can get right with God by a decent and upright life." Some years ago Walter Carlson of Chicago's WMBI took his roving microphone into the city's Union Station and asked passers-by the question, "How does a person get to heaven?" For a half hour a parade of travelers responded with such answers, "Obey the Golden Rule," "Be good to your neighbor," "Go to church," "Do good," "Pay your bills." These answers are natural for all people, also for us. We are all born with a good opinion of ourselves, with the idea that we are able to satisfy God with our own efforts. This is our natural bent—we think that we are something.

Furthermore, doesn't it seem reasonable to believe that one should receive some credit from God by being good, by leading a decent life? After all, doesn't this principle hold true in everyday life? We pay and are paid for goods delivered and services rendered. You can get just about anything, it is said, if you are willing to pay the price. We like to follow this same reasoning in religion. Doesn't it seem fair that if we have sinned against God we must and can make up for our sinning by a sufficient number of good and laudable deeds? A pet approach of Satan is to assure us that our sins really are not so bad considering all the good things we do!

In our text the apostle Paul comes to grips with the ever-recurring question, "How can I get right with God?" Paul gives an answer to this question that the human heart will rebel against, but an answer that is God-given. Man can get right with God not through works but only by faith. This is the heart and center of the

Christian Gospel. This is God's answer to the ever-recurring question, "How can a person get right with God?"

A few verses previous to our text, Paul had made the emphatic declaration, "For we hold that a man is justified by faith apart from works of Law" (Rom. 3:28). To demonstrate and confirm this teaching that man is saved by faith, Paul in our text refers to the case of Abraham. "What then shall we say about Abraham, our forefather, according to the flesh?" (v. 1).

Abraham stands out as one of the greatest people of God of the Old Testament. He had the honor of being the Father of the Jewish people and the spiritual Father of all believers. Abraham so dominates the history of the Old Testament that God even names Himself the "God of Abraham."

Abraham was truly a man who distinguished himself by his good life. God called Abraham to leave his father's house and country and to journey to a strange land that God did not at the time reveal to him. Abraham obeyed God without question and started the difficult journey to the strange, unknown land. Abraham was a person of deep devotional life. Wherever Abraham pitched his tent, he built an altar at which he and his family might worship God. Abraham was also an unselfish person who gave first consideration to others. To further peace with his nephew Lot, Abraham made the unselfish offer that Lot could choose any portion of the land that God had promised to Abraham even though Abraham had every right to first choice. Towering above Abraham's many works was his implicit obedience to God's command that Abraham sacrifice his only son Isaac in whom lay his hope of the fulfillment of God's promise, "You shall be the father of a multitude of nations" (Gen. 17:4).

These were only some of the works and virtues of Abraham. Abraham was a man of many works. In fact, in the eyes of the Jewish people Abraham was a "work's" hero. What shall we say of Abraham according to the flesh, according to his own achievements? If anyone could be saved by his works, Abraham was a prime candidate for this way of getting right with God. Then Abraham would have had much reason for glorying and boasting before God.

Now Paul comes with the verdict of Scripture as to how Abraham got right with God. "For what does the Scripture say, 'Abraham believed God, and it was reckoned to him as righteousness'" (v. 2). Here is God's judgment of Abraham as set forth in God's own Word (cf. Gen. 15:6). As great and good a man as Abraham was, yet the infallible verdict of Scripture is that Abraham was not saved by works. Abraham possessed righteousness before God but that righteousness he obtained by faith.

The entire case of Abraham's salvation rests on faith and faith

alone. "Abraham believed God." And what did Abraham believe?
He believed the promise of God. God had appeared to Abraham and
showed Abraham the countless stars in God's heaven. God told
Abraham, "So shall your descendants be" (Gen. 15:5). That was an
almost unbelievable promise, for at the time Abraham and his wife
Sarah were well advanced in years and still had no son or heir. But
Abraham believed God. And this faith the Lord counted to him for
righteousness.

But Abraham believed more. With the eye of faith Abraham
looked out across the centuries and saw the seed of the woman,
namely, Christ. Jesus Himself gave this interpretation of Abraham's faith when He said to the unbelieving Jews of His day, "Your
father Abraham rejoiced that he was to see My day; he saw it and
was glad" (John 8:56). Through Christ Abraham would become the
spiritual ancestor of many people. Through Christ the blessing
would come to all people. And this blessing would essentially
consist in this that Christ would redeem destruction-destined
mankind from sin, death, and the power of the devil through His
suffering and death on the cross as the sinners' substitute. This
faith in God's promise in Christ was reckoned to Abraham as
righteousness. Abraham's certainty of salvation rested on the
future Christ whom he possessed by faith.

Abraham possessed righteousness before God but that righteousness he obtained by faith. He had not merited it by works.
"And to one who does not work but trusts Him who justifies the
ungodly, his faith is reckoned as righteousness" (v. 5).

Not only for Abraham but for all people of all time, God's answer
to the ever-recurring question, "How can I get right with God?" is
always the same. To him who places no worth or value to his works
but casts himself upon the free mercy of God in Christ by a living
faith, such a faith is counted for righteousness. Faith has nothing
to add to what Christ has already done, but faith is merely the hand
that receives the forgiveness and salvation which God offers us
through Christ His Son who lived, died, and rose again for all
people.

Our getting right with God by faith and not by any works or
merits of ours is the most relevant and most momentous thing in
our lives. But how often does Satan not try to trick us into thinking
that our getting right with God is due entirely or at least partly to
our own efforts. To follow Satan's line of thinking is dangerous. It
destroys us and robs God. It takes the meaning from Jesus'
sacrifice on Calvary's cross. We must be on guard against it.

One day a pastor was called to minister to an aged grandmother
who had become seriously ill. On his way to her bedside the pastor
thought, "Here is a fine Christian. Ministering to her will be easy,
simply a matter of strengthening her faith and making heaven

more real to her." But the minister was to experience a sad disappointment. This pious grandmother told him, "Yes, Pastor, I am sure I will go to heaven. I was always a member of the church, and I always did what I thought was right."

Here was a person who had heard Sunday after Sunday the central teaching of the Christian Gospel that we are saved before God only by faith. Yet, despite this oft-repeated testimony, this pious grandmother trusted in her own personal goodness for salvation. Fortunately, through the Holy Spirit working during the eleventh-hour efforts of her pastor, this grandmother came to see clearly that faith alone saves. We wonder how many members of Christian congregations approach death and the Judgment believing that they are saved entirely or at least partly by their own efforts.

In answer to the ever-recurring question, "How can I get right with God?" God's inspired apostle Paul answers clearly. Man is saved before God not by works but by faith.

Paul further reinforces this teaching by stating that Abraham and his descendants did not receive the promise of a future inheritance on the basis of the works of the Law, but through the righteousness of faith (v. 13). Paul here refers to those promises of God in which Abraham is promised the possession of the land of Canaan. And yet to Abraham the pledge of an earthly Canaan was only a pledge of the better, perfect inheritance, the heavenly Canaan. Abraham "looked forward to the city which has foundations, whose builder and maker is God" (Heb. 11:10)

Final salvation consists in possessing and enjoying the future world, the heavenly inheritance. Man never comes into possession of the heavenly inheritance by the Law or its works. If this were true, then faith becomes empty and meaningless, and the promise is made of none effect (v. 14). Furthermore, the Law only brings upon man God's anger, the opposite of blessedness (v. 15).

Without any regard for man's works or conduct, God by grace gave the promise of a heavenly inheritance so that it might be sure and certain (v. 16). If it were in any way dependent on man's deeds and conduct, it would be uncertain. But God's promise is absolutely certain. We can in faith confidently trust in God's promise. And for all believers God's promise is sure and certain—not only those who possess the Law, the believing Jews, but also the believing Gentiles.

Paul finally says of Abraham, "He is the father of us all" (v. 16). Abraham is the father of all believers, of the Jews and Gentiles. Abraham is that for two reasons. All believers have the faith of Abraham and, as Abraham, are saved through faith. Second, all believers as Abraham receive the heavenly inheritance through faith.

The ever-recurring question, "How can I get right with God?" shouldn't be an ever-recurring question. God has settled this question finally and forever in His infallible Word. Many people will rebel against God's answer—salvation by faith and not by works. They will keep insisting on paying their own way through their own efforts and works. In the process of paying their own way, they are always in a state of tormenting doubt because they can never be sure whether they have done enough good.

The supreme glory and comfort of the Christian Gospel is this: righteousness, forgiveness, peace, salvation, heaven—all are yours, not by works, but by faith in God's Son Jesus Christ who by His life and death as the sinner's substitute secured righteousness, forgiveness, peace, salvation, and heaven for all sin-lost mankind. We are saved by God's mercy, not by our merits—by Christ's dying, not by our doing.

This, God's plan of salvation, is the only plan that saves. This is the only plan that brings about a blessed certainty. This certainty was well expressed by a Christian pastor who lay on a hospital bed critically ill. The pastor's doctor who had a very close relationship with the pastor informed the pastor, "Pastor, you won't live much longer. If you have any accounts to settle, you had better settle those accounts soon." Here was the pastor's calm and confident reply, "Doc, I paid all my bills to men when they came due. And my Savior Jesus has paid in full my sin-debt with God."

This pastor experienced the supreme comfort of the Christian Gospel—that we are saved before God by faith. Can you echo the confident words of that pastor? The pastor's confidence and comfort will also be yours as you believe God's Gospel promise of salvation through faith in the Savior Jesus Christ.

> No condemnation! My debt is now paid.
> My sin all on Jesus, the Savior, is laid.
> Justified freely, by faith I'm His heir.
> Secure in His love, I His righteousness share!

The Call of the Cross

THIRD SUNDAY IN LENT
EPHESIANS 5:8-14

Richard P. Musser

Never has an emblem of torture and death been so magnified, so displayed, and so glorified as that ancient instrument of execution known as the cross. It has been presented in sizes from a 96-foot structure on a mountain peak in South America to a quarter-inch lapel cross made of gold. The cross has been immortalized in poetry and prose and has inspired composers to fill Christian hymnals with scores of melodies whose lyrics bespeak praise and thanksgiving to God. The cross is displayed in millions of homes, worn as adornment by men and women, tops the steeples of churches around the world, and marks the location of a million graves.

Yet, it is not the cross that we worship, but its symbolic meaning. We sing, "In the cross of Christ I glory," but we really mean, "In Christ, whose atoning death has won eternal heaven for all, I glory"—we mean "In Christ, Savior and Redeemer, I glory." So the cross is symbolic of the atoning Christ, who paid the full price for the sins of mankind. Thus, we can say, "I am saved by the cross of Christ," and we know exactly what is meant.

During this Lenten Season we magnify the cross as in no other season of the church year, and we learn many things about its meaning. In a similar way St. Paul taught his congregations at Ephesus. In his letter to them he spends a great deal of time informing his readers about the atonement that was made for them by Jesus at Calvary. In our Epistle for today, Paul teaches that the cross of Christ is a call to remind us of some very important and significant items in the living of our life. So we consider

The Call of the Cross
I. The Cross Calls Us to Remembrance

First of all, the cross calls us to remembrance. Now, what are we to remember? Are we to remember the death of Jesus, as we do in the Lord's Supper? To be sure, we dare never forget that, but we are to remember vastly more. We are to remember the cause of the cross; why was the cross necessary? Listen to St. Paul as he tells his Ephesian congregation, "Ye were sometime (at one time) darkness." Paul, here, is speaking of spiritual darkness, and this darkness is best explained in contrast to Christ who is called the Light of the world. Scripture often uses darkness and light to symbolize the godly and the ungodly. Paul describes this condition best in this same letter, when he uses phrases like, "Ye were dead in trespasses and sins, . . . having no hope and without God in the world." Truly, the cross calls us to remember also our sins.

Sin, however, is a most unpleasant subject to speak about, especially when it is our sin. The word itself is becoming less frequent in American pulpits today. Some time ago a leading New York newspaper reviewed the sermons of thirty-two leading clergymen of the city. In only one was there found a reference to sin. Unpopular indeed, for the word s-s-sin has the hiss-s of the serpent in it, the Old father of Lies that beguiled the world's first humans and brought spiritual darkness into the world. As death passed upon all men, in that all have sinned, it was necessary for a loving God to swing into action for the souls of mankind. It was necessary for the cross of Christ to become an historic fact, that the world by it might be redeemed. So the cross of Christ calls us not just to remember sin in general, not just a few misdemeanors, but our own personal sins, as Paul reminds us, "You were . . . darkness."

Far above and beyond a remembrance of our sin, the cross calls us to remember our transformation. The text puts it this way: "Now are ye light in the Lord." Praise God, the cross of Christ shouts a clarion call to remember that "Ye are washed, ye are sanctified, ye are justified, by the blood of Christ."

This transformation from darkness to light, from sinner to saint, was accomplished without any merit, any worthiness, or even any desire on our part. This transformation was wrought solely and alone by God's free grace. The phrase, "In the Lord"— "Now are ye light *in the Lord,"* is not here recorded by accident or incident. The water of a thousand Niagaras, the power contained in a hundred hydrogen bombs, the learning received from ten thousand universities, cannot cleanse one single soul from one single sin. Only the blood of Christ can remove the stain and the sting of sin.

Do you feel sinless? Do you feel like the children of light, whose fruit is "goodness and righteousness and truth," as the text says. How God can look upon us as transformed beings is precisely the miracle of faith. When God's mighty Spirit worked a saving faith in our heart through the washing of regeneration in Holy Baptism, we were transformed and we stood clothed in the righteousness of Christ. Also as the Holy Spirit, through the mighty Word of God, daily rekindles this faith in our hearts, we remain transformed and stand before God in the righteousness of Christ Himself. This is the transformation we are called to remember as we view the cross of our Lord Jesus Christ. This is the change from darkness into light that St. Paul also demonstrates in the last verse of our text as he says, "Awake thou that sleepest, and arise from the dead, and Christ shall give thee light." Only the message of the Gospel, only the preaching of the atoning Christ can bring about such a transformation. And as we view the cross, symbolic of the atoning Christ, we are to bring to remembrance this glorious transformation from darkness unto light.

II. The Cross of Christ Calls Us to Action

No one, who by the Holy Spirit's power, understands this transformation from sinner to saint, from darkness to light, can escape a feeling of gratitude. When St. Paul was hurled to the ground on the Damascus road, when it was revealed to him that Jesus whom he was persecuting was the Christ of God, he could force no other words from his lips than, "Lord, what wilt Thou have me to do?" The answer, in essence, was "Action!" As gratitude and thanksgiving well up within our hearts, as we ask the same question the great apostle asked, the answer is no different. So, the cross of Christ also calls us to action. The text says we are to "walk as children of light," then adds, "proving what is acceptable unto the Lord." The original implies our lives as Christians ought to prove what is God's will.

How desperately we need to portray the will of God in our lives as we live in a world which is fast going to hell. Our walk as children of light is to reflect God's will which is "goodness and righteousness and truth"—three words that form a blueprint for life. Outside of God's will there is no true happiness, no true peace, no true joy. Outside of God's will the world lives only in constant turmoil. And where do we learn of God's will? From the ancient philosophers, from the cults that are springing up throughout our nation? The psalmist gives us the clue when he says, "Thy word is a lamp unto my feet and a light unto my path."

Where else can we go to find hope for a dying world, to experience true peace and joy and happiness? What about education? Our nation holds two historic world records: We are the best educated nation in the history of the world, and we are also the possessors of the highest crime rate in the history of the world. Now, I am not saying that education breeds crime, but simply that it does not diminish it. The uneducated thief will steal from a bank, but the educated fraud will steal the whole bank.

Neither can we look to science for a better society. While we thank God for all the blessings received through scientific advancement, we must understand that science is nonetheless fallible. Science gave us the A-bomb, the H-bomb, and now, the neutron bomb. Science has invented radar to keep our highways safe, but is has also invented the "fuzz-buster" to allow speeders to escape the radar. In scores of other ways the incongruities of science have not only helped but also hindered the advancement of peace and tranquility within and without.

Nor can we depend upon diplomacy for a world of peace and harmony. History has given us ample proof of that. Only God's Holy Word can guide us and lead us to walk as children of light in all goodness and righteousness and truth. Only the Word of God can insure us a life of true joy and peace, as it presents to us the atoning Christ who has made us one with our God and has established an eternal peace between God and man. The cross of Christ ought to remind us of this and call us into action so that we may walk in the full light of God's saving Word and reflect the will of God, to His glory, in all that we do.

A negative action is yet called for by the great apostle. Call it isolation, or separation, or whatever. He says, "Have no fellowship with the unfruitful works of darkness, but rather reprove them." These words echo the same advice Paul gives his Corinthian congregation when he tells them, "Come out from among them and be ye separate, saith the Lord." As the line which marks right from wrong is becoming fast erased, a call to regrouping and separation is indeed in order. The television, the movies, and the theater have so filled our minds and, unfortunately, our homes with a godless philosophy to such an extent that the very definition of sin has been lost. As worldly ideologies permeate our society we find that God's Word and will is fast being replaced by the thoughts and actions of recording and television stars and movie idols. A way of life is becoming established in which even Christians desire to look like the world, act like the world, dress like the world, and play like the world. Meanwhile, God calls us to reprove the world, to correct the world, and to remove ourselves from the influence of the world.

There is one final call of the cross implied: A call to repentance. The Ephesian Christians had to be reminded again and again to walk as children of light, to forsake the world and its influence, to remember their glorious transformation through the atoning Christ. They had to be reminded of it because they did not always heed the call of the cross. Shamefully we too must confess that our response to the call of the cross leaves much to be desired. But joyfully, we review the precious Gospel of our Lord and Savior Jesus Christ, which announces God's unconditional grace to all who will contritely fall before the cross, and we are assured of the only answer possible from heaven's highest court of appeal, "My son, My daughter, thy sins be forgiven thee."

The Dynamics of Salvation

FOURTH SUNDAY IN LENT
ROMANS 8:1-10

Richard P. Musser

The Scripture says, "Christ died for all," yet everyone knows that all will not be saved. We read, "God so loved the world that He gave His only-begotten Son," yet the Bible teaches that the majority of the world will be eternally lost. God's revealed will announces, "God would have all men to be saved," and at the same time informs us that only a few will enter heaven. The word of the Lord reminds us that "God sent His Son into the world not to condemn the world, but that the world through Him might be

saved," yet we know that the world will not be saved. What about
this seeming contradiction?

Most Christians see the fallacy of such questions. We draw on
our confirmation instruction and recall God's universal grace for
all mankind—yes, for the whole world. We assent to the objective
character of God's plan of salvaton for all men—it is for all. We
affirm, "God does desire all men to be saved." We firmly believe
that Jesus' death at Calvary was made for all. God does love the
world, and He sent His only-begotten Son to save each and every
person in it, but, we answer, "You must accept Jesus as Savior. You
must believe He lived and died for you. You must have faith." To
emphasize this we complete the passage quoted above: "God so
loved the world that He gave His only-begotten Son, that whosoever *believeth* in Him shall not perish, but have everlasting life."
We listen to Jesus' own words, "He that *believeth* and is *baptized*
shall be saved, but he that believeth not shall be damned."
Therefore, we conclude that the gift of God's atoning Son was given
for all—for every single person on the face of the earth. This
salvation won by Jesus is there for all to receive and accept by faith.

You might well ask, "Now we have another dimension not
previously stated. The concept of faith is brought in." Well, what
does "have faith" mean, what does faith do? How am I saved
simply by faith in Jesus as my Savior? What happens, either on
God's part or on man's part when I have faith? To answer these
questions we, under God's guiding Spirit, consider

The Dynamics of Salvation
I. The Law Fulfilled

Have you ever wondered about your eternal salvation? Have
you ever doubted that you would be saved? Should you be called to
stand before God this day, are you certain you would be judged
acceptable for heaven?

Perhaps we should first ask, "What keeps people out of heaven?"
Listen to the Lord Jesus in His account of the judgment speaking to
those who will inherit eternal damnation. To them Jesus says,
"Depart from Me ye cursed of My Father, into everlasting fire,
prepared for the devil and his angels." Now what reason did Jesus
give for this scathing pronouncement of condemnation? They had
failed to preform the will of God. Jesus says to them, "I was
hungered, and ye gave Me no meat; I was thirsty, and ye gave Me no
drink; I was a stranger, and ye took Me not in; naked, and ye clothed
Me not; or sick, or in prison, and ye visited Me not." Then the Lord
explained that their failure to minister to the least of Jesus'
followers was also a failure to minister unto Him. The account in
essence concludes by Jesus pronouncing condemnation to sinners

and salvation to the righteous. From this we are able to determine that it is sin which bars the gate to heaven. Throughout the Word of God are statements such as, "The wages of sin is death," or "The soul that sinneth, it shall die." These pronouncements and a host of others leave no doubt about the fact that sin blocks the entrance to heaven, and no sinner will ever enter.

In addition to this, the Word of God informs us that "all have sinned and come short of the glory of God." You are a sinner! I am a sinner! We begin to doubt the very logic of heaven as Scripture tells us no sinner can enter into eternal life, and at the same time, every human being on earth is a sinner. Logically, we have every right to doubt our salvation. Knowing the condemnation of God's law, we have no choice but to doubt. Knowing that God's law demands perfect obedience and perfect adherence to God's precepts, we have no other choice than to abandon all hope for heaven.

See for a moment, just how this hopelessness could affect our everyday life. Boarding a jet for a distant city, the thought of an airline tragedy, though remote, is nonetheless always present in our minds. In a matter of minutes we could stand before God. What hope do we have? God condemns sinners, and we are sinners. We may face serious surgery. No doubt it will be successful, for we have a specialist. Yet, we cannot ignore the possibility that something could go wrong. This could be our last day on earth. How can we be sure God will accept us? We sin daily, we have not fulfilled God's commands, and we have done what God has forbidden. In every sense of the word we are sinners, and God's law condemns sinners.

Yet, our God through St. Paul, in our text today, reminds us, "There is therefore now *no condemnation* to them that are in Christ Jesus." How can this be? How can the whole law of God, which condemns every sinner so completely, be totally nullified and pronounced void? True, no one can nullify God's law. No one, not even God, is able to wipe out what God has spoken. The law stands, the condemnation of all sinners stands. To be sure the Law is real and it is true. It's pronouncements, it demands, as well as its condemnations cannot be nullified—*they can only be fulfilled!*

This is precisely what has happened—Christ Jesus has fulfilled to total Law perfectly. Listen to the Word of our text: "The Law of the spirit of life in Christ Jesus hath made me free from the Law of sin and death." Now hear how God Himself has made us free from the condemnation of the Law. "For what the Law could not do, in that it was weak through the flesh, God sending His own Son in the likeness of sinful flesh, and for sin, condemned sin in the flesh, that the righteousness of the Law might be fulfilled in us." To state these words more simply, Jesus, because our sinful flesh was too weak to be able to fulfill the Law ourselves, took our place under the Law, was subjected to all its demands and fulfilled them perfectly in our stead. What we could not do because of our sin, Jesus did for us. He became our Substitute, entered our world, in the flesh, fulfilled the Law, and even suffered the total, torturous condemnation of the Law through His God-forsaken death at Calvary—all this for us. That's total fulfillment! Fulfilling the Law completely, fulfilling the condemnation of the Law totally.

II. A Spiritual Transformation

Now comes the question of the ages: "How do I receive all these benefits which Christ Jesus has gained for me?" Subsequently we have a right to ask, "How does Jesus' perfect fulfillment of the Law become effective in me?" And, "How does Jesus' death become beneficial for my soul's salvation?" The answer to these questions would explain our first concerns about faith: What it does—what happens when we possess faith—how we are saved simply by faith.

We have already discussed the seeming contradiction between universal grace and individual forgiveness. We discussed, at length, the fulfillment of both the demands of the Law and its punishment by our dear Savior. Now we need to know of a tool—a method—a mechanism—a something that will transfer or transform Christ's fulfillment of the Law to us. This is precisely the activity of faith. It transfers—we say appropriates—Christ's work of redemption to us, as though we did it. Thus, St. Paul could say, "I was crucified with Christ." Faith transforms Jesus' holiness and righteousness to us, and we become holy and righteous in God's sight.

When speaking of faith, above all else, we had better know how to get it. That's just the point, you don't "get it." Faith is a gift of God—it is given.

Our text uses some very informative terms to refer to those in faith. St. Paul calls them "those who walk after the Spirit," or those who "are in the Spirit." He also refers to the faithful as those who have "the Spirit of Christ." All these expressions give us a clue to the fact that faith is a working of God's Holy Spirit. We read in the Holy Scripture, "No man can say that Jesus is Lord but by the Holy Ghost." Dr. Luther presented this truth in another way: "I believe that I cannot by my own reason or stength, believe in Jesus Christ my Lord, or come to Him, but the Holy Ghost has called me by the Gospel, etc." In other words, we do not resolve to believe and accept Jesus. None of us woke up one morning to say, "I think I'll become a believer in Jesus today." You and I were not brought to faith by our own resolution. Already as infants many of us, by our baptism, were brought to a saving faith in Jesus Christ. Also, through His Holy Word He has kindled and strengthened us in a faith that appropriates or transfers Christ's perfect holiness to us. Brought to faith by the Spirit of God, we now live in that Spirit, and enjoy the fruits of that Spirit, which St. Paul speaks of in our text when he says, "To be spiritually minded is life and peace." In addition, the Holy Spirit daily, by Word and Sacrament, keeps us in the faith. This simply means constant continued forgiveness for all our sins. Paul tells the Roman Christians, and us, that "the righteousness of the Law is fulfilled in us." Christ Jesus fulfilled the Law, suffered the punishment, brought us to faith, and we stand justified, redeemed, and ransomed. We are free from the curse of the Law, we are in a Spirit-walk which sees our whole spiritual life as God's free gift of grace. We did nothing to deserve it, we can offer nothing to pay for it. We can only, and this, too, by God's grace, give thanks for it.

Now, step into any jetliner, anywhere, with perfect confidence in your destiny either here or the hereafter, and in perfect peace with God. Now, enter any hospital for any illness, encounter any trial and any heartache with perfect acceptance of God's promise, "There is therefore now no condemnation to them that are in Christ Jesus."

Do you now see or have you been reminded of God's great plan of salvation for you? Do you now know the power of Jesus' life and death? Do you now understand faith's role in transferring and transforming all the work of Christ to us, individually? Then, let all these precious truths transform our lives in a Spirit-filled walk of praise and thanksliving.

On the Way to Real Living

FIFTH SUNDAY IN LENT
ROMANS 8:11-19

Elmer A. Neitzel

"You say John just died? Only yesterday I saw him in church!— Well, that's life!" Living and dying are an everyday experience. In truth, as David says, "There is but a step between me and death" (1 Sam. 20:3). In the midst of life we are in death.

However, in another sense the reverse is also true. In the midst of *death* we are in life. In this section of Romans, Paul develops the great theme of the Christian's freedom. In chapter 6 he voices the claim that a Christian is free from sin. In chapter 7 he shows how a Christian is free from the Law. In chapter 8 he insists that a Christian is free from death. In His life and work Jesus Christ overcame sin, fulfilled the Law, and destroyed death. Everyone who is in Christ is freed from their power. Because he is a "spiritual" being through Jesus Christ, the Christian has been released from all that tied his life to sin and death. Paul in this text indicates that the Christian, in pursuit of this freedom from death, is

On the Way to Real Living

A New Dimension in Living

Dominating Paul's inspired thinking in this text is, first, *the truth of a new dimension in living* for those whom the Spirit of God has made alive. The selfsame Spirit that raised Jesus from the dead gives life through His indwelling. Although the mortal body is dead because of sin, it is alive because of Christ's righteousness earned on the cross. "He was delivered because of our offenses," Paul says earlier in this letter to the Romans, "and raised again for our justification" (Rom. 4:25). A new creation of God has been started to give to man the original righteousness he had in Eden. A sense of newness comes into his life. A release from the burden of sin and guilt is offered to him. In the court of God's justice he has been pardoned through Christ and declared by God to be innocent of the charges brought against him. The sentence of death for his sins was carried out in Christ's substitutionary death on the cross. Not only has God's justice been satisfied but man's old sinful nature has also been put to death with Christ. Once before this in Romans Paul reminds us that in Baptism we have died, been buried, and raised up and given a new spirit. A new life in Christ has been conceived.

All of life by itself is a gift of God. Living from day to day reflects the goodness of God for all of His creation. The new life in Christ is ours as a gift of our faith. It asserts that man is on the way to real living. It denies, as many believe, that death itself is the end—an exit into nothingness. It says that man is more than merely mortal who will live on because of some "divine spark within." It confirms, as Paul says to the Corinthians, "If any man be in Christ, he is a new creation. The old has passed away and the new has come" (2 Cor. 5:17).

The way to real living, then, is more also than a variety of bromides of our day which offer a new vitality for body, mind, and spirit—a "recharging of our batteries." Nor is it a rejuvenation of the physical frame offered by hosts of health centers for tired men and women. Nor is a life-style of unrestrained flamboyance, characteristic of our jet-age, suggested. Paul's prescription for real living in this text is the only answer to much of the aimlessness of 20th-century life. Indeed, it is the newest and most up-to-date model of Christian living, which is found only in those whom the Spirit of God has made alive and transformed into the image of His Son Jesus Christ. Such people are on the way—on the way to real living.

Lest Paul, however, be thought of as indulging, perhaps even of over-indulging, in theological idealism, he proceeds to say in the beginning of v. 12: "So then, brethren!" In view of everything that has been said about a new dimension of Christian living—so what?

Evidence of This New Life in Christ

He proceeds to show in our text, in the next place, that there is *tangible evidence of this new life in Christ*. There are certain "vital signs" of this spiritual experience. Beating in every spiritual breast is a pulse of our being alive to the promptings of the Spirit of God. He says: "We are debtors, not to the flesh, to live according to the flesh—for if you live according to the flesh you will die, but if by the Spirit you put to death the deeds of the body you will live. For all who are led by the Spirit of God are sons of God. For you did not receive the spirit of slavery to fall back into fear, but you have received the spirit of sonship. When we cry, 'Abba, Father!' it is the Spirit Himself bearing witness with our spirit that we are the children of God, and if children, then heirs, heirs of God and fellow heirs with Christ, provided we suffer with Him in order that we may also be glorified with Him."

One "vital sign" of this new life in Christ is the awareness that you are indebted to the flesh, which has been killed in you. Why pay heed to something that has been put to death by Christ? Any sense of obligation to our flesh and its carnal influences is only slavery all over again. The influence of the flesh only brings death. Therefore remember, says Paul, "If by the Spirit you put to death the deeds of the body you will live." Falling back into former patterns of living is not only lapsing into the enslavement of desires of the flesh but into a direction of life also which focuses only on one's self. The Christian life must be a constant "putting to death" of that self. "Daily repentance and contrition," Luther calls it. Coping day by day with such lapses is one such evidence of life in the Spirit. Reckoning from time to time with the reality of our old evil nature coming to the surface is a vital sign, not of death, but of spiritual life.

The throbbing impulse of God's Spirit is another vital sign. "Led by the Spirit of God," is Paul's perception of it. *"Driven* by the Spirit of God" is a more appropriate translation, as if driven by some great force. As often as we hear the Word of Jesus in the Gospel, this awareness of the Spirit's promptings becomes evident to us. "The words that I speak unto you, they are spirit, and they are life," says Jesus (John 6:63). Paul in our text is alluding to the witness of the Spirit's presence, when the assembled congregation of Roman Christians publicly gives expression to the acclamation "Abba Father!" When that happens, Paul says, "It is the Spirit Himself bearing witness with our spirit that we are the children of God." When we are alive in Christ, through the Spirit we become increasingly aware of our new relationship to God. Indeed, Paul is careful in his vocabulary to make us even more aware of this relationship when he calls it "the spirit of sonship."

This vital sign of our relationship is stimulated through the use of this footnote, so to speak. Children of God, yes, indeed, that we are, but even more so "sons" of God. Sonship is a term that designates children who have advanced in their relationship to God and have come of age. They are on the way to real living. They are steadily advancing to the time when an inheritance is coming to them. Their hearts beat faster in anticipation of that which lies in store for them. As heirs, and joint-heirs with Christ, they are looking forward to the enjoyment of inestimable wealth.

The Spirit is the moving power to make us over into truly living people, sons and daughters of God, sharing an expectation of an inheritance which is "imperishable, undefiled, and unfading, kept in heaven for you" (1 Peter 1:14). To slip back into the enslavement of works of the flesh or to put our trust in riches and treasures, which moth and rust corrupt, is to jeopardize that which is given us in prospect for the life to come. We have much dying to do before our body fails. In so doing we shall find new areas in which we can truly live and not be under the dominion of death.

Yet, notwithstanding, everything that has been said by Paul regarding the Spirit's witness that we are God's children, there are those who seem to have no evidence of their relationship to God. To say to them that they are on the way to real living is hollow mockery. Their lives are torn asunder and surrounded by evidences of death and reverses. Suffering of body, mind, and spirit is their lot. They say: "Where is the evidence of God in my life of pain and agony? I have prayed for help and God has not answered." On the other hand there are those who view suffering in itself as a sign of God's favor, qualifying them for a special entrance into the kingdom of heaven. In answer to these considerations Paul gives his proviso: "Provided we suffer with Him (Christ) in order that we may also be glorified with him (Christ)."

Let those who think that the life in Christ, Paul means to say, is a promise of immunity from suffering come to understand that Christian suffering can be further evidence given by the Spirit of God that we are children of God and fellow-heirs with Christ. The Spirit bears witness to them that God is disciplining and correcting His children. The Spirit bears witness to them that God in love is using suffering, as well as all things in the Christian life, for their eternal good. The Spirit bears witness to them that God is bringing His people into fellowship with His Son Jesus, who suffered sin and death for all mankind. The Spirit bears witness to them that "we must through much tribulation enter the kingdom of God" (Acts 14:22). It is the cross in the Christian life which ultimately leads to the crown of eternal life. Our crosses and sufferings all serve to lead us on the way to real living in eternal glory.

Unveiling God's Eternal Plan

Finally, then, Paul says that *these very sufferings for the Christian begin to unveil God's eternal plan for His people.* "I consider that the sufferings of this present time," he says, "are not worth comparing with the glory that is to be revealed to us." Compared to the glory of the life to come, our sufferings are as nothing. They weigh much less in the balance of what God has planned in eternal life for those who love Him. Yes, the fires of suffering are all quenched by the promise of the glory to be shared with Christ in the life to come. In the experiences of life we are advancing step by step to the final unveiling of God's full glory prepared in the mansions above. Calculated in terms of earthly time, "our light affliction is but for a moment, and works for us a far more exceeding and eternal weight of glory" (2 Cor. 4:17). From a distance we see the promised land of our heavenly Canaan, as Moses did, and, overwhelmed with the awesome sight, the wayfaring Christian exclaims: "O Lord God, thou has begun to show Thy servant Thy greatness, and Thy mighty hand" (Deut. 3:24)! Truly, the weary pilgrim is on the way to real living.

The unveiling of God's complete eternal plan is awaited with eager longing. "The creation waits with eager longing for the revealing of the sons of God," Paul indicates in the closing words of our text. The description of all of God's creation in the section following our text pictures all of nature and even beasts of the field as "groaning in travail," waiting for their final liberation. Disturbances in nature, such as earthquakes, drought, storm, and tempest, are, so to speak, waiting for their "redemption." Man himself who is destined to dust and ashes, plagued with disease and death is awaiting the full redemption of his mortal body. For that final hour of liberation the word is simply: "Death is swallowed up in victory!" The final hour has come when the full power of the resurrection will be unveiled for all to behold.

One commentary refers to this unveiling of God's eternal plan as the "Christian apocalypse." The full redemption of our bodies is drawing nigh. Betimes it is partly hidden from human view. Now and then we perceive its beauty and luster. "It does not yet appear what we shall be, but we know that when He shall appear, we shall be like Him, for we shall see Him as He is" (1 John 3:2). The redemption of our body—what is meant? Briefly, it is the removal of sin and its consequences. Our deliverance from every yoke and burden of this life. In short, it is the abolition of death. It gives meaning to everything that our Savior says in today's Gospel at the open grave of Lazarus to Martha: "I am the resurrection and the life; he who believes in Me, though he die, yet shall he live, and whoever lives and believes in Me shall never die" (John 11:25).

Surely, Paul in this chapter of our text in Romans, in speaking of the Christian's freedom from death, brings a winsome and compelling statement to show that the Christian is on the way to real living. His walk in the Spirit not only gives the Christian a new dimension of living for all of his sojourn in this world. Tangible evidence there also is for him during his earthly pilgrimage to hearten his spirit along the way as the Spirit of God thwarts any possible lapse from life to death. Also, a glorious unveiling of God's eternal plan for him is repeatedly given in God's message of the Gospel, so that he knows he is always on the way to real living forever and ever.

Palm Sunday and the Drama of Holy Week

SUNDAY OF THE PASSION
PHILIPPIANS 2:5-11

Elmer A. Neitzel

Palm Sunday in the Christian calendar is the occasion to set the stage for Holy Week and, especially, for the events of Good Friday and Easter Sunday. World-famed Passion plays in Europe and in this country are helpful in their portrayal of our Lord's Passion and in their devotion to keep alive the message of God's love in Christ's redemption for all mankind. Each year the drama of Holy Week and Easter is unexcelled, as it provides a panoramic view of the mystery of Good Friday and the triumph of Easter.

The triumphant entry of Jesus into Jerusalem as one of the first events of Holy Week, reported in today's Gospel, is not without its dramatic overtones. Although misinterpreted by the populace of that day as a spectacular opportunity to make Jesus an earthly king, its far deeper meaning is woven into the whole fabric of Christ's redemptive act. St. Paul in the Epistle for this Palm Sunday gives meaning and substance to everything we witness in the events of Holy Week. This portion of his Epistle to the Philippians, which is our text, gives his audience of Greek Christians an opportunity to perceive the real message of

Palm Sunday and the Drama of Holy Week

Paul does this, first, by casting Jesus in the role of the obedient and suffering Servant of the Lord and, second, in the role of the exalted Lord of heaven and earth.

The Obedient and Suffering Servant

"Christ Jesus, who, though He was in the form of God, did not count equality with God a thing to be grasped, but emptied Himself, taking the form of a servant, being born in the likeness of men." The inspired apostle in this text pictures Christ as God in His preexistent state from eternity assuming the role of an obedient and suffering Servant. He leaves His royal throne in the heavens and is clothed with the garb of our humanity in order to suffer and die as a real man on the cross. It is said that Peter the Great of Russia at one time during his rule laid aside his royal garments and traveled to Holland to learn the art of shipbuilding for his people. Like any other workman in the ship yards, dressed in workman's clothes, his identity was not known as he learned his trade and labored as a commoner for the eventual benefit of his people. He willingly assumed the most menial tasks to preserve his anonymity and to learn the full measure of laborious toil. Although this may be a faltering illustration of Christ Jesus assuming the role of an obedient and suffering Servant, it gives us a measure of insight into His humility.

He laid aside his glory, yet He continued to possess all the attributes of His divine glory. He did not simulate divine power but thoroughly possessed it. He was not some actor playing the role of President Roosevelt, as it were, but FDR himself. He not only stood on a level with God but was identical with God. Nor did He flaunt His divinity and make a show of it in order to gain favor or make an impression. He did not advertise His deity and put it on display for curious admirers. Above all, He did not exploit His role to capitalize on His ministry for self-gain.

Indeed, the burden of His ministry and His redemptive work was that "He emptied Himself" of His power and glory, that is to say, poured out their contents but not their substance. He renounced their use for the time being and voluntarily divested Himself of their unbounded and continual use. Although He assumed a servant's role, this does not mean that He could help Himself on occasion. His assuming human flesh—His incarnation—was not necessarily demeaning degradation. His likeness in sinful flesh meant that He assumed the ordinary miseries of mankind in order to suffer pain, to endure hardship, to experience poverty, to hunger, to thirst, to weep, and to die—yet Himself to be without sin. He had the form of God in His divine nature and the form of a servant according to His human nature. He was divine and human at the same time.

Finally, in His role as the suffering Servant He assumed the ultimate stage in becoming obedient unto death, even death on a cross, as St. Paul says in v. 8 of the text. "And being found in human form He humbled Himself and became obedient unto death, even death on a cross." Here He took on the most serious ill of all—death, the sum total of all of the evil of sin. He died the death of a criminal. Death on a cross especially was considered to be a special curse. The applause and pageantry given to Jesus on Palm Sunday with waving of palm branches and hosannas are contrasted sharply with His rejection and death a few days later. On Good Friday He did not suffer as a hero, receiving great admiration and support. There was no halo of earthly glory surrounding His death as with a martyr. He was regarded as suffering without honor, and His death was one of a despised and rejected criminal.

"Have this mind among yourselves, which you have in Christ Jesus," Paul says in verse 5 of the text. He says this to the Philippians in urging upon them and upon us also a humble concern for others. In a real sense this is the servanthood of every Christian. This should be the model of every Christian community, namely, the mind of Christ in His obedient role as the suffering Servant of the Lord. Here Paul portrays the highest pattern of self-forgetfulness. A personal regard for the best interest of others was the character of our Lord's ministry and mission. This ought to be also the image of Christ's church in the world today. Since the church, as people in whom Christ lives and who live in Christ, is the body of Christ in the world, the church will also strive to empty itself of ostentatious power and authoritarianism and increasingly remember its role as a servant. The church has called this servanthood the *kenosis* of Christ (from the Greek word for "emptied"). No one who has been around for a while can say that the church has always achieved that kind of "kenotic" look. Nor is it easy to achieve. Yours for a more kenotic look! (Reflections by Dr. Martin L. Kretzmann in "FOCUS on People in Mission," Feb. 2, 1979).

This mind of Christ ought to enforce our personal posture as Christians. Christ laid aside His glory and assumed a servant's role. What other role is there for a Christian? Possessing the mind of Christ we ought, above all, remove all pompousness and vainglory and seek a more accurate estimate of our role as Christians. From the words preceding our text Paul is urging the Philippians to do just that, vs. 1-4: "So if there is any encouragement in Christ, any incentive of love, any participation in the Spirit, any affection and sympathy, complete my joy by being of the same mind, having the same love, being in full accord and of one mind. Do nothing from selfishness or conceit, but in humility count others better than yourselves." Increasingly we ought to learn as servants of God to serve Him and not our own selfish interests and goals. Our expectations in life often are motivated by self-interest rather than interest for others. After all, in the sight of God, all of us are only beggars. We shall come to discover this more meaningfully when we look at the next scene in the drama of Holy Week in which Paul casts our Lord.

The Exalted Lord

The solemn yet triumphant commemoration of Jesus' victorious entry into Jerusalem on Palm Sunday might be characterized as dramatic foreshadowing. Paul reflects this in the use of the connective "therefore," in v. 9, as he writes to the Philippians: "Therefore God has highly exalted Him and bestowed on Him the name which is above every name, that at the name of Jesus every knee should bow, in heaven and on earth and under the earth, and every tongue confess that Jesus Christ is Lord, to the glory of God the Father." Here Paul portrays Christ in the role of the exalted Lord of heaven and earth. His advancement to the full use and possession of His divine honor and glory is declared and affirmed.

So-called "bit" players dramatizing, for the most part, their rejection of the suffering Servant at the foot of the cross have dispersed and disappeared since Good Friday. The supporting cast of those who do acclaim His lordship covers every realm in heaven and on earth and under the earth. The inevitable recognition of His status is proclaimed by all. At the mention of His name every knee bows its allegiance. Every tongue confesses that Christ is Lord. All inhabitants of the far-flung corners of heaven and earth feel the greatness of His power and majesty. Angels and the whole company of heaven sing their hosannas. Saints above and below sound forth in songs of victory and in paeons of praise and thanksgiving. Even Satan and his legions acknowledge their defeat. Even unbelievers so vehement in their confession of unbelief shake their fists and thereby admit that Jesus Christ is no insignificant personality to reckon with. In the end every tongue will confess that Jesus Christ is Lord!

Indeed, Jesus Christ is Lord! This simple statement was the earliest confession of the early Christians. Disciples of our Savior, like Thomas, cried out: "My Lord and my God!" Today yet it is also the most recent and up-to-date statement of faith. After all of these centuries Christ has never been dethroned. It will also be the last acknowledged confession of faith that the world will make, when finally, in its complete collapse and from the ashes of its judgment, it acknowledges what it always denied before—Jesus Christ is Lord! This simple four-word statement is the chart and compass of every Christian's life. It is this simple statement of faith, which lies lodged in this text, describing our Lord's humiliation and His exaltation—"Jesus Christ is Lord!" From the morning of creation to the day of consummation of all things Jesus Christ is Lord! When He intersected human history and appeared in servant form, He

was born in swaddling clothes at Bethlehem. He was raised in
Nazareth. He gathered several fifth-rate characters who were His
disciples. He kept strange company with the lowest of the lowest
and finally brought upon His head the wrath of the establishment.
Thus He died at the age of 33. And from there we operate by faith.

It is faith that asserts it is not an overstatement to say that
Jesus Christ is God, equal with the Father and the Holy Spirit.
Faith affirms that "for us and for our salvation He came down from
heaven, incarnate of the Virgin Mary." Faith affirms the purpose
of His coming—to identify with us, to be our Brother, to assume our
burden, and to incur the wrath of God's righteousness against our
sin and for our ransom. Faith asserts that He is God who came in
human form as a servant, in meekness and humility, not waving
banners to exploit or commercialize the glory He possessed.
Sneering unbelief, of course, asks: "And who is this?" as Jesus this
Palm Sunday rides a mule in majesty, and faith replies that Jesus
Christ is Lord! The skeptic blasts, "You gotta be kidding!" and faith
replies, "You better believe it!" for, if it cannot be said in faith, it will
be said in judgment, "Jesus Christ is Lord!" (Alton Wedel, Senior
College, Fort Wayne, Baccalaureate sermon, 1973)

On this Palm Sunday in a special way we are drawing aside the
curtain on the center stage of all human history. It is not some
isolated little playlet or one little scene or act in the human drama of
sin and death. Christ's suffering and death are not some sideshow
for curious spectators. It is not something akin to a Greek tragedy
enacted for its moralistic focus on the tragedy of human existence.
It is not a melodramatic farce portraying the futility and hopelessness of human life. It is the true-to-life dramatic portrayal of every
human being, with bit players and supporting cast, up-staged by
Him alone, who is the Super-star in the galaxy of the heavens and
Himself the Author and Finisher of our faith. When the curtain
finally closes on the whole stage of human history, the grand finale
of the eternal Easter will commence and linger forever and ever.

Shall we attempt to take a glimpse of that which "eye hath not
seen, or ear heard, or entered into the heart of man" (1 Cor. 2:9)?
Paul lets it be known that this sweeping statement of Christ's
exalted status is no starry-eyed and elusive hope of the Christian's
faith. The mind of humility in Christ is a pattern for the Christian's
earthly life. But there is a sense in which Jesus is our example even
in His exaltation. His redemptive work is a confirmation that we
shall "be like Him and see Him as He is" and share in His glory.
"Where I am, there shall also My servant be," says Jesus. In eternal
glory we also shall be a part of that great company of angels,
archangels, and saints in heaven, bowing the knee and with our
own tongues confessing that Jesus Christ is Lord, to the glory of
God the Father. Even if we here suffer with Him and tread in the

valley of humiliation, He will also let us see, and share in, the glory of His exaltation. As much of Christendom traditionally on this Palm Sunday is clad in robes of white, with palm branches in their hands, the vision of St. John in the last book of the Bible comes to our mind's eye: "After this I looked, and behold, a great multitude which no man could number, from every nation, from all tribes and peoples and tongues, standing before the throne and before the Lamb, clothed in white robes, with palm branches in their hands, crying out with a loud voice, 'Salvation belongs to our God who sits upon the throne, and to the Lamb!' And all the angels stood round the throne and round the elders and the four living creatures, and they fell on their faces before the throne and worshiped God, saying, 'Amen! Blessing and glory and wisdom and thanksgiving and honor and power and might be to our God for ever and ever! Amen'" (Rev. 7:9-12).

It's Time to Remember

MAUNDY THURSDAY
1 CORINTHIANS 11:23-26

Erwin J. Kolb

A ten-year old girl was moving with her family from the Midwest to California. This meant, of course, that she would be separated from her playmates, especially her closest friend, a neighbor girl named Kay. On the day the family left, she gave her special friend, Kay her best bracelet and said, "Keep this to remember me by. Everytime you look at it, think of me." So Kay in the Midwest looks at the bracelet on her arm and remembers her friend thousands of miles away in California. She remembers her love and friendship and the good times they had together.

Do you have any objects or special customs which help you remember loved ones who have moved away—or who have died? I have on the wall of my study at home the bronze plaque of the Lord's Supper that was on my father's casket at his funeral, and when I look at it I remember my dad. On my shelf is the German Bible and hymnbook that belonged to my mother, and when I see them I remember my mother.

When our Lord planned His departure from His friends on earth and thought of those who would be His followers throughout the centuries, He wanted something by which they would remember Him and why He came, so He instituted what we now call "The Lord's Supper," or "The Last Supper." He did that on the Thursday of Holy Week, the week that ended in His death on the cross. It was

Thursday, the night before He was betrayed that He was celebrating the Jewish Passover with His disciples when He took a piece of the matzoh, the unleavened bread, and gave it to them to eat—and remember; remember me, remember my body was broken for you. He took a cup of the wine and gave it to them to drink—and remember; remember that My blood was shed for your sins.

Tonight is Maundy Thursday, and we do what He said and remember. Our text is from the words that describe what He did that first Maundy Thursday; they are called the Words of Institution. Matthew, Mark and Luke, the gospel writers, each describe the scene in their own way, some including details which others do not have. But our words are from the pen of St. Paul who, in writing to the congregation at Corinth, describes that scene in complete detail. He wasn't there, so God had to reveal to him what to write. He says, "For I received from the Lord what I delivered unto you."

The Lutheran Church is known throughout the Christian world for its special emphasis on the Lord's Supper on the real presence of the body and blood of Christ, that Christ's body and blood are really present, as Luther said, in, with and under, the bread and wine. Some churches emphasize the "remembrance" aspect of the Lord's Supper and consider it more like a memorial meal. Tonight as we celebrate Maundy Thursday, may we not only stand on the Lutheran doctrine of the real presence but also emphasize the "remembrance words" that Jesus used and think of tonight as a "time to remember."

A Time to Remember

I. More than a Sentimental Remembering

The Taj Mahal in India, considered by some to be one of the most beautiful buildings in the world, was erected in memory of a faithful and loving wife. Stanford University in California, renowned for its magnificent buidings, was built by some parents in loving memory of their only son who had died. Today when someone thinks of Stanford University, they no longer think of the son; a tourist to the Taj Mahal does not think of a faithful and loving wife unless someone explains and tells him.

Our Lord on that night in the Upper Room when He gave bread to His disciples and said, "This is My body," added, "Do this in remembrance of Me." When He gave them the cup that was His blood, He said, "Do this, as often as you drink it, in remembrance of Me."

2. A Remembering of Deliverance

Bread and wine were ideal memorials to help us remember Him and His death. He could have used other memorials. God had been doing this since the beginning of time. When He lead His chosen people out of the slavery of Egypt on the way to the Promised Land, He wanted them to remember the mighty act that climaxed His feud with Pharaoh. In the series of plagues, which peaked with the slaughter of every firstborn of the Egyptians, the Hebrews miraculously escaped. The angel of death passed over every house that had the blood of the sacrificial lamb on the doorpost. First, God spared their lives from the angel of death, and then from the army of Pharaoh by the parting of the Red Sea. He wanted them to remember so He said, "This day shall be to you a memorial, and ye shall keep it as a feast to the Lord throughout your generations" (Ex. 13:14). Still today faithful Jews celebrate the Passover at this time of the year and thank God for their deliverance by the power of God.

In the wilderness when God cared for His people with manna from heaven, He had them fill a jar with manna and keep it in their tabernacle, that as we read in Exodus, your generations may "see the bread with which I fed you in the wilderness when I brought you forth from the land of Egypt" (Ex. 16:32). When He led His people through the Jordan River by dividing the waters like He had done at the Red Sea, He told them to take 12 stones, one for each of the tribes of Israel from the middle of the river bed, where the priests had stood while the people passed through, and to use those stones to build a memorial, a monument. He said, "These stones shall be for a memorial unto the children of Israel forever" (Joshua 4:7).

Even the clothes which God's people in the Old Testament wore were to help them remember God's great act of deliverance. They were to have four fringes or tassels on the four corners of their outer garment or mantel fastened with a ribbon of blue. He said, "It shall be to you a tassel to look upon and remember all the commandments of the Lord, to do them" (Num. 15:39).

God could have chosen many things to help us remember His great act of deliverance through the death of His Son, but He selected the simple bread and wine from the Passover meal. Thus the two acts of deliverance were tied together, the deliverance from slavery in Egypt to go to the Promised Land and the deliverance from the slavery of sin to lead all people on the road of salvation to the promised land in heaven with God.

3. A Remembering of Christ's Death

The deliverance from sin to salvation was accomplished through the death of God's Son on the cross of Calvary. That is why the bread and wine are so appropriate, the ideal way for us to remember. We take bread and hear the words "This is My body," and we remember. We remember that He was the sacrificial Lamb of God. He was without blemish. Not a bone of His body was broken, like the Passover Lamb, even though He was whipped and tortured and crucified, hung up to die like a common criminal. We receive as we eat that bread the very body of Christ. We receive wine and hear the words, "This is My blood," and we remember. We remember that His blood oozed from the wounds on His scourged back; it dripped from His head crowned with thorns; it flowed from His pierced side.

To eat and drink bread and wine and at the same time receive the body and blood of Jesus Christ is a miracle beyond our mind's comprehension. But it is not necessary to understand it. We only receive it and believe it. Martin Luther and Zwingli met at the castle in Marburg, Germany, to discuss their various teachings based on the Bible. they agreed on all points—except this one about the real presence of the Lord's body and blood. Zwingli said to Luther, "Then you believe that your teeth are chewing and your stomach is digesting the body of Christ?" Luther replied: "That's what Paul implies. Would you trample God's Word because you cannot understand it? My faith does not make the sacrament, it merely accepts it." That's the way a little poem that some have attributed to Luther puts it:

> He the Word that spake it,
> He took the bread and brake it
> And what His word did make it
> That I believe and take it.

4. A Remembering of the Forgiveness of Sins

That's what I do when I eat the bread and drink the wine. I remember that His body was broken for me and His blood was shed for me. But why? That I might have the forgiveness of my sins. I remember my sins and receive the assurance that through His body and blood my sins had been forgiven. In the account of the Last Supper given by Matthew, he adds these words of Jesus when He gave the cup, "which is poured out for many for the forgiveness of sins" (Matt. 26:39). That is why He died. That is why He wants to be remembered, for there is no other name under heaven, Peter said, given among men whereby we can be saved (Acts 4:12). And it is in remembering that story of His death, in hearing His words that it was to pay for my sins, that the Spirit of God created the faith for me to believe. Through that faith in Him I receive the forgiveness of sins and life and salvation.

5. A Remembering of the New Covenant

This new life and salvation which I receive puts me into a new relationship with God. St. Paul records the way Jesus said it, "This cup is the New Covenant in My blood." The Old Covenant in the Old Testament depended on the priests in the temple to make sacrifices for the sins of the people. Forgiveness was received through that system of keeping the laws and doing the ritual that pointed forward to the coming of the Messiah. But Jesus has come and fulfilled it all. Now there is a New Covenant, a Covenant that depends not on the blood of the sacrifices at the temple but on Jesus' blood, the death He endured on the cross for all people for all time. The Old Covenant was fulfilled. We have been given a New Covenant in which we are free from the obligations of the sacrifices and rituals and strict keeping of special laws. We are under a covenant of grace in which through faith in the death of Christ we receive continual forgiveness of all our sins.

Maundy Thursday and every time we receive the Lord's Supper is a time to remember that death. We sometimes have a problem with that because we have covered over the Lord's Supper with traditions and liturgies and customs, so much so that we miss the real value of it as the means by which God gives us the forgiveness and assurance of our place in the New Covenant. It could be compared to the famous painting of the Last Supper by Leonardo da Vinci in the Santa Maria Church in Milan, Italy.

Over the centuries since the original painting was made, it deteriorated, cracks developed in the wall where it was painted, blisters formed on the plaster. Repeated efforts were made to restore it to the original. Five separate times when the colors faded, it was overlaid with new paint. In recent times it has finally been completely restored through the voluntary work of a brilliant painter named Mauro Pellic](ioli. For seven years he worked. He scraped the wall down to the original work done by Leonardo da Vinci and repainted that original.

There has been much controversy about the Lord's Supper throughout the history of the church. In the Lutheran Church customs have developed at different times, and the way we take communion has varied from church to church. On this Maundy Thursday, as we remember the original event in that Upper Room, scrape off any hindering traditions and misconceptions and listen to the words of Scripture. A time to remember. "This is My body ... Do this in remembrance of Me ... This cup is the New Covenant in My blood. Do this, as often as you drink of it, in remembrance of Me."

Today in Gethsemane

GOOD FRIDAY
HEBREWS 4:14-16; 5:7-9

Richard G. Kapfer

Although Good Friday takes us to the foot of the cross where our Savior bled and died, our Epistle for this day of sorrow takes us first to the side of Jesus in the Garden of Gethsemane. The writer to the Hebrews in our text for today is recalling the Gethsemane event as a crucial one in the Passion of our Lord. Jesus was there alone, with no human friend to help Him. Off in a corner His three closest friends, Peter, James, and John, slept.

We read the description of the suffering Jesus in our text: "In the days of His flesh, Jesus offered up prayers and supplications, with loud cries and tears, to Him who is able to save Him from death, and He was heard for His godly fear. Although He was a Son, He learned obedience through what He suffered; and being made perfect He became the source of eternal salvation to all who obey Him." Something happened that evening in Gethsemane that is vitally important for us. In fact it is the beginning of the drama of God's mercy and grace that led to the cross. On this Good Friday it is the cross that we stand under, thinking, reflecting, yearning, and believing. It is the cross that casts its shadow and power over Gethsemane.

The first Gethsemane and Calvary event is over. But the final triumph day begun by the cross and open tomb has not yet come. It's going to. We're part of it now. Yet this world of Caesar and Pilate, Caiaphas and mob continues on. And Jesus is *still* in Gethsemane, a spiritual one, pleading for us, hurting with us, living with us and for us. But this Gethsemane is different. We are there too. We're part of the new age. We're called to be wide-awake Gethsemane watchers and proclaimers. Listen: "Since then we have a great high priest who has passed through the heavens, Jesus, the Son of God, let us hold fast our confession. For we have not a high priest who is unable to sympathize with our weaknesses, but one who in every respect has been tempted as we are, yet without sinning. Let us then with confidence draw near to the throne of grace, that we may receive mercy and find grace to help in time of need."

This is why we title our Good Friday message "Today in Gethsemane," because the first Gethsemane that led to the cross and tomb places us by faith into this second Gethsemane by the side of Jesus. Let's look first at the Gethsemane of yesterday and then the Gethsemane of today.

I. Yesterday in Gethsemane

If anyone doubts that Jesus Christ, who is true God from all eternity, is also true Man; if anyone thinks that "Passion of our Lord" is not a fitting title; then let that person listen to Jesus in Gethsemane. The battle against evil is about to begin. The whole weight of evil will soon be placed on God's Son. God has chosen to find Himself guilty of your sins and my sins, guilty of every cruelty, every moment of cheating, lying, adultery, covetousness, and everything else that we have ever done. He has done this by sending His own Son. The Son is obedient to the Father's will. This is the Father's plan unfolding, His answer to evil and sin that is not of His making, but ours; here the plan that is not rightfully His concern, except that God loves so much.

So the plan of God uses the evil intentions of humans to take His Son to the cross. Jesus is in Gethsemane. He has concluded the Passover meal with His disciples and has celebrated with them the meal of Holy Communion. Soon Judas, the betrayer, will arrive. But now is a time for groans and for agonies. The obedient Son cries out: "Father, if Thou be willing, remove this cup from Me. Nevertheless, not as I will, but as Thou wilt."

This is for real. Jesus of Nazareth, true Man, is praying and pleading. The Incarnation of God's Son is not a matter of God putting on a costume. The Lord did not turn aside from being a human being in the midst of this very human world of sin. The Son of Man had to bring to His lips the bitter cup of evil and the results of evil. My sins, every one of them, and your sins, all of them, are there in that cup. The sins of the world—of every injustice and every cruelty and the cry of every sufferer and every mourner are there. All of that was focused on Jesus in Gethsemane who will be stretched out on a cross and then completely abandoned by His Father.

The message from the first Gethsemane, then, is that "in the days of His flesh" Jesus was born, grew, learned, lived among us, and then, through cries and tears became obedient even unto His brutal and ugly death. Because of His obedience in the place of all of us who constantly disobey, and because of His acceptance of the Father's will in the place of all of us who are rebels against God's will, He became "the source of eternal salvation to all."

There is yet a second message. It is the response of the man and woman and child of God who live the new life in the crucified and risen Christ. It has to do with the realization that the victory is guaranteed by the cross, the victory over sin, evil, and death. But that victory has not been realized completely. Evil's days are numbered. Sin or evil will be completely destroyed in the final resurrection on the last day. God knows when it is time to bring down the curtain. But we live in the meantime, and in the meantime we need to look carefully at—

II. Today in Gethsemane

In commenting on the death of millions of Jewish people and others under the Nazis of Germany, Emil Fackenheim wrote of the dilemma of the holocaust. He noted that the holocaust was an epochal point in history. For many people the dilemma became this: God is either uncaring or He is helpless. To have lived through the holocaust, as many Jews did, brought many of them to that dilemma. God either did not care about the atrocities that had occurred, or God cared but could do nothing about it.

This points up the power of evil and cruelty contained within the human mind as an instrument of evil. St. Paul was not simply using picturesque language when he wrote that "We are not contending against flesh and blood, but against the principalities, against the powers, against the world's rulers of this present darkness, against the spiritual hosts of wickedness in the heavenly places" (Eph. 6:12).

When we view the enormity of evil in our world, we begin to appreciate in just a small way the enormity of what was contained in the cup that Jesus had to drink and of the depth of His suffering as He took that cup to His lips.

It is said that in the Warsaw ghetto there was a message scrawled on a wall: "God was put on trial here and found guilty." A play was written partly in response to that message with the title of "The Sign of Jonah." In this play the sufferers of the world assembled and put God on trial for all of the evils that they and others had suffered. They then passed the sentence that God would have to suffer all of the things that they had to suffer. In this play God stepped into their midst in the person of Jesus Christ to hear the sentence and to declare: "I have taken the suffering of the world upon Myself. I have drunk the bitter cup." That reveals the heart of God. In the midst of suffering and evil, faith is turned to Gethsemane and to Calvary. *That only* makes sense out of senselessness. God came. He is neither helpless nor uncaring. He acts. He cares in sending His own Son to take upon His innocent body the sins and the ugliness and the cruelty of all the world and of all the ages.

There is a second part to this. It is found in the words, "In the days of His flesh, Jesus offered up prayers and supplications, with loud cries and tears, to Him who is able to save Him from death, and He was heard for His godly fear," and the words, "For we have not a high priest who is unable to sympathize with our weaknesses, but one who in every respect has been tempted as we are, yet without sinning." The struggle of Jesus against the evil vividly seen in Gethsemane and worked out for our salvation at Calvary on that first Good Friday points up the fact that evil is *never* God's will or intent. He can, in this fallen world, fashion His will even out of evil. He did this with the evil intentions of Caiaphas in order to work out His will for our salvation. But God is never the author of evil. He hates it as much—more—than we do. God is mad also at injustice. God is sad also at sorrow. God is happy also with beauty and truth.

That brings us to Jesus in Gethsemane today. He is still with the sufferers. He is still pleading, praying, working, and acting on our behalf. The battle against evil still rages. The difference is that the cross and the tomb guarantee the ultimate victory for God's faithful people. Until the final victory at the end of time, Jesus is in Gethsemane today, and so are *we* to be in Gethsemane with Jesus. He stands at the tomb of the Lazaruses and weeps with every mourner. So are we to be there where He is. He stands at the side of every parent and joins in their sorrowing anger over a wayward child. So are we to be there where He is. He hears and feels the rage of the oppressed and is also outraged. So are we to be there where He is.

The companions of Jesus in Gethsemane slept. We cannot clutch our faith and life to ourselves and sleep. We cannot sing our little songs in drowsy cadence and pretend that the battle is over. It is not. Not while holocausts happen again and again; not while people are hungry, thirsty, sick, and imprisoned; not while the world—for which our Savior wept, bled, died, and rose—doesn't know the victory is theirs by faith in the obedient Son of God. It isn't over until His kingdom comes and His will is done on earth as it is in heaven. In the meantime, we go to Gethsemane with our Lord, for we are His followers. He cares; we care. He suffers; we suffer. He acts; we act. That is our privilege and our mission until the Lord Himself says it is now complete and He gathers His yearning people into His arms where "They shall hunger no more nor thirst anymore, and God will wipe away every tear from their eyes."

New Clothes for the Easter Parade

THE RESURRECTION OF OUR LORD
COLOSSIANS 3:1-4

Jaroslav Vajda

What a day! What an event! We have all the makings of a parade. A special occasion that deserves a celebration! Someone to honor who

has just come from a decisive battle as a conqueror! An event that
promises hope and new life not to just one person or family or even a
nation, but to the entire human race, past, present, and future! It's a
time to dress up in new clothes and come out for a parade in great
numbers. A time to sing magnificent songs and to play triumphant
music. A time to display flowers and greet one another with a
special greeting. It's Easter! Let's have a parade!

New Clothes for the Easter Parade

I. The Christian Easter Parade Celebrates
the New Life in Christ

Someone said that if there were no Savior, the world would have
to invent one. Let me suggest that if there were no Easter parade,
Christians would have to invent one. And that is exactly how the
whole idea of an Easter parade originated.

The earliest Christians, those who lived within several generations of our Lord's crucifixion, resurrection, and ascension followed
the Lord's Great Commission and fanned out from Jerusalem to
Samaria and outward to all parts of the world, lighting fires of faith
wherever they settled by announcing the Good News of salvation in
Jesus Christ.

The world around them was almost totally pagan. Super-
stitious! Fearful! Suicidal! Those who were born slaves could expect
to die slaves. Life was cheap. Women had little value. Crippled
children were left to die out in the wilderness. The emperor's word
was law. Taxes were draining people. If people got bored or
frustrated, they got drunk. There were no hospitals to take care of
the sick. The average life expectancy was about 40 years. The world
was swarming with all kinds of prophets, messiahs, and philosophers, each offering some kind of understanding of life, but none of
them able to deal with the facts of sin, and death, the result of sin.

In that rather hopeless society the Christians were a peculiar
group, different from everyone else. They worshiped a God-Man
named Jesus Christ, who was crucified shamefully like a criminal
under the governorship of Pontius Pilate in Jerusalem, and was
said to have risen from the dead three days later. These followers of
Jesus Christ, who were called Christians, had been eye-witnesses of
their Lord's death and resurrection, and they were telling anyone
who would listen that this Christ had come into the world from God
the Creator, to redeem the human race from sin and death by His
innocent suffering and death, so that whoever would believe in that
holy Savior would not perish but have everlasting life.

Those who were attracted to this new religion asked the messen-
gers or apostles how they could become members of this unique
society or community of believers. And there were told: "Whoever

believes and is baptized shall be saved." And they asked: Believe what? And, What is baptism?

And they were told: We will teach you what it is that saves you. It is all contained in the Creed. Learn it, and when you know what it is all about, if you believe it to be true, you may be baptized.

And so they took instructions for one or two years, and then they asked to be baptized. Once again they were asked: Are you sure you want to be baptized? Do you know what this means? It means renouncing allegiance to the prince of this world and all his values and ways and his control over your will, your thoughts, and actions. You will be swearing allegiance—that is, total, exclusive loyalty—to Jesus Christ as your only Lord and Savior. Are you willing to be baptized into the death of Jesus Christ, thereby dying to the world and its ways? Do you want to be a new and different person at any cost? And if they said yes, that they wanted this with all their heart, the leaders of the Christian community would put them through the final exams in the weeks before Easter, for as Easter marked the resurrection of Christ from the grave and His victory over death so their first Easter as Christians would also mark the death and resurrection of their old self to a new life.

The date for the Baptism was the evening before Easter. All night long they observed the Easter vigil in the company of other Christians, listening to the Scriptural accounts of God's deliverance of His people from the slavery of Egypt and likewise the deliverance of the world from the bondage of sin, death, and the devil. And then would come the time for the new birth by water and the Word. The candidate would be given a white gown or robe to wear instead of the old clothes and would be baptized either in a river or a large pool, or have water applied in the name of the one true God they had just confessed in the words of the Apostles' Creed or its equivalent.

In that baptism one was symbolically drowned—to indicate the dying of the old person—and a new person emerged from the baptismal waters. "For when you were baptized," Paul reminds the Colossian Christians, "you were buried with Christ, and in baptism you were also raised with Christ through your faith in the active power of God, who raised Him from death" (2:12). The drowning was like Christ's burial, and the emergence was like His rising from death to life. At Baptism the candidate was given a new name, a Christian name, and joined the other baptismal candidates and those who were baptized formerly, in a procession with the Paschal candle to greet the Easter dawn with hymns and shouts: "Christ is risen! He is risen indeed!" All the Christians who had been previously baptized came to the vigil dressed in new clothes and would take part in what later came to be the Easter parade.

The baptismal candidates wore the white robe for the next 8

days. And what they had privately vowed in the warmth of that friendly company of Christians, they were now parading publicly before a questioning, mocking, or hostile world. People at work or on the street would stare at them, some making derisive comments, others were drawn to them by curiosity as to what it was that would transform them like this—much as we are made curious by the sight of the Hare Krishna sect today.

In some parts of the world, even today, Christians gather for the Easter vigil to receive new members by Baptism or to remember their own baptism, their new birth, their transformation from the old life to the new life, and then they greet the Easter dawn with the ancient greetings: "Christ is risen! He is risen indeed!"

In many parts of the world today it is dangerous and costly to take part in such an Easter parade. In Russia and other communist-ruled countries (and perhaps soon in Muslim countries), you would be as conspicuous as the early Christians wearing their white robes if you uttered the greeting, "Christ is risen!" on Easter Sunday, or if you joined in the worship of the risen Christ with fellow-believers. It is as though your baptism were showing, like the well-defined lines of a cattlebrand. And even if a Christian in that part of the world didn't take part in the Easter celebration, he would still be betraying the new life in him by his attitudes, his behavior, and his values in his daily work and associations. And if you were to ask any of those people: Why do you act or live as you do in a world that is so different, they would tell you: I can't act any other way. The new life in me has to express itself. It has control of me. I am the follower of the risen Christ. I have died to the old life and my life is now hidden in Christ. My baptism makes me His, and when He comes I will share His glory.

II. The Easter Parade Demands New Clothes

"You have been raised to life with Christ," St. Paul tells the Colossians who could remember their Easter vigil and their baptism but who may have forgotten how drastic a change this was to make in their lives. The glow of that experience may have faded under the daily darkness of their surroundings and the pressures of the death-dominated world in which they continued to live and work. Isn't it like that with us, too? Some of us don't remember the day of our new birth, our resurrection to life with Christ in holy Baptism. Many of us do not even know the day we were baptized. And the new life that was begun in us in that sacrament has taken a daily beating since that time. We get tired fighting the good fight. We lose sight of our ultimate goal. We fail to rekindle and feed our faith with Word and Sacrament. We grow weak in our allegiance to the Prince of Life and the King of kings. We are drawn to lesser attractions. We identify more frequently with the way of death around us than with the way of life opened to us at Easter. Our life is downbeat, sterile, boring, and joyless. Our remembrance of our baptism is hazy, the impact of Easter has been dulled.

We need to relive our transition from death to life by such recollections as the observance of our Lord's Passion and death. We need to see the horror and despair and hopelessness of life without Christ in order to appreciate the hilarious joy, the lively hope and the power of the resurrection. We need to be told the same thing as the Colossians: "You have been raised to life with Christ." Remember? Let this day's miracle relight that flickering flame of faith and hope!

Once we realize this, the only logical thing to do is to follow the suggestion of Paul: "Set your hearts, then, on the things that are in heaven, where Christ sits on his throne at the right side of God. Keep your minds fixed on things there, not on things here on earth. For you have died, and your life is hidden with Christ in God. Your real life is Christ."

This is a text to be taken literally, which means, we must understand exactly what it says. Paul is here not saying, Fix your hearts on *heaven* itself—although we are to have heaven as our goal. He is deliberately saying here and repeating: Set your hearts on the *things* that are *in* heaven. Keep your minds fixed on *things* there, not on things here. He is recommending that we be preoccupied with heavenly things rather than with heaven itself. Neither the Colossians nor we are to imagine that we can live in this world as Christians dreaming only of heaven. But with heaven assured for us as it is by Christ's resurrection, we don't have to worry abut this life. We can be carefree and live already now by the ideals and values and principles that are going to govern our existence in heaven. In fact, that is why we are not suddenly raptured and whisked off to heaven the moment we are baptized. We are to live that heavenly kind of life in Christ here and now and until we are finally called to enter our eternal mansions.

That means that the heavenly things are to mark us as Christ's people here on earth, like new clothes give away the person who is celebrating something, like the white robes gave away the newborn Christians in the early church. "You are the people of God," Paul tells the Colossians later, "He loved you and chose you to be His own. Therefore, you must put on [get the image of new clothes?] compassion, kindness, humility, gentleness, and patience" (v. 12). The old rags are identified as "earthly desires, immorality, indecency, lust, evil passions, and greed" (v. 5). "But now you must get rid of all these things: anger, passion, and hateful feelings, insults and lies" (vs. 8, 9).

Christ's death and resurrection can change our values and outlook on life drastically from "Let us eat and drink, for tomorrow

we will die" (1 Cor. 15:32) to "He died for all so that those who live
should no longer live for themselves, but only for Him who died and
was raised to life for their sake" (2 Cor. 5:15).

One of the effects of the earliest Easter parade was that the
world could see visible evidences of a commitment that was made to
the risen Christ. The dying, hopeless, pagan world saw the white-
robed Christians, happy in their Lord, sure of peace with God and
eternal life with Him, and they marveled at the way this life with
Christ hidden in God revealed itself, and they said: "See how they
love one another!" So when we wear the new clothes of Christ's
righteousness, and when the heavenly virtues and values pre-
occupy and control our minds and hearts, the world will see our
good works and be led to glorify our Father who is in heaven.

There is not a trace of sorrow or despair or mourning in this
festival service today. It is like that all over the world where
Christ's people are celebrating His victory over death. This is a
newsworthy event that can fill so many people with an unspeakable joy and with the hope of everlasting life. We praise God for
Christ and for His resurrection. And we thank Him for our new
birth in Baptism. We are His own. Death itself has no power over us
any more, and His life is in us now and for all eternity! What
reasons for a lifelong Easter parade!

Happy Easter! Let any new clothes you are wearing today or will
ever wear be an object lesson to you and to the world, that they are
the symbols of your new life in Christ, and let the heavenly things
Christ has in store for you adorn your life already now so that all
may know the miracle that has taken place in you and that they
may yet find the same joy in the same risen Christ.

Happy Easter! Let's learn to say the ancient greeting and
response of this great day: "Christ is risen! He is risen indeed!"
Let's say it with a heart full of appreciation: "Christ is risen! He is
risen indeed!" "Christ is risen!" (Congregation responds: "He is
risen indeed!") And again: Christ is risen! (Congregation: "He is
risen indeed!") Hallelujah!

The Christian's Hope a Living Hope

SECOND SUNDAY OF EASTER
1 PETER 1:3-9

Hans F. Bruss

When my ship comes in, I find myself saying, my wife and I are
going to take a Caribbean cruise or spend a winter in the sun or

whatever I'm dreaming about at the moment. Well, my ship hasn't come in yet, and it probably never will. That's not being very optimistic, you say.

There is a difference between hope and a baseless optimism. Take the Cargo Cults of the South Pacific. The white man who came to these islands constantly talked about cargo. When the ships from the West would come in with their important cargo: pickles, cloth, tobacco, scissors, beer, whiskey, or whatever they needed, then everything would be all right again. Eventually the majestic ships sailed into the harbor with their precious cargo. The white man's hope and expectations were fulfilled.

The islanders, the natives, however, were deeply impressed by the ships, and they watched their white bosses closely to discover the secret of Cargo or Kago as they would say in pidgin English. Eventually from what they observed, they evolved various symbolic activities, decorating their villages with flowers because the white man kept flowers in vases, imitating their white bosses in other ways, even destroying their own wealth and traditions in an effort to create a situation in which Cargo would come for them, too, and not just for the white man.

The Cargo never came. The final stage common to all Cargo Cults is despair and ultimately collapse. Optimism differs from hope in that optimism of this kind can exist without truth. It's a dead hope, not a living hope.

The Christian's Hope Is a Living Hope

I. It's Based on a Firm Foundation and Therefore Realizable

St. Peter says in our text: "Blessed be the God and Father of our Lord Jesus Christ! By His great mercy we have been born anew to a living hope through the resurrection of Jesus Christ from the dead" (v. 3 RSV).

People who build their hopes on wealth, on station in life, on their ancestry, or their own special virtues, their accomplishments, will in the end be classed as ships that have foundered at sea. The final message over the wires will be: "There is no hope of rescue." How tragic!

But our hopes are centered on Jesus Christ. St. Peter reminds us of the importance of Jesus' resurrection from the dead on Easter, because this is the very foundation on which our faith rests. If He had not risen from the dead, our faith would be in vain. We would still be in our sins. But our faith is not founded on someone who is dead. Our Redeemer lives! Our hopes rest on the living Christ, who was "declared to be the Son of God with power, according to the Spirit of holiness, by the resurrection from the dead" (Rom. 1:4).

Our Lord was also raised for our justification. Jesus bore the burden of our sins. He, the just one, died for the unjust. He atoned for our sins. His resurrection is eloquent testimony that the heavenly Father was fully satisfied with His atoning work. The Father raised His own Son and caused Him to sit at His own right hand as the King of kings. What comfort!

His own resurrection is the guarantee of our resurrection. You and I have this guarantee. We're not hypnotized by an empty dream. We're united with Christ by a faith that tells us that we follow a Savior who will surely bring us to heaven. We have Christ's promise: "Because I live, ye shall live also" (John 14:19).

St. Peter says: "By His mercy we have been born anew to a living hope" (v. 3 RSV). It was not our merit, not our goodness, not our performance, but it was His infinite love that laid the foundation of our hope. Hence the foundation of our hope is not in ourselves, but in God, in God's own heart, where our salvation was planned and prepared. Thank God, because there in God and in His work the foundation is sure, firm, and solid.

From God it has come to us through the Good News, that is, through the Gospel, and through Baptism, so that the Holy Spirit working through the Gospel, through Baptism, has caused us to be born again to a living hope, that is, to become believers in Christ as Savior and Lord.

Because the Christian's hope is built on a solid rock, on the living Christ, His resurrection, His atonement, the Gospel promises of God, the Holy Spirit's work through the Gospel and Baptism, it's a living hope. It's realizable. If you're looking for some evidence of all this in your own life, St. Peter says, see how the Spirit has worked in you and caused you to be born again to this living hope: "We have been born anew to a living hope through the resurrection of Jesus Christ from the dead" (v. 3). If you're looking for proof that you have been born again, well, you believe in Christ, don't you? You love Christ, you worship Him, you follow Him, you rejoice in what Jesus has done for you, you rejoice in His daily care. St. Peter says it this way: "Without having seen Him you love Him; though you do not now see Him you believe in Him and rejoice with unutterable and exalted joy" (v. 8 RSV). Because God is at work here, it's realizable. And you may ask

II. Exactly What Is Realizable?

What do you really mean by the Christian's hope? The hope, the living hope, to which we have been born again is that "inheritance incorruptible" "reserved in heaven" for us according to what St. Peter says in our text. If you ask me to describe it for you, then St. Peter would say, its splendor is difficult to describe adequately in human language.

It's incorruptible, not subject to decay nor corruption. It's undefiled, not tainted as some ill-gotten earthly inheritances sometimes are. It's pure, unspotted, holy, perfect like the inheritance of the saints in light should be. It does not fade away, it's unfading, retaining the freshness of beautiful flowers forever in bloom with everlasting fragrance.

Before His ascension Christ told His disciples that He was going to prepare a place for us in His Father's house, beautiful mansions. Well, this inheritance is even now ready for us. The testator who wills it to us has died for us on Calvary's cross. Hence His last will and testament is in effect. This inheritance waits for us. The Lord is ready to receive us, that we may be where He is.

The Christian's hope is not an empty hope, but a living hope. It will be realized. It's realizable, because (1) our Redeemer has gone before us and we are joint-heirs with Christ. This inheritance is a gift from our heavenly Father by virtue of Christ's atonement. Christ died for you and for me, that we might live. It's realizable because it is a gift of His grace. We could never merit it by our works.

(2) This inheritance is "kept in heaven for you," reserved for you and me. When the Christian comes to the Father's house, finally checking in, there's no chance that your reservation has been lost or cancelled. The heavenly Father sees that you are coming in His Son's name, and He will welcome you cordially to enter into the joy of heaven.

The Christian's hope embraces all of life: not only the life to come, but also the life that now is. The Christian's hope embraces the special care which the heavenly Father devotes to the members of His family. You enjoy this special care. You could undoubtedly as well as I relate how He has protected you, fed you, sustained you, directed you, sometimes miraculously. Therefore you could instantly relate to St. Peter when he is speaking of the inheritance being reserved for you and he goes on to say: "It is kept for you in heaven, and you, because you put your faith in God, are under the protection of His power until salvation comes—the salvation which is even now in readiness and will be revealed at the end of time" (v. 5 NEB), when Christ shall return. If we enjoy happy days with many blessings, thank His goodness.

If we are called upon to suffer various trials, our hope rests securely in the knowledge that it will be "for a little while" only. These trials serve the purpose of testing our faith, strengthening it, refining it as the assayer tests a piece of precious metal to get the pure gold by fire. In this connection we are talking about the pure gold of faith. The Father will be with His children now in their tribulations. It's not only together with our Lord in the mansions above, but together with Him now.

III. The Christian's Hope Animates All of the Christian's Life

When we reflect upon the Christian's hope in this way, we see that it's such a vital hope. St. Paul also talks about hope often. In Rom. 8:24 he exclaims that we are saved by hope. In 1 Cor. 13 he ranks hope with faith and Christian love, saying: "So faith, hope, love abide, these three; but the greatest of these is love."

The Lord has provided us with real hope for this life and for the life to come. That's why St. Peter began our text by saying: "Blessed be the God and Father of our Lord Jesus Christ!" Let us bless, praise, thank God and the Father of our Lord Jesus Christ. We live in a day when cynics, nihilists, and doomsayers abound. The Christian's prospects for the future, however, are splendid. Praise Christ our Lord!

When we hurt, or smart from the sufferings we may have to endure, the inclination may be there to murmur, to complain, but if we'll just be patient and try counting our blessings for a change, we'll find good things to delight in each day. Even at midnight when things seem darkest, we'll be able to sing psalms or praise to the Lord like Paul and Silas in the prison at Philippi.

Since our hope is not an empty, but a living hope, resting on a secure foundation, "this is cause for great joy" (v. 6 NEB). We rejoice, because we know that we won't be disappointed.

Not only does this hope produce great joy, it's dynamic. What can stir us up to fight more than the assurance of victory? Christ will help us to overcome. What can make us more steadfast in our pilgrimage through this world than the certainty of reaching the goal? We may become travel weary, sometimes ready to throw in the sponge, but when we see the spires of the Heavenly city in the distance, we shall be spurred on to reach it. What will better destroy the fascination of the glittering temptations of this present world than the conscious possession of better things, the knowledge that an incomparable inheritance awaits us above?

What comfort in grief and sorrow to know that our Savior Jesus will receive us in the Father's mansions, there to wipe away all our tears. This hope makes us act like the new beings we are in Christ Jesus. This living hope makes lively Christians. Our earthly dreamships may never appear on the horizon, but this ship, the ship of Christian Faith and Christian Hope—when we get into this ship with Jesus Christ as our Pilot—will sail safely into that Harbor above with its precious cargo. "And a joy, unspeakable, and wonderful, fills you with delight as you get what by faith you're looking for—your salvation" (vs. 8, 9 AAT).

The Greatness of Our Redeemer's Work as Impelling Motive for Christian Living

THIRD SUNDAY OF EASTER
1 PETER 1:17-21

Hans F. Bruss

Do you remember the reverence with which the people in Iran in early 1979 looked upon Ayatollah Khomeini? Ayatollah means the reflection of Allah. Khomeini, a frail old man in his late seventies, wearing a black turban and ankle-length robes, often seen holding the Koran in his hands, returned by jetliner from Paris to Teheran after 15 years in exile. The cry went up: "The holy one has come!" The welcoming committee of one thousand or so chanted rhythmically: "Allahu akbar! Allahu akbar!" (God is great! God is great!) Iran went wild.

There were those who denounced Khomeini as a fanatic, saying that he cashed in on the people's hatred for the Shah. But the majority in Iran admired, adored, and revered him not only for his impeccable integrity and honesty, but especially for his uncompromising stand against the Shah's government. Reverence for Khomeini moved the people in Iran into new directions.

While reverence for someone, whether right or wrong, is an animating principle, St. Peter pointed out in this first chapter how the Christian's hope rests securely on a firm foundation. He tells how it can be realized. The knowledge of his hope inspires the Christian to follow after his Lord and Savior, to do what St. Peter says in our text: "Pass the time of your sojourning here in fear." Expressing this as a theme, let us reflect on

The Greatness of Our Redeemer's Work As Impelling Motive for Christian Living

I. The Realization That It Is Only by Grace That We Have Been Saved from the Judgment Evokes Both Gratitude and Deep Reverence for the Redeemer

St. Peter says in our text: "If you pray to a Father who judges men by their actions without the slightest favoritism, then you should spend the time of your stay here on earth with reverent fear" (v. 17 PHILLIPS).

St. Peter quotes from Lev. 19:2 before our text: "You shall be holy; for I the Lord your God am holy." Recall how Israel in the days of Moses saw the judgment of God fall upon the Egyptians who worshiped idols. However the Israelites themselves had been saved from the judgment by the shed blood of the Passover lamb brushed on to the doorposts of their houses. God saved them from the bondage of Egypt and from the judgment. He chose Israel and in choosing them He brought them unto Himself at Mt. Sinai and made them His own people.

If they were to be His people, then they were expected to be like Him. This is why God said to them: "Be ye holy for I am holy. "By His law, by His commandments to them He spelled out for them exactly what he had in mind. He left nothing to their imagination.

When the Israelite therefore reflected upon what God had done for him, when he considered how in mercy he had been saved from bondage and from judgment, and how God in His covenant with Israel had brought him into a special relationship with the Judge of all the earth, that was cause enough for him to commit himself unto the Lord and to live in humble reverence of his Redeemer.

Of all people today Christians should know that God will judge all people without exception. At the end of the world we must all appear before the judgment seat of God. There is no escape. We won't live forever. In the words of St. Peter, we are sojourners, temporary dwellers here, pilgrims. No one will escape death, and after death comes the judgment.

St. Peter emphasizes that there will be no special privilege in the presence of the Judge of all the earth. His justice is perfect, absolute, and final. It will be useless for anyone to boast of his ancestry as did the Jews in Christ's day, saying: "Abraham is our father" (John 8:39). It will be futile for anyone to plead his own special virtues or merits.

God's will is clear. As the holy God He insists on holiness. Whatever objects or people He takes unto Himself and designates as His very own, to that He imparts holiness. Thus Jerusalem is holy, because He chose it to be His city, so is Mount Zion, and so is the Holy Temple. Israel is holy because God chose this people to be His people, and He chose to dwell in their midst. Since God is holy, He expects His people to be holy, to be like Him, to worship Him and keep His commandments.

How grateful we Christians should be, that we have been redeemed by our Savior from the bondage of sin, death, and the devil. By being born again into God's family, that is, by becoming believers in Jesus, we know that our sins are forgiven, and we can now count on Jesus as our Advocate to represent us before the bar of divine justice. Incredible, but true: in Jesus' name, confessing Him as Savior and Lord, we can now come before the Judge of all the earth and call Him Father. What grace! What a privilege!

There is nothing, however, in all that I have said, that should ever cause any of us to treat our great Redeemer as the heathen treat their idols—bring Him a little offering now and then, kneel a little while before Him now and then, sing Him a song of praise whenever we feel like it, and then go off and live our lives as if Jesus never lived or as if He had never died on Calvary's cross for us. Or imagine that we can do no wrong and that in the end the Lord Jesus as the Judge of all the earth will put His stamp of approval on what we know deep in our hearts to be shenanigans.

Shouldn't the greatness of our salvation cause each one of us to look upon Jesus with gratitude and reverence? Shouldn't we be spending the days of our pilgrimage in being the kind of people He expects us to be, in serving Him?

II. St. Peter Tells Us to Consider What It Cost Jesus to Save Us

St. Peter sums up Christ's work this way: "For you must realize all the time that you have been 'ransomed' from the futile way of living passed on to you by your fathers' traditions, not with some money payment of transient value, but by the costly shedding of blood. The price was in fact the lifeblood of Christ, the unblemished and unstained lamb of sacrifice" (vs. 18, 19 PHILLIPS).

St. Paul also states this briefly and clearly: "Ye are bought with a price" (1 Cor. 6:20). All the wealth in the world could not have bought our salvation. Only the Lord Jesus could have paid the price, and He paid it with His own lifeblood. He paid it in full with His innocent suffering and death.

Sometimes young people do not realize the cost of their education. Only later in life their eyes are opened to what it cost father or mother, what sacrifices their parents made to put them through school. Then their respect and their reverence for their parents has deepened. Or an aged person may not realize what it is costing son or daughter, or their children, to take care of them in their old age, until one day somehow they see the truth of their own situation. Then love, respect, reverence, appreciation, and gratitude for son or daughter, or for their children, wells up in them and grows.

What it cost our Lord to redeem the world, you and me, taking our place under the Law, is beyond description. Only His love for us, unworthy sinners, could have moved Him to suffer all this.

There is this familiar story of the Christian missionary in pioneer days, who was speaking to his Indian friends about Jesus. In the midst of the sermon the Indian chief rose, walked forward, and laid his tomahawk before the missionary saying, "Indian chief give his tomahawk to Jesus Christ."

The missionary spoke on the love of God in Christ Jesus and how great this love was. Rising from his seat again, the old chief walked forward, unwrapped his blanket from his shoulders, and laid this, too, at the missionary's feet, saying this time: "Indian chief give his blanket to Jesus Christ." Then he sat down.

The missionary preached on, as missionaries do, about how God had not even spared His Son, but sent Him into the world to redeem lost mankind. This time the old chief rose and left the meeting. Well, that seemed to be the end of that, but suddenly the old chief reappeared. He came leading his pony to the missionary. He said loudly for all to hear: "Indian chief give his pony to Jesus Christ." Those present looked at each other and silently agreed that this was quite a gift.

The chief returned to his seat. It seemed that he had given just about all that he had. But the missionary wasn't through, he was just coming to the heart of what he wanted to say: how Jesus came and how, because Jesus loved us so much, He willingly took our place under the Law, kept it for us, and then took our burden upon His own shoulders, your sin and mine, shed His very lifeblood to redeem us.

Deeply moved, the Indian chief, his eyes moist, a tear or two running down his ruddy cheeks, came and knelt reverently before the missionary, simply saying with a trembling voice: "Indian chief give himself to Jesus." That, of course, was the ultimate commitment, what Jesus is looking for from each one of us.

When we consider that tremendous sacrifice, the price which He paid for us all, for each one of us, what else is there for us to do but to give ourselves wholly to Jesus and to spend our days trying to be the kind of people He wants us to be and to serve Him in those ways He expects from each one of us.

III. Shouldn't the Tremendous Prospects the Sacrifice of Jesus Has Opened Up for Us Deepen Our Love, Our Gratitude, and Our Respect for Our Great Redeemer?

Since he has so graciously provided us with a new status in God's family and made His rich resources available to us, shouldn't this cause us to make the most of the days of our short stay on this earth? St. Peter reminds us that the atonement took place that our "faith and hope might be centered in God." And what a hope the Christian's hope is, not an empty hope but a living hope: God's constant, special care of the members of His family in this life, and that special, incorruptible inheritance reserved in heaven for us.

God's eye sees everything: past, present, and future—in an instant. God saw the problem and planned our salvation before creation. Incredible but so reassuring! When the fullness of time was come, God executed His plan in Christ and published it through the precious Gospel. If Christ had not been chosen as the

Redeemer from the beginning, the patriarchs could never have obtained forgiveness and justification. All this was done, revealed, published in these last times, as Peter says, "for your benefit" and for mine.

How sad it would be, then, in view of what we have been redeemed from, in view of what it cost Jesus to redeem us, and in view of the tremendous prospects that He has opened up for us, to waste, squander the time of our pilgrimage upon this earth in an empty life, in chasing like a butterfly after the vain things of this world, in the worship of the idols of this world. If we trust Him, believe in Him, love Him, if we appreciate, are grateful, and reverence His name, shouldn't we truly strive to be His people, live like His people, serve Him in every way we can?

The Straying Sheep Returned to the Shepherd

FOURTH SUNDAY OF EASTER
1 PETER 2:19-25

Norbert H. Mueller

The portrayal of Jesus as the Good Shepherd is a picture that affords comfort and assurance to God's people. Whether young or old, man, woman, or child, married or single, who of us can resist picturing themselves as the lamb securely embraced by the arms of the Shepherd. In this portrayal the Lord provides us with the answer to a need basic to our happiness: the need to be secure, free from anxiety and threat. God provides us with that sense of security that frees us to live a life in response to His grace. Yet while rejoicing in the shepherd-lamb relationship, how often we find ourselves straying. How good it is to hear Peter remind his readers, as he does remind us today, "The Straying Sheep Have Been Returned to the Shepherd's Care."

I. The Straying Sheep

Echoing the words of Isaiah, "all we like sheep have gone astray" (Is. 53:6), Peter reminds us of something that at times we tend to ignore or fail to realize, that we have a tendency to stray. It isn't something that we did once and had done with. It is rather something that we continue to do again and again. We keep on straying. This is not done in ignorance. It isn't that we don't know better. Even though we have been called from darkness into his light and are done with the old way, we often do battle with the temptation to go on straying.

You and I do this even while recognizing that we are to blame for the consequence of that straying. Sunday after Sunday we confess: "O almighty God, merciful Father, I, a poor, miserable sinner confess unto Thee all my sins and iniquities with which I have ever offended Thee and justly deserve Thy temporal and eternal punishment." Each and every one of us can give meaning to those words on the basis of our experiences. We can define for ourselves what it means to have been disobedient to His will, refused to listen to His promises, tended to live out our lives as if God didn't exist. How many decisions do we make, how many things do we do, how many conversations do we enter, without regard at all for the fact that we belong to the Shepherd?

There are certain consequences of our straying that we have also experienced. When we stray from the fold of the Shepherd, we also lose the sense of protection and security that comes about when we leave and remove ourselves from the care of the Shepherd. We forfeit the care of the Shepherd. We become insecure and defensive. We assume the burden of providing our own care and security, rather than rejoicing in the care of the Shepherd. We become vulnerable. The promises of our God no longer ring true to us when He says, don't worry about what you need to eat, or drink, or what you need for clothing. Your Shepherd knows you need them and has promised to provide them.

Going out from the fold we forfeit these promises, bringing down the anxiety and worry that goes along with forfeiture. Often we become defensive. With the result that our lives take on actions and attitudes that are decidedly un-Christlike. Rather than taking the things in life in stride, they upset us and we strike back. Rather than coping with the persecutions and jeers of the world with the sense of ultimate victory in Christ, we tend to respond in kind. Rather than remaining faith witnesses to our Lord and God, we are forced into words and actions we decry yet feel necessary if we are to survive. If we feel insecure and threatened, everything, even the little things, becomes a threat to us. Indeed, we may even feel that we are "without God and without hope in the world."

Peter knew well what he was writing. He was no stranger to succumbing to the temptation to stray and experiencing firsthand the consequences. The promises of God had become so remote for Peter that in the face of the accusations of the servant girl in the courtyard of the High Priest, he felt so threatened that he not only denied his Lord but cursed and swore to emphasize his denial. Have we ever climbed out on a limb so far that, rather than swallow our pride and admit we were wrong for fear that we would lose respect or admiration, we persisted in our folly, shouting that we were absolutely right; even cursing for emphasis? How many of us have found ourselves in threatening situations in our marriage, in our jobs, in the classroom, where every little look, or whispered word is viewed as a threat and we strike back with a torrent of language, in the end to be mortified and ashamed? All because we feel insecure, we become defensive. The ultimate consequence is when we become so lost and alienated from the Shepherd that we become lost eternally.

This is a far different picture of us as a little child in the care of a loving father going out to the barn at night, dark and threatening, with perhaps a storm coming up and the wind swirling around. It didn't really bother us because our hand was in the hand of our father. As long as he was there we were safe. There was nothing to worry about. We were secure in the care of a loving father. So it is that when we are in the care of the Shepherd, we don't need to be afraid, nor to become defensive. We don't have to worry about getting lost, or not finding the way back. We don't have to strike back or do those things that are a consequence of our leaving the Shepherd's care. It is a precious promise that Peter speaks when he reminds us that although we keep on straying, we have been returned to the Shepherd's care.

II. Returned to the Shepherd's Care

"Now you have been returned to the Shepherd and Guardian of your soul." Often sheep today are left pretty much to fend for themselves. While driving in the country, it is not unusual to see a few or many sheep out in pasture, protected by fences but with not a living soul around to watch over them or care for them, and this, night and day. I am sure that someone checks on them periodically to make sure they are getting on all right, but the relationship is rather casual. How different this is from the time of Jesus Christ. What a different view of shepherding now from that projected as typical of the shepherding Christ. In New Testament times each and every lamb was precious in the sight of the shepherd. There was an almost personal relationship between the shepherd and the sheep. Indeed the shepherd knew each of them by name. The sheep on the other hand knew the shepherd's voice. A strange voice would scatter them. They would follow only the voice of the shepherd they knew. The shepherd assumed total responsibility for the well-being of the sheep. When the sheep would be gathered at night into a stockade, the shepherd would sleep across the gateway and literally become the door to the sheepfold through which no enemy could pass, and through which no sheep could wander to be exposed to danger. Indeed the shepherd's commitment was to lay down his life, if necessary, for the sheep. Jesus describes Himself as the Good Shepherd of the flock of God:

I am the Good Shepherd; the Good Shepherd lays down His life for the sheep. . . . I know My own and My own know Me. . . . My sheep

> hear My voice and I know them, and they follow Me.... I give eternal life to them, and they shall never perish; and no one shall snatch them out of my hand. John 10:11, 14, 27, 28

We have experienced this and more, for He is the Shepherd who leaves the ninety and nine and goes after the one that is lost. By faith in the Shepherd who gave up His life, upon whom the Lord laid the iniquity of us all, we have been returned to the Shepherd's care. We have been returned to the care of Him who has fullest knowledge of us, of our souls. He knows every inner secret that we have. He knows what is best for us. This Christ brings us back into His fold, for by His stripes we have been healed, by His wounds we have been forgiven.

Fulfilled are the words of Ezekiel:

> "I will feed My flock, and I will lead them to rest," declares the Lord God. "I will seek the lost, bring back the scattered, bind up the broken, and strengthen the sick;"... Ezek. 34:15, 16

Jesus brought us back, returned us to the fold of God through His death and resurrection by which that which separated us from God is forgiven and we are restored to the sheepfold, the family of God.

Because of this once-and-for-all act of sacrifice that assures us that we are members of the flock, Jesus continues to be the seeking Shepherd. As often as we sin, as often as we stray and keep on straying, the Shepherd continues to call us back, to come after us and draw us again and again into his care and security. No wonder, then, that the life of the believer is one of daily repentance, of putting the old man to death, so that the new man in Christ might rise and live in righteousness and purity, safe in the Shepherd's care and concern. Drawn into this relationship with our God we live out our lives free of anxiety; free to the leading of the Holy Spirit; free to respond to the divine purpose revealed most perfectly in the death and resurrection of the Shepherd. The people of Peter's time like us felt threatened. For them the threat of persecution and deprivation was very real. Many of them had been driven from their homeland to be dispersed throughout the empire. They had suffered loss of home, employment. They had no real prospects for improvement, only more of the same. Many also faced the loss of life because of their faith and loyalty to Jesus Christ. Peter tells them, and reminds us, that they can meet these things and whatever else may come their way in the firm confidence of victory in Jesus Christ. They had been begotten "unto a living hope." They were heirs of an eternal inheritance that would not fade—or change or decay. They had the assurance that this inheritance not only was kept—guarded for them in heaven—but that they also would be kept by the power of God unto the time of Jesus' appearing. In this confidence and faith they could bear what they were bearing, and endure anything else that came their way as Christ did, patiently without striking back in kind, for they had heard the voice of the Shepherd. He had given unto them eternal life. Nothing could pluck them out of the hand of the Father. The Shepherd would guard and keep, care and provide, and finally bring them to Himself in heaven—there Jesus would be in their midst. There God would wipe every tear away from their eyes.

Peter knew whereof he wrote, for he, too, had experienced in his own life this kind of victory over threat. The same Peter, who had denied later when confronted with the threat of harm, even death, if he persisted in bearing witness to Jesus the crucified and risen Lord, answered, "for we (Peter and John), cannot stop speaking what we have seen and heard" (Acts 5:20). Peter strayed, but the Good Shepherd had returned him to His care through His seeking and forgiving grace.

That same Shepherd has returned us to His care through the forgiveness of our sins. That same Shepherd has begotten us again to the living hope of an eternal inheritance. That same Shepherd lets His voice be heard, which we hear in faith, and He gives us eternal life. That same Shepherd promises us power to guard and keep us unto the day of His coming again. That same Shepherd promises that nothing shall pluck us out of His hand.

Standing assuredly in the power supplied to us by the Holy Spirit, we too can meet with confidence and hope, with patience and endurance whatever the world places upon us. We can meet it without fear and anxiety. We can meet it in a Christlike strength and humility, for we have been returned to the Shepherd and Caretaker of our souls, bearing witness to the things that we have "seen and heard" in Christ Jesus. We are secure, for even when we stray or fall, the forgiveness of our Shepherd, secured by His shed blood, restores us again and again to His fold and to His care unto everlasting life.

God Calls Us His Church

FIFTH SUNDAY OF EASTER
1 PETER 2:4-10

Norbert H. Mueller

Emily Dickinson said it so well. The way we so often feel, I mean. "I'm nobody! Who are you? Are you nobody too?" Have we not often found ourselves in the same dilemma, wondering who we are, and clearly connected to that question, "What am I good for?" In this Easter season we celebrate anew how our lives are inseparably bound to the risen Christ; and it is well for us to remember the words of St. Paul: "We are buried with Christ by Baptism into death, that, like as He was raised up from the dead by the glory of the Father, even so we also should walk in newness of life" (Rom. 6:4).

Peter, in the text before us today, in his very own way answers the questions for us. He reminds us that we are "somebodies" and that we serve an important purpose in God's scheme of things. Because of our relationship with Him through Christ Jesus, God calls us His church.

I. Made of Living Stones

Peter, even though he is referring to them as stones, is really talking about people. In our everyday life to be described as a stone or rock can be very unflattering. We at times describe people as having "hearts of stone." Or we can refer to a person as being stubborn as a rock. If a person is slow to pick things up, he may be referred to as not having "all his marbles." On the other hand, calling a person "rock-like" can be very flattering. We admire a person who is as "strong as the rock of Gibraltar"; or as dependable and "solid as a rock."

"Living" is not the way we usually describe stones. We can often describe rocks or stones as being sharp or smooth; flat, round, or jagged. Rocks are pretty. They are cold. They are unusual in shape. We can define or describe them in geological terms. But how many of us ever think of stones as being alive? Yet this is the way that Peter describes us—people to whom something has happened; people in whom the spirit and the power of the risen Lord reigns and has an affect; people who have come to experience the dynamic of the risen Christ in their everyday life.

At this point we may be tempted to consider ourselves in terms of anything but a "living stone." We feel anything but alive and dynamic. It isn't that we consider ourselves as inanimate, bereft of life, yet there are characteristics of "deadness" or lack of dynamic and responsiveness to the Gospel of Jesus Christ. The power, presence, radiance, or warmth of our Christ seems to be far removed from our life. In some of life's bleakest moments, for all intents and purposes we seem to be without God and without hope in the world. We can pick up our newspaper and read of a suicide, a tragedy, people who really are bereft of any hope. But, it is unimaginable for us to conceive of life without God and without the hope that He gives. Yet there is enough of the Old Adam in us that drives us to say, "What have you done for me lately, Lord?" But Peter would remind us that we are the people of God. We are what he describes us to be, "living stones." And this because of our relationship to Jesus Christ who is *the* Living Stone.

The stone of whom Peter speaks is none other than Jesus Christ. The psalmist centuries ago had written of that "stone which the builders rejected." It became "the chief corner stone" (Ps. 118:22). In prophecy the psalmist spoke of the Messiah's coming and what would happen to that Messiah at the hands of the "builders." Peter identifies that Messiah as Jesus Christ. The "builders" are the leaders, those who had the care of the church. It was from them that Jesus received His greatest opposition. Those who were to build rejected the most important, indispensable "stone," Jesus Christ. Although rejected by men and cast aside, He it is who came as the one chosen by God from eternity, who received divine approval, "This is My beloved Son in whom I am well pleased"; and upon whom the Holy Spirit was poured out; and in whom the fullness of the Godhead chose to dwell.

This Jesus Christ, precious to God, comes into the world to become precious to us. It is through His great redemptive act of death and resurrection that we have been reconciled to God by the forgiveness of sins, claimed to be God's children and named to be His heirs, for time and for eternity, of all those things that God has in store for them that love Him. Although there are people yet today who reject Jesus and His claims and what He accomplished and offered; although the Gospel of Jesus Christ is still foolish to the worldly and a stone of stumbling to the Jew, for us this Gospel is the very power of salvation. He is precious to us who believe, for it is through His life that we have life now and eternally.

II. Fashioned into a Living Temple

"Living Stones" becomes an apt description because of our relationship with *the* Living Stone, Jesus Christ. We find ourselves numbered with all the other "living stones" that go to make up what we confess to be "the holy Christian church, the communion of saints." This is the church, that "spiritual" temple of the Lord, built upon the apostles and prophets, Jesus Christ being Himself the chief Cornerstone without whom there is no church at all. "Living stones," these are people to whom the Lord is so precious, for we recognize what we were and what we are now, "for," as Peter says in our text, "you once were not a people, but now you are the people of God; you had not received mercy, but now you have received mercy." Our identity question is answered. We are the people of God, who have experienced His mercy in Christ Jesus. Our identity comes out of our relationship with God. Our relationship comes also out of our relationship with one another, brothers and sisters in Christ, bound together by a mutual faith, a mutual concern, by a mutual love and hope, by a mutual purpose. It is God who redeemed us with the precious blood of Christ, claimed us as His own, and named us to be His heirs. No wonder Peter is led to call the people of God "a chosen race, a royal priesthood, a holy nation, a people for God's own possession. We are a spiritual temple, called to be a holy priesthood, to offer up spiritual sacrifices acceptable to God through Jesus Christ."

III. Existing to Do God's Will

The church finds its reason for being in the realization that it exists to do God's will. "A holy nation" is a people "set apart" for God's own purposes. You will recall that Paul in writing to the Roman Christians says, "I urge you therefore, brethren, by the mercies of God, to present your bodies a living and holy sacrifice, acceptable to God, which is your spiritual service of worship" (Rom. 12:1). Peter in our text resonates the same theme saying that "as living stones built up as a spiritual house to offer up spiritual sacrifices . . . set apart for the purpose of proclaiming "the excellencies of Him who has called you out of darkness into His marvelous light."

This means in part, Peter says, that as "aliens," "in the world but not of the world," we will avoid those things that "wage war against the soul," those passions of the flesh, sins and short-comings that so easily beset us and undermine our relationship with God, jeopardize our eternal destiny, and betray our Godly parentage. These are the cravings and desires aroused within by the animal nature described by Paul in his letter to the Galatians as evident in the deeds of the flesh:

> . . . immorality, impurity, sensuality, idolatry, sorcery, enmities, strife, jealousy, outbursts of anger, disputes, dissensions, factions, envying, drunkenness, carousing, and things like these . . . (Gal. 5:19-21).

Placed in contrast to the fleshly lusts, our text speaks of the "spiritual" sacrifices we are to offer. Free gifts are produced by the power of God Himself; they are acceptable to Him because they are prompted by and come out of the new relationship that we have with Him in Christ Jesus. It is the living out of a life responsive to the will of God whereby the name of our God is glorified. "Spiritual sacrifices" are understood in the quality of life that we exhibit; the kind of attitudes we project; the kind of caring individuals we are; the kind of priorities we set. People can perceive by observation a sense of victory, of hope, joy, caring, concern, forgiveness and warmth; a confidence born of the resurrection of our Lord and measured in terms of our devotion to Christ and our concern for people.

We are to "proclaim the excellencies of Him who called us out of darkness into His marvelous light." We are to be a saving remnant to the world. The Lord here in His Word is not asking us to bear witness to something that we have not experienced. Jesus, "precious in the sight of God," is also very precious to us. We who were once no people now are the "people of God." We who at one time had not received mercy now "have received mercy." Daily and richly we experience the grace of God as He forgives all our sins, lifts us up as His children, and sends us forth in His name. As we daily experience anew God's rich grace and mercy, we share it among ourselves, "teaching and admonishing one another with psalms and hymns and spiritual songs"; we daily share it with others as we seek to be instruments of our Lord in drawing others into that fellowship of the people of God in Christ Jesus.

As we ponder how often we have forgotten who we are and what a great task and purpose God has summoned us to fulfill—in spite of the fact that we have forgotten, and failed to fulfill God's purposes and expectations—the forgiveness of our Christ, secured for us on the cross, still embraces, still lifts, and still sends us forth. Indeed the power and dynamic of the living Christ can and does work in us. We are "living stones" called for "spiritual worship," "to proclaim the excellencies of Him who called us out of darkness into His marvelous light." We are the people in whom by God's grace, the power of Christ will live and be active, now and until the day of His coming for us.

Where There's Hope, There's Life

SIXTH SUNDAY OF EASTER
1 PETER 3:15-22

Henry A. Simon

"Where there's life, there's hope." That saying from *Don Quixote* almost has become a proverb. Baseball fans know that the game isn't over until the third out in the bottom of the ninth inning. Many persons with a terminal illness hope science will produce a cure in time to help them. The apostle Peter would reverse that saying for Christians, based on his words to us in today's Second Lesson. He would say that Christians who live as Easter people believe that "where there's hope, there's life."

I. Where's Hope?

A. The Glow of Easter May Be Fading as Problems Keep Coming

Easter Day Was More Than a Month Ago

Peter's words are important for us to hear today. We celebrated our Lord's resurrection on Easter Day more than a month ago.

Easter is the joy and highlight of the church year for Christians. Perhaps part of the reason for that joy is that Easter has remained a Christian festival. Easter is not commercialized like Christmas. Persons who were in church on Easter were confronted with the Christian claim that Christ has won victory over death through His death on the cross. Yet even that great good news and the glow it brings to our faith tend to fade as the days go by.

Day-to-Day Problems Bog Us Down

Easter is very important to the Christian faith, but it didn't stop the bills from coming this month. We joined in the shout of faith, "He is risen indeed!" but we still have problems loving that person with whom we work, the one who gets under our skin. The hangings in the chancel stay white during this Easter season to remind us of the purity of our Lord, but you and I still need to confess our sins every time we come to the Lord's Table. If Peter is serious—and he is—in talking about our hope because of Christ's resurrection, then that hope seems to shrink as we get farther from Easter Day.

B. Peter Assumes Christians Will Suffer for Doing Right

Be Prepared to "Make a Defense of Your Faith

Such problems with keeping the Christian hope glowing in our lives would not surprise Peter. In the Second Lesson for today he tells us several times to be aware that our hope and the faith on which it is based will be questioned and even attacked. "Always be prepared to make a defense to anyone who calls you to account for the hope that is in you" (v. 15), he urges us. Defending yourself isn't necessary unless someone attacks you. Peter is sure that the Christian will be attacked. We can be certain that some people will wonder whether we Christians aren't a little bit foolish, if not stupid, when we place our trust in Jesus Christ. Because we believe on the basis of faith and not scientifically provable fact, we sometimes will not be able to answer their questions to their satisfaction. Often the best we will be able to do is to share our faith.

We Will be "Abused"

Sharing our faith—and the "good behavior" which Peter says goes with our witnessing—won't always get us off the hook. Peter assumes that we will be mistreated for the Christian witness of our lives and lips. "Keep your conscience clear," he says, "so that when you are abused, those who revile your good behavior in Christ may be put to shame" (v. 16). With such blunt words from the inspired writer, you and I might begin to wonder just how we can have the hope which Peter is talking about. Smiling isn't very easy when you're being punched in the mouth, whether with words or with a fist. Instead of helping us to see how we can have hope, Peter seems to be causing us to question even further. He adds, "For it is better to suffer for doing right, if that should be God's will, than for doing wrong" (v. 17).

II. There's Hope!

A. Christ Died for Our Sins

Christ Suffered So That We Would Not Have to Suffer

Just when the situation seems the darkest, the Christian can see the light of the Savior shining—even if that light seems to our eyes to be only flickering. Peter provides the light of our Lord when He continues, "For Christ also died for sins once for all, the righteous for the unrighteous, that he might bring us to God" (v. 18a). When hope seem gone, Peter points us to the cross. There we see God's Son, and learn what it really means to have hope disappear. "My God, my God, why have you abandoned me?" Jesus cries out from the cross. Our Lord experienced the horrors of hell, the total absence of all hope and life, for your sins and mine. If we think that we have problems, the cross quickly and sharply can remind us what real problems are all about. Those real problems were ours, until Jesus Christ took care of them for us.

The Righteous One Gave Himself to Bring the Unrighteous to God

Peter uses several words when talking about Calvary that remind us just how unexpected it is that we can have hope. Jesus was "the righteous" dying for the "unrighteous." If we are tempted at times to look at the problems which sap hope from our lives and feel that life is unfair, Peter here reminds us that Jesus Christ had the unfairest life of all. He did not deserve what happened to Him. The suffering and death of Jesus Christ belonged to us. We are the unrighteous, those who deserved the punishment. But Jesus Christ, the perfectly holy and righteous Son of God, was punished so that we might become righteous in God's sight.

B. We Have the Hope of Heaven

That Hope Is Ours Through the Rebirth of Baptism

Because of Christ's sacrifice for us, Peter can begin this letter by talking about how "we have been born anew to a living hope through the resurrection of Jesus Christ from the dead" (1 Peter 1:3). The new birth through which we receive the living hope is Baptism. Peter's fellow apostle Paul makes that point several times in his New Testament letters, especially in Rom. 6. By our baptism, Scripture teaches, we share in the benefits of Christ's death and will share in the glory of His resurrection. We have a "living hope."

Our Hope Is That We Will Share in the Resurrection

The Easter season reminds us of just what our hope means. In the Creed we confess our hope in the resurrection of the body and the life everlasting. Easter reminds us that even though one day our names will be listed in a newspaper obituary column, that is not the end. The promise of never-ending life which continues after death is stated strongly by St. Paul in 1 Cor. 15:19: "If our hope in Christ is good for this life only and no more, then we deserve more pity than anyone else in the world" (TEV). But then Paul goes on, "But the truth is that Christ has been raised from death, as the guarantee that those who sleep in death will also be raised" (1 Cor. 19:20). The Christian hope is that when the Last Day comes, we shall be raised in glorified bodies like our Lord's. Our hope is "there"—and "there" is our heavenly home.

III. Here's Hope!

A. We Have Hope and Life Here and Now

The Easter Victory Has Been Won

The sure and certain hope of the resurrection which Christians have is one of the most valuable treasures of our faith. That hope is more than just nice-sounding words. Our Easter hope means that the victory has been won. The battles continue in our lives with sin, death, and the devil and their allies—but the war has been won. We can hold out until the final victory is ours because of that belief. We may ponder Christ's suffering and death for 40 days during Lent, but we remember Christ's victory over death for 50 days, because Easter is greater than Good Friday. We can proclaim our Lord's death in Holy Communion and we do so "until He comes"—and He cannot return unless He is risen.

Jesus Christ Is Lord

Peter reminds us of what Christ's resurrection means for us at the start of our Second Lesson. "In your hearts, reverence Christ as Lord," he says (v. 15). "Jesus is Lord" was one of the earliest Christian statements of faith. Christians by those words said there was someone who ruled in their lives besides the emperor, of whom it was said, "Caesar is Lord." That Someone else was Jesus Christ. He is Lord because he gives us not only the hope of heaven, but also help here and now. That help comes through our baptism, through which we can be sure that God has claimed us as his own. That help comes through the Holy Communion, where our Lord assures us of His forgiving love by sharing His very self with us. That help comes through the Holy Scriptures, which teach us about salvation and God's will for our lives. Because Jesus Christ is Lord, we can have hope and life as we follow Him.

B. We Show Our Hope Through Our Life

Peter Assumes People Will Look to Us
to Display Our Hope

What does having hope "here" mean until we die and then realize the hope is "there" in heaven? The story is told about a Christian college student who worked for a summer in a rough mining camp out West. A friend greeted him upon his return to school in the fall, and asked how things had gone. "Oh, quite well," came the reply. "But what happened when they found out you were a Christian?" the friend wanted to know. "Oh, they never found out." This is the trap into which we sometimes fall. We have our hope—and we keep it inside, like a painting by Rembrandt hidden away on a closet wall. Peter knows that mature Christian hope will be displayed in our living, without our even trying to do so. The only Christian sermon many people hear is "preached" by our lives. Our lies demonstrate the hope we have in Jesus Christ through what we say and do.

We Strengthen Each Other with That Hope

A little girl recently provided a reminder of what we as Christians can do to share our hope. While worshiping in a midwestern Lutheran church she saw two people in the chancel. "Is that Jesus?" she asked her mother about one man. "No," she was told. "Is that Jesus?" she asked, pointing to the other man. "No," she heard again. "Then why are we here?" she wanted to know. You and I are here for the same reason that little girl and her mother were in church: to share with one another the good news of Jesus Christ. We share that message of salvation through our worship and celebration. Then we go out to share that good news in lives of witness and service. Jesus Christ isn't here in person. He is risen. But the hope and new life of Easter is here in person, in every person here who confesses Jesus Christ as Lord. We will want to share that hope here and now in our worship, and then in our daily life in as many ways as we can. That's because where there's hope, Christian hope, there's life, life in Christ. In the name of the Father and of the Son and of the Holy Spirit.

Living Under Our Ascended Lord!

THE ASCENSION OF OUR LORD
EPHESIANS 1:16-23

Henry E. Simon

It is forty days after Christ's resurrection. He has led His disciples out of Jerusalem to Bethany.

He gives them final instructions. I have all power in heaven and earth, He tells them. You go into all the world to share My gospel. Be My witnesses. I'll be with you always.

They hear. And they watch. He raises His hands in blessing. Slowly, majestically, He begins to ascend. Spellbound, they see that holy body rise, until it disappears into a cloud.

The disciples keep staring upward. They hear voices. Two men, clothed in white, have a message for them: "Men of Galilee, why do you stand looking up into heaven? This Jesus, who was taken up from you into heaven, will come in the same way as you saw Him go into heaven" (Acts 1:11).

It is God's gentle way of bringing their thoughts down to earth. Their continued staring upward is understandable. They want another look at their Lord. They can't, however, do much witnessing, looking up into the sky. They have a life to live for him on earth.

So did the Ephesians, to whom a few years later, St. Paul sent the message of our text.

And so do you and I, whom God in His miraculous love has called out of darkness into His marvelous light. We pray the Holy Spirit, through this text, to teach us more about

Living Under Our Ascended Lord

We might summarize the teaching of our text in two sentences. Living under our Ascended Lord is a life of knowing and growing in our awareness of our heavenly hope. It is also a life of knowing and growing in our awareness of God's caring and providing power.

There is heavenly hope for us. Heaven is real. God's desire and intention to have us there someday is a fact. Shortly before our Lord went to the cross to make it all possible, He gave His Word to all who believe in Him: "I go to prepare a place for you, ... I will come again, and I will take you to Myself, that where I am you may be also" (John 14:2-3 RSV).

Aware of Our Heavenly Hope

St. Paul speaks of this wonderful truth in our text. He expresses the prayer that his readers might be enlightened to know more fully "the hope to which He has called you—the riches of His glorious inheritance."

St. Peter says it, too (1 Peter 1:3-4 RSV): "We have been born anew to a living hope . . . to an inheritance incorruptible, undefiled, and unfading, kept in heaven for you."

So grand and glorious is that heavenly inheritance awaiting every believer that St. Paul figuratively just shakes his head in amazement and cries out: "Eye hath not seen, nor ear heard, neither have entered into the heart of man the things which God hath prepared for them that love Him" (1 Cor. 2:9 KJV).

The Bible describes it as being with Christ, beholding His glory. We're told there will be good pleasures at His right hand forevermore, with no night and no tears. God Himself will take care of that.

When we're strongly attracted to the good things of earthly living, Scripture reminds us that being with Christ is "far better." On the other hand, when our living is loaded with troubles and woes, the Holy Word bids us remember, with St. Paul that "the sufferings of this present time are not worth comparing with the glory that is to be revealed to us" (Rom. 8:18 RSV).

Heaven is, indeed, real. And it's for us. It's our heavenly Father's good pleasure that we have it. It's as real as any inheritance any child has ever received from a parent.

This is true, even though most of us have acquaintances who may shake their heads in pity if we talk about this. People who don't believe in Christ cannot understand this eternal hope of ours. To them such hope has to be, at best, escapism. True, they may not discourage it. What's the harm, they may think, even though they feel there's nothing to it, but they won't believe it. And if we want to be utterly honest, most of us will have to admit that while we wouldn't dream of denying it, we sometimes live as though this earthly life is what matters most. We, too, lose sight of the hope of heaven.

This hope of heaven is no pipe dream. It is not a sentimental or emotional journey into fantasyland. It's as sure as God is sure, and He clearly wants us to have this hope.

It is true that for now we "walk by faith." Sometimes that walk takes us through pain-filled valleys, across doubt-ridden ditches and over storm-tossed waters. God does not see fit always to show us why He permits troubles to come. He does, however, assure us that we have heaven ahead. He does most surely promise us that "in everything God works for good with those who love Him" (Rom. 8:28 RSV). And He reminds us that what He promises He has both the almighty power and the loving will to bring about.

That's a second great truth of our text. Living under our

Ascended Lord is a life of knowing and growing in our awareness of God's caring and providing power.

Our Lord had told this to His disciples shortly before His ascension. "All authority in heaven and on earth has been given to Me" (Matt. 28:18 RSV). In our text the Holy Spirit has St. Paul literally heap phrase upon phrase to stress the utter limitlessness of that power.

He talks of the *immeasurable greatness* of His power to us who believe, according to the working of His *great might* ... far *above all* rule and authority and power and dominion, and *above every* name that is named, not only in this age but also in that which is to come, and He has put *all things* under His feet and has made Him the head over *all things.*"

Reassured by His Immeasurable Greatness

Notice that St. Paul isn't just talking about Christ's power within the church. He declares Christ has absolute, utterly total authority over everyone and everything, now and forever, everywhere, authority so stupendously complete that it is immeasurable.

The amazing truth is, however, that this boundless power exists in the interests of the church and of the individual believer. Christ is "head over all things for the church," says our text. It talks of the "greatness of His power in us who believe." One of the Bible paraphrases says that this power is "exercised for us believers."

It is good for us to remind ourselves that our lives have been touched by that divine power. It not only raised Christ from the dead, it raised us from spiritual death. He who "commanded the light to shine out of darkness, hath shined in our hearts to give the light of the knowledge of the glroy of God in the face of Christ Jesus our Lord" (2 Cor. 4:6 RSV).

The Holy Spirit used divine power in working the miracle of our conversion. He continues to use it, coming to us over and over in Word and Sacrament, to nourish and strengthen our faith in this glorious, heaven-providing, all-loving, almighty Lord.

The earthly church does not always have smooth seas to sail. Sometimes God permits those waters to become violent. We may feel that we are in such turbulent times at this point in our history.

Perhaps, but we do not have to depend on fluctuating feelings to know that Christ, in all His immeasurable power and saving love, has invested Himself in the church. It is His body, "the fullness of Him who fills all in all." The holy church will overcome. The very "gates of hell" will not be strong enough to withstand its God-given strength.

And as far as each of us individual Christians is concerned, what is true of the church our Lord certainly would have us take for ourselves. With the poet we can confidently sing: "On Christ's ascension I now build the hope of mine ascension!"

We live under our Ascended Lord. It is a life filled with more than enough burdens and perils. We worry too much and, sometimes, in worrying we sin. As we know and grow in our awareness of His providing power, however, we can join St. Paul with ever-increasing confidence to declare: "I am sure that neither death, nor life, nor angels, nor principalities, nor things present, nor things to come, nor power, nor height, nor depth, nor anything else in all creation, will be able to separate us from the love of God in Christ Jesus our Lord" (Rom. 8:38-39 RSV).

That gives us what we need, not only for today, but for tomorrow, and next week, and next year. We'll keep on having troubles—that's life—but we'll also and always have our greater Christ. We'll fail sometimes, you and I. We'll drift into sin. It shouldn't happen, but, like St. Paul, we'll sometimes not be doing what we should, and doing what we shouldn't.

That's when we'll especially remember that this great almighty Lord of ours went to the cross "to prepare a place for us," enroute to His ascension. He died there, utterly forsaken, so that we might never be forsaken. He rid us of the guilt of our sin by taking our sin upon Himself. He willingly gave up using that immeasurable power of God (by which He could surely have spared Himself) in order to spare us the fear that God's saving power would ever be withheld from us.

It won't be. "You . . . by God's power are guarded through faith for a salvation ready to be revealed in the last time" (1 Peter 1:5 RSV). No "ifs." It's absolutely true.

What a God we have! What an almighty, all-loving Lord to live under! What a glorious heaven to look forward to!

And what a privilege that you and I, knowing and growing in our awareness of these priceless blessings, can share them with our loved ones and our neighbors, in community and world!

Come Down out of the Grandstand

SEVENTH SUNDAY OF EASTER
1 PETER 4:12-17; 5:6-11

George H. Beiderwieden Jr.

Can you feature someone who'e enlisted as a soldier and then gets real good at pinochle? He feels like a pretty fair success. He sings the battle songs. And learns all the tricks of pinochle! And he wonders why the army's not more effective and the world's not nicer.

Some of the songs we sing here are pretty tall, like: "The Son of God goes forth to war ... who follows in their train?" "This day the noise of battle ... the next the victor's song." "Fight the good fight with all thy might!" Is that where we stop?

The Lord today calls us to

Come Down out of the Grandstand

Is our Christianity merely a spectator sport? Is it just one hour on Sunday mornings and no more? Do we just go through some pious motions there, expect to be titillated? Is our support, in time and treasure, little more than an afterthought? Yes, if we were arrested for being Christian, would there be enough evidence to convict us?

I. Christians Called to Suffer

In our text the Spirit has St. Peter remind us that we believers are called to pay a price, to suffer. As one has correctly observed: The water of life is free, but the piping costs. Peter clarifies by beginning with the other side of the coin: What is *not* the price. "But let none of you suffer as a murderer, or as a thief, or as an evildoer, or as a busybody in other men's matters" (v. 15). The apostle calls us to live carefully.

Now the Spirit doesn't indicate why He here picked these particular areas of conduct. The first two might seem a bit obvious. A believer will certainly realize he is not to be a murderer or thief. Perhaps the cue to this category is indicated in the third item "or as an evildoer." Pretty plainly, we are not to be a lawbreaker. Remember that's what they accused our Lord of before Pilate: "If He were not an evildoer, we should not have delivered Him up unto thee" (John 18:30). So St. Peter here exhorts us believers to observe the laws of the land. We should be law-abiding: observe the speed limit, pay taxes, vote.

The last item here is the interesting one. St. Peter bids us Christians make sure that we do not suffer "as a busybody in other men's matters" (v. 15c). Such would bring upon the Christian a definite social odium and render him generally unpopular. Meddling, offering advice where it was not warranted, displaying a sense of superiority in so doing would be galling to those of another mind, perhaps foisting his convictions upon another.

We Christians are to live carefully, for we are engaged in a campaign for the souls of men. And the battle is to the death. The stakes are extremely high. St. Peter reminds us of that when he adds: "For the time is come that judgment must begin at the house of God: and if it first begins at us, what shall the end be of them that

obey not the gospel of God" (v. 17)? They who oppose God's cause
will suffer consequence. And woe to them if they repent not of such.
"And if the righteous scarcely be saved, where shall the ungodly
and the sinner appear" (v. 18)? The Christian "must through much
tribulation enter the kingdom of God" (Acts 14:22). Then imagine
the consequence to such as refuse God's escape! St. Peter seeks here
to deepen our concern. Fearful is the consequence of refusal of God's
Christ. Let not anything in your conduct be responsible for such
refusal. The foreign missionary was expressing concern that not
more natives had a copy of the Bible. A native convert observed:
"Oh, they need no Bible. You are their Bible. As you live they see our
Jesus." And it is reported the missionary did not sleep so well that
night!

II. Partakers of Christ's Suffering

But the price asked of us is something else than just avoiding
something. "Rejoice, inasmuch as ye are partakers of Christ's
sufferings" (v. 13a). Now partaking of Christ's sufferings is pretty
much! When you recall the spit, the mockery, the crown of thorns,
even crucifixion! Again—"if ye be reproached for the name of
Christ" (v. 14a); and, "if any man suffer as a Christian" (v. 16a).
These Christians, believers to whom St. Peter is writing originally,
are about to get it. Nero and the imperial government in Rome are
taking a hostile attitude toward Christians. They are treating it as
the "religio illicita." The worst is to be expected. The Roman
authorities in the provinces will soon adopt the same attitude.

Well, that was the first century. We're living in the twentieth.
And this is America. "I doubt that this Scripture even applies to us
today!" There is no suffering for Christ now. Sadly, that's probably
true. But is that because of our country or is it because of us? Let's
check that for a moment. Do we not oft hide our Jesus? Couldn't
someone some day say at our office, school, or shop: "Why, I didn't
know you were a Christian!" Don't we freeze up at a lot of openings
to advertise Him? "Thank God! I'll pray about it!"

Then there's our language. Is it always distinctively Christian,
different today? Do our morals profess loyalty to Him? How about
our business ethics? What places do we frequent? Try this one on for
size: When did you last say: "No, I couldn't do that. Jesus wouldn't
like it!" And how about our material philosophy or our outlook on
things. To the unbeliever, things, money, this life is all there is. So
naturally, he majors in such. He evaluates his own happiness,
success, contentment thus. He measures others thus. Are we 20th-
century Christians so different? Really? Would we rather win one
for our Christ, or get a raise in pay? Grow in Jesus, or get a new car?
Have all our children in glory, or get a fine new home? Why is
stewardship of treasure so disturbing in the church? Tithing is a

bad word! Is this our reaction to the One who gave one hundred percent for us?

No. We're not "partakers of Christ's sufferings," we aren't "reproached for the name of Christ," we don't "suffer as a Christian" because we're not that concerned for our lost relatives, friends, and neighbors. So we don't stick our neck out. We don't mention the name of Jesus. We play it safe. We don't witness much. If we did, if we seized our opportunities, if we let our identity be known generally, if we pleaded sin and Savior, we'd suffer all right! The world is no more friendly to Him today. Then we would suffer ridicule. Some would write us off as unintelligent. Some, as old-fashioned. Some, as brainwashed. What fools! We would then suffer some social ostracism. We "always talk religion" because we mentioned it once, in context. And so we wouldn't any longer be welcome at a party or card club or golf foursome. And then, if we began to show our true colors, we should probably suffer even some material loss; maybe miss a promotion by the pagan boss; or lose friends who could benefit us financially. No, this Scripture isn't outdated at all. It's as relevant as tomorrow's headline. If . . .

III. Christians Committed to Suffering

But that's so alien to our thinking today. Ours is a day of self-service. You got to get for me. It's a sensate culture. Now! Everybody's out for fun. You avoid pain at all costs. Why should we Christians court discomfort? Do and say what you can bet will "rock the boat"? St. Peter cites the heaviest push when he says: "You are partakers of Christ's sufferings" (v. 13a). For us, that takes only a mention. We're moved. We know He patiently endured all those, for us. It was the price of our sin. He did not wish us to have to pay it in all eternity, to go to hell. So, He assumed that payment. Recall just a bit of what "Christ's sufferings" all involved. He left the mansions of Glory, the perfect company of the Father. He came all the way down here. He the Creator became not merely a creature but the lowliest of creatures. A baby. An unknown teenager. A humble carpenter's apprentice. Though God was in the flesh, He did not push His weight around. Showed very little clout. How lonely He must oft have felt! He offered Himself and how few accepted His generous offer! No wonder He sobbed. And we have not even yet come to Gethsemane, and the Praetorium—or Calvary. Oh, what a price! What a continuing paying! "Christ's sufferings"!

It is this One who asks you and me, Christians, share His sufferings. "Ye are partakers of Christ's suffering" (v. 13a). He asks that we be in on the campaign for the souls of our contemporaries. Remember, He said once: "The disciple is not above his master, nor the servant above his lord. If they have called the master of the house Beelzebub, how much more shall they call them of his household?" (Matt. 10:24, 25). Remember when He assured James and John: "Ye shall indeed drink of the cup that I drink of; and with the Baptism that I am baptized withal shall ye be baptized" (Mark 10:39).

And thus we suffer for our witness to Him; for our claimed relation to Him, we shall bring glory upon God. "If ye be reproached for the name of Christ . . . on your part He is glorified" (v. 14a, c). "If any man suffer as a Christian . . . let him glorify God on this behalf" (v. 16). Our brave witness, our Jesus-observation inserted in due time . . . will be used of the Spirit. Friends, relatives, neighbors will be converted. And heaven's chorus of "Worthy is the Lamb that was slain!" will have been expanded by just that much. More glory upon God.

But can we risk it? St. Peter insists: You bet! "Wherefore, let them that suffer according to the will of God commit the keeping of their souls to Him in well doing, as unto a faithful Creator" (v. 19). We cannot know how effective our witness may become. "One soweth, and another reapeth" (John 4:37). Nor can we predict how vicious opposition to Christians may yet become in our lifetime. But we have One who has never lied to us. He has never failed to keep His word. Ours is a "faithful Creator" (v. 19c). We can safely entrust the outcome to Him. Ours is only to speak, to witness, to identify.

And then one day comes the climax. "But rejoice, inasmuch as ye are partakers of Christ's sufferings; that, when His glory shall be revealed, ye may be glad also with exceeding joy" (v. 13). Consider Stephen, John Hus, and all the martyrs. The missionaries who invested their very lives for Him and the souls of men. How they praise Him now . . . His love having constrained them. I can't remain up in the grandstand. Stay in the safety zone . . . no matter? Never! Sacrifice for me . . . like His . . . I can't resist! Can you?

Words! Words! Words!

PENTECOST
ACTS 2:1-21

George H. Beiderwieden Jr.

Play this little game with anybody. "List five things you know about God the Father." Oh, He's the Creator of all. He loves humans. He sent the Son. He is the One to whom we pray in the Lord's Prayer. And, let me think, we become His adopted children by faith in Christ.

OK! "How about ten things about God the Son?" That's easy. I can name twenty. "I'm sure you can. I believe you."

"How about three things you know about God the Holy Spirit?" Say, that is rough, isn't it?

Yes, I could echo St. Paul: "I beheld your devotions . . . To the Unknown God. Whom therefore ye ignorantly worship, Him declare I unto you" (Acts 17:23).

Let's call it . . .

Words! Words! Words!

I. Gathered About God's Word

Yes, "of making of many books there is no end!" (Eccl. 12:12b). Whatever happens anywhere in our world today is reported over and over again many, many times for a week. The President has a press conference. And then the commentators must explain in many words what he said, what he meant, what significance each part of it has politically, internationally, economically. We surely get sick of words!

And yet God has decided to work through words. "It pleased God by the foolishness of preaching to save them that believe" (1 Cor. 1:21b). "My Word shall not return unto me void" (Is. 55:11). Paul insisted: "I am not ashamed of the Gospel of Christ, for it is the power of God unto salvation" (Rom. 1:16). We are bidden: "Preach the Word!" (2 Tim. 4:2).

And the Word that God has given us humans in His Scriptures has power to save. That Word reveals our true nature, our condition in the eyes of a holy God: our guilt and need of forgiveness. That Word then also introduces us to God's answer, His Son Jesus. And then that Word spells out the reacting conduct. And that Word not only informs, it convicts and it convinces. It can do that because God the Spirit deigns to work through this channel, God's Word to us. "No man can say that Jesus is the Lord, but by the Holy Ghost" (1 Cor. 12:3b).

What does all this add up to for us? Isn't it: Where does the Spirit come? Under what circumstances will He do this His blessed work with us? Where? Our text insists *He comes where the believers are gathered about God's Word.* Listen: "And when the day of Pentecost was fully come, they were all with one accord in one place. And suddenly there came a sound from heaven as of a rushing mighty wind, and it filled all the house where they were sitting. And there appeared unto them cloven tongues like as of fire, and it sat upon each of them" (vs. 1-3). "They were all with one accord in one place" (v. 1b). The New International Version tells us "they were all together." "The assembling of ourselves together" (Heb. 10:25)! I'm sure you'd agree they probably weren't merely having a potluck or playing bingo! This wasn't some sort of committee meeting. This was per their custom: "They continued steadfastly in the apostles' doctrine and fellowship, and in the breaking of bread and in prayers" (Acts 2:42). They were assembled for worship. And *then* the Spirit came!

Isn't the lesson obvious? If we wish the Spirit to work His blessed salvation and transformation on us, we'd better be where He comes and that is to the worshiping assembly. Remember Thomas? How much he missed Easter Sunday nite? When they had to report of him: "But Thomas was not with them when Jesus came!" (John 21:24)? Thomas missed the Risen Lord. And he spent a dark, dark week because of His absence.

Is the cause of so many of our heartaches today right here? The Lord comes to the worship hour. He speaks by His Scriptures to those assembled. The Spirit carries His Word deep into hearts and out to all of the persons present. They're changed for the better in many ways. They come in heavy and go out buoyant. They come in frightened and leave triumphant. And we miss that! Did you know that only forty some percent of professing Christians are in their pew each Sunday. More of them miss than attend worship. And these are professing believers! Is it any wonder "many are weak and sickly among you and many sleep" (1 Cor. 11:30)? Marriage breakups are on the increase, even among Christians. There are more and more problems with children. Fear abounds and cynicism is rampant. "Rejoice in the Lord" sounds Pollyannaish to many. Prayer is relegated to the spot of desperation.

Is it any wonder? The Holy Spirit comes to the assembly with heaven's gifts and more than half of us are missing. We are majoring in our favorite minor.

II. Speaking God's Word

And what is the Spirit's major? I think even a casual reading of this account would have that pop out at us. Listen: "and they were all filled with the Holy Ghost and began to *speak* with other tongues as the Spirit gave them utterance" (v. 4). Again: "Every man heard them speak in his own language" (v. 6b). Again: "and how hear we every man in our own *tongue,* wherein we were born" (v. 8)? Differently, but they all spoke. And "we do hear them speak in our tongues the wonderful works of God" (v. 11).

The Spirit obviously enables the believers to *speak.* These early ones needed that. Before Pentecost their record wasn't too great. They all ran from Christ in Gethsemane. No one offered the Lord any defense, in any of His trials, though they had the best Client ever. None spoke out for Him at Calvary, though many shouted against Him. The Good News was going to die in the first century. God had to do something. It was absolutely essential these be "given utterance" (v. 4b). They were given courage; backbone was engrafted this day. Watch them after this coming of the Spirit! Peter and John are hauled before the authorities and "commanded not to speak at all nor teach in the name of Jesus." But the believing insist: "We cannot but speak the things which we have seen and heard" (Acts 4:18, 20). And when they return to their believing company, these pray and note for what: "Lord, grant unto Thy servants, that with all boldness they may speak Thy word" (v. 29). And the Lord authenticates their priority: "the place was shaken" (v. 31b). Again the apostles are imprisoned. An angel releases them with definite instructions: "Go, stand, and speak in the temple" (5:20). The authorities have them picked up with, "Did not we straightly command you that ye should not teach in this name" (v. 28)? The apostles insist: "We are His witnesses of these things" (v. 32a). And the authorities recognize there is only one way: "They took counsel to slay them" (v. 33b). Then there's Stephen: "They were not able to resist the wisdom and the Spirit by which he spake" (6:10). Only forcibly silencing his voice would do it. So they stoned him.

Have we recognized that Satan's strategy remains unchanged? God's plan is to save and transform by His Word, empowered by the Holy Spirit. That Word must be spoken by the witnesses. Satan knew well that entire great plan could be negated, if only the apostles could be kept silent. Be quiet. That's all. That strategy of negation remains in force today.

How successful has it been with you? Does anyone say of you: "I never knew you were a Christian"? Imagine anyone saying: "I didn't know you were a Cub fan!" "You don't show much enthusiasm for the Packers!" Are you saying that you're afraid you'll say the wrong thing? Have you never heard that he who makes no mistakes makes nothing? Do you excuse yourself by saying that you won't know all the answers? You've forgotten that the assignment is not: "Ye shall be lawyers!" but rather "Ye shall be witnesses unto Me." Have you eased your conscience by saying: "I tried to talk Jesus once and nothing happened. I've never seen any results." Jesus promised: "One soweth, another reapeth" (John 4:37). Remember, "God does not gather all His harvest this October!" Maybe, just maybe, you haven't spoken enough!

It's not too late. So much, so very much depends upon our speaking. We don't have to be "preachy" and mount a soapbox. We only need to watch for opportunities. Keep our eyes peeled. Opportunities to speak a "word in due season" there are aplenty! We work with people who suffer affliction periodically. When they lament and share their burden with us, then we have the perfect opening. Tell them about being "in Christ" and having a forgiving heavenly Father who has a plan for the life of each of His children. "All things work together for good . . . " (Rom. 8:28). "Whom the Lord loveth He chasteneth . . . " (Heb. 12:6a). It's a "soft-sell" way of witnessing to Jesus. Or maybe someone close to us shares worry. We have a perfect opening for: "I used to be a worry-wart until Jesus found me. And I learned He loved me so much He gave His life for my forgiveness." And Paul's logic I can't refute: "He that spared not His own Son . . . how shall He not with Him also freely give us all things" (Rom. 8:32)? So I try to remind myself: "Which of you by taking thought can add one cubit unto his stature" (Matt. 6:27)? Worry is futile and, with Jesus, unnecessary. A purposeless life confided, offers opportunity. "I am the Life." They who have Jesus, have Prayer Privilege. Instead of "luck" or "the breaks" or "I must be living right," we can say: "Thank the Lord!" or "Thank God!"

III. Word with the Spirit

The Spirit caused a furor. "And suddenly there came a sound from heaven as of a rushing mighty wind" (v. 2a). The report spread rapidly. A crowd gathered. They each heard "the wonderful works of God" in his own way. "And they were all amazed and were in doubt, saying one to another, 'What meaneth this' " (v. 12)? Then Peter got up and explained what had happened. He found the answer in the Old Testament. All along God had had big plans for "the last days" (v. 17a), the New Testament era between when the Son came to earth at Bethlehem and when He would come again in Judgment. The prophet Joel had described it: "I will pour out of my Spirit upon all flesh" (v. 17a). He could have said: "The Spirit will come upon everyone who is repentant and has faith." Now that had just been fulfilled: "How hear we every man in our own tongue" (v. 8)!

And when the Spirit comes, what follows? "Your sons and your daughters shall prophesy" (v. 17b). "Prophesy" is to preach, speak of Jesus, witness. And as the Spirit enables us to speak, what follows? "Your young men shall see visions, and your old men shall dream dreams" (v. 17c). "Visions" and "dreams" of what? "Whosoever shall call on the name of the Lord shall be saved" (v. 21b). The results of Spirit-enabled speaking will exceed the imagination.

People are rescued eternally. We can't even begin to appreciate what all that involves. Humans destined by the hand of the Maker for God's company and glory! And for their rebellion now headed for everlasting rejection and darkness! And Christ came. He paid the bill. And the Spirit moved someone to tell a fellow. The Spirit accomplished faith. And hellbent has become heaven-bound. And that's to be forever. No wonder Charles Spurgeon opined: "I should be very disappointed had God intended my son to be a missionary and he became only king!" Visions and dreams! Souls saved for glory!

And, of course, that sort of reversed course for the everlasting has its radical effect on the days and weeks and years of here and now. "If any man be in Christ, he is a new creature" (2 Cor. 5:17). "He died for all that they which live should not henceforth live unto themselves but unto Him . . . " (2 Cor. 5:15). We hardly need Scripture proof, do we? Someone saved from drowning has now an indebtedness. One rescued from a burning, collapsing building knows he lives on borrowed time. Mondays, Tuesdays, and Thursdays are changed. Self as king has been dethroned by the Rescuer. Sunshine looks different. Affliction doesn't seem the same. Life's purpose has been elevated immeasurably. "Lord, what wilt Thou have me to do?" "I live by the faith of the Son of God who loved me and gave Himself for me" (Gal. 2:20b). Imagine being in on effecting such a change in another human!

Doesn't our culture set the stage for a chief aspect of that transformation? Everywhere around us it's "get." The material ratrace. You're evaluated by the things you possess. And things don't do it. The American experience surely validates that—our affluence and our restlessness, discontent, rising suicide. If the Lord's edict needed a demonstration, we're it. "A man's life consisteth not in the abundance of things which he possesseth" (Luke 12:15). In the midst of that context you and I can be used by the Spirit to change getters into givers. And, oh, the joy! Real satisfaction! Making a contribution. As Peter Marshall used to say: "Life is measured not by its duration but by its donation." Wouldn't you like to help throw that switch for some friend, relative, or neighbor?

And our God is so generous that, as we speak of His Son as He's asked of us, we're "paid off" overtime and double time. Our own appreciation of Jesus is deepened and purified. How surely some have experienced this! Our worship and communing, our Bible study take on a new dimension. Besides feeding, it's now also enabling. It's different when you kneel and ask during this hour for total commitment to Christ. By faith you then receive His body and blood as "laborer in the vineyard." Eagerly! Purposefully!

The "Unknown God" who operates through Words . . . Words . . . Words . . . is really significant, isn't He! We're glad today that someone spoke the Word that He could save us and now still transforms us steadily, aren't we? May we not allow the chain to be broken! May He enable each one of us to speak till visions and dreams take on flesh and bones that one day shall be glorified eternally.

What More Can You Ask?

THE HOLY TRINITY
FIRST SUNDAY AFTER PENTECOST
2 CORINTHIANS 13:11-14

Arthur O. Kaul

Some people are backslappers and public relations people. As such, they may overreact or they may not always be sincere. Or they may have found a way to twist someone's arm to promote their purposes or their organizations.

The apostle Paul wasn't like that. He was always sending heartfelt and sincere greetings to people. Sometimes greetings of hello, or at other times, farewell greetings.

In the last chapter of the Book of Romans, read the long list of people who send their greetings to the Christians in Rome. One can almost feel the warm promptings of this great missionary as he records the names of various associates whom he includes in greetings to these faithful Christians.

When Paul says farewell to the elders of the church at Ephesus (Acts 20:36-38), it was a scene filled with deep feelings and the power of that great emotion—love. When you read it, you almost feel as though you too were there.

Paul concludes the second epistle to the Corinthian church. Then he says, "Finally, brethren, farewell" (v. 11). And again he couldn't keep from saying, "All the saints greet you" (v. 13).

In a few other statements concluding his epistle, Paul hands out some good advice. Briefly he speaks of relationships between Christians and God. Self-evidently it's not only a matter of how to live with others but—

I. How to Live with Yourself.

There are some people who find it hard to get along with other people. One of the reasons may be that they have never learned to live with themselves. If you are a child of God, don't put yourself down. It doesn't have to be conceit to have a good impression of yourself. Every person is very important in God's sight. We are children of God, redeemed by Christ and therefore very important to Him. The gospels in the New Testament illustrate how Jesus took time for everyone, the "little people" and what we would call the "important people," because of the possibilities Jesus saw in everyone.

In his message Paul gives some good advice. He says, "Mend

your ways" (v. 11). Let me show you how this works with a true story. Some years ago I was a tent evangelist in Southern Illinois. In a certain town we were looking for a lot on which to pitch our tent. After finding one, we needed help in getting the weeds cut. The owner of the lot asked one of his employees to do the weed cutting. He was an outspoken atheist. As he cut the weeds, he cursed our mission, God, and the church. To add to his feelings, we invited him to our services. The first night he stood across the street and listened. The next night he was on our side of the street. The third night he was in the back of our tent. By the last evening, he was sitting in the front row, a brand new Christian. This man had a foul mouth. But quit cursing. He used to say, "I never quit cursing, God just took it away." His dress was always sloppy, his face unshaven. That changed too. His drinking habits were drastically altered. One day I purchased some paint in a store in this town. The owner said, "No charge, because I am so impressed by what happened to that man in the tent." This man became a leader in the church and each day he was a living example of what Paul meant when he said, "Mend your ways" (v. 11). What More Can You Ask For?

What was Paul's advice to the Corinthian church? He said, "Heed my appeal" (v. 11).

Christian congregations are far from perfect, because the people in them are not perfect. The Corinthian church was no exception. The people in it, like all of us, had so many shortcomings. Paul urges these people to let Christ truly live in them, and by His power to "become perfect" (v. 9). To put it in Paul's own words, he writes, "Not that I have already obtained this or am already perfect" but I press on to make it my own, because Christ Jesus has made me His own" (Phil. 3:12).

On some occasions for instance, they had grossly misused the Sacrament of the Lord's Supper. Paul urges them to be repentant in heart. His appeal was always through the power, grace, and mercy of Jesus Christ. Paul not only shows these people how to live with themselves, but also how to live with others. He has a trio of suggestions, the first being "agree with one another" (v. 11).

If this were heeded on an international scale, we would have world peace. If this advice were followed in families, there would be less chaos and more love. If this advice would be taken seriously between two people, our world would be a better place in which to live. Listen carefully to the newsbroadcasts on radio and television. You will note that wherever there is trouble in our world, it is because individuals or groups disagree with one another.

What does it mean "to agree with one another" (v. 11)? I don't always agree with the opinions of other people, not even with my wife. However, as Christians filled with the love of Christ, we are to discuss our differences. We should look at all the various sides of the subject and then, to the best of our ability, arrive at a common consensus. This isn't always easy. We may not always be successful. One of the most difficult things for a person to say is, "I'm sorry, I was wrong." But this is still how to live with others. Disagreements continue when there is no communication. When couples come to me with marital problems, one of the first things I note is that communication between the two people has usually ended. Communication with words, ideas, and thoughts are bridges we can build to each other.

We are to "live in peace" (v. 11). Do you remember that great sermon Jesus preached on the mountain side? In it he said, "Happy are those who work for peace among men; God will call them His sons" (Matt. 5:9).

To live in peace, we have to work at it. I recall counseling a couple whose marriage was in difficulty. The wife kept saying, "He just won't let me have any peace." And yet this couple hadn't spoken to each other for many weeks. Their problem was that they hadn't worked at being at peace with each other. We are to work for peace in every situation, and let the love of Christ motivate our lives in that direction so that we can "live in peace" (v. 11). The lack of peace between people and the failure to strive for peace can even lead to physical and nervous ailments and disorders.

We don't generally go around and "greet one another with a holy kiss" (v. 12). Another translation of this verse reads, "A handshake all around, please" (Philipps). I'm sure that all of us have attended churches where almost immediately you feel at home. There is warmth and friendliness all around. By contrast all of us may also have been in churches where the people seem cold and distant. Could this be a reflection of our attitude towards Christ? We Christians have a reason to have a twinkle in our eye and a spring in our step. We are God's people, here on a mission, with love that should overflow to others. The next time you are in church, why not make a special effort to greet someone and to make new friends? Frequently our attitudes will need changing or be changed.

The apostle Paul told one of his congregations that their love was known throughout all of Asia. To me it seemed not so remarkable that these people loved one another, but that they showed and demonstrated this love. How can someone know that we love them if we never outwardly show that love? Love is a most powerful and effective emotion. However, for love to be love, it must be active. Love is far more than a word.

II. Living Under God's Triple Blessing

In order to live life as it ought to be lived with ourselves and with others, we need outside help. Our own techniques and devices will never succeed. On this Trinity Sunday, what more can you ask for than this triple blessing, "The grace of the Lord Jesus Christ, the love of God and the fellowship of the Holy Spirit be with you all" (v. 14).

It is the grace of God that enables us in our total behavior. St. Paul's great desire for these Corinthian Christians and for us is that the blessings of God's grace be conferred upon us. When we by faith receive Jesus Christ, His mercy, forgiveness, and grace, then we can say, "What more can you ask for?" St. Paul wants us to have all that God has provided for us. Not just small bits and morsels, but all of God's gifts of grace in super abundance.

Martin Luther once said, "The grace of God first shames us and then it saves us." We could perhaps look into theological books and find a detailed explanation of what the grace of God means. However, the best way to understand the grace of God is to experience it.

When the angel appeared to the Virgin Mary, the angel told her she would bear the Son of God. He would be a king like David. His kingdom also would never end. Mary did not grasp the full implications of what she was told, so she replied, "How then can this be" (Luke 1:34)?

Jesus told Nicodemus, "I tell you the truth, no one can see the kingdom of God unless he is born again" (John 3:3). When Nicodemus could not grasp this truth, he replied, "How can this be" (John 3:9)?

When we read the gospels, we can be amazed at the words and works of Jesus. People were surprised at the circumstances of His birth. They were astonished at His preaching. His miracles fascinated people. Men were frustrated at His ability to read the thoughts of their minds. They could not understand His love for sinners of every description. When he healed the sick and raised the dead, they became speechless. The crowds were awed at His death and dumbfounded at His resurrection. Again and again there is complete surprise about the words and the works of Jesus Christ.

However, the greatest miracle for each of us is found in these words, "The grace of the Lord Jesus Christ be with you all" (v. 14). The wonder of wonders, "God has shown us how much He loves us: it was while we were still sinners that Christ died for us" (Rom. 5:8).

Not because we are good, but because of the goodness of God, the Innocent One dies for the guilty. The only compulsion being the "love of God" (v. 14).

John, the beloved disciple, was overwhelmed by this love so that he wrote, "See how much the Father has loved us! His love is so great that we are called God's children—and so, in fact, we are" (1 John 3:1).

When we realize the enormous price paid for our redemption and that it came about without anything that God saw in us, but only by

His love, then we begin to grasp the meaning of the word "grace." Someone has described evangelism as one beggar telling another beggar where to find bread. Two pastors were walking down the street. Lying on the sidewalk was a poor drunken derelict. The one pastor said to the other, "There, but by the grace of God, I am lying." This describes the grace of God in a practical way.

Martin Luther summed it up so well when he wrote, "I believe that I cannot by my own reason or strength believe in Jesus Christ, my Lord, or come to Him, but the Holy Spirit has called me by the Gospel." There it is in a nutshell. "The fellowship of the Holy Spirit" (v. 14). It is the Holy Spirit who reveals Christ to us. It is the Holy Spirit who brings us to faith, so that we experience the grace of God.

Our real strength and our spiritual strength is given to us by the outpouring of God's Spirit and grace upon us. Oh, that all of us might be made thirsty and say with the Samaritan woman long ago, "Give me this water"; then truely what more can we ask for?

We need to meditate more and thank God more for His Word through which the Holy Spirit works. Thank God for the Gospel through which the Holy Spirit works. Thank God for the blessed Sacrament of Baptism through which the Holy Spirit works. Thank God for the Sacrament of Holy Communion through which the Holy Spirit works.

It is this fellowship of the Holy Spirit in our hearts that will keep our faith from becoming dull, dry, uninteresting and ultimately dead.

For where the Spirit is, there is life. We have that life of the Spirit in Christ by faith. "What more can you ask for?"

God's Plan Better Than Man's Plan

SECOND SUNDAY AFTER PENTECOST
ROMANS 3:21-25a, 27-28

Arthur O. Kaul

Some time ago I wrote a tract titled, "You're Right, Nothing Works." In the opening paragraph I said the following: "Nothing makes sense. Nuts to it. Jump in the lake. It's your fault. I told you so. I've had it. You can't believe anybody. Everybody's out to get you. You're a liar. I got gyped. I thought you were my friend. That so-and-so. I just fixed it, now it's broken again. You know where you can go."

Each of us have either made statements like this or thought them. Why? Because we are by nature alienated from God. We are all sinners. We mess things up. We make our own rules and plans for living. We do things our own way even though they never seem to work. So our world has become disjointed and out of order. Because of our vast news networks connected with radio, television, and the printed page, every day we know what's going on in our world. Looting and rioting in one country, an attempted coup in another, an army invasion in yet another . . . on and on the story goes. It's far easier to point to these things and say, "there's the problem." The finger really should first be pointed at ourselves. Purchased by Jesus Christ, as we have been, we still carry around our old evil natures. Each day this nature wants to dominate our lives.

Just before the lines of the text, St. Paul gives us a clue to the problem. We've broken God's laws, and now our own plans don't work. He writes, "What anyone does to keep the Law will not make him righteous before God, because the Law shows us our sin" (Rom. 3:20).

Then these words, "but now." Something better is in the works. God has a plan, and it's better than man's plan.

I. What Is Man's Plan?

If you gathered together several dozen people and asked them to name some of the most subtle sins that afflict them, you'd come up with an array of answers. I tried this once when I was in evangelistic work. I got answers like, "cursing, lying, laziness, temper," and many others. Seldom if ever would anyone tell you that pride is one of their sins. Yet it afflicts and harms us all. This is one sin the devil has succeeded to camouflage as few others. Few of us recognize it for what it really is; the devil has given it a real face lift.

Sometime ago a noted psychiatrist asked the question, "Whatever became of sin?" Another question worth asking today is, "Whatever became of the devil?" He's as real today as he was when he caught Adam and Eve off guard in the garden long ago. He used a double strategy on them. He does the same today.

First, he will get you to doubt. Do you ever have doubts about God? Do you ask, "Is He real? Does He really care about me? Does He love me? Is the Bible really God's Word?" That was the tactic the devil used on our first parents. The devil said, "did God really tell you what you shouldn't do?" He casts doubt about God and about His Word.

Then the devil proceeded to tell our first parents the advantages of yielding to his seduction. They would be like God. Here was a powerful appeal that caught them off guard. It tempts us all, and often traps us. It was an appeal to pride.

Had it stopped with our first parents, there would be no problem.

It didn't. It has crept down through the centuries and now afflicts us. St. Paul takes our pride for granted. He writes, "What then becomes of our pride?" Paul excludes no one. He indicts the whole human race. "There is no difference. All have sinned and are without God's glory." What a statement! There's no difference, educated or uneducated, rich or poor, all have sinned.

Through pride our world is in trouble. Pride spawns other evils.

A woman came to my office. She was troubled about the world we live in. She said, "There is so much war, poverty, hatred and violence." Then she asked, "But why?" There is no profound philosophical answer. God's answer is man's sin, man's pride. Until God's plan is put into action in our lives, man remains proud and haughty. All of man's plans just won't work.

Solve the problem of sin and you will close every jail, dismiss every physician, close every hospital, dismantle every war machine, close every gun shop, and repeal every law.

Pride is like a germ. It spreads. It breeds other evils. "What then becomes of our pride? is it excluded? How? By the way of works?" Pride and good works, as a way out of our dilemma, are twin evils. one gives birth to the other.

Our natural inclination is to try and pull ourselves up by our own bootstraps. I've heard this said by people, "I don't want to brag, but let me tell you what I've done or what I'm doing." The inference is, "Isn't that great!" or "Look at my good works. God has to be pleased with me."

"What then becomes of our pride? Is it excluded? How? By the way of works? No, by the way of faith. We are convinced anyone is righteous by faith without doing what the law says."

II. Here We Have God's Plan for Each of Us

"But now God has shown us His righteousness."

Have you ever thought about what God is really like? None of us have seen Him. Without Jesus Christ none of us would know what God is like. Jesus is God's greatest revelation of Himself. It is in the Word of God that we discover God through His Son.

Without this revelation, we would be like the two blind men trying to describe an elephant. The first blind man felt the elephant's tail and said an elephant was like a rope. The second blind man felt the elephant's leg. It felt like the trunk of a tree, so to him the elephant was like a tree.

How old is God? I look at Jesus Christ and find that death could not keep Him in the tomb, so I know God is eternal. Is God all-powerful? Jesus changed water into wine at the wedding of Cana. He stilled a storm on the Sea of Galilee. He walked on water. On and on the Scriptures relate the power of God through Jesus Christ; the power to lay aside the laws of nature He Himself had imposed. Is

God loving? Does He really care about people? About you? Jesus took time to love the loveless, the sick, the forgotten people. I know God cares, because I know Jesus Christ cares. Is God holy? Jesus Christ said, "Which of you can prove me guilty of sin" (John 8:46). Not only did He say this, but from that time until now, no one has been able to find fault in Jesus Christ. Sunday after Sunday, we therefore confess, "I believe in God the Father Almighty"—almighty in perfection, love, and power. This is the righteousness of God. As the Scripture says, "God has shown us His righteousness." He surely has!

Here is God's plan for each of us: "God's righteousness comes to all who believe, just by their believing in Jesus Christ."

I'm sure that some of us have heard this for most of our lives, but what does it mean? God tells us "we become righteous by a gift of His love, by the ransom Jesus Christ paid to free" us. In that little book of Philemon with only twenty-five verses tucked away in the New Testament, we have a beautiful story. A runaway slave has come to visit Paul. He sends the slave back to his master with these words, "If he cheated you or owes you anything, charge it to me" (v. 18). Jesus Christ paid the ransom on the cross to free us from sin. Like the runaways we all are, Jesus said, "Charge it to Me."

A God who can love is a person. Just imagine falling in love with a raindrop, or thinking that a raindrop can love you. It is impossible. It can't be done. Behind love there has to be a person with a warm, loving heart. Jesus is the gift of God's love.

God says, "righteousness comes to all who believe." Man is lost. That's why his plans won't work. God gave Jesus up to a sacrificial death on Calvary's cross for all men that "everyone who believes in Him should not perish, but have everlasting life" (John 3:16). Some years ago I heard about the deathbed statement of one of my former seminary professors. As he lay dying, he began to talk about believing in Jesus. Then he said, "Oh, that everyone would believe and have eternal life."

What is it to believe in Him? It means to put your soul's confidence in Jesus Christ, to trust Him, God's blessed Son. There is a Scottish translation of the New Testament where the word "believeth" is not found. Instead there is the Scotch word "lippen," and it means "to throw your whole weight upon."

Have you been struggling, working, fussing, trying to give up this or do that? Whoever throws his whole life upon Jesus will receive the goodness, the righteousness of Jesus. He won it for us upon the cross.

John, that beloved follower of Jesus wrote, "But to all who welcomed Him, who believe in His name, He gave the power to become God's children" (John 1:2). It has been said that there are just five letters to the word Jesus and they mean this: "Jesus Exactly Suits Us Sinners."

We are poor, lost, guilty men and women, but He is the Holy One, who endured the cross; bore our sins; died for us and rose again.

A surety is one who stands good for another. We might do this for a friend, but not for a stranger unless we're prepared to lose. But it was when we were strangers and foreigners and enemies, alienated from God that Jesus became our surety. "Christ died once for our sins, the righteous one for the guilty, to bring us to God" (1 Peter 3:18).

"By the way of faith" we become righteous before God. What is faith? Scripture defines faith this way: "Faith is being sure of the things we hope for, being convinced of the things we can't see" (Heb. 11:1).

Faith is believing, and faith is a gift to be received. We have to distinguish Christian faith from other faith. I can have faith that it will not rain tomorrow, but it may rain. However, our Christian faith is based on a historic fact. The fact that Jesus came to earth, lived a perfect life, died for our sins upon the cross, and arose from the grave. Would you like to have that faith? Perhaps you do. How about a greater faith? God's formula for believing is that "when we tell people" the Good News of Jesus, "they believe, and we tell them by letting Christ speak" (Rom. 10:17). Coming to God's house to hear the Good News isn't just something to do haphazardly or once in a while. In God's house, we hear the good word of Jesus Christ. Perhaps also nothing is more personal than Holy Communion. In this act, God speaks to each of us personally and says, "Take eat, blood shed upon the cross for you, for the forgiveness of your sins, for the strengthening of your faith." What an opportunity, what a blessing!

The Bible is a book filled with life and truth. Centuries before Jesus Christ walked upon earth, the "law and the prophets tell about it."

Speaking of Jesus, Moses told his people, "The Lord your God will raise a prophet for you, one of you an Israelite like me: listen to Him" (Deut. 18:15).

Perhaps no prophet spoke more clearly about Jesus than did Isaiah. Luther says of Isaiah, "He seems to have seen more clearly than any of the other prophets, the suffering servant of Jehovah." Isaiah gives us an exact picture of Jesus.

Other prophets spoke of the place of His birth and many other details.

God's plan for each of us is a wonderful plan that begins in the here and now and reaches into eternity with the gifts of eternal life. It's too good to miss. Not our works, not our efforts, but God's gift, Jesus Christ, received by believing through the gift of faith.

Roy Palmer was right when he wrote:

> My faith looks up to Thee,
> Thou Lamb of Calvary
> Savior Divine . . .
> O let me from this day
> Be wholly Thine.

How Can I Be Right with God?

THIRD SUNDAY AFTER PENTECOST
ROMANS 4:18-25

Eldor W. Richter

Man's basic question is the question Martin Luther asked, "How can I find a gracious God?" But modern man is not asking that question much any more. Rather, modern man is asking, "How can I live with myself? How can I cope with my fear and anxiety? How can I get along with others?" God is easily dismissed. He is no longer relevant for many people. The question of God has been taken care of. "God is loving—everyone knows that. Man is good— at least he's pretty good, at least not so bad, at least good enough so that he's not damned. All the religions of the world are the same, so who worries about God? All is well between me and God—at least I think so." Our text confronts us with the basic issue of man's relationship with God once again. It raises the question, "How can I be right with God?" The answer of our text is, Abraham believed in the promise of God and "it was reckoned to him as righteousness" (v. 22). Have faith in Christ as Abraham had faith, and you will be right with God.

I. God, Myself, and Others

Modern man searches for harmony with self and a harmonious relationship with others; but really can this search be separated from the quest for a relationship with God? Can I separate myself and others from God? The Old Testament says, "You shall love your neighbor as yourself." And then it adds, "For I am the Lord your God" (Lev. 19:18). The two relationships are bound together. Jesus sights the two great Commandments and says, "The first is, 'You shall love the Lord your God with all your heart and with all your soul and with all your mind,' " and then He was quick to add the second, because the two are inseparable, "And the second is like unto it, 'You shall love your neighbor as yourself.' On these two Commandments depend all the Law and the prophets' " (Matt. 22:37-40).

You see, when we ask the question, "How can I have a right

relationship with self and with others?" It is directly related to the question, "How can I have a right relationship with God?" "How can I get right with God?"

Is There a Righteous Man?

Was there one person in the Scriptures, in the history of man, who was righteous and right with God? Both the Old and New Testaments say, "Yes, there was one. His name was Abraham." How did Abraham get right with God? We might think, "He was obviously a good fellow, one that was a notch above other people." Let's look at the record. Was he really that great in himself? Let's look at his background. He grew up in the heathen land of the Ur of the Chaldees. No doubt he worshiped the gods of the land, the moon god in particular. We are told that the God of glory appeared to him and called him out of this idolatry (Acts 7:2). When he moved to the land of Canaan, was he any better? He knew the true God, but was he a man who was righteous in himself? A famine came, and he and his wife Sarah had to seek food in Egypt. Sarah even at 65 years of age was a beautiful woman, and Abraham was afraid that the Pharaoh would want Sarah to be his wife and that Pharaoh would kill him. Abraham, therefore, said to Sarah, "Say that you are my sister." She was his half sister, but the fact is she was his wife, and it was deception to say that she was not.

Abraham was as human as any of us. He was selfish and wanted to save his own skin. Nor did he consider the feelings and reputation of Sarah. Later on in life Abraham repeated the very same deception. Righteousness was not something he had in himself.

Abraham's Faith

Well, how then is it that he became righteous? Both the Old and New Testaments tell us, "He believed the Lord and He (God) reckoned it to him as righteousness" (Gen. 15:6). Our text in Rom. 4: 20-22 says, "He grew strong in his faith, and he gave glory to God, fully convinced that God was able to do what He had promised. That is why his faith was reckoned to him as righteousness." There you have it! Abraham was righteous by faith, faith that had been created by the grace and promises of God.

Again and again the Scriptures tell us of the faith of Abraham. The God of glory appeared to Abraham in the Ur of the Chaldees and said, "Go from the land into a land I will show you" (Acts 7:2-3). And Abraham believed and went by faith.

First Abraham and his father went to Haran in Syria, and God said to him, "Go from your father's house to a land I will show you ... I will bless you ... and in you all the families of the earth shall be blessed" (Gen. 12:1-3). Abraham believed and went by faith.

When he was in the land of Canaan, God said, "Lift up your

eyes. Look to the north. Look to the south. Look to the east. Look to the west. All the land which you see I will give to you and to your descendants forever. Walk through the length and breadth of the land, for it is yours" (Paraphrase Gen. 13:14-15, 17).

Sometime later God said, "Look toward the heaven, and number the stars, if you are able to number them. So shall your descendants be" (Gen. 15:5). And Abraham believed the Lord, and it was reckoned to him as righteousness (v. 6).

When Abraham was 100 years old and Sarah 90, God said, "I'm going to give you a son" (Par. Gen. 17:16). Abraham laughed for joy. He believed! He believed that God could "call into existence the things that do not exist" (v. 17); that God could call into existence a son from a barren womb. God could do the impossible. "In hope he believed against hope, that he should be the father of many nations" (v. 18).

II. Saving Faith Believes God's Promise

Saving faith, the faith that makes us righteous before God, first of all believes the promise of God. What is that promise? That Jesus was "delivered up," the original says (v. 25). He was "delivered up" as a lamb to the slaughter (Is. 53). He was "delivered up" for our transgressions. He was "delivered up" by Judas. He was "delivered up" by Pontius Pilate. Faith believes that. It does not doubt. It believes as Abraham, who did not "waver concerning the promise of God" (v. 20). Faith says, "Yes," to the act of Christ. Saving faith says, "I am right with God, because God has forgiven me for Christ's sake, as the Scriptures plainly promise."

Saving Faith Believes the Impossible

Second, saving faith believes that Jesus Christ was raised for our justification. Abraham "in hope against hope believed" (v. 18). He believed that God could raise from Sarah, who in child-bearing was as good as dead, a child (v. 19). Our faith is likewise reckoned as righteous when we believe in Him who raised Jesus our Lord from the dead (v. 24). Such faith believes that life came from the womb of the grave as surely as Abraham believed that life could come from the dead womb of Sarah. "In hope Abraham believed against hope" (v. 18). In hope we also believe that God raised Jesus and that we, too, shall be raised. This we confess when we say, "I believe that on the third day he was raised from the dead . . . I believe in the resurrection of my body and the life everlasting."

Saving Faith Gives God the Glory

Third, faith that saves and is righteous before God gives God the glory. Abraham never said, "Look at how great my faith is. What a great person I am since I believe." Abraham gave God the glory (v.

20). He knew that without the promise of God and without the grace of God shown him, he would still be in the Ur of the Chaldees serving the idols of his fathers. Righteous faith gives God the glory. It keeps its eyes on the death and resurrection of Jesus our Lord and says, "What a great God I have that He would do all this for me, though I do not deserve it."

Such Faith Is Reckoned as Righteousness

Fourth, such faith—which believes God's promise, which believes the impossible, which gives God the glory—such faith is reckoned as righteousness before God. It is "reckoned." The word that is used is one used "to tabulate or compute." No longer are my sins "computed" against me. Rather Christ's righteousness is computed toward me (2 Cor. 5:19, 21). Christ wonderfully takes the "print out" of my sins, which the Law tabulated against me. In exchange he "reckons" to me the righteousness of His suffering, death, and resurrection. What joy there is to receive such an exchange by faith. What confidence and peace it brings to our hearts!

III. Am I Right With God?

How easy it is to begin trusting in self once again. Recently this Pastor visited a family that had not attended worship for some time. The father was a good father in every human sense of the term. Yet he was neglecting "the one thing needful." We talked about God, and he assured me that he believed in God. I then asked him how he looked upon God. He said, "Well, I believe in God. I don't believe in heaven or hell. I don't believe that God governs everything that I do. He does help out once in a while when I need Him." I asked him whether he felt that he lived in a daily relationship with God. This took him by surprise since he had not thought of a daily relationship with God. I asked him whether he ever confessed his sins to God. He replied that he did not often think about it. I asked him if he was sure that he would be with God when he died. He said, "I figure that God and I will talk it over and then he will decide." I then told him that there was a way he could be sure. God had given him life in His Son. It was a gift because all of us are sinners. After recalling the Ten Commandments and the life and death of our Lord, I pulled out two chairs from the kitchen table and said, "There are two ways a person can live." Sitting in the first chair I said, "One can live pretty much without God. He can say, 'I believe in God. I try my best. I will take my chances when I die.' " Moving to the other chair I said, "The other way is to live by faith, to believe that Jesus atoned for our sins, that we can't save ourselves, that Christ in love has saved us. Through faith in Him we live in a personal relationship with God our Father. It is a whole

new way of living. It is the way of faith, and it is a wonderful way."
After I had finished, he thought quietly for a long time, and I could
see that he was deeply moved. He said, "I was sitting in that other
chair, wasn't I?" I said, "Only you can say, but God this night is
calling you to faith in His Son and to live your life by faith in Him."
He said that once again Christ would be the center of their lives and
that things would change. Happily from that time there has been a
marked change in his life, evidenced by faithful worship atten-
dance. Once again he was living in the saving faith of Abraham.

There was a man who came from a very fine religious family. He
went to a top university of his day. He sat at the feet of one of the
most learned teachers. He led a good life. He fasted and prayed. He
sought peace with God. In so doing he made life miserable for
himself and everybody else.

And then he met Jesus Christ and this is what he says,

> For His sake I have suffered the loss of all things, and count them as
> refuse, in order that I may gain Christ and be found in him, not
> having a righteousness of my own, based on law, but that which is
> through faith in Christ. (Phil. 3:8-9)

This man was Paul. He wrote our text. Through faith in Christ
he was right with God.

This Pastor recently received an urgent phone call, "My husband went out in a boat. It's been hours, and they are unable to find
him. Please come." I went to the distressed family. Speaking to the
wife I said, "Your husband is safe. If they find him alive and well,
he is safe. If he has drowned, he is safe with God. In either case he is
safe with God." Speaking to the children I said, "Your daddy
believed in God. He is safe." Daddy's faith was like the faith of
Abraham. It saved. Through faith in Christ he was right with God
and safe in the ultimate sense from sin and death.

> Lord, give us such a faith as this;
> And then whate'er may come,
> We'll taste e'en now the hallowed bliss
> Of an eternal home. (*TLH* 396)

The Greatness of God's Love for Sinners

FOURTH SUNDAY AFTER PENTECOST
ROMANS 5:6-11

Eldor W. Richter

One of the most dramatic pictures that I have ever seen shows a
Roman Catholic nun and bishop dead on a lonely road in Rhodesia.
The nun's name was Sister Marie Francis and the bishop's name

was Bishop Schmitt. They had been ambushed and shot by guerrilla terrorists on Dec. 5, 1976. What leaves an indelibile impression upon my mind is that Sister Marie Francis with arms outstretched had flung her body across the body of Bishop Schmitt in a vain attempt to shield him from the terrorists' bullets. It is a picture of sacrificial love and devotion. The apostle Paul states, "Perhaps for a good man one will dare to die. But God shows His love to us in that while we were yet sinners Christ died for us" (v. 8). How Great is God's Love!

I. While We Were Yet Helpless . . .

"While we were yet helpless, at the right time Christ died for the ungodly" (v. 6). A family was stalled on Interstate 80 in the worst winter in the history of eastern Iowa. All night they huddled in their automobile. In the morning they decided to form a human chain and walk to a restaurant located at the nearby exit. In the human chain that they formed was a small boy, Jason, three years old. As they groped their way through the snow storm, the human chain was broken. Each group thought that the other had Jason with them. When they arrived at the restaurant, they discovered that Jason was missing. Hurriedly they retraced their steps and found Jason huddled up against a large tire of a stalled semi truck. He was severely chilled. One of the men took him into his arms and ran back to the restaurant, breathing warm air into his mouth. Back at the restaurant they placed Jason in warm water. As he began to thaw out, he began to call for his "mamma." Jason, who was helpless, and without hope, had been rescued in the nick of time.

"While we were yet helpless, at the right time Christ died for the ungodly." We were spiritually helpless. We were lost and unable to find our way back to safety. Not only were we helpless, but we were numbered among the ungodly. We were broken off from God and His people. But at God's right time, and in the nick of time for us, Christ died for us and rescued us. He brought us once again into the safety and warmth of the Father's house. How great is God's love for the helpless and ungodly!

While We Were Yet Sinners . . .

"God shows His love to us in that while we were yet sinners Christ died for us" (v. 8). Perhaps we took note of the fact sometime ago that Patty Hearst and Susan Ford married their bodyguards. At first this may strike us as strange. They come from prominent and wealthy families. Why would they be attracted to marry their bodyguards? On second thought, it may not seem so strange. After all these men are willing to "take the bullet" for them. They are men who are so committed that they are willing to die for them. Such commitment is bound to create admiration, if not love.

"God shows His love to us in that while we were yet sinners Christ died for us." God's love was so great that He sent His Son to "take the bullet," to take the curse and the spear for us. This He does for sinners, for those who are bound under the curse and the power of sin and who consistently "miss the mark" of His perfect Law. How great is God's love for the sinner!

While We Were Yet Enemies . . .

"While we were enemies, we were reconciled to God by the death of His Son" (v. 10). National television showed twin brothers about eight or nine years old. One, because of a kidney disease, was considerably smaller than the other. Once he had been weak and sickly, but now before the cameras he played and chattered away. Why the improvement? Because his brother had given him his kidney and saved his life. His brother was asked what kidney he gave. He replied, "My right one." "Why your right one?" he was asked. "Because I am right-handed, and I figured that my right kidney was my best kidney." What an example of love! His parents said that it was his own idea to give his kidney and that his love was free and generous toward his brother. Yes, for a good man, for a bishop or for his brother, a person might be willing to die. But, God shows His love for us in that "while we were enemies we were reconciled to God by the death of His Son" (v. 10).

A study of Lutherans a few years ago revealed that 18 percent of Lutherans believed that they first had to come to faith and love God before God would love them. The Scriptures say that God loved us while we were yet enemies. Before we ever came to faith and before we ever loved Him, God loved us and reconciled us to Himself by the death of His Son.

We may object and say, "How could I be an enemy of God? I have never murdered, committed adultery, or embezzled another. Perhaps not, but all of us must confess to the sin of indifference. Would you call it love if a husband or wife lived in the same house, but never inquired concerning the other's welfare, or expressed affection, or showed kindness, or paid any attention to the other? Would you call it love if he or she went on their way day after day and were indifferent? Hardly.

Thus, it is that when man does not seek after God and when he goes his own way as if God did not exist (Ps. 14:2 and Rom. 3:11), he is clearly in "enmity against God" (Rom. 8:7). When man is indifferent, he is in opposition to God. Jesus said, "He who is not with Me is against Me" (Matt. 12:30). God looks at man's heart and finds "They have all gone astray, they are all alike corrupt; there is none that does good, no, not one" (Ps. 14:3). Even the child of God must in sorrow confess such indifference in his heart.

II. We Were Reconciled . . .

But God shows His love in that "While we were enemies, we were reconciled to God by the death of His Son" (v. 10). God indeed was for us, but He had something against us—we were His enemies. Yet in His immeasurable love and in His infinite wisdom He found a way whereby we might be reconciled to Him. It was through the sacrificial death of His Son, so that now we are "justified by His blood" (v. 9).

A popular notion is that all is well with us if we just tell each other so. All we have to do is affirm that we are valuable human beings, and everything will be okay. Certainly it is true that we are valuable human beings, created by our gracious God, but that does not change the fact that we are sinners. I may come to you and say, "I really feel terrible about what I did and what I said to the person whom I love." You may say to me, "That's okay. You are still a valuable human being to me." So I am a valuable person; the fact is that I have acted in a terrible way. We may tell each other, "I'm okay and you're okay," but does that remove the guilt?

But if God (who has the authority to forgive) says, "On the basis of the death of My Son and by the shedding of His precious blood, I declare your sins to be forgiven and everything to be okay," then indeed it can be believed. Then there is a basis for our mutual affirmation, for this affirmation comes from God Himself. Then it can be believed, for the wrong has been paid for. It is not mutual self-delusion, but rather an absolution, an absolution as real as the death of Christ. And it is valid, as valid as if God Himself were speaking to us. How great is the love of God which pronounces a former enemy to be His friend!

Much More . . .

But there is more. "Since we are now justified by His blood, much more shall we be saved by Him from the wrath of God" (v. 9), and "much more shall we be saved by His life" (v. 10). Jesus not only died for us, but He now lives for us.

> I know that my Redeemer lives;
> What comfort this sweet sentence gives!
> He lives my kind, wise heavenly Friend,
> He lives and loves me to the end. (*TLH* 200, 1, 6)

With Christ living as our Friend, there is no need to fear anything in the present. And there is no need to fear death or judgment in the future, since we are already friends of God. If God was willing to go to such lengths while we were His enemies, surely He will not forsake us now that we are His friends and numbered with His people. If everything is okay now, surely we can count on everything being okay in the future. He will not forsake us in our time of need, in the hour of our death, or on the Day of Judgment.

A pastor friend of mine told the story of his grandfather dying. He recalled that when he was a little grandchild, his father and the other children gathered about his grandfather's deathbed singing hymns of comfort. As the time of death approached, the grandfather with outstretched arms said, "The Lord is calling me now. He is calling me. I am going home." And with that, as Stephen, he died. The Lord had been with him as a Friend all of his life. Now he was going to be with the Lord. There was no fear.

How great is God's love to us as the helpless, ungodly; to us as sinners; and to us who were His enemies. Therefore, "We rejoice in God through our Lord Jesus Christ through whom we have now received our reconciliation" (v. 11). The original says, "We boast in God." We do not boast in ourselves, or in our own merits, but we are proud of our God. Even as Scripture says, "Let him who boasts, boast of the Lord" (1 Cor. 1:31). We boast in the love of our God. We boast in the reconciling death of His Son. We boast in the cleansing blood of Christ's cross. And we join all of Christendom and all the saints in exclaiming,

> Unto Him who loved us and washed us from our sins in His own blood and has made us kings and priests unto our God and His Father to Him be glory and dominion for ever and ever. Amen (Rev. 1:5-6).

Possibility Living

FIFTH SUNDAY AFTER PENTECOST
ROMANS 5:12-15

Richard H. Warneck

John Claiborne, general manager of the St. Louis Baseball Cardinals, was fielding questions from a radio audience before the 1979 baseball season. Listeners inquired about the possibilities of several rookies making the team at the close of spring training. Mr. Claiborne repeatedly emphasized that the eager hopes of the fans or the ambitions of any young player to break into the line-up of a major league team must always be realistic.

As he spoke, Mr. Claiborne seemed to describe three kinds of rookie players. The first is the young man who has done well ever since batting the ball around on the sand lot as a youngster. Yet, he is unrealistic about the competition, and his own preparedness to play with the pros. He is gripped by illusion. The second type is the young man who discovers he has been illusionary about his ability. He encounters superior competition in the tryouts and calls it quits. He is realistic. He doesn't have it for the majors, and he bows out early. The third player Mr. Claiborne described is the young man who discovers the reality of his inadequacy and settles for a berth with a farm club, applies himself over the years, steadily improves his skills, and waits for his day when they will call him up to the big league. He patiently works with his potential.

You readily recognize three traits manifest in these aspiring young ball players. There is first, illusion. Then, there is reality. Finally, there is possibility. These same traits apply to the person becoming and growing as a Christian. And that is what St. Paul writes about in Romans 5. He addresses the illusion men hold about their own goodness and righteousness. He confronts them with the reality of their spiritual inadequacy. Finally, he poses the possibility for sinful men through the grace and righteousness of Jesus Christ, the power to bring an illusionary and realistically hopeless sinner to newness of life.

I. Illusion

The verses of today's Scripture from Romans confront us with this trio, illusion, reality, and possibility. First is the shocking explosion of illusions about ourselves and our sinfulness. No man is an island to himself. He may think that he is able to rise above the nature of his fellows, but he is always confronted by reality. He is inextricably bound to the human race and the human condition. Let him plummet to the ocean depths, let him soar to the loneliness and detachment of outer space and set foot upon the moon, he is man. No circumstance may deprive him of that nobility. Neither can he escape the folly and tragedy of the human race. And the human race cannot escape the tragedy of the first man, Adam. The apostle says clearly, "Sin came into the world through one man ... all men sinned" (Rom. 5:12).

The apostle's words are confirmed in our personal experience. Still, we run away from this reality. We tend to be illusionary about the open Bible and its teaching about sin. Holding fast to our illusions, we often dismiss the apostle's frank words about our sin as ancient and meaningless vocabulary of the traditional church. We hear the words, we say them in the Confession, but the meaning, the judgment of God which they speak, does not easily penetrate our illusions.

The 20th century is marked by world conflict, man's inhumanity to man. Still, we have not awakened to admit that the human race is impelled by something other than its own goodness on a road to so-called progress and utopia. Unable to resolve the most elementary human conflicts and disagreements, we look hopefully to such folk heroes as Superman, the bionic man or bionic woman, as if science or at least science fiction may feed our fantasies of a human being capable to resist evil and choose good, defeating corruption, saving the race. There must be more than passing significance attached to countless self-help and self-improvement techniques ranging from pursuit of yoga or raquet-ball twice a week to programs for weight watchers. And then there are the psychic phenomena, meditation techniques, self-hypno-tism, the transcendence disciples, and the like. Can all these pursuits reflect the hope of many that a better specimen of human being may evolve in a human race on the way to becoming more ideal, more perfected? Are not such absorbing interests of modern people the very fabric of an illusion about ourselves, our bond to the human race, its tragedy, its one progenitor, Adam, through whom sin passed upon all?

The illusion is everywhere perpetrated, and always meets a listening, sympathetic ear. "We can lift ourselves out of ignorance, we can find ourselves as creatures of excellence and intelligence and skill. We can be free! We can learn to fly." These words are from Richard Bach's best selling book, *Jonathan Livingston Seagull.* In Bach's book, Jonathan is an aspiring seagull who wishes to rise above the normal activities of other gulls by embarking on a self-improvement program. Of course, Mr. Bach is writing his little parable for us. And one of the themes of his book is that all apparent limitations of human nature are just illusions of the mind!

II. Reality

But the confidence in man's own ability to surmount his limitations may, in fact, be the greatest illusion of all. The truth spoken by St. Paul shatters this illusion perpetrated by Bach and believed by so many persons who hedge on honesty. He writes in terms of universals, but not at all in generalities. We like to treat sin as a general condition which either excuses personal involvement and responsibility or poses the probability that man may solve any general surface malady himself. It is easy to be flippant about sin until we meet head on the direct words and their universal implications. "Therefore," says St. Paul, " . . . sin came into the world through one man and death reigned through sin, and so death spread to all men because all men sinned" (Rom. 5:12)! We cannot be illusionary about Adam, about the first man, the first sin. Can we afford to be illusionary about the results of that first sin? Yes, sin came from without, but passed upon the entire human race by the instrument of the first man, Adam. Sin may not be the intrinsic fabric of human nature, but since Adam, sin has per-meated the human race through and through. We live under the reality that sin grips our lives so pervasively as if it were, indeed, part of our very nature from the beginning. Sin is inextricably bound up with our thinking, our actions, so that from honest examination of ourselves we see that we are included in Paul's universal conscription. "By one man's disobedience, all were made sinners" (Rom. 5:19a).

We resist that judgment. We do not want to believe that our separateness from God is also an active and aggressive alienation. We cling to the illusion that ego bolstering efforts of physical development or pyschic discipline or identity with heroes real or otherwise may temper that condemnation; but, our life day to day confirms the words of the apostle, ". . . sin spread upon all men." We are baffled by our behavior. Have you returned from a party, eager to sleep and forget it all, except that reflecting on the way you acted and the words you spoke, you want to say, "Why, that is not me at all!" There are embarrassing moments. A popular radio personality in a major city, provoked by the Internal Revenue Service, goes on the air and comes off badly with language which is not representative of his usual good program material. Who is to judge? It happens every day. Explain such behavior as a dip on one's bio-rhythm chart, or an off day, or blame someone else. St. Paul removes all the illusions. He says, sin entered the world by one man and touched the entire human race, and we are all inextricably bound up in sin.

Still, these words from St. Paul about our human condition are received like so much rhetoric, like preacher talk. They do not hit home. It was me at the party, yes, and a host of other people too. So bad language comes over the radio, you hear it everywhere, all the time. We tend to elude accountability for our own sin, as if the law of God did not mark and charge sin against us. We rationalize to a point that we are not unlike the hardened criminal mind convinced that society's standard of right is all wrong, and what is deemed wrong in society is perfectly acceptable behavior. He lives in an upside-down world. It is not only his right to be antisocial, it is his duty to pursue his own contradistinct values. Many have similarly repressed consciousness of God's law. They avoid hearing God's "do's" and "don'ts" in the hope that both consciousness of guilt and accountability to God will disappear.

It is an illusion. There was a time in history, the long centuries between Adam and Moses, when there was no external law by which sin could be measured and imputed to the sinner. Still, during that time, death reigned. And death reigns always among men who care nothing for God and His law. If we are compelled to believe that death passed upon all men, then we ought to be convinced beyond a shadow of doubt that sin also passed upon all men, for death came and death reigns because of sin. Finally all the illusions are shattered, dashed away, and we are confronted with two realities. First, the soul that sins also dies (Ezek. 18:20). Second, I, too, have sinned because death passed on me.

III. Possibility

Like the young aspiring baseball players in spring training, we hold many illusions about ourselves, and they are disclosed as illusions when we face reality in the light of God's law and the stark presence of death. But the Letter to the Romans has not survived these many centuries as God's white paper, His divine put-downs, His judgment of the human race. No, this great Epistle survives because it clearly declares something new and alive and exciting, that there is a new possibility for men whose illusions are shattered and broken under the harsh realities of sin and death.

But the possibility lies not in our own thinking or self-improvement or even self-realization. There is no discipline or pursuit, physical or psychic, which is capable of providing that hope, that possibility. It comes from outside the realm of sinful men. It comes to us by grace through Christ Jesus who is the counterpart to to the first man, Adam. And what Christ effects is counter to the effects of our bonds to Adam and a sinful race. This is what St. Paul is really talking about. Everything he says in these verses about Adam as the one man by whom many were implicated in sin only serves as a pre-figure, pointing to another, to the God-man, Christ Jesus. Paul speaks in universals again. He uses Adam and the passing of sin over all to show by comparison that Christ came and affected the lives of all, but in another way. From one man, Adam, came sin and death. Now enters Christ into the world, and with Him some things new. In place of sin and death, He brings righteousness and life. The apostle says it this way, "Then as one man's trespass led to condemnation for all men, so one man's act of righteousness leads to acquittal and life for all men" (Rom. 5:18).

The illusions about ourselves shattered and destroyed, there is only one possibility for you and me, the possibility which dawned upon the human race when that second man came and lived and shed His blood on the cross, bringing righteousness and peace between us and God by the forgiveness of sins. The only person who cannot be affected by this grace of the Lord Jesus, though His grace abounded for all, is the person who does not want it, who either evades the reality of sin, or, in spite of sin, or because of sin, is convinced that there is no hope.

"But as many as received Him, to them gave He power to become the sons of God, even to them that believe on His name" (John 1:12). Those words from St. John's Gospel always invite us to believe and trust that second man who entered our world from above, who came in likeness of our flesh, and suffered and died that in Him, we might die to sin and live in righteousness and for eternal glory. Even people who mistakenly hold on to the illusions which met the severe judgment of God, even they are included under the canopy of grace through Christ unto righteousness and life.

One last phrase dare not escape our attention today. St. Paul says, "much more" did grace and forgiveness of sins and the Holy Spirit abound toward us in Christ Jesus. How hard the reality of sin, how pervasive its influence, how final God's judgment of sin, how eternally ruinous is death which came by sin! We see sin all the time, everywhere. We are fearful in the face of it, we seem helpless to avoid it, we ourselves cannot escape sin, and the proof positive is the vast reign of death from which there is no refuge. But where sin abounded, and it certainly does abound, grace did much more abound (Rom. 5:20)! And that grace abounds the more in Christ for you who have sunk in despair, crushed by the reality of sin. However intense and pervasive sin may be, however severe the ravages of guilt have taken our own hearts, the more, yes, "much more" does grace and mercy abound in Christ Jesus! Whenever you are overwhelmed and can only believe that sin reigns supreme, St. Paul bids you to consider the "much more" of Christ, His grace and righteousness unto eternal life (Rom. 5:21).

Conclusion

That "much more" of Christ, His grace and righteousness before God for us, are so profound and compelling that we are constrained to change our terms at the last. The reality of sin never gets the best of Jesus Christ. The possibility in Him becomes a new and abiding reality of a victorious life as sin yields to the upper hand of Christ. Be rid of illusions about your so-called better self! It is by itself not so good. Be rid of the reality of the dominion of sin. Begin to live the possibility of life afresh, anew, awakened to God by His everlasting grace unto righteousness through our Lord Jesus Christ.

Christians Alive

SIXTH SUNDAY AFTER PENTECOST
ROMANS 6:1-11

Richard H. Warneck

Seeking authentic and genuine experience of faith in their personal lives, many ask, "How may I become a better Christian?" Much so-called Christian behavior is insipid and colorless, little more than vague Americana, doing what is expected of any law-abiding citizen. Are you looking for a vibrant, more sincere Christian life?

One popular answer to our quest is this formula, "Turn every-

thing over to Jesus and ask God to come into your life!" That
invitation seems helpful, except some persons are not in the asking
mood. They are not convinced God would set foot in the door of their
lives even if it was open to Him. Another response to the quest for
genuine Christian living says that we should abandon the search
altogether. Do not bother yourself with Christian living. Grace
abounds all the more as sin abounds. The Russian monk Rasputin
held that those who require the most forgiveness will receive
comparable grace and forgiveness.

This notion that God's grace affords liberty to sin is quickly
corrected by St. Paul. To that rhetorical question, "Shall we
continue in sin, that grace may abound?" the apostle answers with
a resounding "No!" God gave His Son for sinners, but He did not
waste His Son so that you and I may continue in sin. And to the
other question, "How may I become a better Christian?" St. Paul
furnishes a radical answer from the death and resurrection of our
Lord Jesus Christ.

I. Death

No one may become a better Christian until he comes to grips
with sin in his life. He must own up to it, and something must be
done about it. Have you a program for grappling with sin? We share
in Adam's fall, and our propensity for sin is called "sinful flesh" in
the New Testament. There is no good in it, says St. Paul (Rom. 7:18).
You may call it "the old Adam," "Old nature"; and, unless it is
broken and defeated, there is no helpful answer to the question,
"How may I become a better Christian?" If you are not asking that
question, you may be more seriously enslaved to that inclination to
sin than you realized.

Can your repress the old nature, can you rise above it, can you by
sheer will power and resolve escape its power and domination over
your life? The years have taught us the futility of such efforts. A
more radical solution is called for. And St. Paul sets it before us.
There is an expression you hear sometimes among unhappy
employees in a company or among restless students in schools. You
will even hear it in the church. When people are frustrated with
central administration and leadership of an institution, you may
hear it said, "There is nothing wrong here that a few funerals would
not help!"

That is morbid, grotesque! It should not be said at all, except St.
Paul is saying, what prevents you and me from becoming better
Christians could be resolved by a funeral! Yes, the funeral of our old
sinful nature would be the greatest help to living Christianity. St.
Paul is not speaking of the funeral cited by notices in the
newspaper. True, death may excuse us from many obligations of
life, but sin is a debt that will not be buried in the grave. Sin follows

us into eternity unless it dies a radical death while we are yet living this side of the grave.

How does that work? Hear the language of the apostle: " ... we are buried with Him [Christ] by baptism into death" (v. 4a); " ... our old man is crucified with Him that the body of sin might be destroyed" (v. 6); " ... we have been planted together in the likeness of Hs death" (v. 5a). Christ the Son of God became involved with our sinful nature, not as sinner, but as Sin-Bearer when He lay down His life on the tree of the cross (1 Peter 2:24). Whether we are in the flower of youth or the prime of life or the crown years of advanced age, there must be a funeral conducted for this sinful nature. It must be united with Christ in His death on the cross, or we may give up seeking to become better Christians!

That does sound a bit radical! Are there other ways to handle the old nature? Mostly, you want to repress inclination to sin, and you think you are successful. But it comes back to haunt you. Or, you try another method. You substitute another pattern of behavior. If you are selfish by nature, you try to be more outgoing and generous. It works, until you go back to the dog-eat-dog competition in a world where survival of the fittest is no game for good hearts and gentle people. The old flesh wins again. We learn the hard way that the old nature is tough. The old Adam will not listen to us. It will not be scoulded, restrained, or repressed. It yields nothing to will power. Neither can we close our eyelids in death and be rid of it. So, we must deal with it now. To delay is dangerous. There is only one thing to be done. The old nature must die!

So, it happened that a funeral was arranged for this rebellious sinful nature, the old nature which embarrasses you and spoils your best intentions to be a better Christian, the nature pulling you back two steps for every step forward in Christian life. And that funeral occurred simultaneously with Holy Baptism. "Know ye not, that so many of us as were baptized into Jesus Christ were baptized into His death" (v. 3)? We are not observers or onlookers at Calvary where Christ died for our sins! There were no bleachers at Calvary. Rather, by baptism, we are drawn into the history of those redemptive events, united with Christ.

Travelers to the Holy Land are deeply affected by the places where Jesus Christ lived and spoke and ministered to people. Who would not be impressed and deeply moved, standing where the cross stood, bearing the body of the Lord, who bore our guilt and sin? Or, stand at the sepulcher from which sprang life eternal for you and me when He rose from the grave. And the words from the Sermon of our Lord flood the mind when one walks the hills above the towns surrounding the Sea of Galilee!

Still, it is much more personal to recall that, "We were there!" In such a dynamic way, in Baptism by water and the Word, we were drawn to the cross. Our old sinful flesh died in the redeeming death of the Lord Jesus. A new person emerges, the power of sin broken by His death, sealed forever in defeat by His burial. And we were quickened to transcendent everlasting life by faith in God's operation through our Lord's rising from the grave. When from the cross He cried, "It is finished!" our sinful nature was finished, washed up. When He gave up the spirit and died, our sinful flesh gave up power and authority over life. United with Christ in His death by our baptism, the old nature is truly, "crucified, dead, and buried!"

II. Life

Holy Baptism is no trifle! While many Christians could not adequately explain their own baptism, nor even express the blessings they enjoy in Baptism, St. Paul makes it abundantly clear that in this Sacrament there stands tall the cross of Christ, the axis around which turns the Christian life, yes, even the better Christian life. If you are not yet baptized, something can be done about that! But, baptized and forgetting your baptism or neglecting it or going through life misunderstanding its application day by day, that is to invite back the free reign of the old nature which makes you a slave to sin!

When that funeral is conducted for the sinful flesh, a birthday is celebrated at the same time, for "we believe that we shall also live with Him" (v. 8b)! Do you share the apostle's faith? Are you alive in Christ because the power of sin is broken? To be alive may mean to be done with some things of which we are ashamed as well as others of which we have mistakenly become proud. There are places we will not traffic, things we will not do. There are lines to be drawn and boundaries to be fixed.

But the Christian who is alive is also open to new vistas of living he never saw before, pathways of love turning into service and bringing joy never before experienced. Turned out from the death of our dominant sinful self to new life, baptized into Christ and putting on Christ, the heart soars to new heights as our hands reach down to new depths helping and restoring where we never had either thoughtfulness or time heretofore. And the time we have, long or short, is crowned with living hope in the Lord who brings us along into His life and His eternal kingdom to rule and reign with Him for eternal ages.

Pipe dream or possibility for you, this new life in Christ? Some of you are weary of the battle of life. You say it is too late for change. You are too rigid for something so radical as death to the old nature by Baptism and a new life in Christ and the power of His resurrection. So, you cannot teach an old dog new tricks. Agreed, you cannot teach the "old," but the "new," that person can learn, that person can put on Christ, and with Christ righteousness and holiness and hope! And you, if you be a man or woman or child in Christ by Baptism, you are new, so very much spanking new!

Be what you are, be alive as a "new" Christian! It is the apostle's fervent plea. The documentary film, *Scared Straight,* was produced at Rahway prison in New Jersey where life-term prisoners attempt to literally scare the crime out of juvenile delinquents who have been flirting with serious crime on the streets. The prisoners are men dedicated to sparing the younger generation of the years of misery and defeat they suffer in the penitentiary. When they bring these young people into that room deep within the walls of the prison, they lean on the young offenders with a heavy hand. They are so intense, so urgent. They describe so vividly conditions in the prison, the crimes abounding against person and personhood. They tell about the bestiality, the abuse, the hopelessness, the fear. And all of this to plead with the young people to choose life and not death!

The apostle Paul pleads with every Christian reader of Romans chapter 6, reckon yourselves, consider yourselves dead to sin and alive to God! The shackles of sin are broken, be free in Christ to live the Christian life each day better than the day before. Now, you may even be prepared to ask God into your life. Once Christ, in Baptism, has taken you to His cross and raised you with Him out of death, you are alive like you never lived before. Look alive, alive to God, alive now and to eternal ages.

Christ Will Deliver Me

SEVENTH SUNDAY AFTER PENTECOST
ROMANS 7:15-25a

Rudolph A. Haak

The devil made me do it! Now and then we hear this almost flippant quip from a youngster who is momentarily faced with the pressure of having to give an account of himself in some kind of immoral, sinful situation. He cannot plead ignorance of knowing the right. His Christian parents gave him all the knowledge that he needed to live an upright life. His sinful act was executed in spite of an inner voice that hold him not to do it. But he did it anyway.

The easy, hurried excuse for his wrongdoing is primarily a "cop-out." It is an attempt to be at least somewhat relieved of the responsibility of the wrong action. It is a kind of panic, last resort to preserve some kind of dignity in an otherwise hopeless situation of guilt.

Without trying to draw a clear picture of what brings such a response we do find in this illustration a sample of the struggle that goes on in the life of a Christian person. Of all people, the apostle Paul says, "I do the very thing I hate." "I do not understand my own actions" (v. 15). After describing further the lines of battle and the awful dilemma in which he finds himself he finally exclaims, "Wretched man that I am! Who will deliver me from this body of death?" (v. 24). He answers his own questions in the very next sentence. "Thanks be to God through Jesus Christ our Lord!"

Christ Will Deliver Me
I. The Agonizing Conflict

The conflict is set in motion and kept going through the activity of Satan on the one hand and the Holy Spirit on the other.

Since the fall of man into sin (Gen. 3), Satan has laid claim to every human being. In setting the trap of temptation, he was successful in bringing about the fall into sin. He was successful in wrenching God's people from Him and bringing them into the kingdom of darkness and death. He keeps very many in the delusion that all is well even while they are far from God and headed in the direction of eternal death. In fact, as long as God's law is not held up before them to threaten and condemn, they are often lulled in their spiritual slumber and blindness, quite unaware of the hopeless position in which they exist and unaware of the awful death which will surely overtake them. It is no wonder that such as are captives of Satan and sin often feel no great struggle going on inside. They often seem to be quite content to the casual observer, because the Spirit of the Lord has not yet revealed to them the demand of God's law, nor has He yet entered their hearts to oppose Satan and all his wicked works.

Not so with Paul! In him the battle rages with all its fury. In the midst of the fray he calls out, "Wretched man that I am! Who will deliver me from the body of this death?" (v. 24).

This is no longer Saul—the persecutor of Christians. This is no longer the Saul, who with calm and skill, with a planned, orderly program methodically brushed Christians out of his way—and pursued them unto death. This is no longer the Saul who was seeking to challenge the God of the Christians in order to disprove His power and existence.

This is the Paul who fell into the hands of the Lord's Christ Himself—on the Damascus road (Acts 9:1-9). Here the Holy Spirit began the battle with Satan, and the sinful nature within Saul. The battle was so furious that Paul fell to the ground, and for the first time he recognized the voice of his Lord. There was never any doubt as to the outcome of the battle within. That battle over Satan was won by Jesus Christ on Calvary's cross. The battle within Paul was only to have the devil yield to His maker the person whom God Himself had redeemed.

From that time on the conflict within Paul goes on. Sometimes seeming much subdued—only to burst into open fury again when Satan (reluctant to acknowledge defeat) would again challenge the victor.

Dear friend—this should tell us much about the origin of the conflict. Do you identify with Paul at times? It is a part of the trick of the devil to have you feel guilty about these "goings on" inside of you. It is part of Satan's battle strategy to even question your faith and security in Christ as you observe what's going on inside your heart and soul. But surely Paul's experience is recorded in our text in order that all Christians may not be deceived. Those in whom Christ dwells will surely experience something of the battle which ensues when Satan challenges the Lord, whose we are.

This account of Paul surely also helps us to understand the fury of the battle and the vigor which is demonstrated by the antagonists. The devil's last chance to get you is now, before you are snatched into your eternal home. He won't spend himself with those who are already his. He will give himself fully to the task of drawing such to him as are in God's family and are serving Him daily.

Opposing him is our gracious and loving God. His Spirit will not permit Satan's efforts to prevail. The victory is already won by Jesus Christ. But Satan needs to be convinced of that victory again and again.

It's a mysterious duel. Every attempt at explanation leaves unanswered questions. I am one person. I am not two, much less three. How can I identify myself in the conflict? Something of me seems to be an ingredient on both sides of the struggle. Or is the real me entirely apart from the struggle? I don't want to be a part of the devil's tool. Yet I so often do his bidding. I know God's will. I want to be His servant, yet I so often do contrary to His will. How will I ever unravel the mess?

I won't. Paul couldn't understand it all (v. 15). We don't need to. Our gracious God understands it—and takes care of it. We follow Paul, who in a kind of futility cry says, "Wretched man that I am! Who will deliver me from the body of this death?"

II. The Glorious Deliverance

He answers his own question when he says, "Thanks be to God through Jesus Christ our Lord" (v. 25a). There lies the complete and satisfying answer. It is Jesus Christ who "delivers me from the body of this death." You will notice that a part of Paul's wrestling in the early verses of the text had to do with his attempt to so find his

place under the Law that he might find some reasonable justification of his life responses (or lack of them). In fact, in all of chapter 7
he emphasizes the fact that the Law is good. It is from God. It serves
a very important function. From all this it follows that those who
love the Lord must follow it and keep it. No matter how carefully
Paul would analyze the Law—and his behavior—it always came
out the same. Paul was a sinner! So am I! So are you! All attempts to
muster some dignity and self-worth by placing ourselves alongside
of God's law are futile. Thanks be to God who gives us the victory
through our Lord Jesus Christ.

The whole discussion about the Law and its meaning for the life
of the Christian is sandwiched between two beautiful Gospel
sentences. Don't miss them!

"The wags of sin is death, but the free gift of God is eternal life in
Jesus Christ our Lord." (Rom. 6:23).

"There is therefore now no condemnation for those who are in
Christ Jesus" (Rom. 8:1).

Whatever lies shrouded in mystery of chapter 7 is cleared up
with those two precious Gospel promises. It is as though Paul would
let no one approach the contents of chapter 7 or leave it without
relating the words directly to Jesus Christ and His redemptive
work.

Therefore Jesus Christ delivers me—and you—and all people
from sin, death, and the devil.

He delivers me from sin in that He takes away my guilt. For God
has made Jesus to be sin for us, even though He had no sin in
Himself. In this God made us to be righteous. Thus the Law no
longer condemns us because in God's eyes we are righteous. The
guilt of doing those things that are of the flesh and against God's
law is not meant to be carried by us. The devil says, "I am guilty"
because I have sinned. I agree with the verdict—but only until I
hear God say, "You are guiltless and just." God's Word stands. This
is the victory over the guilt of sin. And this is not a confrontation on
God's part because all who are in Christ Jesus are holy by faith in
Him. For Christ is the end of the Law for righteousness to everyone
that believes.

In Christ Jesus is victory over the punishment of sin. Indeed the
sins of all must be punished. God, who is faithful has done precisely
that. He took the sins of Paul, of you, and of me, and of all the world
and placed them upon Jesus Christ. He bore the punishment that
was due because of these sins. He suffered. He died for all—for you,
for me. Paul summarizes this in the last verse of chapter 6 of
Romans, "The wages of sin is death, but the free gift of God is
eternal life through Christ Jesus our Lord."

In Christ Jesus there is victory over the slavery of sin. We no
longer need to yield to every whim and passion and base desire

which would draw us into sin. In Christ Jesus we have implanted in us a new mind and a new will which seeks to serve God, not sin. And when we do fail in such service God is not pleased to have us tremble and hide in fear and shame, but quickly fall to the open arms of His grace and mercy.

Thanks be to God for His victory over death in Christ Jesus. Indeed we die a temporal death, but this need no longer cause us to fear. For death has become the doorway through which we pass to eternal life. Christ has abolished death and brought life and immortality to light through the Gospel.

And though Satan lives, and though he is very strong, and though he is still very active in his effort to steal Christ's people, he will not prevail. For Christ has subdued him and chained him. Walking close to Jesus we may indeed be tempted, but the victory is ours through our Lord Jesus Christ.

Paul in chapter 7 is engaged in careful examination of self in the light of God's law. It is a wholesome, necessary exercise. It is good for every Christian to go through a similar process every day. But it is meant to be a relatively brief process. On this level of "looking at self" is not where God means for life to be lived. This level can only yield bewilderment and "wretchedness" as it did with Paul.

God means for His children to live the victorious life above the human reality of sin and a life related only to the Law. God means for us to live a victorious life *in Christ Jesus*. To dwell on our guilt, on our sins; to live in fear of failure and punishment is the road to death, no matter how sincere the intent. For this reason Paul urges elsewhere that we keep our eyes fixed on Christ Jesus who is the Author and Finisher of our faith.

Christ has delivered me! I am free, victorious in Him! Thanks be to God! That's life! Live it, won't you?

Groanings on Tiptoe

EIGHTH SUNDAY AFTER PENTECOST
ROMANS 8:18-25

Rudolph A. Haak

In the early morning hours a fire broke out in an apartment building trapping a number of families. With hallways ablaze and filled with smoke, a family waited frantically for rescuers to reach them from an outside window. In their efforts to protect the children, the parents were already overcome with smoke. The two children, horrified with such an experience, stood on tiptoe peering through the window watching the rescue operation below. In these horrible moments of waiting their great and exciting hope was that the rescuers would reach them—in time. They watched, as they waited on tiptoe, and emotionally labored with every move of the rescue team until they were finally snatched from the trap of death. Their confident, watchful waiting had helped to prevent them from a foolish dash onto the stairway or a leap from the window—which would have meant certain death.

This simple example is something of a picture of all of life in the world. People and all living things see death and destruction all around them. All of life seeks deliverance, a rescuer, a way out of the dilemma. All of life is "standing on tiptoe" hoping to see some rescue apparatus functioning that will enable them to believe that deliverance is sure and near. So the Scripture lesson before us gives a picture of

Groanings on Tiptoe

I. Whence These Groanings?

Our text talks about suffering (v. 18). Creation waits with eager longing (v. 19). The whole creation has been groaning in travail together (v. 22). Even Christians are groaning inwardly (v. 23).

The groaning in futility and pain is found in every living creature. In the Christian the pain is felt when he finds himself being less than God has meant for him to be. The Christian knows God's will for him. The Spirit of Christ in the Christian wants to do God's will. But time and again the Christian still finds himself doing the very opposite, namely fulfilling the desires of the flesh. This produces the pain of guilt, the pain of bringing shame upon the Savior whom we love, and the hurt of failing to fulfill the task in life to which we are called. So in the Christian the battle between Spirit and flesh rages on bringing weariness, pain, sighs, and groanings. Oh, when will deliverance come from the body of this death?

The unbeliever often goes through much of life without the pain and longing for deliverance. The spirit of gain often drives him into a flurry of action that promises deliverance from whatever hurts. Much of life for him is spent in pursuing happiness and fulfillment in getting more for himself of money, goods, pleasure, fame, ease, or power. The spirit of Satan and the flesh often so fill his life with pursuit of these that he may not even feel the pain. If there is some pain, he dulls the senses with drugs or alcohol, or with some other device to escape from reality.

But when finally, sometime, somehow the discovery is made that life does not consist in the abundance of things to be possessed, then the groanings set in. When the mad pursuit stops long enough for him to become aware of a God to whom he is accountable—and of a devil who has tricked him—then the pain and the groanings set in. Then the guilt, the shame, the hopelessness, the futility become immeasurable—and the groanings are often so desperate that they are silenced only in death.

Where is the root of all this? It is our inheritance from our first parents whose disobedience to God in the Garden of Eden brought sin into the world. The pain and the groaning of every human being has its roots in sin. By nature, sin is a part of our very being. Thus the sinful thoughts, desires, words, and deeds become a very part of the expression of that nature. It is an attempt to live life apart from God. It is an attempt to demonstrate to self and others that we are in charge of our own lives and do not need God. All pain, futility, groanings, and despair have their roots in sin. And the greatest longing in every heart is to find deliverance from all of these.

This struggle, these groanings are not only to be found in people, but they are a part of the existence of every living creature; every plant and animal. Our text says that "the creation was subjected to futility" (v. 20). Creation itself will be set free from its bondage to decay (v. 21). The whole creation is groaning in travail together until now (v. 22).

The permanent stain of sin has spilled over beyond the human race on to all of God's creation. Among all living things there is an inescapable tyranny of sickness, deterioration, and decay. It is a kind of universal travail among all living things, both plants and animals. It is as though the pain of birthing and giving expression to life is immediately overtaken by the dying process. It is a pain that yields nothing but death. And the only prospect seems to be that the cycle will continue to repeat itself. So creation was "subjected to futility" (v. 20). This condition was not something which creation brought upon itself. But the One who made all living things put them under the management of human beings. God's hope for living creatures to fulfill His purposes lay in His primary creation, man. He had glorious things in store for people. Other living creatures had an important part in His plan. But man incurred a great loss because of his rebellion against God—with this came also the loss of God's intended hope for all living creatures. So thorns and thistles infest the ground. So every plant and living creature soon moves into the path of disease, deterioration, death, and extinction. So all of life becomes for such creatures a struggle for survival. Such living is painful, futile. It is lived with groaning and longing for deliverance. Thus the deteriorating life, loss of vitality, being victimized by disease or "natural" enemies, and all other descriptions of the dying process are finally also linked to the catastrophe of human sin. So indeed, all of creation is groaning in pain, all is living in a futility cycle, yet "standing on tiptoe" as it were, hoping and watching, and in some cases believing, that the rescue operation is at work and there is early deliverance.—In this tiptoe peering ahead there is hope.

II. The "Tiptoe" Glance of Hope

For the Christian the hope is a certain one. Its certainty lies in the accomplished fact of Jesus' payment for sin, His victory over death and the devil. The fact that Jesus lived in our stead to provide righteousness for us is a foundation for certain hope. The fact that He suffered and died to take the punishment for our sins and satisfy the wrath of a just God—this is solid foundation for hope. The fact of Jesus' resurrection is evidence that God accepted the sacrifice of His Son. This is sure foundation for Christian hope. The testimony of His Spirit in our hearts as to the truth and reliability of all this is foundation for hope. The changed heart by which we are now able to love the Lord and desire to serve Him—this is undeniably the fruit of the Spirit of Christ working in our hearts and the evidence of His presence. This is solid foundation for hope. And in this hope we are saved (v. 24).

This is indeed a prolonged "glance." It is a vision, though still a vision of the eyes of faith. That's why it is still hope. And the fullness of the deliverance has not yet taken place. The hidden and vague lines of the future reality of deliverance will all become clear when the Christian is delivered, body and soul, from this life to life eternal. There the "tiptoe glance" of hope will burst forth into complete, experienceable reality. In this reality there will be no remembering of the "sufferings of this present time" (v. 18). In this hope fulfilled, any thoughts of past suffering and groanings will quickly be abandoned as being worthless, because this will be God's full and complete revelation of the sons of God. In this act of complete deliverance God's glory will be revealed. Oh, the joy of that time!

But God did not mean for us to wait until we experience this fully before we rejoice and use it. That's why He has given us hope. That's why He has given us a "tiptoe look." He wants us to use it now.

A youth leader had taken a group of children on a wilderness trip to teach them the techniques of survival. The camp area was so remote that it could only be reached on foot. An unseasonable storm forced them to stay in camp much longer than they had planned. Thus food and supplies became short. Some children were sick. All of them were homesick. The spirits and morale of the children were at rock bottom. In this condition they began to walk the long journey through snow and debris back to civiliization. As they trudged slowly on, one after another stopped in exhaustion only to be carried by the braver and stronger. The hope of reaching home before some would die from fatigue, illness, or frostbite seemed to diminish each moment.

At this point the leader asked them to stop in a sheltered area. For one-half hour he engaged them all in planning a party for some future date. When the planning was near completion, they ventured on their journey again. From that time on there was lively conversation about a funtime, good hot food, a roaring bonfire, etc. All were able to walk, and soon all were home safely. They were enjoying the party in anticipation of the event. The party was of greater value to them before it happened than when the event actually took place.

In much the same way the Lord would have us anticipate the joyous deliverance which is now only our sure hope. The contemplation of this joy makes the sufferings of this present time unworthy of comparison.

But in the "tiptoe glance" of the world, the view is much more dim. People who do not know Christ Jesus as Savior do not have the eyes of faith. They therefore miss the meaning of the vision of Jesus' coming, His life, His death, and His resurrection. In their glance they see only you and me. If they stood on "tiptoe" today and saw me—would any clear vision of Christ in me show through? The only voice of Jesus they hear is mine. The only hands held out to help are mine. The only heart to love is mine. For it is through me that God rescues them. When they stand on "tiptoe" to get a good look at me, will hope increase? Will faith be awakened or strengthened? Will their glance at me enable them to believe that deliverance will surely come—in time? Or will their countenance darken? And will they then sink in despair, futility, and death?

O Lord, make me Your person to bring hope to silence the groanings before death overtakes and silences them!

All creation waits—with eager longing—for the sons of God to come into their own. Yes, one day they will see it in all its fullness, when Jesus comes again in glory. But God hasn't meant for them to wait that long. The redeemed children of God are meant to act the part now, here in this life. God's order of His children being managers of all created things is still in force. All of life on earth depends upon the good management of God's managers of all created things. The weak and the sick and the dying plants and animals look to us to deliver them. Their "tiptoe glance" is meant to show them something of God's goodness and mercy as His children manage life on earth. All of the cosmic agony we see finds its roots in man's guilt. All relief, and healing, and loving care, and tender cultivation is meant to come from the redeemed child of God who lives by faith in Jesus Christ. He is appointed to lead others to know the treasure of God's creation of life.

And so the blade of grass, the stalk of corn, the fruit tree, every animal on the earth, every fish in the sea, and every bird in the air looks at me (and you) with wistful, longing eye in the hope that it might have just a taste of the glory which shall be revealed by God on the last day when Jesus Comes to gather His own.

What will these living creatures see with their "tiptoe glance" when we pass by? Will our presence, our actions, give them hope?

God counts on it!

When We Think We Can't Pray

NINTH SUNDAY AFTER PENTECOST
ROMANS 8:26-27

Jack Breznen

It is late a night. Everyone else is asleep, and the lights are out. You are awake, lying on your back in bed, and very restless. Your evening prayers have concluded, at least those regular prayers that you pray every night. You have already thanked God for the many blessings you and your family have received. You have already brought your regular petitions to Him, that long list of friends and relatives, church members and non-members that you systematically place before His throne. You have been taught to cast your burdens on Him, and have done so once again. But there is still that restlessness. No matter how hard you try to sleep, you are unable, for more and more names in need keep coming to mind.

There was a letter that arrived that day, from an old friend back home. She had written of her concern for her son who has completed another term at college. He had recently returned from school on a semester break and informed his parents that their Christian faith was just wishful thinking. He had told them of their sheltered lives under the shadow of the church; and as far as he was concerned, he wished they would stop nagging him about going to church.

And then you think: "Lord, lead John back to You. Remind him of his confirmation vows. Continue to call him by the Gospel and open doors for someone to minister to him." You have placed the matter in God's hands, but the restlessness continues.

Bill and Marge had been over earlier that evening. What had begun as a casual conversation turned into a bitter verbal battle between them. This husband and wife of twenty years turned on each other with all the ferocity and four letter words of a street fight.

And then you think: "Lord, what causes a Christian couple to act like that toward each other? What could I have said to alleviate

the tension? What should I say tomorrow when I see Bill at work?"
And the restlessness continues.

Then there's the disagreement over the vacant church property
that has caused a slight division in the congregation. And there is
Aunt Sue struggling for life in the nursing home, and Phyllis
suffering with a terminal malignancy, and the ridicule that Jerry
faces at school because he refuses to do things that he knows are
wrong.

And then you think: "Lord, it just seems endless. There are so
many people with so many needs, and I don't know how to express
them all to You. It's so frustrating! It seems as if I just keep saying
the same list over and over to You. It gets longer and longer. With so
many of these people, I don't even know exactly what I should be
praying for!" And the restlessness continues

When We Think We Can't Pray

Nearly 2,000 years ago the apostle Paul wrote his letter to the
Christians at Rome. Paul faced the same problems, and he knew
that God's people everywhere also faced afflictions and weaknesses. In the eighth chapter of this letter, used as our Epistle lessons
during a four-week period, we take a close look at the comfort God
offers. We are reminded that even though there will be sufferings on
this earth, we have the hope, the assurance, that is in Christ Jesus,
our Lord. Nothing will ever be able to sever that love, for we are
adopted sons of God, as He has called us to be His children.

Strength in the Midst of Weakness

The Lord knows that we will have those occasions when we are
frustrated and restless. "Likewise the Spirit helps us in our
weakness; for we do not know how to pray as we ought, but the
Spirit Himself intercedes for us with sighs too deep for words." The
Holy Spirit helps us to bear the weakness that we have. It may be
physical infirmity or emotional illness. It may be spiritual trouble
or a desire for another to receive God's love. But He helps, and with
divine strength sufficient for us. God declares, "My grace is
sufficient for you, for My power is made perfect in weakness" (2 Cor.
12:9).

That's why God sent His Son into this world. That's why the
Word became flesh and dwelt among us. That's why Christ, our
Redeemer and Savior, true God and true Man, showed us the way to
live. That's why our Lord Jesus is seen so often in prayer. That's
why in our human weakness we are taught to look for divine help.

There are many Greek words which when translated mean "to
help." It's interesting to note that this particular word in our text is
used only twice in the New Testament. It's not the type of healing

that we would associate with doing a favor for someone. It doesn't imply taking someone else's place or filling in for another. It specifically means to share a duty with another. The other passage records Martha asking the assistance of Mary to help with the work, to share in the serving. Likewise the Holy Spirit helps us in our weakness. We know from Scripture that God will never leave us nor forsake us. He is with us always. "In Him we live and move and have our being" (Acts 17:28). He is there to help with His strength when we are weak.

The specific example Paul gives is prayer. As he readily admits, "we do not know how to pray as we ought." If it were left entirely up to us, we wouldn't even pray at all. But having been motivated by the love of God, we offer our prayers of thanks and place our petitions of request before Him. Even then we conclude so often by saying "if it be Thy will." There are instances where God's will is made very clear to us through the Scriptures, and we dare not ignore His commandments by tagging on this phrase in those situations. And yet, so often we don't know how to pray for specifics. We don't know what things are really necessary, "but the Spirit himself intercedes for us with sighs too deep for words."

The prayers which come out of the depths of our souls are initiated by the Holy Spirit. But it is not the Holy Spirit that sighs, for the Spirit doesn't groan. It is we who do the sighing and groaning from within our hearts. It's that frustration that comes from an inability to put into words one's innermost desires and feelings of love and concern. We can't find the right words to adequately express ourselves, and so our hearts respond where our lips are unable to articulate.

Weakness Supplanted by Strength

This is a phenomenon that is not uncommon. Jeremiah lamented, "My anguish, my anguish, I writhe in pain! On, the walls of my heart! Behold, O Lord, for I am in distress, my soul is in tumult" (Jer. 4:19; Lam. 1:20). Peter writes of faith in Christ: "Without having seen Him you love Him; though you do not now see Him you believe in Him and rejoice with unutterable and exalted joy" (1 Pet. 1:8). Through the ages God's people, prophets, and patriarchs have experienced the same. We read of the laments of David in the royal palace, the moaning of the souls of Isaiah in the temple, and the unutterable groans of the multitude of the faithful suffering under the taskmasters' whips in the mudpits of Goshen. They are feelings that can't be uttered in any language, silent sounds heard only by the Almighty. As we are children of God, this is the activity of the Spirit of God within us.

There is no possible way to describe the mystery involved, but the method is similar to that of a stage actor. The actor has learned his lines well, with a great deal of practice and preparation. He has even performed the same production many times before. But, human as he is, his memory fails him, he gropes for the right words, stuttering, unable to speak what He knows. His lips and his heart are unable to synchronize. And then, unseen, from behind the curtain comes the prompting that he needs. Instead of disastrously babbling the wrong words, he is set at ease, for the prompter has provided the necessary assistance.

In a way far more important, the Holy Spirit prompts us or intercedes for us, with gentle whispers and sighs too deep for words. Our memories are moved to remember God's working in the past, how we have witnessed the power of prayer through direct unmistakable divine answers. Our thinking is stirred to the promises of God from Eden to even now as we stand in the long line of faithful. Bible passages we had memorized as children are recalled to soothe and bring comfort. The weariness of a morning prayer becomes refreshing when the Spirit prompts us with a reminder of who we are, then also helping us recognize the One who supplies the lifeblood that runs through our bodies and pulsates our souls. The exhaustion of an evening prayer becomes relaxing and encouraging as the Spirit prompts us to recall, "for into Thy hands I commend myself . . . let Thy holy angel be with me, that the wicked Foe may have no power over me."

Notice that the text states: "He who searches the hearts of men knows what is the mind of the Spirit." God searches the *heart*! He doesn't grant one man's prayers over another because one is more articulate than the other, because one individual is more fluent with phrases than another. I once read of a certain clergyman who was said to have given the finest prayer ever offered to a Boston audience. Possibly true. But's that about as far as the prayer ever got—the Boston audience received it and there it ended. Evangelist D. L. Moody said the best prayer was one that was cut on both ends and set on fire in the middle. Famed Lutheran Hour speaker Walter A. Maier wrote that "no exceptional ability, no technical preparation, is required to express the simple sincerity of effectual prayer." True prayer is not just words. As a matter of fact, true prayer can be without any words at all. Shakespeare wrote: "Words without thoughts never to heaven go."

The Spirit's Strength Motivates

God searches the hearts of His sons and daughters, and He discovers unutterable sighs and frustrations from an inability to put those prayers into words. And although there may be no verbal activity on our part, those sighs and frustrations are heard, understood, and answered by God's almighty power. Because the Spirit intercedes, our weakness is known and is in accord with His will. Didn't Jesus say, "Your heavenly Father knows of these things even before you ask of them" (Matt. 6:8)? Charles Spurgeon compared this relationship to that of a defendant and the best attorney available. The defendant has chosen to plead his own case, but he is unable to put the situation into the right words. He knows very little about the law, and the prosecutor is cunning and crafty. But he has the best attorney available who uses all his knowledge in the case. This counselor suggests the plea, arranges the arguments, and puts his client at ease. When the case is eventually won, the testimony of the client has proven crucial, but it was the counselor who provided the impetus and the instruction.

Within our weakness we plead to the Lord for all sorts of assistance in this life. And we are aware of the simplicity of our prayers, and our lack of Scriptural knowledge. But because the Spirit intercedes for us, we are taught how to pray, how to plead. Those prayers are heard, and we are thankful for the testimony of the Holy Spirit, our Counselor.

Paul is truthful when he writes, "we do not know how to pray as we ought." As children of God we ought to pray regularly and grow in our prayer life daily. When we think of what our Lord Jesus has done for us and how He continuously pours out His blessings, we should be moved to prayer by pure thankfulness and love. When we think of His constant offer of forgiveness and the promise of eternity, we should be motivated to prayer by the Gospel and nothing less.

Luther stated that "it is a good thing to let prayer be the first business of the morning and the last at night. Guard yourself carefully against those false, deluding ideas which tell you, 'Wait a little while. I will pray in an hour; first I must attend to this or that.' Such thoughts get you away from prayer into other affairs which so hold your attention and involve you that nothing comes of prayer for that day" (LW Vol. 43, p. 193).

If you are not now *daily* setting aside a few moments to be alone with God in prayer, then do it! And I don't mean just at meals when you give thanks for the food on the table. I mean a private talk with God. Set aside a segment of time to perhaps read a portion of one of the gospels or a psalm, and then speak to the Lord in prayer.

For all of us, there will come those times when we are unable to express ourselves in words to our heavenly Father. We are sinful, weak human beings, and we will experience frustrations and restlessness. Our concerns for our family and friends will be with us throughout the day, and, at times, even keep us awake at night. But as redeemed children of God and with a firm faith in our Lord and Savior Jesus Christ, our hearts and minds are open to Him. We have received the free gift of His Holy Spirit.

He hears those sighs and groans. He sees the deep concerns we have, even when we think we can't pray. Our hurt is so deep over the marital strife between Bill and Marge, we are unable to form a prayer; yet as He was bruised, wounded, and afflicted, His love for us is so great He is aware of that unspoken prayer. He knows the anguish we feel over John's desire to turn away from the faith, for He felt the agonizing pains of love on a pair of crossed beams. As we toss and turn in our bed, thinking of Phyllis and Aunt Sue suffering and struggling for life, unable to lift a finger to help, they are nonetheless in the hands of the Great Physician. There should never be a time when we think we can't pray.

"Now to Him who by the power at work within us is able to do far more abundantly than all that we ask or think, to Him be glory in Christ Jesus to all generations."

Those Who Love God

TENTH SUNDAY AFTER PENTECOST
ROMANS 8:28-30

Jack Breznen

While growing up with brothers and sisters back in Ohio, our family encountered the usual amount of solemn moments in life. There was the sudden unexpected death of a close relative, grandmother's lingering illness in a nursing home, the tornado that ripped through town leaving a trail of destruction on whichever side of the street it chose to set down. These were serious times and all of us faced them. There's probably not a soul here this morning that hasn't asked himself or herself, "Why is all of this happening to me?" For some it was getting a draft notice and the eventual orders to report for overseas duty. For others the crisis was a period of hospitalization or even a trip to the doctor to check out a newly formed lump on the chest. For still others it was the attempt to heal a serious difficulty in the marriage over a period of time. These are solemn moments in life. But they are not all past history. They happen now. They are within our families. They are serious situations and crises that we must face. The comfort that is supplied by God is recorded throughout the Scriptures and is certainly found in the truth of these words: "We know that in everything God works for good with those who love Him." We realize that Christianity takes man beyond tragedy and that the hand of the Almighty guides.

Those Who Love God

There are those who don't love God, who choose not to realize their blessings. They remain steadfast in their unthankfulness. Tragedy presents no problem for the fatalist or the atheist. The atheist, on the one hand, concludes that everything happens by chance anyway, and there is no sense or rhyme or reason in the world. Therefore, he has no explanation. The fatalist, on the other hand, says that everything happens according to some plan over which there is no control whatsoever, that all things happen according to the stars or some other fatalistic force. They say they have no problems.

But the Christian in his thoughts and prayers and theology does have a problem when he considers the entire realm of suffering and evil. For the Christian has concluded from the beginning that God is a God of love and grace. When confronted with evil, the Christian is also confronted with God's love in the face of the problem of evil.

Face Tribulation Under God's Care

There isn't a single detail in life that ultimately works for evil to God's people. The Scriptures only speak of good for those that love God. God doesn't punish us with sickness, infirmity, disease, or death. He doesn't take loved ones from us in order to hurt us. The God of all creation is not a destructive divinity who punishes people when it pleases Him.

"In everything God works for good with those who love Him." Paul is by no means saying that everything that happens in life, each event and experience on earth, is necessarily good. There are certainly miseries and troubles and times of deep depression and unhappiness. All sorts of emotions and experiences touch our lives: birth and death, richness and poverty, happiness and grief, joy and tragedy. Each of these comes to our families, our friends, our homes, and ourselves.

The hurricane winds of the east coast affect the trees and roofs of all the buildings. The winter influenze touches all of the schools. The spring flood waters flow into homes on every street in the coastal lowlands. All things come to all people. Even our Lord Jesus spoke about the two homes in the rainstorm. Although the foundations were different, one built on rock and one built on sand; it was the same rain that fell on both homes. Our Lord told of the wise man who was prepared for tragedy.

Christianity takes man beyond tragedy! Despite what men do to themselves and to each other, God still reigns and His mercy is still sure. God still answers that prayer: "Stretch forth Thy right hand and help and defend us." Christianity takes man beyond tragedy to the place where God comforts. A skeptic will ask: "What good does it do a suffering person to hear that?" It will do him good if he understands that evil is significant merely in terms of our response to it. Christians are those who know this truth. Christians know that trust in God can bring them through this experience into a far greater one. And here is the question that all of us have heard too often: "Why is it that it's always the good people that have to suffer?" The answer it this—that this is the reason they are "good," because they have gone beyond tragedy into the hand of God. They have lived through something. They have seen God in the midst of it; and they have come safely on the other side. "Yea, though I walk through the valley of the shadow of death, Thou art with me." Saints are not those that have lived sheltered lives. They are those who have gone through something, and they have come through glowing, assured that God has had His guiding hand on those who love Him.

Joseph was sold into slavery by his brothers to the Midianites and eventually was imprisoned in Egypt. How he must have wept over that turn of events. His own brothers had sold him and now he was a slave. Eventually he rose to a position of power. Instead of seeking revenge against his brothers, he realized that the position enabled him to help his entire family. Joseph states: "Fear not, for am I in the place of God? As for you, you meant evil against me; but God meant it for good" (Gen. 50:19-20).

Saul of Tarsus was persecuting Christians around Jerusalem and was even present at the stoning of Stephen. The church was scattered and fear of oppression and persecution reigned. But within a few short years those events planted the seeds of growth. The Jerusalem church, forced to scatter in all directions, was now springing up throughout the entire Mediterranean; from Galilee to Galatia, from Alexandria to Antioch. God had worked mightily even through the Roman persecution, using the very force that sought to oppress the Gospel, to actually transplant the church in every direction. And what of Saul of Tarsus? This was now the the mighty Paul, powerful penman, preacher, and personality of the Apostolic Age. The same man who breathed "threats and murder against the disciples of the Lord" could now preach "What no eye has seen, nor ear heard, nor the heart of man conceived, what God has prepared for those who love Him" (1 Cor. 2:9; Is. 64:4).

Move Along from Faith to Faith

God most certainly has prepared things for them that love Him. Even when our working gets in the way, God makes all things to work together. Paul writes, "We know" this. When used in the Scriptures, the phrase "to know" many times means a most intimate relationship, almost synonymous with love. He knew the condition of Adam in the Garden, and He knew the hearts of the children of Israel in bondage in Egypt. To Jeremiah He says, "Before I formed you in the womb I knew you" (Jer. 1:5). Paul writes to the church at Corinth: "But if one loves God, one is known by Him" (1 Cor. 8:3). To Timothy he writes: "The Lord knows those who are His" (2 Tim. 2:19).

"For those whom He foreknew He also predestined to be conformed to the image of His Son, in order that He might be the Firstborn among many brethren." We are speaking about the faithful, all those throughout the ages who acknowledged the one, true God as He has revealed Himself to man. According to His purpose He has revealed Himself through His works, events, in the heart of man, in the written Word and the continuing Gospel of Jesus Christ. Throughout history He has revealed Himself through people; Abraham at Ur, Jacob at Bethel, Moses in the Sinai, Paul on the Damascus road, all according to His purpose.

One of the key words to this section of Scripture is the word "those." Paul specifically writes "those who love Him." Every mention of the word "those" refers to "those who love Him." There are teachers and theologians who would have us believe that God predestines all people, that the day we are born we are predestined to either heaven or hell. There is no such teaching in the Scriptures. "God so loved the world . . . whosoever believes . . . shall have everlasting life." Our Father wills that all men are to be saved. His love reaches out for everyone. We can say that God damns nobody to hell. What it comes down to is that an individual chooses to live without God on earth, takes no time for the Lord in his life, and turns his back on the Almighty, all the while hardening his heart to the Holy Spirit. He has no use for God on earth, he has chosen to be separate from God. He himself has thus also chosen to separate himself from God in eternity.

This portion of Scripture deals with those who love God, "those who are called according to His purpose."

In His omniscience He sees beyond ages and eons, even to eternity. The psalmist writes "The Lord knows the way of the righteous." The effect of this knowledge has everlasting significance for those who are faithful.

"And those whom He predestined He also called; and those whom He called He also justified; and those whom He justified He also glorified." We are called because of God's love for us, which we in no way deserve. That is what we call grace. He knew all He called, and to those who were faithful to His calling came the destiny of being conformed to the image of His Son. Those who accepted this calling, not by any personal strength, reason, or deed, are justified "by His grace as a gift, through the redemption which is in Christ Jesus" (Rom. 3:24). God never excluded anybody, but many chose to exclude themselves. Recall how Jesus lamented, "O

Jerusalem, Jerusalem, killing the prophets and stoning those who are sent to you. How often would I have gathered your children together as a hen gathers her brood under her wings, and you would not! Behold your house is forsaken and desolate" (Matt. 23:37, 38).

The text concludes with the words, "those whom He justified He also glorified." What a crowning conclusion of comfort for us all. This is the final step that is not in this world. John writes: "Beloved, we are God's children, now, it does not yet appear what we shall be, but we know that when He appears, we shall be like Him, for we shall see Him as He is" (1 John 3:2). This comfort is throughout time and yet timeless. For gathered in heaven will be all the saints, all the faithful from the vast span of earthly millennia, covering hundreds of generations, all glorified. "These are those who have come out of the great tribulation; they have washed their robes and made them white in the blood of the Lamb" (Rev. 7·14). There are those who are not yet called, those who are not yet justified, those who are not yet even born. It all works together according to God's purpose for those that love God.

So we have the absolute promise of salvation through Christ Jesus, eternal life. But that doesn't come without an earthly death. We can talk about glory and crowns and faithfulness. But they are intertwined with graves and caskets and funerals. God's Word is not something far removed from our everyday lives, rather it is unmistakably intertwined in all that we do. There is no guarantee that Christianity is going to isolate any of us from grief and sorrow and sadness. But we are guaranteed that all things work for good for those that love God, and we are given the strength to see through those times of trouble. Notice that I didn't say we have the strength to overcome them. There are hardships and burdens that we can't overcome and no amount of positive thinking is going to overcome them. Sometimes we must learn to live with those difficulties. Arthritic hands may afflict through a period of many years, but they will never hurt enough to keep us from prayer. Eyesight and hearing may dim with age, but the blessed Gospel we have heard and read cannot be taken from us. Emotional aches and mental agony will bring tears and torment to our hearts and homes, but we are comforted with the constant presence of a Creator who cares. We are taken beyond tragedy, secure in the hands of the Almighty, knowing everything works for good, for those that love God.

Your Loan Is Guaranteed!
Go Ahead with the Building!

ELEVENTH SUNDAY AFTER PENTECOST
ROMANS 8:35-39

Robert R. Krueger

The couple sat uneasily in the outer office of the loan officer at the local bank. They had been in to see him a few days earlier with their request for a loan for the construction of their new "dream home." They had filled in all of the necessary papers, gathered all of the supporting information required and had handed it over to him. "Come back and see me in three days," was his parting comment to them. Here they were, again—waiting! Finally, his door opened and they were invited in. They were seated in front of him. He opened their file, studied it for a few brief seconds, looked up at them, with a smile, and announced: "Your loan is guaranteed! Go ahead with the building!"

Some of us have gone through identical or similar experiences. I have lived through two such experiences in church building programs. It is not difficult at all for us to identify with that couple and to know and sense the exhilaration, joy, and unconquerable feeling they must have had as they left the bank that day.

Multiply their exhilaration, joy, and unconquerable feelings to the nth degree, and we will be at that level of spiritual sureness that St. Paul would bring us to in the Epistle for this day. The Epistle, our text, stands as a peak in the midst of this Letter to the Romans. For the better part of the first half of that Epistle Paul is building to this text, and what follows in the remainder of this Epistle is predicated upon the sureness stated in this text.

Watch how Paul builds up to this text: the opening three chapters of Romans sweep all of mankind under the blanket of sin, first Gentile, the Jew, then all—regardless; from there he moves to God's gracious action of setting sinful men right with Himself— men "are justified by His grace as a gift, through the redemption which is in Christ Jesus" (3:24); "For we hold that a man is justified by faith apart from the works of the law" (3:28); on, then, to the examples of Abraham and Adam (chs. 4 & 5); further along, the Good News that the believer escapes the curse of sin by being brought to Christ in faith; this "justification by faith," which is instantaneous and complete, produces and calls forth the "sanctification-struggle," which is ongoing for the remainder of the Christian's life.

Now, in the words of our text, Paul assures that the purpose for this "sanctification-struggle" is to replace any doubt that might assail us with that joy, exhilaration, and unconquerable knowledge that our salvation is guaranteed. And so,

Your Loan Is Guaranteed!
Go Ahead with the Building!

I. Have No Doubts About Lesser Persecutions, Such Shall Not Separate You

Relying on the God-revealed and Christ-won act of justification by faith, spoken of in the verses preceding our text, Paul silences those voices that would accuse us of not being worthy of the sureness of our salvation. Such sureness God wants each of us to have! We will be directly or indirectly assaulted in our "sanctification-struggle." Yes, what about those specific assaults against us and against our faith?

"Big deal" (to borrow from a younger generation), responds our text. "Who shall separate us from the love of Christ?" And now, a listing of those assaults uselessly aimed at dislodging us from the nail-scarred hands of our Savior: "Shall tribulation, or distress, or persecution, or famine, or nakedness, or peril, or sword?" Was Paul, already a tested veteran of the cross, reflecting here on some of the assaults that had already been launched against him? Was he looking back, remembering "tribulation," "distress," "persecution" already experienced *and* conquered (2 Cor. 11:24 ff.)? Was he, also, by some special gift of insight granted to him by his precious Lord, looking ahead when he spoke of the assaults of "peril or sword?"

If these assaults are personal remembrances of Paul, and I believe they were, then he reaches back to a special psalm, a psalm that prays for victory. Paul quotes from that psalm the Scriptural understanding that such seeming assaults are not to be viewed as signs of God's anger toward us, but rather tests of love toward and discipleship of the Lord Jesus. The faithful who prayed that prayer for victory (Psalm 44) in the Old Testament could look back in the midst of being attacked and say: "Our fathers have told us, what deeds Thou didst perform in their days" (Ps. 44:1b), and they were given unconquerable joy. So, also, Paul could be in the midst of being attacked or could still be smiting under recently delivered attacks and could recall, "As it is written . . .." (v. 36).

We, too, whether being assaulted or still reeling from freshly delivered assaults against our spirit's life, can and ought and must reach back and allow the assuring statements of God's Word to ring again and again in our ears. "It's guaranteed!" "As it is written . . ." "We know that in everything God works for good with those who love Him who are called according to His purpose." "It's guaranteed!" When the question is asked, "Who shall separate us from the love of Christ?" this is no theoretical question. For it is a question by which the world and our own sinful flesh needle us each and every time we are so assaulted.

"Hey, Christian, if God really loves you, how come you're having such a rough time?" ... "'Take no thought for the morrow,' now that is a pretty stupid statement with which to plan college educations, retirement years, and old age, isn't it?" ... He said He would give me 'peace' unlike anything the world had to offer. So how come I am so torn up, confused, and uncertain?" Against these and an ocean more that the world and our flesh would fling against us, our text responds. It enables and empowers us to shout out, "NO!" in answer to the question: "Will anything ever make Christ stop loving us?" "Your loan is guaranteed!"

II. Have No Doubts About Greater Powers, Such Cannot Separate You

That's easy for Paul, almost 2,000 years removed from the closing years of the 20th century, to speak about being sure of Christ's love when attacked and assaulted. We are dealing with bigger and more frightening events and forces than just "distress," "peril," and the "sword." Was Paul ever confronted with runaway inflation, a nosediving recession, living in the shadow of nuclear warfare, an energy crisis, mind-paralyzing drugs or soul-crippling cults?

He did not have to be confronted with such things in order to bring us this Word of conquer from God! He picks up that infallible Word and, again, begins knocking down anything and everything that might cause us to doubt the love of Christ toward us or that might try to make us doubt the sureness of our salvation. And he seems to begin right where he left off, before making that quick turn back into the Old Testament. . . . Then he adds that clinching statement of specifics that shall not separate him from God: "For I am sure that neither death . . . (v. 38) or sword . . . (v. 35) shall separate me from God. Why mention "death" a second time? Could it be, as some have said, "Death is perhaps man's greatest fear"?

I'll admit it to you—"I fear death." No, I did not say that I am afraid to die, I said: "I fear death." There is some difference between those two statements. I fear death for one, rather obvious, reason—I have never done it before! But I also had a certain "fear" of leading two congregations into multi-thousand dollar building programs until the word was received, "Your loan is guaranteed! Go ahead with the building!" Likewise, while I might still have a certain "fear" of death, I am not afraid to die because I have received the Word—and you have received it too—"through death (Christ) [destroyed] him who had the power of death, that is, the devil" (Heb. 2:14). And, because we have received that Word, we can and do join with Paul in shouting still another word into the teeth of death: "O death, where is thy victory? O death, where is thy sting? . . . But thanks be to God, who gives us the victory through our Lord Jesus Christ" (1 Cor. 15:55-56). Did you hear the good Word? "Your loan is guaranteed!" "Yes, though I walk through the valley of the shadow of death, I will fear no evil; for Thou art with me; Thy rod and Thy staff, they comfort me" (Ps. 23:4).

So what of those inscrutable, elusive, unidentifiable "powers" that might attack and might cause us to doubt the love of Christ toward us and might lead us to doubt the sureness of our salvation? Name them: " . . . neither death, nor life, nor angels, nor principalities, nor things to come, nor powers, nor height, nor depth, nor anything else in all Creation . . ." Whew! Paul has run out of breath. He leads us to look in each and every conceivable direction we can and then, just to make sure that we have not missed anything, he adds, "nor anything else in all creation." Yes, that is an impressively frightening list of enemy powers that could and would, that can and will attack us. Make no mistake about it, there is an entire universe out there, and they are our enemies. None of the faithful before us were immune from attack by them, and we can expect no special treatment from them either. But, and at the the same time, make no mistake about this either—over and against all of these enemy powers and powerful enemies that are definitely against us, stands our powerfully loving and lovingly powerful Lord Christ! He is for us! We have God's Word on it! For thus saith the Lord: "If God is for us, who is against us?" (v. 31).

I love this personal confession of sureness of salvation that the blessed apostle is led, under certain inspiration, to make to us. I love it because he makes it more than his confession of salvation surety. He slips his arm through our arms to link us with him and the confessing church of all ages when he says, "I am sure that (nothing) . . . will be able to separate us from the love of God in Christ Jesus our Lord." It is an exhilaration. It is a joy. It is an unconquerable feeling and knowledge to be assured that nothing will ever make Christ Jesus stop loving us! It is an exhilaration. It is a joy. It is an unconquerable feeling and knowledge to be able to hear Paul assert so unwaveringly: "Who shall separate us . . .? . . . we are more than conquerors . . . and . . . I am sure. . . ." We want to, we need to add our "We are sure too!" to such surety of salvation, and so. . . .

III. Go Ahead with the Building

Go ahead with the building! Keep going in that "sanctification-struggle" which God's act of justification by faith has brought to

your life. Our text, as I said at the beginning, is the culmination of
some eight chapters of this letter to the Romans. And now, we are
urged on and into the remaining eight chapters: chapters that urge
us to "go ahead with the building": chapters that carry us unto our
relationships and attitudes toward the descendants of God's Old
Testament people , our responsibilities within the church, within
the state, our responsibilities as individuals.

Yes, "your loan is guaranteed!" and, yes, there is absolutely
nothing that can separate us from the love that Christ has toward
us—except ourselves, our sinning, our refusal to "go ahead with the
building." Of this danger and in counteraction to it, we have
correctly said and confessed in The Formula of Concord: "That the
good work which [God] has begun in [us] He would strengthen,
increase, and support to the end, *if* [we] observe God's Word, pray
diligently, abide in God's goodness, and faithfully use the gifts
received."

We, easily, identified with that couple—their exhilaration, joy,
and unconquerable feeling—after they had been told, "Your loan is
guaranteed! Go ahead with the building!" But what would we think
of them if they went back to their rented apartment or back to their
present, much-too-crowded home and just sat down to TALK about
their guaranteed loan, but never got around to "getting on with the
building?"

To paraphrase The Formula of Concord—that "loan" which
God has guaranteed us: namely, the adoption of sons through the
suffering, death, and glorious resurrection of Jesus Christ, He does
want to bring to fulfillment—go ahead with the building! Observe
God's Word, pray diligently, abide in God's goodness, and faithfully use the guaranteed loan.

"Your loan is guaranteed! Go ahead with the building!"

Don't Think of Praying a "Crazy" Prayer

TWELFTH SUNDAY AFTER PENTECOST
ROMANS 9:1-5

Robert R. Krueger

Recognizing that the chapter and verse divisions of Holy Scripture
are human "additions" to God's Word, we read and hear the words
of today's Epistle right on the heels of last Sunday's Epistle. In his
rising *Te Deum* to God (last Sunday's Epistle), we can still hear
Paul speaking confidently concerning his and our assurance of
salvation. From that tremendous high, we move right on into this
day 's Epistle. (Read the text from An American Translation.)

Wow! Such apostolic anguish is heard and felt in those verses. Though Paul speaks in love for his "fellow Jews," his "own flesh and blood," it is a love that is hurting him. He hurts over the rejection of Christ by his own. In the Old Testament Lesson, in the Gospel, and in our text, the Epistle, there is a sameness of message uniquely told. Elijah, losing "sight" of God, bemoans in a cave (1 Kings 19:9-18); Peter losing "sight" of Christ, cries out as he sinks (Matt. 14:22-33); Paul, almost tempted to think that "God failed" (v. 6), is battered with a "great sorrow" and "pain that never leaves" when thinking of his rejecting relatives.

And what of us, who soared with Paul on the assuring words and confident convictions of last Sunday's Epistle? When we look at the spiritual state of Israel today, the very people to whom was given "the glory, the covenant, the Law, the worship, and the promises"; when we consider folks who have knelt at this very altar on the day of their confirmation, but now rarely, if ever, kneel here or at any altar; when we give thought to individuals who have stood within God's house and have sung with us, "Thee will I love, my Strength, my Tower . . . Thee will I love, O Light Divine, so long as life is mine" (*TLH* 399 v. 1), and now we rarely hear them so singing or see them so living within our parish family. We, too, can identify with Paul in feeling that "great sorrow, that "pain." However, with Paul, let's not make the mistake of praying a "crazy" prayer.

Don't Think of Praying a "Crazy" Prayer

I. The "Craziness" of That Prayer

Paul had such heartache for the Jews that he says: "I could wish myself cut off from Christ and damned for my fellow Jews, my own flesh and blood" (v. 3). One highly respected Biblical commentator has called this statement of Paul's "a crazy prayer" (R. C. H. Lenski, *Interpretation of St. Paul's Epistle to the Romans,* page 584). To be sure, as the original Greek of this text indicates, Paul never prayed such. Even the English usage, "could," carries that flavor. For Paul knew that it would bespeak "spiritual insanity" and "theological craziness" to so speak or pray.

Luther saw this "wish-offer" of Paul's as being beautiful but impossible. He said "For such men (Paul, in this case) freely offer themselves to the entire will of God, even to hell and eternal death, if that is what God wills. . . . It is impossible that the man should remain outside of God who has so completely thrown himself upon the will of God. For he wills what God wills; therefore he pleases God. And if he pleases God, he is loved by Him; and if loved, then saved." (Luther's Works (American Edition), Vol. 25, p. 381.)

While Paul's "wish-offer" is a divine impossibility, it does echo and reecho the great concern he had for the eternal state of his kinsmen. He even goes further than his predecessor, that Gothic man of God, Moses. Moses stood before God as God's anger raged over the golden calf incident. Moses pleaded, "But how, if Thou wilt forgive their sin—and if not, blot me, I pray Thee, out of Thy book which Thou has written" (Ex. 32:32). Moses' love for his people was so great that he did not want to be saved without them; Paul's love soared higher in that he considered the salvation of his "fellow Jews" even at the cost of losing his own standing in eternity.

I can only begin to imagine how many mothers, how many fathers have also thought as Paul did. To see a son who eighteen or nineteen years ago was in your arms while God reclaimed him and in and through the saving waters of Holy Baptism, now disclaiming any rights that God has on his life or disavowing any responsibilities he has toward God moves a parent close to uttering, "I could wish myself to be cut off. . . ." To agonize over the unknown whereabouts, geographical or spiritual, or both, of a daughter, who seventeen, nineteen, twenty-two years earlier used to "crash" through the family room singing, "Jesus loves me, this I know," and now is in the damning clutches of some Christ-mocking cult or sucked into the sewers of an intellectualism that has "outgrown" its need for a God, the very God who receives sinners and justifies penitents. Such agony undoubtedly brings that "great sorrow" and afflicts with that pain that never leaves."

But just as Luther spoke of the impossibility of Paul's potential prayer and another referred to it as "a crazy prayer," and even as Paul would not, could not bring himself to such praying, so also none of us dare ever come to such "craziness." Such an offer would not only be at the top of the list of ridiculousness, worse yet, it would be a Christ-denying action. It is Jesus Christ and Him alone who was asked by the Father to allow Himself to be "cut off" and "damned" for the sake of Jew and Gentile alike. It is Jesus Christ, and Him alone who willingly accepted the terrifying task of atonement and who asked in the darkness of Golgotha, "My God, My God, why hast Thou forsaken Me?" And it was of Jesus Christ, and of Him alone, that the answer to that question was given, because "God was in Christ making friends of all men through Christ . . ." (2 Cor. 5:19).

The "craziness" of such a potential prayer, the divine impossibility of such a "wise-offer" is only worsened if we are misled into thinking that the door of grace has now been closed to some.

II. The "Craziness" of Thinking That the Door of Grace Is Closed to Some

As is always the case in reading Holy Scripture, a section of God's Word dare never to be read in isolation or naked from its context. Such is true with our text. Our text is the opening of three chapters treating with the alleged failure (?) of God. Seemingly, all of God's laboring throughout the Old Testament era has failed! Time and again throughout the pages from Genesis through Malachi, God stated His "covenant." He gave and reiterated His "law." He manifested, with high regularity, His "glory." He was beautifully and majestically present at His "worship," Beginning with Abraham, He reminded them again and again of His "promises." How very, very often had He not told them that they were His "people"? And what was it that greeted His ears on that porch of Pilate? "Crucify Him! Crucify Him!"—and—"His blood be on us and on our children!"

Indeed, from an earthbound line of vision, listening to those catcalls from Calvary, viewing the vast rejections of Christ by the Jews, and agonizing over those gone AWOL from within His army of today, one is tempted to conclude that the plan of God has failed. But no sooner does Paul vantilate that possible allegation within the verses of our text, but that he immediately presses on and in the verses following our text states with the same confident boldness as was heard at the conclusion of chapter eight that God's plan has not, in fact, failed but is proceeding on schedule. Listen! "It doesn't mean God failed to do what He said. Not all who are descended from Israel are the real Israel, and not all who are descended from Abraham are for that reason His real children" (vs. 6-7).

The promise of salvation was and is made to the SPIRITUAL descendants of Abraham, but not the physical! The only thing that has failed as far as the "Jewish connection" is concerned is that the Jews have failed. They have failed to trust Him, into whose "family" they were called; trust Him, whose "glory" they saw; trust Him, whose "covenant" they affirmed; trust Him, to whose "Law" they said "Amen"; trust Him, at whose "worship" they bowed; trust Him, whose "promises" they were to accept. God's plan has not failed. They very opposite is true. Within these ninth, tenth, and eleventh chapters of his Epistle to the Romans, Paul speaks not of the eternal destiny of individuals but of the role of individuals within God's plan of salvation.

As far as the role of the Jews within that plan of salvation, Paul says: "Did they stumble, I ask, to be lost altogether? Certainly not! By their error salvation has come to the non-Jews . . . " (Rom. 11:11). And so, with this warning against the "craziness" of thinking that the door of grace is closed to some, we and the immediate hearers of Paul, the saints in that Roman parish, are cautioned against thinking that all is lost and useless and hopeless for the Jews. Rather, Paul concludes these three chapters by saying: "You see, God has put all people in a prison of disobedience *in order to be merciful to all*" (Rom. 11:32).

Paul knew that the door of grace was not closed to his "own flesh and blood." He, the great apostle and missionary to the Gentiles, says that one of the reasons why he works as hard as he does in bringing the gospel of Jesus Christ to the Gentiles is his hope to " . . . make my fellow Jews jealous and save some of them" (Rom. 11:14). In his missionary tactics and strategy, Paul "fleshed out" that statement. Almost without exception, upon arriving at a new town, he would immediately go to the local synagog to proclaim Jesus Christ and Him crucified, risen and coming again. What was his motive? To inflict beatings, stonings, and imprisonments upon himself and those laboring with him? Hardly! But, always and again, to invite and assure those Jews that the door of God's grace was open to them as it had been open to their fathers, Abraham, Isaac, and Jacob. No matter that beating, stoning, and imprisonments might result! Then it was on to the non-Jews with dual motivation: as missionary to the non-Jews with the gospel of Christ Jesus; as "flesh and blood" relative to the Jews with the same desire, " . . . to make my fellow Jews jealous and save some of them."

Our beloved Synod has recently affirmed the "craziness" of thinking that the door of grace is closed to some when, in solemn convention in 1977, we declared our God-directed intent to speak the Word of God's reconciliation to the contemporary descendants of Paul, the Jews of our day and age. This is not to be seen as "specialized evangelism" but rather an action done within the boundaries of apostolic action. Nor is this to say that we, as a Synod, have embarked upon something new in the evangelism thrusts of our church, as though witnessing to "the people of Israel" (*TLH* p. 13—The General Prayer) was novel or never done before. The now-sainted Francis Pieper said in his *Christian Dogmatics*, "It may be correct to say that since the first Pentecost proportionately as many Jews as Gentiles have been converted to Christ if we compare the relatively small number of Jews in the world with the great number of Gentiles" (Vol. III, p. 533).

But not just the Jews only! Indeed, it is "craziness," it is Scriptural insanity, to think that the door of grace is closed to some. So long as their hearts still beat, so long as their lungs still fill with the air of God's creation, so long as their brains are still functioning, and, of highest importance, so long as Jesus Christ is Lord— the door of grace is still open to all! Our's is not to wonder "how" or "why," nor is our's to plumb the pain of God in putting "all people in a prison of disobedience." Rather our's is to be the rejoicing in the fact that He has done all of this "in order to be merciful to all."

So, if we feel that "great sorrow," if we smart with that "pain," let us not think of praying a "crazy" prayer, but rather, learning from the mistakes of Elijah and Peter, keep our eyes on Jesus and lose not the courage that our faith in Him gives us to rejoice in the certainty of our salvation and, at the same time, to continue and increase in our efforts of calling out to others that the door of God's grace is still open to them.

A Special Word to Gentiles About Jews

THIRTEENTH SUNDAY AFTER PENTECOST
ROMANS 11:13-15; 29-32

Bruce J. Lieske

Frederick the Great, King of Prussia in the 18th century, once asked his court chaplain to give him a proof that God exists in one sentence. The chaplain said, "The Jews." Even though we may know very few Jewish people personally, we are aware that history and current events are filled with famous Jewish people. Among them are Felix Mendelssohn, the famous composer, Albert Einstein, the pioneer of the nuclear physics, and Doctors Salk and Sabin who gave the world the vaccines that have made it possible to eliminate the dread disease of polio. This tiny minority of people numbering only 14,000,000 in the world today continues to make history. Even in the world of entertainment in the United States, it is estimated that 80% of the professional comedians are Jewish.

Scripture itself indicates that a special identity is to be given to Jews. Paul says in our text, "Now I am speaking to you Gentiles," and then he goes on to speak about the Jews. God has indeed through His apostle given a special word to Gentiles about Jews.

The Paradox of the Jews

There is a striking paradox about the Jews that almost defies explanation. On the one hand they have experienced remarkable successes in the world, but on the other hand incredible failures. The Jewish doctors Salk and Sabin gave us polio vaccine, but Karl Marx gave the world the godless system of communism.

Our text speaks of "their rejection." At first we are puzzled by this expression. Does it mean that God has rejected the Jews? Or does it mean that the Jews—overall—have rejected something? It cannot mean that God has rejected the Jews, Israel, because He is faithful to His covenant with them. Through His covenant with Abraham, Isaac, and Jacob God made them a chosen people. The prophet, Jeremiah, spoke to the idolatrous and apostate Israel of his day.

> Thus says the Lord: "If the heavens above can be measured, and the foundations of the earth below can be explored, then will I cast off all the descendants of Israel for all that they have done, says the Lord" (Jer. 31:37).

Paul in Romans says: "I ask, then, has God rejected his people? By no means" (11:1). When our text speaks of "their rejection," it means that Israel has rejected their Savior, Jesus, not that God has rejected Israel. This does not mean that every Jewish person has rejected the Messiah, Jesus, but that *most have*. Here is a most amazing paradox. Jesus Christ is the best known person in the whole world, even among unbelievers. And Jesus is Jewish! The aged Simeon took the baby Jesus into his arms, blessed God, and said of Jesus that He was "for glory to thy people Israel" (Luke 2:32). What a paradox it is that most of the Jewish people reject Jesus as their Messiah! This rejection, this unbelief, is the great failure of Israel.

In the Bible the relationship between God and His people is frequently described as a marraige. God with His love courts mankind. I'm sure many of you can recall your own courtship. Perhaps the man was at first rejected, but he persisted in is attention and love, and finally the young lady of his intentions accepted his offer of marriage. Israel is like that. Israel has been rejecting the courtship of her Messiah, Jesus, for almost 2,000 years. But the Bible tells us that the time is coming when she will accept. Our text hints at this when it says, "For if their rejection means the reconciliation of the world, what will *their acceptance* mean but life from the dead?"

And this is what the prophet Hosea predicts:

> The children of Israel shall dwell many days without king or prince, without sacrifice or pillar, without ephod or teraphim. Afterward the children of Israel shall return and seek the Lord their God and David their king; and they shall come in fear to the Lord and to his goodness in the latter days (Hosea 3:4-5).

"David, their king" is Jesus, the descendant of David, the King of kings. We shall say something later about how this will happen, that Israel will come to accept Jesus as Savior. But let us turn our attention now to another paradox.

Jewish Unbelief Brought the Gospel to the Gentiles

The twelve apostles were all Jews, and the early Christian church in its formative years was largely Jewish. The apostle Paul, God's great missionary to the Gentiles, proudly tells us that he was "circumcised on the eighth day, of the people Israel, of the tribe of Benjamin, a Hebrew born of Hebrews" (Phil. 3:5). But the good news about Jesus, the Gospel, was meant for all people—Jew and Gentile alike! That is why Jesus told his Jewish apostles: "Go therefore and make disciples of *all* nations" (Matt. 28:19).

God has indeed given a special identity to the Jews, as a people, but when it comes to our personal problem with sin, and our relationship to God, there is no difference between Jew and Gentile. Paul says in Rom. 3:

> What then? Are we Jews any better off? No, not at all; for I have already charged that all men, both Jews and Greeks, are under the power of sin, as it is written: "None is righteous, no, not one." (Rom. 3:9).

"Not one!" The observant Jew, with his phylacteries and prayer shawl, praying in the synagog, eating only kosher food, regularly keeping the sabbath—is not righteous and therefore cannot approach the Almighty, or really know Him. The religious Gentile, with his generous tips to the waiter in the restaurant, small favors done to his neighbor, and kindness to his dog imagines that *he* is righteous. God's Word cuts through all our shallow imagined righteousness and speaks: "None is righteous, no, not one" (Rom. 3:9). There is no difference between Jew and Gentile "For God has consigned all men to disobedience, that he may have mercy upon all."

How disappointing it must have been to God that most of the Jewish people rejected the Savior. But he *used* that very rejection that he may have mercy upon all! Our text says "their rejection means the reconciliation of the world." Because Israel, the Jewish people, rejected the Gospel, then the emphasis turned towards presenting the Gospel to the Gentiles. We see that this is what happened in the ministry of St. Paul. In Rome he proclaimed Jesus as the Savior to his Jewish kinsmen. When most of them rejected Jesus he said: "Let it be known to you then that this salvation of God has been sent to the Gentiles; they will listen" (Acts 28:28). It was Jewish unbelief that caused the Gospel to go out to the Gentiles.

We said before that God has not given up on Israel, that He has not rejected them, that He continues to court them with His love. God is not pleased when men say "Judaism is the religion for Jews, and Christianity is the religion for Gentiles." Through his prophet Isaiah God speaks: "My house shall be called a house of prayer for all peoples" (Is. 56:7). The one God has one true religion for all peoples—Jew and Gentile alike. And God has not forgotten His people Israel, even though they have rejected Him. He has a way of courting them, of loving them, of winning them!

Gentiles Bring the Gospel Back to the Jews

Paul speaks to the Gentile Christian about the Jews when he says: "They have not been disobedient in order that by the mercy shown to you they also may receive mercy." God's plan is for the Gentile Christians to bring the Gospel back to the Jews.

You wonder how you can do that. You know that Jewish people resist attempts to convert them. Paul does not give up. He tells us: "I magnify my ministry in order to make my fellow Jews jealous, and thus save some of them." What is it that he did that made Jewish people jealous and caused some of them to believe in their Savior?

He lived in the reality of the cross! He knew that Jesus had died upon the cross for his sins. He knew that the cross was empty—that Jesus was not only raised from the dead, but *with him*. And Paul was not ashamed to speak of that cross, and of the living Lord Jesus to others. That is what we mean by living in the reality of the cross.

We have all heard people say ugly words in anger like, "God damn it," or even "God damn you." Perhaps we have even said those phrases ourselves, and broken the second commandment by using God's name in a vain and blasphemous way. When Jesus, the Son of God, died upon the cross, He was actually damned by God. He had to be damned by God in order to take upon Himself your sins. O how it bothers us when we are accused of doing something that we did not do, or when we have to suffer unjustly. We cry out, "Unfair!" We protest loudly. Yet Jesus was *damned* by God the Father, and he had done nothing except to love, to heal, to help other people. He had done no acts of violence. He had spoken no lies. Yet He did not cry out in protest—because He loved us. He was willing to bear our sins upon the cross. He was willing to be damned so that we would not be damned.

Because Jesus was damned in our stead, we do not have to live in fear of damnation. We know that our sins have already been punished. We cannot be punished for them again. We claim by faith what Jesus did for us, and it is ours! We are acquited by the Judge of the Universe in the heavenly courtroom.

The cross is empty. Jesus is risen. Where is He? He is with us, not visibly, but invisibly. Even though we—out of weakness—continue to sin, He still chooses to dwell with us. But as we become more and more aware of His presence, we become more and more like Him. Jesus loved sinners. He talked to them, he ate with them, he died for them. He did not judge them, or hate them, or talk about them behind their backs. As we become more and more like Jesus, we will be able to love sinners better—to stop judging them, to stop despising them, to stop talking about them behind their backs. And those sinners will sense that, and they will wonder why it is that we seem to love them better than they love themselves. They will want what you have. What is it that you have? You have Jesus! Perhaps one of those sinners may be a Jew.

Reach out to him in love. Tell him about that empty cross. Tell him about that long-promised Messiah. Let him have what you have. You, Gentile Christian, bring the good news of Jesus *back to the Jews*. Christians are not in agreement whether or not most of the Jews in the end times will accept Jesus as their Savior. But our text hints that it is possible, and Hosea says "the children of Israel

bodies as a living sacrifice, holy and acceptable to God, which is your spiritual worship."

Once you are right with God in Christ, once you are converted, once you are born again of water and of the Spirit, then you have the basis on which to act. "Present your bodies a living sacrifice." There is now an urgency that you do something, having become a believer in Christ. The policeman who was in crowd control at a very busy intersection approached some folks and said, "If you are going to stand around here, you just have to keep moving." When you become a believer in Jesus Christ, then you present your body, that is, your whole self, before the Lord and put it at His disposal.

There is some powerful, picturesque language used her in the term "living sacrifice." It does not speak as clearly to us in our culture as it did to the Jewish Christians who heard the apostle saying to them: For your worship is no longer the offering up of the life of another creature in sacrifice, such as the lamb, a dove, but it is the dedication of your life to God. This living sacrifice is called "spiritual worship." New Testament worship is a new living worship. Notice how the word "worship" is used here in the broad sense of the whole life, all of it, not just the time spent in private prayer, in Bible class, in the Sunday morning worship hour.

Let's take a look at the Sunday morning worship hour. What happens there? God comes to us in His word with His message of the Gospel that tells me that my sins are forgiven in Christ. God comes to us, and we respond to Him. This can be illustrated by two arrows—the first one pointing down (God comes to us) and the second alongside of it pointing up (our response) (⇕) . In the worship service we hear God in Word and Sacrament, and we respond to that with praise, petitions, thanksgiving, and our offerings. Now St. Paul tells us in our text that our whole life is a response to God's coming to us.

B. Is Expressed in the Renewal of the Mind

What does this mean, and how is this to be expressed? St. Paul continues in our Epistle lesson: "Do not be conformed to this world but be transformed by the renewal of your mind . . . " There is some powerful stuff here. With all the dynamic theology of the Epistle to the Romans as a background focusing on how we are justified before God by grace through faith in Christ, we are reminded that a person who experiences conversion is one who also experiences change. Paul specifically says that a converted person, one who has accepted the Christ who died for our sins and is now the resurrected living Lord, is a transformed person, therefore, be what you now are—live a changed life. Paul expressed the same thing in Eph. 5:10: "Walk as children of light . . . and try to learn what is pleasing to the Lord."

This does not happen by some magic process, some sudden stroke of the Holy Spirit with lights flashing and bells ringing. There is nothing mysterious here, for St. Paul tells us, "Be transformed by the renewal of your mind." This is a conscious, working, responsible action performed by the power of the Holy Spirit. The mind is not disengaged as though it were in some kind of neutral stage while the Holy Spirit works his miracle of faith. The apostle says that the mind is "renewed," made like new, for the new life in Christ comes from the Christ who died for us and rose again.

The renewed mind of the Christian is a valuable asset to the kingdom. It is a pity that the Christian church at times gives the impression that it has a low regard for cranial activity. In reality, the Holy Spirit gives man the capacity for expanded mental activity. Now we can have sanctified common sense and view life in all of its dimensions—physical, mental, and spiritual. The flatness is gone; it has depth.

Your Body Life Is in the Body of Christ

II. Body Life Is According to Faith

A. Faith Is Individual

The apostle continues his description of the new life of worship by pointing out that we are to live our life "each according to the measure of faith which God has assigned him." Faith is the basis for all activity. Of course, you remember that all faith is a saving faith, no matter how weak it is, and here the apostle uses the expression "measure of faith," and this refers to the functioning of our faith in service to others according to the gifts that God has given us. A little later on in v. 6 he speaks about us as "having gifts that differ according to the grace given to us." In 1 Cor. 12, we are reminded that God gives every person some gifts, but He "apportions to each one individually as He wills." The apostle is here emphasizing the variety of the gifts and places no value or prestige on any specific gift.

B. Faith Combats Pride

However, with the bestowal of these gifts comes a warning from the apostle: "I bid everyone of you not to think of himself more highly than he ought to think." Did you notice how this is addressed to "everyone." All need it. It is very easy for us to build a tower of pride on the talents or gifts that we possess. All of us are soloists by nature, but life is never an individual performance. Pride and self-centeredness is a constant danger. Perhaps you read about the prominent political leader in Washington, D.C., who was spending an evening at home and during the TV commercial turned to his wife and said, "My dear, do you know how many truly great men there are in the world today?" Without hesitation she responded, "No, I don't, but I do know there is one less than you think there is." Many of us have this problem of the ego. We think of ourselves more highly than we ought, and pious pride is the nastiest kind. History tells us that St. Paul wrote this epistle while he was living in Corinth, and he could speak from the background of personal experience in that congregation where individual gifts were misused for personal gain. That solo spirit was present in Corinth, and now he warns the Christians in Rome that life is not a solo sport, and there is more to it than the solo performances of tennis, golf, bowling; you soon run out of one-man performances.

C. By Faith We Are Members of One Body

1. We Have a Relationship One to Another

But how do you handle pride? God tells us through the apostle that we are to remember who we are now that we have been converted and renewed in our mind. Remember, you are a member of the body of Christ. "For as in one body we have many members, and all the members do not have the same function, so we, though many, are one body in Christ, and individually members one of another." The Scriptures use many pictures to describe the kingdom of God, the church, in its visible form here on earth. Here we are referred to as members of the body of which Christ is the head. Members have no life apart from the body. In Christ we are one organism, functioning on the basis of His life, and we are also to function as one unit with many members.

The picture of the church as the body of Christ shows us in some kind of relationship to one another, related in such a way that if any one of us was missing, then the body would be incomplete. This may sound a little too ideal to you, for it may appear that we are not such a unified body at times; we may look more like feuding clans than loving families. And while this may well be true, in spite of our ineptness at being the body of Christ, we are still the body of Christ because our Lord Jesus Christ has said so, and St. Paul reminds us of it again in the text when he specifically says, "So we, though many, are one body in Christ."

St. Paul had a rich background of experience with the congregation in Corinth on the bais of which he could write. That church in Corinth was really quite a church, they had Jews and Greeks, slaves and free people, rich folk and poor folk, people having trouble with their marriages, people going to court to sue one another, there were factions and quarrelings in the congregation. It has a somewhat familiar ring, doesn't it? Well, we have a broad cross section of people too. We have people of great faith, and we have people of a weak faith. Sometimes we Christians become so interested in our growth and developing and maturing in our Christian life and faith that we become impatient with the slow growers, the later bloomers. We express disapproval of those whose lives are less than what we think God expects them to be. Just because you yourself sometimes may be uncomfortable in the presence of the weaker Christian and may want to separate yourself from him, or you are faced with a Christian family that has so many complex problems and you feel so inadequate to help them that you simply want to run away and hide. Well, I know how you feel—because we have all been there at one time or another. We have all wanted to get away from it, to cut out, to simply split. But that solves nothing. You are a member of the body of Christ, and God wants you to fulfill your role and function in the body of Christ, particularly over against the other members of the body.

The emphasis in our congregation recently has been on our youth program as it relates to high school youth, college youth, and young adults. These young people are also members of the body of Christ, but you would hardly know that from the amount of attention that our church gives to them in terms of program and staff time. Sometime check and see what percentage of our budget is set aside for these members of the body of Christ. You almost get the impression that we think we can get along without one another. That's just the opposite of what St. Paul is talking about here in our text when he reminds us that we are members of one body. He expands upon that thought in his First Epistle to the Corinthians, chapter 12, where he reminds us that just to say that one is not a part of the body does not remove a person from being a part of the body, "If the ear should say, because I am not an eye I do not belong to the body, that would not make it any less a part of the body." He also reminds us that we cannot say that we have no need of a part of the body, "The eye cannot say to the hand, I have no need of you." And yet by our inaction in the area of our youth we are acting just exactly that way. We have been insensitive to the needs of these people.

Someone has likened people who remain insensitive to the needs of others to two shipwrecked men sitting together at one end of the lifeboat doing nothing. They watched intently as the people at the other end bailed furiously trying to keep the boat afloat. One man says to the other, "Thank God, that hold isn't in our end of the boat."

2. Each Member Has Distinct Gifts

This kind of insensitivity always leads to inaction. The fact is that each member of the body is unique, and the very uniqueness of each member ought to be appreciated by us. Remember, it is your differences, the thing that makes you different from the person sitting next to you, that is what makes you, you. The eye is unique, the ear is unique, and our feet are unique, and the unique arrangement of all these members with their distinctive gifts make it possible for each member to be of benefit and help to the other member. So God has given you gifts according to His grace; He has graced you with yourself, your age, your education, your experiences in life, your personality and He has fit you into the body. We need to appreciate this about ourselves and about others, and then we can begin to be sensitive to the needs of other members of the body.

In summary, then, we note that only the unique "you," with your special gifts, is able to meet the needs of your fellow members in the body of Christ. This is God's arrangement, and if you do not fulfill the purpose and role God has given you, no one else can take your place.

Our text speaks clear, strong language, and there is no room for the slush of sentimental love which promotes situation ethics and works to the hurt and harm of the church. Become what God intends for you as you accept the redeeming and living Christ in your heart by faith. We are always becoming what God has called us to be. You will find that your real life begins in the body of Christ, as you present your bodies as a living sacrifice, which is your spiritual worship.

The Christian and the State

SIXTEENTH SUNDAY AFTER PENTECOST
ROMANS 13:1-10

Elmer W. Matthias

Kurios Christos (Christ is Lord) was the creed of a group of people in the Roman Empire in the late first century A.D. This Christian group was far more politically concerned than its simple faith formula might suggest. They lived in a time and in a place where all loyal, patriotic citizens were required to assert once every year, "Kurios Caesar," which means "Caesar—the State—is Lord." So, when these Christians pronounced their creed, "Kurios Christos," they were not only saying "Christ is Lord," but they were also saying, "the State—Caesar—is not Lord." They were affirming what the Lord had told their Jewish forebears on Mount Sinai, "Thou shalt have no other Gods before me." We will have no other gods before the one true God.

St. Paul must have had something of this in mind when at the beginning of Romans 13, our text for today, he continues to describe the life of faith, which earlier he had described as true "spiritual worship" in which people presented their bodies to God as a "living sacrifice." Here Paul is not talking about relationships the Christians have to each other in the body of Christ, but their relationship to the environment. Now it would seem that there are aspects of this life which are not fit material for spiritual worship, too rough and stiff to weave into the seamless robe of the new life in Christ. It would also seem that the Roman government might be such an institution because it was completely identified with pagan worship and activity. To the Jews it was a revolting and abnormal thing for the chosen of God to live under Roman rule. After a fashion the Sadducees had come to terms—the Pharisees looked upon it as a judgment form God—the Zealots resisted and spoke the language of revolution. What was the new Israel, the renewed mind, the members of the body of Christ, what was this gorup to do? In the previous chapter, Paul had said: "Bless those who persecute you" (v. 14). "Repay no one evil for evil" (v. 17). And, again, "Avenge not yourselves" (v. 19), so violence and revolt were out of the question. Does this mean then that the Christian is simply to be neutral? Is he merely to express a resigned passivity? That is not sufficient. The Lord has something to say about that.

The Christian and the State

I. The Origin of the State

A. The State Exists by Divine Institution

Paul comes directly to the point. He calls for every individual to be subject to governing authorities, and not just because it is the prudent thing to do, but for religious reasons. "Let every person be subject to the governing authorities. For there is no authority except from God, those that exist have been instituted by God." That was a powerful challenge for the Christians of that day. In the verse prior to the beginning of our text St. Paul says, "Do not be overcome by evil, but overcome evil with good." You see, the Roman State had such a reputation for evil that it was very natural for Paul to switch from the topic of evil to the subject of the state. What makes this such a powerful challenge to the Christians is that in spite of all the evil trappings of this Roman government it still existed by divine right, and the citizen was not excused but was directed to be subject to that govenment. Paul told the Christians of that day and us that the source of authority for government comes from God. The governing authority that confronts us is His.

Paul hammers away at this by referring to God's ordinance and authority six times within seven verses; count them sometime this week.

B. Resistance to Government Is Impiety

There is the direct statement: "Therefore he who resists the authorities resist what God has appointed, and those who resist will incur judgment." Resistance to the state is impious. You may get away with it on the human level; you may not get caught; enforcement may be lax; but you never get away with it on the divine level. Disobedience does not come from faith, but our obedience is to be an expression of our faith in our Lord. In His Word we are given directives for our conduct also in relationship to the state. The question is: Are we listening? Do we say: "Speak, Lord, your servant is listening."

During World War II, the German government distributed to the people radio sets that would receive only the official Nazi stations, thus preventing them from hearing other versions of reality. We are to be like single station radio sets that are continually tuned in to the divine transmission of Scripture so that we can share in the blessing. But many of us are not receiving the complete transmission, and it is not because God is not sending the signals or that His signals are weak—they are strong and clear. But we frequently practice selective tuning, and God's message is either garbled or ignored.

However, for all of Paul's insistence on obedience to the state, remember that he is still saying all of this against the background of *Kurios Christos* (Christ is Lord). Under no circumstances are we ever to obey an edict of the state when it is in conflict with the law of our God. We owe Him primary allegiance in all circumstances and, in the power of the Spirit, stand ready to suffer all the consequences.

II. The Functions of the State

A. It Promotes the Good

Not only does St. Paul remind us here that the state exists by divine authority and institution, but he also points out by divine inspiration the function and purpose of the state. First of all, it is to promote the good. "Then do what is good, and you will receive his approval, for he is God's servant for your good." The state is always intended by God to be a blessing to the human family.

You can think of the state as an afterthought of God. It was not a part of His original plan of creation. There was no need for it until after the fall and sin, when God recognized that He would have to establish an authority which would now curb the base and evil inclinations of people. Some system needed to be developed to promote and encourage the good. Wicked and evil as the Roman state was, Paul still saw how God used its cumbersome machinery to protect him at various times as he made appeal to Roman authority.

B. It Curbs Evil

Not only does the state promote the good, but it curbs the evil. "For rulers are not a terror to good conduct, but to bad ... but if you do wrong, be afraid, for he does not bear the sword in vain; he is the servant of God to execute His wrath on the wrongdoers." The state bears the sword to execute God's wrath. Paul's use of the word "sword" gets its impetus and meaning from the fact that the Romans used the sword as the instrument of execution. It was a symbol of retributive justice. The right to inflict capital punishment was called "the right of the sword." This is God's annihilating reaction against those who spurn Him.

It remains the Christian citizen's responsibility to uphold the right of government to punish the evildoer. The relationship between crime and punishment is determined by the severity and enormity of the criminal act. Justice and fairness must prevail, and punishment must be in proportion to the evil done. When this is properly in balance, the power of the law as a curb to evil acts will be evident. Fair enforcements of the law with proper punishment builds fences of protection around the citizen.

III. The Christian's Response to the State

A. Obedience

The words, "Let every person be subject," were addressed to Christians of Paul's day and to us. In verse 6 Paul continues: "Therefore one must be subject, not only to avoid God's wrath but also for the sake of conscience." Obedience is the response of the Christian to the state. Obedience promotes the common good; it is the basis for a happy and productive life for us and for others around us. To be disobedient is disastrous.

Soren Kierkegaard, a 19th-century religious philosopher (some call him a theologian) disturbed the church leaders of his day when he vividly portrayed the disastrous consequences of not obeying the Lord's teachings. For example, he described the people who come to worship every Sunday as a gaggle of geese. They come to church, and they listen as one of the ganders gets up and preaches the sermon. (As Kierkegaard put it, he "preachifies" every Sunday.) This gander struts up front and preachifies to people about how much God loves them, and every time people hear this they bow their heads and do other pious things. And he goes on to say that the God who loves you so much has given you wings, and if you will practice and learn how to use them, these wings will make it possible for you to fly off to distant places. There you will fulfill the destiny of your being by becoming the totally beautiful creature you have been created to be. It is a moving and a thrilling sermon, but then Kierkegaard goes on to say that the geese all go waddling back

home to a big meal and sit around talking about what a great
sermon it was and how they intend to start using their wings "one
of these days."

He was right. We can identify with this. We say, "I've got to start
working on this." But nothing happens. We waddle in the next
Sunday, and we hear a sermon on the same theme, and we waddle
home again and talk about what a great sermon it was—Sunday
after Sunday we do this. And then Kierkegaard said we do this until
we get fat and juicy, and then we are slaughtered and sold by the
pound in the market place. Now, there is a part of us that says,
"What a clever story that is," but there is also a part of us that
squirms a bit because we know it strikes a little too close to home.
We know what our responsibilities over against the state are. Some
of the problems we have in government today exist only because
Christians have not acted upon their good intentions of getting
involved. How many more sermons are you going to have to hear on
the Christian's responsibility to government before you actually
respond?

B. Good Citizenship

Yes, good citizenship, involvement on our part is "not only to
avoid God's wrath but also for the sake of conscience." This is all
part of St. Paul's appeal at the beginning of the 12th chapter, "To
present your bodies as a living sacrifice, holy and acceptable to
God, which is your spiritual worship." There are no options here.
Being in Christ, a member of the body of Christ, we have a special
relationship to another one of God's institutions, the state.

Do you notice where Paul says that we are to present our bodies
"a living sacrifice," well, that is a possibility for us only because
Christ first sacrificed Himself for us. Christ came, He lived, He
died, He arose again and is our living Lord; all of this was done to
bring about the reconciliation of the human family to the heavenly
Father. Paul expressed it this way (2 Cor. 5:15), "Christ died for all
so that those who live might live no longer for themselves, but for
Him who for their sake died and was raised." Therefore, if anyone is
in Christ he is a new creation, and all this comes from God who
through Christ reconciled us to Himself and has given to us the
ministry of reconciliation. This makes us ambassadors for Christ,
God making His appeal through us (v. 17, 18, 20).

And now we entreat you not to accept the grace of God in vain, in
fact, in the issue that lies before us, our relationship to the state, we
are to remember that we receive the motivation and the power for
proper and responsible citizenship only from the presence of Christ
in our heart by faith. The love of Christ constrains us.

That is why Paul could say here: "For the same reason you also
pay taxes." When you pay taxes, you pay what is due by divine
right, but just payment is not enough. As redeemed children of God

we recognize the authorities as representatives of God, and you "pay all of them their dues . . . revenue to whom revenue is due, respect to whom respect is due, honor to whom honor is due."

C. Love Is the Governing Principle

Paul goes on to explain how it is possible for a Christian to express a right relationship to the state, even when the state is evil, simply because the believer has experienced the love of God in Christ. Paul had a deep awareness of personal sin and weakness, but he also had an almost overwhelming appreciation of God's forgiveness of that sin through Jesus Christ. This kind of love which Paul experienced from his heavenly Father enabled him also to show love to his fellowman. Therefore, he simply points out that for the Christian, love is the governing principle which guides him in all relationships, also to the state. Faith always works through love. You pay your debts, your dues, you give honor, but that is just the beginning—it is minimal. The Christian goes beyond the demands of the Law; he is interested in more than duty; his spiritual worship is a living sacrifice that is constant and continuing. So, you see, faith never destroys the Law, but upholds it, for when you love your neighbor with a constant love then the Law is fulfilled. In fact, the Law's deepest intention, as Jesus expressed it, is that man should love his God with all his might, and love his neighbor as himself.

"Love does no wrong to a neighbor; therefore love is the fulfilling of the Law." When, by the power of the Holy Spirit, you love your neighbor, then his marriage, his goods, his health, and welfare are as big a concern to you as your own are. When love lives and works the will of God, "what is good and acceptable and perfect" is done. Love, born of faith, puts it all together.

One rainy Sunday afternoon, a father was babysitting his children and had the task of keeping them entertained. He assigned specific tasks to each child. To keep his ten-year-old son busy, he had torn a full page map of the United States out of a magazine, cut it into small pieces, and told his son to reassemble it as a jigsaw puzzle. To the father's amazement, his son presented him with the completed puzzle in just a few minutes. "How did you do it, son?" he asked. "It was easy," the boy replied. "At first, when I tried to fit it together all those little lines and dots and the small print on the map, it looked like an impossible job. Then I saw part of a man's face on the back of one of the pieces. So I turned the pieces over, and when I got the man together, the United States took care of itself."

The sometime jigsaw puzzle of life makes sense, we get it all together, when we live our life against the background of Christ. That is, faith in Christ as Redeemer and Lord makes all the pieces fit. This is especially true in the complex and sometimes confusing area of the Christian's relationship to the state. Our faith in Christ sanctifies our understanding and enables us to see how good Christian citizenship is also to be an expression of our relationship to Jesus Christ.

Through Death, Christ Is Owner and Lord of Everything

SEVENTEENTH SUNDAY AFTER PENTECOST
ROMANS 14:5-9

John W. Saleska

The terrible temptation of strong-minded men is to despise the weak, to ridicule and hold in contempt the "less fortunate." Wherever this proud spirit prevails, class distinctions, endless friction, disharmony, and dissension inevitably occur. And even though we are aware that our inner drive to do this reaps these ugly results, nevertheless all of us having become very practiced at it, are hopelessly caught up in it. We Christians know that we are to love our neighbor as ourself, and yet we often segregate ourselves and behave as if somehow we are inherently better. In our day "self assertiveness" is encouraged. It means putting weaker people down and forcing them to listen to us. We do just that. Instead of loving and helping others, we hurt them. We enslave and destroy them. This "way of disorder" wends inevitably towards alienation and ends in the death of any genuine relationship.

The Way of Disorder

Both the text and context talk about this kind of behavior. In the first four verses of chapter 14 the apostle Paul speaks of our relationship with one another as Christians, and he states simply that we ought to accept one another. And that makes good sense. Of course we should. He also says that we should not judge one another in the everyday affairs of living—that is, in what we, or others, eat or do not eat, or in the days we observe, or do not observe in our everyday behavior (v. 5). Certainly we should not judge one another in such matters. After all, who are we to judge when we, ourselves, do not want to be judged? Our Lord Himself has warned, "Judge not, lest you be judged." (Matt. 7:1). To the Colossians Paul wrote that "nobody should say you are wrong (judge you) in what you eat or drink or do on a festival on the first of the month or on a Sabbath" (Col. 2:16).

Christians are free to make their own decisions about these

things (v. 5b). Why then do we look down our noses at believers who do not behave as we do? Why do we hold ourselves above, and why do we stand apart from people who are not as "pious" or as "holy" as we are? After all, the one who observes a special day honors the Lord in it. And when another eats, he gives thanks to the Lord for the meal, or in not eating he, nevertheless, remains grateful (v. 6).

When a man's conduct is viewed in that light, judgment is absolutely forbidden. So why in the face of a direct command not to, do we do it anyway? Why are we constantly busy at it (context, vs. 10-13)? Isn't it because, as the Deceiver suggested to Eve, "our eyes have been opened to know what is right and wrong, good and evil?" Consequently, men should listen to *us*, shouldn't they? Let *us* lead them? Let *us* determine behavior as we pull the strings to make the puppets dance, or push the buttons to make things come out the way we have them programed. After all, why did God choose us if not for our inherent superiority?

You can almost hear the snake, can't you? "You can be like God" (Gen. 3:5). Man is curved in on himself. In all of this we can see how hopelessly self-centered we really are. How utterly and incurably judgmental. Luther even had a Latin phrase for it: In *curvatus in se*. The noted psychologist, Alfred Adler, called the drive for superiority over others *will to power*. We enslave people by demanding that they hear us and do as we say. We do this over God's own strenuous objections in both the text and context that we not "judge down" our brother and make him subject to our opinions. We are not to practice this kind of "mind control" over those who are weaker than we are. We are not to mold and shape men, to make them over into our image. Men are free to make their own decisions in these matters. "Let every man be fully persuaded in his own mind" (v. 5). All of us, finally, will stand before God's judgment seat and give an account of himself. No one, regardless of his condition or position, escapes. Infants and kings alike stand on equal ground there (context, vs. 10-12). So, then, who are we to judge others?

How can we hope to extract ourselves from this inordinate desire to take God's place as judge and to enslave men and rule their consciences—when this is not only what we do, but how we are? Paul answers that in the text: "For none of us liveth to himself, and no man dieth to himself" (v. 7). In saying that, he eliminates even the faintest notion of a life lived independent of God, or others, and for self only. "A fool says in his heart, there is not God." That is: "Nobody will ever know." No one lives or dies alone. The text and context have clearly established that we are responsible people. "For whether we live, we live unto the Lord; and whether we die, we die unto the Lord: whether we live, therefore, or die, we are the Lord's."

God Owns Us

We may no longer behave as if no one knows or cares. We are someone else's property. We belong to another, whose ownership is timeless: *"Living or dying, we are the Lord's."* He owns *us*. Now there's a thought to make one sit up and take notice, and it could strike terror to our hearts. After all, the One to whom we belong and whose we are may very well demand an accounting of *us*. If we don't measure up, then what? And the text says that living or dying, it makes no difference, we are His. There's no escape from this owner, even our most anxious thoughts about the disposition of the owner towards us are completely, everlastingly allayed when Paul intones the highest note of all Scripture and all theology as he signs: "for *to this end* (for this purpose) Christ died and lived, *that* He might be Lord both of the dead and the living" (v. 9).

That verse (9) clearly indicates that the purpose of Christ's death and resurrection was to establish, once and for all, His Lordship over everything. "For Christ died and rose to life *in order to be* the Lord of the living and of the dead." The goal of the cross and Joseph's Garden was that Christ finally and forever would rule everywhere, as King of kings and Lord of lords. His is a universal dominion. This is precisely Paul's message in Philippians also (2:5 ff), where he says that Christ left everything behind and became not only a human being, but a servant besides; and then humbled Himself and became obedient to death on a cross. Then comes this startling assertion: "Wherefore [that is why] God hath highly exalted Him, and given Him a name which is above every name; that at the name of Jesus every knee should bow, of things in heaven and things in earth and things under the earth; and that every tongue should confess that Jesus Christ is Lord, to the glory of God the Father."

This passage, paired with the statement in verse 9 of the text which says that Christ died and rose *that* He might be Lord both of the dead and living, fixes forever the cause of Christ's glorious reign over all things. Atoms and molecules in the physical world, angels and men in heaven and on earth, as well as the devil and his hosts in the underworld, acknowledge the victory by which He has subdued all things unto Himself. After He was *risen from the dead,* He said: "I have been given all power in heaven and on earth." His death on the cross is the most profound event in all of human history, and nothing in the entire expanse of the created universe can cloud its brilliance. "Through the Son, then, God decided to bring the whole universe back to Himself. God made peace through His Son's death on the cross, and so brought back to Himself all things, both on earth and in heaven" (Col. 1:20 TEV). He died and rose *in order that* He might be Lord everywhere, over everyone—the "living" as well as the "dead" (text v. 9). Through death, Christ is Lord.

God Owns Everything

It is clear, then, that God made peace with an alien dying world through His Son's death on the cross, and in this way restored *everything* to its rightful place, under the Son. The cross touches *all things*. The shadow of the cross invades every domain. Nothing, absolutely nothing, is exempt. No wonder Paul says to the Corinthians: "For I determined not to know anything among you, save Jesus Christ, and Him crucified" (1 Cor. 2:2). And to the Galatians: "God forbid that I should glory, save in the cross of my Lord, Jesus Christ ... " (Gal. 6:14). The cross of Christ is the beacon whose rays sweep into the farthest reaches of heaven and earth and throughout all time and eternity. Christ is the *very God* who is from everlasting and to everlasting, whose glory even the heavens declare, and it is at Calvary that we are brought face to face with such unspeakable glory that with the angels we lower our gaze in wonderment at that bright mystery. This is how and where *everything* is turned "right-side-up."

What Christ did, in a sense, was to stand in front of a speeding train as it hurtled down the tracks toward us and absorb the impact, so that it would not crush us, even though it killed Him. What a marvelous thing to do for another person! To stand there and take those devastating effects (when that is the punishment which we really should have received) defies comprehension. However, that is what He did to save us, and that is why God has highly exalted Him and given Him a name that is above every name. Through the cross, Christ reigns everywhere. of course! He deserves it! All the honor, all the glory, all the power belong to Him. "For to this end Christ died and rose ... " "That at the name of Jesus every knew *should* bow, of things in heaven and things in earth and things under the earth." The text sums it up simply by declaring that Christ died and rose *that* He might be Lord both of the dead and of the living (v. 9).

The story is told of the lad who spent literally a lifetime constructing a replica of a ship he had once seen docked in the harbor near his home. Every sail was intricately cut and sewn exactly to scale and perfectly placed; and every plank was carved and then fastened precisely as it should have been. Finally the time came for the grand launching on a small creek just the right size for such a small craft. During the first moments the ship slid gracefully over the water and rode the slow current the way a finely crafted vessel should. But then without warning the current quickened and suddenly the improbably happened. A gust of wind caught the sails and the ship darted completely out of reach, and in a few more moments bobbed out of sight in the widening stream. The boy was

crushed at this unbelieveable turn of events. All those hours, and
all that work, lost, gone, it seemed, for good! He was heartbroken—
disconsolate. How could this have happened?

But then, some months later he spotted it, in the window of a
hobby shop, his ship! The very ship he had fashioned so pain-
stakingly. And it was for sale. The price was steep, and even though
it belonged to him already, he was still ready to pay anything to get
it back. To him it was a "pearl of great price." So he scraped
together every last penny and bought it. It was his again. And this
time it would not get away.

The whole world is God's by right of creation. He built it, and it
was "very good," precisely as He wanted it. It is also His by right of
"purchase." He bought it! It is His twice, all of it, including you and
me. We belong to Him. We are the property of the Eternal. We are
not even our own. The effect of Christ's death is that we are
redeemed from death and slavery. "He purchased and won me from
all sin, form death and from the power of the devil, not with gold or
silver, but with His holy precious blood, and with His innocent
suffering and death." Why? What was His purpose in this? "That I
might be His own, and live under Him in His kingdom, and serve
Him in everlasting righteousness, innocence, and blessedness."
Paul says to the Corinthians: "For ye are bought with a price:
therefore (for that reason) glorify God in your body and in your
spirit, which are God's" (1 Cor. 6:20). " . . . He died for all that they
which live should not henceforth live unto themselves but unto Him
which died for them and rose again" (2 Cor. 5:15). He died and rose,
not to force us to obey and serve Him; but by such remarkable
service to free us to really serve God and our neighbor, as the whole
text instructs us.

The perfect ransom price for everything has been paid by the
One who is Lord of life and death. When Christ shouted from the
cross: "It is finished!" it really was finished. God could do nothing
more than that for dying sinners. With that one mighty shout, the
walls of the enemy's stronghold crumbled and fell. Prison gates
sprang open, and men walked out into the dazzling sunlight, *free.*
The text says again: "*For to this end,* Christ died, and rose, and
revived, that He might be Lord both of the dead and living." He is
Lord everywhere! The Philippians text (above) says that because of
Christ's death on the cross, at His name, "every knee should bow, of
things in heaven, and things in earth, and things under the earth."
Under the earth! The underworld is also subject to Him. That is why
Christ preached to the spirits in prison (1 Pet. 3:19). He delivered us
from the devil's power to accuse, and "He made a show of them
openly." The Good News Bible translates Col. 2:15 like this: "And
on that cross Christ freed Himself from the power of the spiritual
rulers and authorities; He made a public spectacle of them by

leading them as captives in His victory procession." His victory makes Him Lord everywhere. The devil and his legions are a laughing stock. Christ is the conqueror of death. "For *to this end* Christ died and lived again. . . . "

God Over Us and in Us

So, who can accuse us? Obviously no one, because Christ is on His throne; and everyone and everything answers to Him. He is Lord of the living and of the dead. Paul exults: "Who shall bring any charge against God's elect? It is God who justifies; who is to condemn? It is Christ Jesus who *died;* yes, who was *raised from the dead,* who is at the right hand of God, who indeed intercedes for us" (Rom. 8:33-34). For His sake alone the heavenly Father fully and freely forgives everything. Even though our wicked hearts condemn us, and the whole catalog of the sins which we have committed looms in front of us in all their frightening and hideous reality, we are nevertheless free because of what Christ has done in His death and resurrection.

In view of all that God has done, how are we now to live our daily lives? Are certain foods and beverages forbidden? How are we to view the behavior of our fellowmen in their day-to-day living? Paul answers, "Let every man be fully persuaded in his own mind." Here he is expressing the great principle of liberty of conscience. We are no longer in captivity. We have been freed from the alien powers that once ruled us. The cross is God's declaration of independence, and it is there that we live our lives with respect to everything in *God's good* creation. And it is there that we receive the power to honor and be patient with others. The strong person, rather than ridiculing his weak brother, can now bear with him. He is now willing not only to surrender what he eats or drinks, but also any other permissable behavior in order to hold up and not injure the more fragile fellow-redeemed. This is really the beginning of loving my neighbor as myself. The Spirit of Christ is to seek the welfare of the weaker. I am my brother's keeper—as Christ was and is. Now that the mote has been removed from my eye, the beam in my brother's eye seems so much smaller. How petty the differences that once divided us. It is clear now that we are not enemies but friends. Christ has called us that—His friends and therein friends of one another. The text says that not one of us lives for himself. Paul makes the same point in Philippians (2:3-4): "Do nothing from selfishness or conceit, but in humility, count others better than yourselves. Let each of you look not only to his own interests, but also to the interests of others." And in Romans he says, "But we who are strong must be patient with the weaknesses of the weak and not just please ourselves. Everyone of us should please his neighbor for his good, to help him grow" (Rom. 15:1-2).

Finally since judgment for every single failure has already taken place on the cross—in the death of the Lord of all, can we continue to judge others and try to get them to submit to us? To live as we think they should live? To enslave and burden them? To "Lord it over them?" Never! Especially not now since we have come to know the disorder, discord, and death that self-serving spirit brings! Christ came *"not to be ministered unto,* but to *minister* and *to give His life* a ransom for many." Our Lord has not merely given us an *example* that we should do as He has done to us; but He has also brought with Him the *power* to begin to love as He loved, to minister as He ministered, to care as He cared, to bear as He bore, and if we know these things, happy are we if we do them. That's the only way to "live and let live." That's living as our Lord lived and ministered, by giving instead of saving self. We now live to free people as we have been freed. Our lives are then the victorious lives of those who have conquered death through Him, who because of His death, is Lord of all the living and the dead. To Him be glory and dominion forever and ever.

"Christ" Means to Be Alive, Free, and Together

EIGHTEENTH SUNDAY AFTER PENTECOST
PHILIPPIANS 1:1-5, 19-27

John W. Saleska

Paul pens these words in a prison cell, and yet it is obvious that he is not a prisoner. His thoughts are not at all centered on his condition. He is not in the least wrapped up in his own whereabouts. His eyes are focused outside the cell on the one who has set him free. It is Christ who is in his heart and mind as he writes this letter. The Christ about whom he had written, "For of Him and to Him and through Him are all things: to whom be glory forever. Amen" (Rom. 11:36). It is with such a bold thought in mind, and on that lofty note, that the whole thanksgiving theme of this text commences. Paul is thankful that God had also given the Philippians eyes to look through the bars and view Paul's Christ and the new life of freedom to which He called them. For Paul there is nothing else, everything in heaven and on earth begins and ends with Christ. The theme of his whole life is there in verse 21 of the text: "For me to live is Christ . . . " (v. 21).

Freedom

This was not the first time the Philippians had heard him. A jailer and his family remembered that chilling midnight scene—when the earth trembled, as the God of Paul's prayers shook open prison gates and snapped iron chains—and desperate, despised men walked free. The passing years did not change Paul. His prayers are still for these same people as they were then. "I thank my God upon every remembrance of you, always in every prayer of mine for you all making request with joy, for your fellowship in the Gospel from the first day until now." "Fellowship"—this was a community. They were partners, Paul and the Philippians; and the common interest they shared from the beginning was Christ. His was the joyous free "life" they now lived, bundled together with Him, the Lord, and all those who are alone among the "living." At the heart of this body was the one who holds everything together. Only the "living" can pray and sing joyfully and thankfully with the poet: "Salvation unto us has come; by God's *free grace* and favor."

Paul had, it seems, simply appeared in Philippi carrying this "free grace" in his body, as a gift to these foreigners. And, all of a sudden they were really alive, and life took on new meaning. Now there was a fellowship. Now Paul and these people were bonded together, and they would not be wedged apart. They would let nothing and no one come between them. It was as if they had known him all along, although they had just met him. And after they had met him, they could never forget him; nor he them. No mere human community could ever have offered the concern, the love, the tenderness that this one did. This was how people should really treat people. This is the behavior of men who have been rescued form a common enemy; who have been saved alive from the lion's den, and whose only joy is in reminding one another and telling others of that Strong One who stopped the lion's mouth. They were really one, with an eye out for each other, and Paul is anxious that they continue to "stand fast in one spirit, with one mind striving together for the faith of the Gospel" (v. 27). They were now driven with one holy purpose—to publish the Good News of this "free life" to men bound to die. "Every time I pray for all of you, I always do it with joy because you have shared in telling the Good News from the first day until now" (v. 5).

One verse in the context (v. 6) clarifies completely all of Paul's and the Philippians' inner impulses for this joint life. That is, his thankfulness for them, his joyful requests, their fellowship in the Gospel. In verse 6 Paul states that he is certain of this, that the God who had begun the "good work" in them would continue it until the day of Jesus Christ. It was that "good work" which energized this fellowship. And although as Paul says it had a beginning *in them*, for its real beginning we need to look beyond time and fasten our gaze on eternity. The "good work" that Paul mentions in verse 6 is timeless. He is talking about the Gospel which they shared, and it is the "everlasting Gospel" (Rev. 14:6). This is really the "work" of the eternal Son of the Father. It was that very "work" which inspired the psalmist to write, "O, give thanks unto the Lord, for He is good: for His mercy endureth forever" (Ps. 136:1). It was this Good News which created the community of freed men in Philippi; this was the glue that held the fellowship together. It was that "good work" of Christ which was in all of Paul's preaching and which ties into, and is responsible for, everything that follows in the text.

Paul could not have breathed one prayer, he could not have talked about living or dying as he did; and he could not have scratched out one word on that parchment in front of him about confidence in the future, without that "good work," the Gospel, in which he and the Philippians and all of us are free and alive together (v. 5). That "good work" was finished outside of him and all of us in eternity. The Good News which Paul and the Philippians shared was of the "Lamb of God which takes away the sin of the world" (John 1:29), of "the Lamb *slain* from the foundation of the world" (Rev. 13:8), who stepped into time and fulfilled *God's promises* by taking our death and imprisonment on Himself.

We too often live as if our final sentence is death—as if sin, death, and hell have won out. As if in this life there is no hope, suffocating in a cell from which no one escapes. Even to us darkness, pain, and death seem to have prevailed. "We're all dead men" is our plaintive cry. We act as if we have been left completely alone. We too often foolishly trust our own strength in our struggle to break free. And we finally find ourselves with the world calling out: "Who will bring us out of this disease-infested dungeon to freedom and new life?" This is exactly the scene Paul saw from his prison cell in Philippi and announced that he had the "key". The "key" God had given him would open the door to liberty and life for all men everywhere. He sang from his cell of the Christ who opens prison gates and ushers men into a new world of light and life. No matter how desperate our circumstances, no matter how evil the demons that strike terror to our hearts, no matter how dark the thoughts form our seamy past that rise up to haunt us, no matter how intense the pain in our disease-ridden bodies, no matter how exasperating the problems at home or work, the "news" that Paul carried to the Philippians and which he brings to you and me is everlastingly good. We need no longer cower and cringe in the face of any of life's worst moments, and even death itself. Christ took on all our foes and defeated them, especially that last one when He rose to life. So for Paul and the Philippians, and for you and me— "to live, is *Chirst,* and to die is gain." *To be with* that Christ is certainly *far better.*

This Gospel (v. 5) is the treasure which Paul carried about with him in his dying body, that house of clay, that he was not at all afraid to move out of (v. 23). It was that very *Good News*, the death of God for a dying world, that calmed Paul's quickened pulse in the face of death's awful darkness. This was the message, the Good News of a new creation, of a Kingdom in which the King himself, died fighting to free his subjects, that the dusty stranger shared with Lydia and the jailor and finally all the others. To them it had been like the announcement of a last minute pardon as they were being led to the gallows, and it was simply too good to be true! And so they sang with the poet: "He breaks the power of cancelled sin. He sets the prisoner free." It was the news of that Kingdom in which men could live in happy harmony and breath freely that Paul spoke; and in that Kingdom both he and the Philippians, living or dying, rejoiced. "Living or dying," either way, it was theirs already. If a man is fighting for every breath and a physician administers an injection that makes him breathe easier, he immediately heaves a sigh of relief. This is what Paul's gospel did. The forgiveness of sins makes men breath again.

Life

In Philippi as also among us the Good News created a living, breathing body of freed men happy to help one another grow in and glorify the Christ who breathed His very own life unto them. This "good work" which God had begun in the Philippians Paul was confident He would finish, since he, God, not only had a panoramic view which permitted Him to see everything from beginning to end, but also the strength necessary to bring it to a successful conclusion. God Himself had begun it, and He could be counted on to finish it. This sublime reality of the full scope of this work of Christ so touched C. F. W. Walther (first president of the Missouri Synod) that he was moved to exclaim: "In view of this, are we not blessed, highly favored men? Our bliss beggars description. Heaven and earth are full of the goodness and grace of the Lord our God. Anywhere and everywhere all things cry to us: You are redeemed; your sins are forgiven; heaven is thrown open to you. Oh believe it, do believe it, and you have this bliss" (*Law and Gospel*, p. 180).

And so Paul too is taken by it completely, fully expecting everything "to turn out victoriously for him" (v. 19). We are left breathless too. And why not? After what God has done. If God "spared not His own Son, but delivered Him up for us all, how shall He not with Him also freely give us all things?" Which means simply that if God would do that "good work," which He, in fact, has done, then certainly He will also see to it that all our little earthly needs are more than met. In the final analysis, the forgiveness of sins brings with it everything else too. "All things are yours" (1 Cor. 3:21). From that verse Luther concluded, and so can we, that the believer possesses with Christ, all things. This was why Paul could be so bold in everything. He knew now that his God could be trusted to supply everything, including, of course, the faith to perservere, to go right on believing to the end. Obviously, Paul could then confidently look into the future, and even stare death in the face, because he knew that the shackles of death which held him securely had been broken in Christ's resurrection. Even though Paul does not mention the resurrection, nevertheless he is talking about it. Listen to him: He does not know whether it would be better for him to stay or to go to be "with Christ," which is far better (vs. 22-23). It is obvious that Paul believes Christ is alive, has prepared a place for him; and since it is already prepared, it is there waiting for him, and Paul is ready to "break free" and move in permanently. The promises Paul trusted are ours too. In Christ everything is sure for you and me.

But, of course, with this reservation: "Thy will be done." That is the spirit of Christ in Paul (v. 19), which says that if it is more important in God's economy that I stay here for a time, then well and good. I will be happy to stay to proclaim the faith, and so help the Philippians grow and rejoice in it. In either case, staying or leaving, I win. The victory has already been achieved and proclaimed. "Death is destroyed; victory is complete, Where, oh death, is your victory? Where, oh death, is your power to hurt? Death gets its power to hurt from sin, and sin gets its power from the Law. But thanks be to God who gives us the victory through our Lord, Jesus Christ" (1 Cor. 15:54b-57)! In the above passage, as well as in the text, Paul is like the baseball fan whose favorite player has just hit a ninth-inning, bases-loaded home run to win the game. He jumps up in joy shouting, "We won!" even though another really did it. The happy effects of the victory leave nothing in Paul's existence untouched. "For me to live is Christ, and to die is gain." By nature Paul was like us, a prisoner to self, selfish, self-seeking, self-centered—completely unable to "leave self behind." But the self-ishness of Christ, Himself literally leaving everything to become one of us, to absorb into His very person our punishment, and to free us so captivated Paul that he surrendered all in order to receive with Christ everything. "Love so amazing, so divine, demands my soul, my life, my all." "The gain of this One Thing all loss can requite..." This *One thing* is God's gift of freedom and life to you and me.

Together

When Paul says finally, "But live as citizens worthy of the good news of Christ..." (v. 27), the natural response is, "Well, after what He has done, who wouldn't want to? Who wouldn't gladly serve a King Who would do what this one has done for His subjects?" This kingdom is unlike any other. Earthly rulers force their subjects to serve. But the Spirit that moves men in this Kingdom is a freeing Spirit that makes men willing and ready to do the will of Another, joined together with, and alive to the needs of others—feeding the hungry, clothing the naked, visiting the prisoner. The gracious words that flowed from His lips, "Son, thy sins be forgiven thee," are words that transform angry rebels who deserve the death sentence into happy friends, willing to "live under Him in His kingdom, and *serve Him* in everlasting righteousness, innocence, and blessedness." "Inasmuch as ye have done it unto one of the least of these My brethren, ye have done it unto *Me*."

So with the Philippians we want to share the Good News that the ruler of darkness, prison, and death has been finally and forever defeated. The one whose hideous wickedness has twisted everything in the world out of shape has been uncovered and his cruel tyranny revealed. Let the hosts of hell rage, they no longer rule anywhere. Another Spirit reigns! Death itself has been destroyed. Every enemy has been defeated. Together we are a nation—the King's sons and daughters who have left the land of slavery and death, passing into freedom and life through the waters in which all of our enemies have been drowned. We are branded "new people" whose lives are a witness of the very "life" of our Leader, and with Paul we carry this "life" with us in our dying bodies. And as the Philippians were happy in their living to "follow the Leader," whether Paul or anyone else was there to watch them (v. 27), so we too now gladly live for Him who has given us freedom and life. This Lord of life and death, who is King of kings, is coming again to take us, as he did Paul, to live together with all pardoned people forever free in the mansions He has made ready for us—and us for them. "Oh, that we were there!"

A Better Way—the Way of Humility

NINETEENTH SUNDAY AFTER PENTECOST
PHILIPPIANS 2:1-5 (6-11)

Paul J. Foust

In these very precious verses of Philippians 2, God is speaking to us on a subject which is not popular. The subject is submission. Who likes to submit? Who wants to be a slave to someone else? The unregenerate world glorifies the man who gives the orders or elevates the champion, it may even picture submission as a weakness. We live in a climate where submission is not really seen as something great!

There is a very understandable reason for this. Ever since that tragedy in the garden of Eden, fallen man has been on an ego trip. Those first two human creatures of God, who were given so much by Him, began to see themselves as little gods! Should they really take orders from the One who put this all together? Should the Lord of all be the Lord, or should they assume this lordship? Did He really have the moral right to guide their lives in His way? Their decision to disobey put them on a course of lording their own life. Submission was lost, and tragedy broke loose! Someone said, "pride is a disease, which makes everyone sick except the one who has it!" The proud man gloats in it and doesn't know the difference.

When this text leads Christians into the path of humility, this may not be popular in a degenerate world, but this is God's way, and it's a better way! May the Spirit of God open our eyes to see and our hearts to accept God's way as we consider the theme:

A Better Way—the Way of Humility

This charming exhortation to humility begins by speaking to Christians. They are the only ones who can understand this kind of language. They have eyes of faith to see things no one else can see. The verse says we who are "in Christ" find strength and comfort in His "agape-love." The word "agape" is a special Greek word for love which is used in the Scriptures when referring to a very special love. It is a love which God has and which He transmits to Christians.

The Better Way Is Rooted in Christ

Here are the footings of this whole concept of humility. There are several levels of love mentioned in the Bible. "Agape-love" is much bigger than the "philos-love" which unregenerate people can have for each other. "Agape-love" is deeper than the "eros-love" which husbands and wives can have for each other. "Agape-love" is the love God has for a whole world of people who had all gone astray but who He, nevertheless, wants back. God loves those who do not deserve to be loved. God loves people no matter how low they have fallen. God loves them anyway! Consequently, His love provided a plan by which everyone could come back. It was a great plan of submission. God's own Son would humble Himself even to the cross to pay the whole price of all sins. His love would hold out pardon to all and plead for a world of lost sinners to come home and be "washed in the blood of the Lamb." In fact, He would draw them back by filling them with this "agape-love" and activating them into a beautiful life of submission.

There is indeed great strength and comfort in this marvelous plan of God. A proud unbelieving world may struggle to come back by themselves, but our salvation is not based on something we have produced with our imperfect sin-infected lives. We are completely incapable of earning our own way back! The Bible says "by the deeds of the Law there shall no flesh be justified." Our salvation is based solely on what Jesus, the perfect Son of God, did for us. Our strength is in Him; we have a sure comfort that eternity cannot condemn what God's Son has already forgiven. This is my great "consolation in Christ"; this is that great "comfort of love." This is the very basis of humility: *He did what I could not do!*

The Better Way Has Fellowship with the Spirit

In this first verse of the text we progress immediately from Jesus and His redeeming love to the "fellowship of the Spirit." One of the beautiful things about the Christian life is that God did not pay the price and then abandon us! God was concerned that those who are bought back should also be drawn back and enjoy a new life, become new creatures; as He said in the Gospel of John, live the "abundant life."

This is why He provided what we call "the means of grace." Through His Word and Sacrament the Holy Spirit would invade our lives and take up residence there, and we would become "temples of the Holy Ghost." This "fellowship of the Spirit" becomes more than a theological cliche. The Holy Spirit enters us and binds us together in a great mission of living for our Lord. We are one in the Spirit! Rebellious ego trips manifest the old Adam still struggling within us, but submission to our Savior is evidence of the Spirit of God at work within us. Paul referred to this frustrating struggle when he said "The god that I would I do not, but the evil which I would not that I do." He also affirmed, "The fruit of the Spirit is love, joy, peace," etc. This influence of God's indwelling Spirit builds a better way! Christians do not rebuild their own life; the Spirit of God does! Give Him the credit. This is humility!

The Better Way Loves People Through Us

Verse one reaches a climax as it speaks of this life with Jesus, which is filled with the Spirit of God, by indicating a wholesome effect in our lives. Instead of being self-centered, Christians become people-centered. Affection and compassion flows from these new creatures. "Agape-love" cannot be dormant. It activates my life. I am caught up in this love of God for people. This kind of love reaches out to other lives; cares about them; sees their needs; expresses by words and deeds a benevolence which the world needs. This is the beautiful progression of the Christian life. The Epistle of John says "Whoso hath this world's goods and seeth his brother have need and shutteth up his bowels of compassion from him, how dwelleth the love of God in him."

There are so many needs in this sin-depraved world. There is sickness, hunger, hurts. There are deprived, disadvantaged, and disabled people. These are all temporary needs, but an earthly life is a long time. These are people who need affection and compassion. Add to this the eternal problems of those who are alienated from the God who made and wants them back. These have even a greater need for affection and compassion!

No wonder the church, the corporate assembly of people, who have agape-love, who have fellowship with the Spirit, have established hospitals, ministries to blind, deaf, mentally ill, orphaned, aged, and counseling for people in any kind of trouble. No wonder we send missionaries to the most remote parts of the world. This is all a manifestation of "affection and compassion."

Let Christians everywhere gladly support all these ministries of mercy to hurting bodies and empty souls. This is all a part of the new life, of the better way; that way of humility which sees others and responds to their needs instead of living for self.

St. Paul lays bare his pastoral heart in verse two when he speaks of his great joy in seeing these Christian lives mature. Paul says, "fulfill ye my joy." Every pastor is highly pleased when such beautiful lives blossom in his parish. This is what the Christian ministry is all about! Lives anchored in Jesus, full of the Spirit and reaching out to love people—and love them with an everlasting love. This is when "agape-love" has accomplished its goal. The target of God's love is people back where they belong, living for Him who lived and died and rose again for them!

The Better Way Unifies Christians in one Mission

Besides the joy which Paul experiences, he also sees the church, the body of Christ, cemented together by all this in a single-mindedness. The mission of the church is clear. The purpose is unclouded. The love of Christ is being delivered. Lost lives are being found and given meaning.

Let congregations which are torn by strife, where individuals are on ego trips and where segments of the church are driven by parochial ambitions or hovering around questionable goals, re-examine their mission! Are they really motivated by the love of Christ? Are they living in this fellowship of the Spirit? Are they bent on an affectionate and compassionate mission which cannot rest until lives are touched and lifted and activated by the eternal love of Jesus?

If you find that your church is not united, that it is torn by disunity, that your strengths are invested in fighting with each other rather than fighting your real enemy, the devil and his forces, you may well find verses 3-4 helpful. Here our Lord is aiming squarely at that same old ugly pride which raised its head in Eden and has caused trouble ever since! "Do nothing from selfishness." Is the better way the way of selfishness or the way of humility?

When individuals are determined to elevate themselves, when the church is dominated by people on ego trips, the Lord of the church is dethroned in favor of little human lords, and the church is fragmented. This is when pride takes over; the humility of the Christian life is missing; regretfully, the unity of the church is lost! This is not the better way!

The Better Life Also Has Christ as the Model

The final verse of this text wraps up the whole concept of the life in Christ—this better way. The text does a complete circle and takes us right back where we started. "Have this attitude in yourselves which was also in Christ Jesus."

Here is both the motivation and the model. The agape-love of Christ has redeemed us by His perfect life and perfect payment. There is no motivation which can replace this in drawing lives back to the God who made us! Jesus said, "No man cometh unto the Father but by Me." The cross still is the mighty magnet; it still draws all men unto Him.

But Jesus Christ is more than our Redeemer, He is also our model. "Let this mind be in you which was also in Christ Jesus." Christians still sing, "I Long to be like Jesus!"

Even the unbelieving world often refers to Him as a great moral leader and as a great teacher. If that is all He ever was, we are in eternal trouble. None of us have been able to measure up to His model of perfection. If He was only a model, we are still sinners in trouble. If He was only a great teacher, we have not been able to live by His perfect teachings. Indeed He was a model and a teacher, but He was also much more! He was our Savior who died that we might have pardon for a lifetime of sins, peace with the God who wants us all back, a life which "fights the good fight of faith" and which "presents our bodies as a living sacrifice," and a heart which confesses that "because He lives I shall live also!" This is the better way; this is God's way!

The Better Way Communicated to Us

There is a story told of a man who sat in his living room and peered through the front window observing a bitter snowstorm. He saw birds, trapped in the wind and snow desperately searching for shelter. Some of them flew against his front window in a vain attempt to get inside. They only fell stunned in the snow. He was moved by compassion and went to the barn and slid open the door and even tried to drive them inside. His problem was that he had a solution for their food and shelter, but he just could not communicate with them. If only he could become a bird and tell them of the haven inside the barn!

Jesus Christ had a great agape-love for a whole world of people who were trapped in the bitter storms of a sinful world. They too have made all kinds of human attempts to escape from their plight. The harder they try, the more they fall stunned by their vain, work-righteous efforts. "They have all gone astray; there is none that doeth good,—no not one."

God knew there was only one place to find eternal shelter. That place was the cross of Calvary. Jesus became one of us, humbled Himself all the way to the cross, and communicated the greatest news human ears have ever heard. That news is, "The blood of Jesus Christ, God's Son, cleanses us from all sins." We have responded by singing, "Beneath the cross of Jesus I fain would take my stand."

This is the better way! God's Son submitted Himself to redeem the world. This is why our strength and consolation is in Him,—not in oursleves! The Spirit of God has humbled us to give up all human attempts. He has drawn us to the cross where we find peace and life. He even dwells within us and produces "fruits of the Spirit." In humility we must give Him credit for any beauty in the life we live. In deeds, we are even moved by agape-love to reach out and love others. We live not unto ourselves but unto Him who died and rose again. His mission to save and love people becomes ours! This is the life of Christian submission.

"Let this mind be in you which was also in Christ Jesus"—this is the better way.

Citizens for Heaven

TWENTIETH SUNDAY AFTER PENTECOST
PHILIPPIANS 3:12-21

Paul J. Foust

In order to enrich our lives, we turn this morning to a text which takes us back to about 60 years after the birth of Christ. The place is Philippi, a city of Greece. It's about five years before the great apostle Paul was executed. Philippi was on a trade route between the east and the west, and it was a center of gold mining.

Paul had come there some 10 years earlier and brought them something much more valuable than gold. He brought them Jesus Christ. Jesus could be theirs eternally and bring pardon, peace, and life blessings which were priceless. Gold would slip away during their earthly life and be useless in eternity. The Philippian congregation was one of those rare ones which seemed to appreciate this! Paul saw them as the dearest and purest of any he had established. When he left, they took a special offering and sent it to sustain his ministry.

He wrote this epistle to say "thank you," but he added a lot of other things they needed to hear. We need to hear these same divine truths.

In the third chapter God is speaking to this congregation of Christians in Philippi, and He is speaking to us through the great apostle Paul. In the early verses of the chapter He talks about the miracle of Christian conversion. Paul uses his own as an illustration. Then in this text he progresses to the next phase of the Christian life: the maturing of the new life with God. We call this sanctification. Finally he launches into the grand finale of it all: the Christian life in glory. All this seems to fit very well under the theme

Citizens for Heaven
The Miracle of Conversion

We will appreciate and understand the text more fully if we look first at the preceding verses and see what Paul went through before becoming a Christian. He tells us of the struggle in his life during those days when he figured a person could work his own way back to God. He had a "confidence in the flesh" and was determined that if anyone could earn heaven, he could! He was born from the chosen people of the Old Testament. He was circumcised as a baby. He drove himself, adding to God's laws all those pharisaical rules. He labored tirelessly to keep them. But then God opened his eyes to see a great mystery!

All those labors in his life were tainted with sin and counted for nothing. He couldn't earn his way back to God if he lived a million years! By the deeds of the law no living flesh could be justified. Paul finally admitted, "I have counted all these things but loss!"

This is a great lesson which every one of us Christians has had to learn. The natural religion has always insisted that man could come back to God without a Savior. He could earn his own way back! The experience and the witness of the great apostle Paul was, "It can't be done!" Redemption was *God's* action for me, conversion is *God's* action in me, and sanctification is *God's* action through me!

The Spirit of God had opened Paul's eyes to see himself as he really was and, more important yet, had also opened his eyes to see Jesus as He really was, the Savior of every sin-infected life. Jesus, God's own Son, did what no one else could do. He paid the whole price of sin. He furnished the robe of righteousness which He holds out to a world of people who need it. It covered the inferior life of Paul and made him acceptable to God, and it made me acceptable too!

Every person gathered in this sanctuary ought to see here the miracle of conversion—lives brought back by God, forgiven and changed and salvaged for eternity.

When that conversion took place in your life is not all that important. In many of your lives it happened longer ago than you can remember, at the baptismal font. The important thing is that, right now, you are convinced by the Spirit of God that your frail sinful life never would have come back by itself. You would have sunk deeper into the quicksand of sin. Jesus Christ did what you couldn't. He paid the whole price and bought you back. God's Spirit opened your eyes to see your hopeless condition and led you to confess "God be merciful to me, a sinner." He lifted you to the cross and moved you to rejoice, "Jesus, Thy blood and righteousness, my beauties are, my glorious dress." That's the miracle of your conversion. We who are attached by faith to Jesus Christ are now, citizens for heaven.

Our Growth in Sanctification

After stressing the miracle of conversion Paul (v. 12) moves immediately into the next step, the fierce struggle which we Christians go through while living, "in the world but not of the world." He reminds us that our life here will not be easy, and it will not be perfect. This is important to understand as we "fight the good fight of faith." There are those who insist that once they became a Christian, they stopped sinning and lived the perfect life. It wasn't this way with Paul. He confessed, "not as though I had already attained, neither were already perfect." It's not that way in your life either!

Indeed, the Christian life is lifted by the indwelling Spirit of God. We are temples of God and have that beautiful motivation which makes us want to worship, want to thank God for daily blessings, and want to please God as we walk beside Him and fight that good fight of faith.

Yet, we still live in a world which is hostile to God and where there are consistent temptations. The devil is still trying with his enormous power and deceptiveness to trip me to stumble and fall. Too often he succeeds! Even my own sinful flesh never gives up, it's a struggle so that "The good that I would, I cannot, and that which I would not, that I do!"

But the very next verse has an answer to all this. God says, "Forgetting those things which are behind." The sins of the past are all taken care of. God has buried them "as in the depths of the sea." Now let's not go fishing them out! Guilt is gone, peace is ours.

"Forgetting those things which are behind, reaching forth to those things which are before."

When the load of sins no longer burdens you, you can really run the good race! Here Paul introduces a picture which was familiar to those Greeks. They were great athletes and knew all about running in a race. Verse 14 pictures the Christian as running a race. The runner is straining every nerve and muscle, giving every ounce of strength, veins bulging with pressure. This was the way Paul ran the spiritual race of the Christian life. "Pressing toward the mark of the high calling of God in Christ Jesus."

What a picture of Christians who are not satisifed to live mediocre lives! These are the real soliders who are not about to sit in the barriers. These are runners who are not content to trail along behind. These are the pacesetters!

Pacesetters are a great example to the weaker Christians who need the strengthening ministry of others. And many a fellow Christian has challenged my life by his example. Paul is an example to all of us. The text emphasizes that those Christians who are spiritually mature should have this "same attitude." Oh, that every child of God hearing this message might thrust forward in this great race. God can use pacesetters! Paul affectionately says "Brethren, join in following my example."

In contrast to all this he points out that there are plenty of people in Philippi who no longer have their eyes fixed on Jesus and on that eternal prize He won for all. They aren't even in the race. These, he says, are living for the base and temporary things of life. He puts it very frankly, "Their god is their belly."

It's no secret that there are thousands of people in God's world today who have not experienced the miracle of conversion, or who have lost their faith. They do not know the joy of running the good race and living for Christ. They have nothing bigger to live for than the things they are going to lose. Paul's words are so descriptive of an unbelieving world, "Whose god is their belly and whose glory is in their shame, who mind earthly things."

But Paul added "I tell you this weeping." It ought to grieve the heart of every Christian so that we cannot rest, until these too are running the race. We ought to be possessed by this conviction, "I've got a secret that I cannot keep." (This is the secret of sin and grace.) "I'm a steward of God's mysteries." "I cannot but speak the things I have seen and heard." When Christians become Ambassadors of Jesus Christ, sharing the mysteries of God, they soon discover that those, "whose god was their belly," are transformed and their God becomes Jesus Christ. Instead of "glorying in their shame and minding earthly things," they are changed to glory in their Savior and to mind heavenly things!

Glory—When Vile Bodies Are Changed

Now we come to the grand finale of this entire text. "Our conversation is in heaven." I like the way the NAS translation puts it. "Our citizenship is in heaven." This makes all the difference in the world in the life we live!

When the runner sees the finish line, it does great things to his sprint! I know,—I've run many a race! I also know what it does to Christian lives when they know for sure that they are citizens of heaven. It does great things in their worship, their conduct, their witness, their service. Their worship takes on new meaning and spirit. Their conduct becomes a daily walk with God. Their witness becomes alive in word and deed. Their service becomes a joy, and they live and labor and give for Him who lived and died and gave Himself for them.

Citizens for heaven know that we have a very limited time left before we cross the goal line. No wonder our pace quickens. This sin-infected world shall be discarded, and this vile body shall become like His glorious body. This Church Militant shall become the Church Triumphant. Strangers and pilgrims shall know the joy of permanent citizenship!

Paul loved those Christians at Philippi. They knew the miracle of conversion. They grew in the sanctified life. Their pace was quickened as they saw the goal line. They are now eternal citizens of heaven.

This morning God has privileged me to bring you a message drawn from the same text that has touched the hearts of Christians ever since that first Philippian congregation heard God speak to them. The love of Jesus, which has reached out to me and made me His, reaches out to you. If Jesus Christ is your personal Savior, then thank God for the miracle of conversion. No, your life is not perfect. God isn't through with you yet! He is drawing you to Himself this morning again, that you may run the good race. Your faith is more precious than gold! The goal line is sure. He redeemed you with His blood. You are citizens of heaven. "Press toward the mark for the prize of your high calling of God in Christ Jesus."

A Life of Consistent Joy

TWENTY-FIRST SUNDAY AFTER PENTECOST
PHILIPPIANS 4:4-13

Arnold F. Krugler

The last half century has been dominated by economic insecurity. Fifty years ago the world was rocking in the midst of the Great Depression.

Some of us remember with acute pain the Great Depression of 1929 when banks closed, savings were wiped out, and once hardworking people lined up for welfare assistance. At various intervals during the past 50 years we have been hit hard by what economists call "recession." Twenty years ago we were beginning a period of runaway inflation.

Whether we are in a period of depression, recession, or inflation, during times such as these people find it very hard to enjoy those blessings they already have received from their God. During times of economic upset, people find themselves almost overwhelmed by concerns for their finances and for their economic future.

In a sense such concerns are very natural, and when we see people acting tense and irritable because of them, we can understand their reasons. We Christians are not exempt from the same worries, pressures, and tensions.

But here, in the midst of such tensions and concerns, St. Paul comes along in our text and tells us to rejoice always. It seems like too much. When he tells us to lead "A Life of Consistent Joy," we are tempted to tell Paul to give this command to someone else, or to come back some other time when we don't have so many financial worries. After all, how can we rejoice when we are surrounded by economic insecurity?

I. Our Inability To be Consistently Joyful

Whether it be depression, inflation, or recession—whether we are talking about the economic fortunes of our nation or merely looking at our own economic troubles—in the midst of such economic trials it is hard, very hard, always to be joyful.

For the sad fact for all of us—and periods of financial troubles only bring this truth home to us more forcefully—is that we can rejoice only on those rare occasions when things seem to be going our way. And it is truly a rare occasion for most of us when we feel everything is going our way.

When our income doesn't expand fast enough to keep up with the cost of living, when we face economic trials, when things don't go well at home, at work, on the farm, at the shop, it is impossible for us to be joyful at all times. We may indulge in a few brief moments of joy. But to be consistently joyful—that's quite another matter.

II. Paul's Secret of Consistent Joy

We need to be honest with ourselves. If we cannot be joyful all the time, evidently we have not yet learned the secret that Paul emphasizes in our text. Paul isn't making a demand that he regards as unattainable. Neither is Paul giving us advice in a matter he knows nothing about. Paul knows how we can attain consistent underlying joy, because he knows how he has attained it himself.

And he realizes that to have that kind of joy is just as possible for us as it was for him.

But first of all we need to realize our problem. Perhaps because we have been living through so much economic uncertainty, we have come to believe that to be joyful we need to depend on things. If we have enough money in the bank, if we have enough insurance for that proverbial rainy day, if we have enough cars, TV's, and other appliances and conveniences, we feel we can be joyful. And if something comes along to threaten our possession of these things, we find ourselves saddened.

But Paul managed to escape from this kind of trap that so subtly and yet so effectively robs us of joy. For in our text he tells us that he had learned first of all to be content, no matter what economic condition he faced. He reminds us that there were times in his life when he had an abundance of goods, wealth, and food. But for some strange reason the Bible is silent about those periods when Paul experienced wealth and superabundance.

Yet there also were times when he went without the necessities and suffered privation, hunger, and pain.

But what he insists on is that, regardless of his own economic fortunes, he could be joyful because he had learned to be content with his situation in life.

But what is of greatest importance for us is *why* Paul could be content. It wasn't because of some strong, inner force—his self-discipline. The reason he could be content is that he knew, no matter what the trial or need, that his God was always near. Knowing this, Paul didn't have to worry about anything. He could go to his God at any time and let his God know what he needed.

The apostle Paul was no Pollyanna. He was no blind optimist who ignored the perils he had to face. Anyone familiar with Paul's writings knows that Paul did experience periods in which he was utterly, unbearably crushed. He had a thorn in the flesh which he begged God to remove. And Paul still heard God deny that request.

But Paul also could say that he knew that God would guard and keep all that he as His apostle had entrusted to His care. For this reason he assures us in the last verse of our text that he could do everything with God's help. For God supplied strength to do what needed to be done.

Paul's life was not a bed of roses. He experienced poverty, weakness, and hunger as well as success, prosperity, and strength. Yet through it all he knew that His God would be with him always, that his God had marked him for His own in his baptism, that his God had died on Calvary's cross for even the foremost of sinners, that his God had made Paul's body His temple. Paul knew that with the gift of Jesus God would give him everything. So what was there to threaten his joy? He was beyond the reach of anything that could try to separate him from the love of God in Christ Jesus.

III. A Joy Resting on God's Promises

It is from this rich and happy experience that Paul tells us we, too, can be joyful always. We have the same promises Paul had. We have the same God who has adopted each of us to be His beloved children. We have the same God who loved each of us so much that He gladly left His throne on high and came to earth as our Brother to suffer and die for us so that we need never fear death or any other tyrant. We have the same God who fills us with every good and perfect gift, not because we deserve His gifts but rather because He loves to give us everything He has that is for our good.

Because Paul knew such a God, he could be content no matter what economic condition he faced in his life. Because Paul knew such a God, he was convinced that he could do everything through the God who gave him strength to face any challenge.

You and I have the very same promises Paul had. Would God have placed more than 7,000 of them in the Bible if He didn't care about our every need, down to the hairs that fall from our head? We can live the same life of confident joy Paul enjoyed. We, too, can always be joyful. But only if we anchor our joy on the fantastic promises our God has made to us.

We don't have to let any worry steal that joy from us when we take our needs, our concerns, our cares to our God.

Paul assures us in our text that our Lord is near. With that assurance we can experience God's peace that surpasses all comprehension and that will guard our hearts and minds through Christ Jesus our Savior and Friend.

It's a wonderful life, a life of permanent joy and of peaceful contentment, when we live life as Paul did, trusting in God's promises.

May that life be ours, now and forever.

Loved by God

TWENTY-SECOND SUNDAY AFTER PENTECOST
1 THESSALONIANS 1:1-5a

Arnold F. Krugler

When two young people fall in love, it seems that within a short time after that momentous discovery, one of them suddenly is troubled by a question that assumes major importance. Put simply, the question is, Why does my beloved love me? Why of all people in the world am I the lucky one? Why me?

Those who are older and supposedly wiser in the ways of the world can smugly smile when they see a person going through the mental and emotional anguish that accompanies this question. Yet we know that all the best advice in the world will not rule out or eliminate the trauma.

No matter what we may feel about such a question between a young man and a young woman, all of us, if we stop to look at ourselves in our relation with our God, will be caught up short with the same question. Why does God love me? Why, of all people in the world, am I the one? Why me? But believe it. It is a fact. God so loved the world.

Paul of Tarsus never was able to overcome his sense of wonder and awe in knowing he was loved by God. And while he didn't know why God loved him, he never would tire of assuring the people he ministered to that it was in fact true that he, Paul, was loved by God. And not only was that true for himself; he also assured his readers that they, too, are in all reality,

Loved by God

I. The Reality of God's Love

When Paul delivered this message of God's love, he was strangely met with widespread unbelief and opposition. It just didn't make sense for a wandering tentmaker to go to a crowd of uneducated peasants and tell them that the God who had created the world really loved them—loved them not just in some sort of vague, impersonal way, but that He loved each of them so desperately, so deeply, that He even gave His own Son into death on a cross so that they might believe and be saved.

This message was regarded as foolishness by some in Paul's day. When we are honest with ourselves, we admit that it is just as difficult to believe in our day.

We con ourselves a little into thinking that God loves us because

He loves all people. But when we take a really good and honest look
at the human race, we find even that can game pretty hard to play.
When we look at the way humans rush to ruin the good earth the
Lord has given us; when we look at the terrible acts of atrocity and
bloodshed and torture being perpetrated around the world, we have
to realize that it is just as difficult to believe that God loves the
whole human race as it is to believe that He loves just one member
of that race.

And so in our text Paul goes on to assure us that we are loved by
God, not because we chose to be loved, and certainly not because we
deserve this love. But the fact of God's love for us remains. We are
loved by God, Paul insists, for one reason and for one reason only—
that God has chosen us to receive His love.

When a young man has just fallen in love with a beautiful
woman and asks himself why he was the one she fell in love with,
the only real answer is that she chose him out of all the other men
she knew.

When God tells us why He loves us, He assures us it is simply
because He chose us, chose us before we were born, before we had
done anything either good or bad.

Certainly if we had to do something to deserve that love we
would quickly be cut off from God and lose His love.

II. Loved by God Because of His Choice

When we search through the Bible, which is God's love letter to
those He loves, we find that God nowhere tells us why He fell in love
with us.

A little one-line rhyme says: "How odd of God to choose the
Jews." Why would he choose a man like Abraham, make of him the
father of a great nation that would torment Him by constantly
rebelling against Him? It is clear that He didn't pick the Jews
because they deserved His love. And after He had chosen them,
they continued to give Him a hard time. And He never did say why
He fell in love with them.

In the same way, He never tells us why He fell in love with us.
Like Israel, we were nobodies and even rebellious when He chose to
set His love upon us. In fact, the Bible describes us then as God's
enemies.

Yet the marvelous mystery remains. God in fact does love us. He
loves each of us so desperately, so recklessly, that He proves His
love for us by sending His only Son to become our brother and to
cement that love by dying for us on a cross that we helped to
fashion. He loves us so much that He adopts us to be His children so
we can go to Him in prayer as dear children go to their true father.
And because of this same love He has sent us His Spirit to be a
guarantee of God's love for us.

The doctrine of election or predestination is something that many Christians are afraid of. They seem to see it as some sort of threat to them.

But it is wonderful assurance to each Christian to know that our relationship with God, His love for us, does not depend upon our ability to choose God or to make ourselves deserving of His rich and wondrous love.

III. Loved by God Because of His Promise

This is the truth Paul asserts in our text when he assures us that we know we are chosen by God to receive His love, because God said so. God tells us that we are His beloved. And Paul hastens to assure us that when we are assured of this in God's Word, we are not merely hearing a vague bunch of meaningless words. For the message of God's love is a message of power, of conviction, and of the Holy Spirit.

No message can make a greater difference in our lives than does this assurance that we are loved by God simply because He chose to love us.

When a child feels it has to deserve the love of its parents, it lives in perpetual bondage. That child is afraid to take any chances or to run any risks for fear he will lose his parent's love.

When a man feels he has to deserve the love of his bride, he too is in endless bondage. Every day he feels he has to do something to earn the love of his bride. And he is in the constant torment that some day he will not be able to earn that love.

People who live with the idea that they have to deserve the love of God are in the same kind of bondage. If we have to deserve God's love, then our every act, our every thought, must be examined carefully to see whether or not it will be something that can gain God's love.

But Paul begins his letter to the Thessalonians by assuring them of God's undeserved love for them so that he can go on from there and expect great things from them.

They already are assured that God loves them at their worst. He loved them while they were His enemies. What they do does not buy God's love.

But see what happens when people like Paul and the Thessalonians appreciate the love of God. Like Paul, they pray for others, for their faith and joy in the Lord, for their comfort and care, for their earthly and eternal welfare. When you love someone, you pray for that person, you want the best of all gifts for that person—the love of God.

And see what happens when the message of God's love—the Gospel—gets rooted in people's lives: "We remember before our God and Father how you put your faith into practice, how your love

made you work so hard, and how your hope in our Lord Jesus Christ
is firm" (v. 3).

It is only the kind of love that comes from the heart of God that
performs such transformations in naturally selfish and rebellious
creatures.

Because they are loved by God, they can now go out and live in
the light of that love. They are now free, because God chose them to
be His beloved, to live as God's beloved children—free to serve Him,
free to give their lives for their fellow humans, free to help one
another. Finally, they are free to live as those who know God loves
them, and for that reason they are free to live, free to serve, and free
to love even as they themselves have been loved by God.

A Sermon to the Faithful

TWENTY-THIRD SUNDAY AFTER PENTECOST
1 THESSALONIANS 1:5b-10

Richard Bauerle

The faithful of God are a unique people. They have great strengths
and gifts of which even they themselves are often unaware. They
should remind themselves and the rest of the faithful of God how
unique they really are. Christians do not speak often enough of
their uniqueness and the gifts God has given to them. Thus they
lose so many opportunities for encouraging each other in the
Christian faith.

At a pastor's conference recently, the speaker asked us: "How
often have you preached an entire sermon about the ninety and
nine righteous who need no repentance?" Theologically, that may
be a difficult sermon to preach, but those are the words Jesus used,
and He must have used them for a reason. Most of the time when we
preach about sheep, we are preaching about the one lost sheep, but
how about the ninety and nine righteous who need no repentance?
Do we neglect these too much? We do have difficulty speaking of our
own gifts and encouraging the faithful to continue what they are
doing, don't we? Do we neglect speaking of our gifts because we are
afraid that the faithful will become filled with pride? Or is it
because we are afraid our people will neglect their prayers of
repentance if we speak to them in a complimentary way? Whatever
it is, we seem to have great difficulty speaking of the gifts which the
faithful have received.

Paul had no such difficulty. Even when he could hardly wait to
attack abuses within the congregations to whom he wrote, he
always began his letters to the churches by complimenting them

for the gifts that God had given them. His first letter to the Thessalonians is only one example of this great man's ability to compliment the faithful. "We give thanks to God always for you all," he says, "remembering before our God and Father your work of faith and labor of love and steadfastness of hope in our Lord Jesus Christ" (1 Thess. 1:2-3). Then he goes on to describe their faithfulness, both to Christ and to him, along with their faithfulness to others. "You became an example to all the believers in Macedonia and Achaia" (1 Thess. 1:7), he said. "Your faith in God has gone everywhere, so we need not say anything" (1 Thess. 1:8). He spoke to them in the most complimentary ways. It was the beginning of his letter to the faithful.

In response to that text, I have the urge to preach a sermon to the faithful to, those ninety and nine righteous, as Jesus described them, who need no repentance. What does one say to you, the faithful of God?

You Have Many Gifts

First of all, we must say that you as God's people have many gifts. Whenever a pastor looks around knowingly at his congregation, he sees so many gifts given to the people of God redeemed with the blood of Christ. These gifts are great gifts. They are the gifts to speak and to teach and to exhort one another, to comfort one another, to heal wounds, and to be able to love one another. They are indeed great gifts! One could not ask for more. They are not always used, but they are great gifts given to us by God.

When Paul wrote his letters to the churches, he very often began those letters with a Greek word that is very difficult to translate into English. It is the Greek word, *Hagios*. Most of the translations say "saints," so that it reads, "To the saints in Corinth, or to the saints in Rome, or to the saints in Ephesus," or wherever he wrote the letter. Other translations use the term "consecrated." Still another uses the phrase "called to be God's dedicated people." It is a hard word to translate because it was a word used in Greek to describe a temple or shrine that was dedicated to the total use of one of their gods. It was a temple or a shrine into which great wealth was poured because nothing was too good for those gods.

By using this word, Paul is depicting the Christian as that shrine of God into which great wealth has been poured. The blood of God's own Son, poured out so freely for our salvation is the most precious gift ever given to the world. It was given to that *Hagios*, making that "saint" a shrine of great value. Paul referred to that another time, when in 1 Corinthians (3:16), he said, "Do you not know that you are the temple of God"? You are a temple into which great gifts have been poured. God gives gifts to His people. You are a gifted people, a great people, a shrine—yes, you, people of God.

You Also Bear Many Afflictions

But we must also say this. With your many gifts, you have many afflictions. Paul writes to the Thessalonians: "You became imitators of us and of the Lord, for you received the word with much affliction" (1 Thess. 1:6). Although we have many gifts, we are also afflicted with a variety of struggles and many enemies to our faith. Many of the obstacles to our faith are simply irritations, but many of those obstacles must be called afflictions, for they have a detrimental influence on our faith to which the Holy Ghost has called us. In fact, those afflictions are often great enemies of our faith. The faithful have many afflictions, both inward and outward. Paul often spoke of the enemies that war against the soul. Those enemies bring great pressure upon us. The pressures and influences to be immoral, to cheat, to lie, or to lose our faith in our Redeemer are intense. It has always been so, and it certainly is no less today. The pressures of our work, the pressures of being criticized, our attempt to please people who cannot be pleased, have never been stronger than today. Those enemies must certainly be called afflictions which attempt to destroy our faith. Webster interprets the word, "affliction," that which causes pain or distress. We do not know the afflictions to which Paul referred, but we certainly know a great deal about affliction in our day.

A few years ago I decided to give up just about everything I enjoy except my wife. I gave up those things because I thought I was too busy. I gave up even my means of exercise, and for a long time I felt quite sorry for myself. One day at a pastor's conference, I discovered that many of my co-workers in the ministry had done the same thing. As we were discussing the reasons for that, we discovered that we had not done that because we were so busy, but because we were afraid of criticism from members of our congregations. We were not that busy! We were afraid of criticism even though the members of our parishes never criticized us for it.

What an affliction for the faithful! The fear of criticism even when there is no reason to fear it! No wonder we fall to the pressures of our work. We have so few reserves left as we try to be righteous and trustworthy and loving and straightforward trying to please people because we are so afraid of being criticized.

In the 1960s when it seemed that people hated one another more than at any other time in history (and we haven't gotten over it yet), there was a form of group counseling invented which was supposed to make people strong. Pastors were urged to do it among themselves. It was to go something like this: From a peer group the members were supposed to choose one person in their midst for each session. That person was to be told by the members of the group what they liked and what they did not like about that person, and what changes should be made. In this way, that person was to reexamine his life through this severe criticism and become a better person.

I was involved with a group at that time which met for breakfast twice a month. One of the younger pastors insisted that this is how we should use our time together. He wanted the chance to tell us what he thought of us! Finally, when we could not put him off any longer, we all agreed that we would begin doing this at our next meeting. At the next meeting, he was the only one there! Just the thought of such a thing destroyed the group. We discovered later that some people had been destroyed emotionally by such an experience. We cannot bear criticism that way. It is a great affliction of the faithful.

When Job in the Old Testament was being criticized so fiercely by his three friends, they told him that all those terrible things were happening to him because he was such a terrible sinner, to them Job said, "There is a path which the eye of the vulture has not seen" (Job 28:7). He was referring to the great vision of the vulture. But that vision sees only what is dead and rotten. That is all he is looking for. There is a path which he does not see. Ah, yes, there are those who see only what the vulture sees in us, and that is a terrible burden for the faithful of God to bear. Others may be able to bear it better than we can, for they are not as sensitive about sin as we are; for we know the price God had to pay to forgive sin. We are the first to admit that we are sinners. Why else was it necessary for the blood of Christ to be shed for us? But that criticism is a great affliction to the faithful, for it takes from us our freedom to be what we are.

But there is another affliction we must also describe for the faithful in our day. It may seem strange to have to describe it as an affliction; yet because of the resentment it builds up within the faithful, it must be considered as such. This new affliction to the faithful is that so-called new convert, who, according to his own words has been "born again." That new convert today is different from the one we used to know. In years past, when one received Christ as Savior that person was at first silently grateful for having come to the knowledge of Christ. Today that new convert claims to have found it himself, so he/she attacks the ninety and nine righteous who never left the flock. After all the trouble those ninety and nine went to for the new convert, and the trouble Christ had to find the lost sheep, collectively some still assume they are the only ones who know Christ. The new convert was the lost sheep who was found, but now he/she is so proud of the fact that he/she is the one who found Christ! Then that new convert attacks the rest of the members of the flock who were never lost!

This is a heavy burden which the Christian who has been a faithful follower of Christ for a long time must carry. What an unusual cross for the faithful! It is a galling burden which has happened seldom in history. However, this cross is something we must learn to carry with grace for their sakes. That weaker brother or sister is spoken of often in Scriptures. They must be nourished and strengthened until they are mature in their faith. They are new in their faith, and they are enthusiastic, just like children when they discover a new truth. It is a truth we have known for a long time, but when they first learn it, they are like children who learn a truth which is new to them. They are so excited about learning that new truth that they cannot believe you already know it.

That weaker brother or sister is not the enemy. The enemy is that inward frustration and anger that the faithful feel when the new convert is full of such pride and arrogance when they have been found, and then they say that they are the only ones who know the whole truth about Christ and the Scriptures. It is a difficult affliction to bear, but we must bear it for their sake.

You Have Much Joy

There are many more things that ought to be said to the faithful of God, but let me conclude with just one more thing. You have a joy that no one can take from you. It is not a fake joy. It is a deep joy. It is not like someone said about a man once: "He smiles with his lips, but not with his eyes." It is not that kind of shallow joy. It is a deep joy which knows that the Lord is dealing with us in a loving way. It is the deep joy in knowing that God proved His love once and for all for us when He sent His own Son into this wayside planet to die for us. It may be true that there is much joy in heaven over one sinner who repents, but while we are on earth, it gives the faithful of God great joy just to be numbered among the faithful.

In one of the great writings called "Orthodoxy" by G. K. Chesterton, he writes about Jesus and why he became a Christian. He was once an avowed atheist who fought Christianity with all his might. He said that there was a mystique about Jesus which no one understood and which was hidden from all men. It was something which was too great for God to show us when He walked this earth. "Then," he said, "as I have studied and re-studied the life of Jesus, I have discovered that the great secret He kept hidden from everyone was His great joy."

Christianity without joy is a betrayal of the One we follow. We are a forgiven, redeemed people who belong to that faithful flock on the way to heaven. We are a people with great joy.

I will always owe a great debt to my supervising pastor while I was on internship. Let me tell you what he had me do my first day with him. He sent me to call on a lady because, he said, she was a shut-in. She was sitting in a chair when I arrived, and I was not surprised when she did not get up as her husband answered the door. She was the most pleasant person I had ever met.

The next day as I sat with my supervising pastor, I said to him that he must be mistaken. That lady should not be on the shut-in list. She is as healthy as anyone, I said. He smiled as he said to me that he was sure I would come back with that opinion because of the way she hides her pain with her joy. He told me that she lives in excruciating pain every single moment of her life. No one could have guessed it because of the joy she displayed as the faithful of God. She had not always been that way, but she had worked through the confusion of why she had to suffer such pain, and she discovered who she was. She was a member of the faithful of God on the way to heaven, and she displayed her joy for just being a member of that great company of elect and faithful children for whom Christ died. God had given Himself to her in a way she could feel. She had a joy that no one could take from her because she knew God loved her and she simply took it for granted that she would spend eternity with Him after the pain. She knew she was loved.

Another such lady for whom I thank God often was my mother. I will never forget the last time I saw her. She had been in an automobile accident. She survived the accident and was on the mend, although we knew she had a bad heart. Four days after the accident, my wife and I saw her in the hospital on a Sunday afternoon as we had done each day since the accident. We were about to leave, and I said to her that we would see her tomorrow. She then said to me, "Aren't you going to kiss me good-bye?" I said, "Of course," and when I kissed her I said to her, "Mom, you know we love you, don't you?" She said, "Yes, I know." It was the last thing she ever said to me. I am so glad we were able to convince her we loved her. That is so important. It is the most important thing in the world, to know we are loved.

So I know my Lord loves me. He has proved it to me over and again, and for that reason, I and the rest of the faithful of God have a joy that no one can take from us.

That Last Enemy

LAST SUNDAY AFTER PENTECOST
CHRIST THE KING
1 CORINTHIANS 15:20-28

Richard Bauerle

The thoughts we have for this last Sunday of the Church Year are moving thoughts, for they deal with the end of things. All of us are intensely interested in the end of things, and the older we get, the more intense are those thoughts of the end of things. What is of special interest to us, of course, is the end of our lives. I often wonder how I will face those last moments of my life. I like to think that I will face those last moments of my life bravely and courageously and that my words to those around me will be filled with great wisdom. But I do not know. Greater men than I have gone whimpering to their death.

That passage, therefore, of Paul in his First Letter to the Corinthians, the 15th chapter, is very meaningful today when he says: "Then comes the end, when He delivers the kingdom to God the Father after destroying every rule and every authority and power. For He must reign until He has put all His enemies under His feet. The last enemy to be destroyed is death" (1 Cor. 15:24-26).

I. The Enemy That Death Is

Ah, yes, that last enemy! What an enemy he is! He entered the world when sin entered it, and that alien, that foreigner in this world has been rooting up and pulling down and destroying ever since he came. Death tears in pieces the great handiwork of God, even the human body which was so marvelously wrought by the fingers of divine skill. That vandal spares no work of life, however nice it is. He makes everything ugly, no matter how beautiful it is. Look at the man whom death has attacked and see how he has ruined this man. How his beauty has turned to ashes, and his body to corruption. Surely an enemy has done this!

He has intruded into everything we call dear, and he has spoiled the whole of life. He is not a part of the great Shepherd's flock, but he is as the wolf that comes to kill and destroy. Nowhere is the work of this enemy not seen. Where is there a field without its grave? What city is without a cemetery? The generations of men lie everywhere. Even the sea is not without its dead.

He has no mercy, this enemy of ours. The tears of the bereaved, the wail of the widow, the moan of the orphan are his song of victory! He cares not that we weep when he appears. When he takes a friend from our side, or a child from our bosom, he does not care how much we cry. Death has no pity for the young and no mercy for the old. He pays no attention as to whether one is good or beautiful. He goes into our garden and cuts down the sweetest flowers as well as the weeds. And even those little fragrant flowers that grow in a sheltered corner of that garden, hiding there beneath the leaves that they may blush unseen, death spies out even these and coarsely says: "Cut them down!"

What an enemy! He cares not if a child is left fatherless with no one to shelter it. He is not moved by the tears of the widow who has lost the light of her life. He is cold to the husband whose house is empty, where little children cry for their mother. He robs them one and all and feels nothing! What an enemy! Even our prayers seem to have no effect on him. We plead for the life of a loved one, we beg him to leave us be, we try to hold him back with our cries, but he comes anyway in his relentless terror. He is a ruthless enemy! He just keeps coming, coldly, and without mercy.

II. The Enemy Destroyed

For those and many other reasons, I am so glad our Savior came to destroy that enemy, death. "He must put all enemies under His feet, and the last enemy to be destroyed is death" (1 Cor. 15:25, 26). It is true, He has not yet destroyed death completely, but it is nearly done for His people. He has so subdued death for His people that they hardly need fear him. Of course, we must die, "For flesh and blood cannot inherit the kingdom of God" (1 Cor. 15:50), but although death still holds dominion over our bodies, our living Redeemer has so changed the face of death that he is no longer death, that fierce enemy, but he is something other than what he appears to be.

Now death is that fiery chariot on which we will ascend to God. Death is now that gentle voice of the great King who says to us at the great banquet, "Come up higher." Death is now those wings of the eagle that fly out and beyond this veil of tears. Oh yes, death still looks like a dragon, even to God's elect, but his sting is gone. He still may be the lion that attacks us, but the lion can only knock us down as he charges at us and strikes us, for his teeeth are broken and his claws are clipped.

Now death is a completely different thing for the people of God. The people of God discover dying is so different from what they expected. They expected death to strike them with a sword thrust; they discover it is only like a pinprick. If death is to the people of God what has been promised to us by God's Word, then we will say on that last day, "Can this have been death? To die is so different a thing from what I expected. I didn't know it would be so light, so joyous, and so easy. Is this the monster I was so afraid of all my life? All I did was shut my eyes on earth and opened them in heaven. Is this what I feared so all my life? How foolish of me!"

I am so impressed with the way the gospel writers describe the first Easter morning. There was so much confusion among the women and the disciples, but at the tomb there was such a relaxed atmosphere. When Mary was weeping in the garden thinking someone had taken the body of Jesus, suddenly Someone appeared to her and quietly spoke her name, and she recognized the One who addressed her. Then He left. It was such a quiet thing. When Peter and John later came to the tomb and looked in, they saw the grave clothes, and the napkin covering the face of Jesus, neatly folded up in a corner. It was all so relaxed. Everything done so neatly and unhurried without panic. Just a sort of leisurely little job done in a matter of fact way. Then when Peter and John came out of the tomb, there sat an angel on the stone that had been rolled away.

I love that! The relaxed kind of thing. The angel just sitting there and asking them what they wanted, as if he were surprised that everyone did not know, and in effect saying to them: "What's the problem? Didn't He tell you He would rise from the dead? He is not here, He is risen, just as He told you He would. Come on, relax, what's the problem? He is risen." That is what death has become to us now, a relaxing sort of thing when we go to sleep to awaken to a better day. The enemy has been subdued, or as Barclay translated it: "Death has been reduced to helplessness." He cannot harm us. We will not be the worse for dying, we will be the better for it. Death's teeth have been pulled and his sting removed. Yes, he will knock us down, but he cannot chew us up.

III. Keep Death for Last

Finally, let me speak to you about one other aspect of the text. Paul says death is the LAST enemy to be destroyed. In God's working in this world through Christ, all the enemies of God and man will go first, and death will be last. Please notice he does not say death is the worst enemy. He is only the last one. There are worse enemies than death. There is sin, a much greater enemy than death, for it stands between us and God. There is Satan, who is only interested in seeing us spend eternity in hell. There are greater enemies than death. Death is just a secondary mischief compared to what sin can do. To be tried by death is nothing compared to being tempted by Satan. No, let the great enemies go down first. Let sin and Satan be smitten first, and save death till last. Then death will hardly be an enemy when the other enemies are destroyed.

There is therefore some practical advice to be given about death. Since death is to be last, then let him be last! Don't get the order of things confused. Don't fret about death before you need to fret about it. Don't try to receive the grace to die before you need that grace. Ask for grace to live while you live, and when death is at the doorstep, then ask for the grace to die. You don't need a boat until you get to a river! Ask for the grace to live, and glorify Christ in your life, and then you will have dying grace when dying time comes. Your last enemy is going to be destroyed, but not today. There are a great number of enemies to be fought today, but not death, so be content to let this last enemy go for a while. God will in due time help you overcome your last enemy, but meanwhile, see to it that you overcome the world, the flesh, and the devil, today. If you live well, you will die well.

It is extremely practical on God's part to let the last enemy be death. Have you ever wondered what life would be like without death? I suspect it would be quite boring, especially since sin entered the world. None of us would try very hard to make something of ourselves, nor would we make such an effort to please God, if it were not for death. The thought of death stimulates us to great things. We know our frailty, and we know we are not going to be around long, so we try so much harder to be something and do things we might never do if we knew we would be here forever. We want to be remembered, so we do nice things, along with evil things. But the problem of being remembered would not be a problem if death were not the last enemy.

Think of the beauty that has come to this earth and to us, given to us by people who were so aware of their frailty they wanted to do something great to be remembered, and we are beneficiaries of all that beauty. Thomas Mann once said that without death, there would not be any poets. I wonder if he is right? Would no one be inspired to write poetry, were it not for our last enemy? Socrates and Plato both said there would not be any reason for philosophy or philosophers if we didn't have to study the problem of death. The first known writing of all literature from ancient Babylon was on death. The great music of the world has as its underlying theme "death." Michaelangelo said nothing existed in him which death had not carved with its chisel. We are recipients of great things because of our constant companion, the last enemy, death, which constantly reminds us of our frailty. So we do the best we can in the few short years we have.

It is also true that if there had been no death, the saints of God would not have their greatest opportunity to demonstrate the faith in Christ which is theirs. It is the highest offering we can make to our God, to say to Him: "Here is my life. You gave it, and I give it back to you." Those martyrs of old gave Christ a glory when they laid down their lives. He would never have had that glory if they had denied Him. But He was their Savior and Lord in life and death. They waded through streams of blood to offer their lives to Him who gave it.

When we die, we can offer the Lord the same gift. It will be the greatest demonstration of our faith and love for Him when we die with the assurance that everything God said to us in love will be done for us. That will be my supreme offering to God when I give my life back to Him freely and without fear. If I can offer my death to Him without fear, that will be my offering of faith He has asked of me. I could not offer such a gift were it not that death is the last enemy I have. I offer my last enemy to God in faith that He will take me with Him into eternal bliss. This is why I will lay me down in peace, for I can offer my last enemy to God. It is the greatest offering I can give to God.

There is a lovely old legend from Greek mythology about the hero Ulysses. It was said of him that one day he returned home from one of his adventures to find that the entire nation was in mourning. When he asked why they were mourning, he was told: "Haven't you heard? Our queen is dead." When he hurried to the palace, he discovered it was true. The lovely queen was dead. She, who was the heart of the nation, was gone. Ulysses then went on his most perilous adventure. He went out to the lonely tomb and wrestled with that ancient enemy, death, and fought death for the life of the queen. He snatched from death the life of the queen and took her back to the palace in his arms, handing her to the king alive. As he handed her to the king, he said, "See, I give her back to you."

In ancient lore, there was never any hope that this story was true. But bring that story over into Christianity, and it *is* true! Our Christ went to that lonely grave and wrestled death and conquered him for us, and as He stood outside that tomb, victorious, He says to us: "I am alive, and because I live, you shall live also." What the Greeks could only wish for in their mythology, we know to be true. Our Lord and Savior, Jesus the Christ, has conquered that last enemy death and given us life forever.

Sermons for Special Occasions

In Flesh and Blood God Destroys Death

REFORMATION SUNDAY
HEBREWS 2:14-15

Robert Kolb

> Oh, then rejoice that through His Son
> God is with sinners now at one;
> Make like yourselves of flesh and blood,
> Your brother is the eternal God.
> "To Shepherds as They Watched by Night" (*TLH* 103, 3)

Martin Luther was a joy-filled man—because he had a friend, a relative, in high places, in the highest of places. They had not always been friends; Luther had not always been eager to acknowledge the relationship. Luther knew for a long time that the other fellow really did not like his attitude, and he knew that he just made a fool of himself every time he tried to make up to the man. But they got to be friends anyway when the other man came to Luther to say, "Things are all right between us. We can be brothers—because I have shared your flesh and blood and died your death. Therefore, I will give you life, and you do not need to break your neck anymore trying to make up to Me."

Luther's "Brother"

The man who said that to Luther is also God. He is God's Son, our brother, Jesus of Nazareth, who chose to make human flesh and blood His own. He came to Luther and introduced Himself so that they could be brothers, just as He has come to us to be our brother too. Jesus made Luther feel quite at home with his Father as well. They talked back and forth all the time. Luther heard the Father speak as he studied the Scripture and as he listened to the message of God in the proclamation and in the conversation of other Christians. He replied to God in prayer, and he did so frequently: it is said that he prayed three hours a day—though not just with hands folded. Luther talked with God as he went about his normal activities. He let his Father and Brother know that he liked what they were doing for him and said thanks. He let them know that he needed something as the occasion arose. He gave them advice on how to help somebody else.

Some people think that God is so special that He must be far away. Luther knew that God is so special because He has come close to us. Some people think that God must be above getting Himself dirty in the muck and mire of this earth if he is going to be great. Luther knew that God is great just because He came to this earth, walked dusty roads as a man, and was laid to rest as a corpse in the earth. Some people think that God has to be invisible and that He has to accomplish what He wants with flashes of lightning, with magic, with overwhelming displays of power, if He is going to be a God worthy of the name. Luther knew that God works through selected elements of His own created order, through human flesh, through human words, through water and wine and bread. Luther knew God comes to us as one of us, and that He does his work for us through other people, whom He has called to do His work for Him, often in little, insignificant ways that some people do not think worthy of someone as important as God.

Martin Luther was a good friend of Jesus Christ, but he never got over a certain degree of awe and wonder when he thought of God who is at one with us in flesh and blood. On the one hand, Luther could speak rather sharply to God when he thought God was not giving him the comfort promised from the empty tomb. He could shake his fist in God's face and point to the crucifix on the wall and say, "You promised," when he felt depressed over his own sins and wanted to be cheered through God's promise of forgiveness in the cross. But, on the other hand, Luther was always amazed and awed by the fact that in the manger, in diapers, had lain a baby who had made the heavens and the earth. He just never got over marveling that on the cross God's own blood had trickled and oozed. God in the flesh, in the streets of the city; God eating grain in the fields; God sobbing before the grave of a friend; God under the whip; God with blood on His face; God crying "It is finished," and dying; the living God with holes in His hands and a gash in His side, saying to His friends, "Because I made it through death, you will, too": Luther could not suppress a joyous laugh, a clap of delight, a happy grin when he thought how God had picked up flesh and blood and bones to deliver us from the mess we have made of our lives.

Luther knew that there is at the right hand of God, in the very counsel of the Holy Trinity, a human being, tugging at the Father's sleeve saying, "I know what it is like to be faced with hunger. I know what it is like to have friends let you down. I know what it is like to be betrayed." Luther turned to Him, the God-man, at the top, his brother and friend in high places.

Luther decided to depend on his own plan for living and then realized he had not been depending on God. He took his guilt to his Brother and said, "God, forgive me. You have already suffered for my disobedience and rebellion against you." Luther used his busy schedule as an excuse for not consoling a person in need of cheer, and he felt ashamed. He turned to his God and said, "I just cannot seem to do the good I want to do, and I always seem to be doing the evil which I would like to avoid." He felt then the hand of Jesus of Nazareth on his shoulder and heard His words, "I accept you, for I died to take away your mistakes and failures." Luther was afraid that Emperor Charles V would send his troops to destroy Luther's church and put him to death, so he turned to his Brother in heaven and asked, "What are we going to do about the big evils out there which are beyond my control and which may well do me in?" He heard the Lord, our Brother, say, "Martin, remember that my death and resurrection put all those evils in the proper perspective. None of them is as powerful as the breath of life blowing out of my tomb." Then Luther remembered that the wind of God's saving power which had blown the rock away from in front of the tomb had also swept all the clouds away from the horizon of his life.

Luther's Good Life Through His "Brother"

God's coming back from death made Luther's life a clear day, and he could see forever, into the stretches of eternity. There he saw that Jesus Christ had prepared the good life for him. He knew he had nothing to worry about. He was confident that his Savior, his Lord, his Brother, would take care of him. He knew that he had been freed from all his need to be concerned about his own failure to serve God, so that he could delight in God's coming to him with forgiveness for his sin and with power which enabled him to serve the Lord after all.

Each day Luther realized that he had botched life once again. He admitted his faults and his failure. He was shaken and shamed by how often he broke God's law and set aside his plans for life. He was chagrined again and again as he realized that once more he had turned his back on his Father and had failed to recognize his Brother as the Lord of his life. But he always felt the joy which comes with the warmth of God's love when we realize that God has reconciled us to Himself and embraced us as His own through Jesus of Nazareth.

Luther marveled at God's love in Christ and at how lovingly God brings us this love and reminds us of it. God uses human language to let us know how He brings us His love, and also to deliver its power and to reshape our lives as He recreates us through it. God uses water with that Word to wash away our sins, to put us to death as sinners that we might be buried in Christ's tomb and be brought out alive as people who in Christ's resurrection have been given a new lease on life. God uses bread and wine and His own body and blood, united together in His own Supper, to bring us forgiveness and strength as it unites us with our heavenly Brother. Luther marveled at God's exhibition of love in the Lord's Supper; he never did figure out exactly how God did it, but he took Jesus at His Word and exulted as he received joy and peace and strength from

Christ's body and blood as he confessed, "No greater love than this could bind us to God: His blood blesses us and sustains us. Here, in this Sacrament, we are reminded that He paid our debts. That makes us at peace with God as we enjoy His favor."

That peace with God, that confidence in His support and power, made a difference in the way Luther lived each day. He knew that God had indeed embraced His creation in love. He had walked among us in flesh and blood so that He might destroy the mightiest enemies of His human creatures, death, sin, guilt, all that disrupts our relationship with Him. To continue the battle against evils large and small in our lives God has further arranged to use the network of his human servants which He had established at creation to meet the needs of His people. Though He has not been on this earth in a manner as visible as He was in the flesh and blood of Jesus, that is, not since our Lord's ascension, He is present as the Holy Spirit commissions our flesh and blood to meet people's needs.

At Luther's time people thought you could please God by doing a lot of religious things and that the help you gave people around you was not as important as the show of religion you made. Luther said that we worship God in church so that we may be equipped to worship God at home, work, and play, wherever we may be in God's creation. Some people at Luther's time thought you served God best by doing something religious, but Luther taught that his Brother who had hung on the cross wanted to be served by us as we stand ready to lay down any part of our lives—money, time, skills—in answer to a call God gives us through the needs of those whom He places within our reach. Luther saw that God calls us to take care of each other as parents, children, spouses in our families, and he glowed with the realization that he and Katie had been called to be co-creators of their children with God and that they were serving the Lord as they played ball and sang lullabies and spanked and cooked and fussed over their children. Luther beamed with delight as he realized that his neighbors had been called to care for God's people by making them shoes or building them furniture and houses. He knew that God feeds us through farmers who plow fields and through butchers who dress meat and through grocers who sell it. He saw that God protects us and helps us as we work together as citizens of our community and our country.

But Luther also knew that each one of us is called in different ways to end the reign of evil in other's lives as He, our elder Brother, brings His Word to hear on the power of death, as He uses us to bring life in Jesus' resurrection to those around us. God calls some of us to proclaim His Word from the pulpit and others to share it at the doorstep. But above all God calls all of us to remind people of their sin and to bring to their minds the fact that God has become our brother to end the power of evil in our lives. We are called to do this at home, at school, at work, on the beach, in the backyard as we encounter people who are despairing in the face of death, who want to dodge their responsibilities toward others, who are separating themselves in pride or in shame from their loving Father and Brother. God calls on us to let people know how delighted we are that our Brother, who is God, has died and has risen to free us from sin and self-centeredness, so that we can be free in the joy and peace we have in Him, free to serve Him as we shine and beam His love through our lives into the lives of others. For that is the way God gets His work done; that is the way He makes sinners die to death and arise to life which has no end.

Martin Luther heard God calling, and the Holy Spirit brought him to answer that call. Because of this he was a happy man. We are filled with joy, too, today because we know that our Brother, eternal God in human flesh, has freed us and forgiven us through His death and because we are confident that he has chosen us to make his love real in the places where we live, where He lives through us.

Can November 26 Really Be Thanksgiving Day?

THANKSGIVING DAY
PHILIPPIANS 4:6-20

Lester A. Wolf

A number of years ago a guest Lutheran Hour speaker delivered a Christmas sermon *in mid-July*. One can have a Christmas Day, he must have felt, even when the trees are not up, when the lights are not on, when the stockings are not filled, when the mistletoe is not hung, when the yulelog is not blazing, when the carolers are not singing. Why, he must have thought, one can have a Christmas Day when *Independence Day fireworks are brightening our nation's skies*.

If such is the case, is it possible to have a Thanksgiving Day in February or in April or in June or in August? A more pointed question: Is it possible to have a Thanksgiving Day, a *genuine* Thanksgiving Day, on *National Thanksgiving Day?* On November 26?

"Yes, yes, yes," cries the Spirit of God, after which He proceeds to tell us how to accomplish this. He seems to say: "Cut the smaller word THANKS out of the larger word THANKSGIVING—and hang that smaller word on your praying hands, on your everyday lives, and on your horns-of-plenty!"

I. Tag Those Hands!

Paul, disgustingly restricted and hampered by his present imprisonment, gets out his paper, picks up his pen, writes by inspiration of God's Spirit, and sends a Thanksgiving Day card, as it were, to his Philippian friends.

Just as a Roman guard is constantly at his side, keeping an eye on him, watching every move he makes, so, Paul suggests, another guard—the peace of God which passes all understanding—stands by his mind and heart, keeping an eye on them, speaking words of hope to them.

What does the divine guard say? This: "God is not fighting you, O tentmaker from Tarsus-town! God has made peace with you, O apostle of the Most High King! God is deeply in love with you, O man of the prison chains!"

So Paul rightly concludes that he can stand before God's throne without a gram of fear; that in everything, in all cases, under all circumstances, he can make known to his Lord the requests of his aching heart; that he can be absolutely sure that God, hearing his requests, will roll up His celestial sleeves and do something about those pleas; that he can therefore pull up the windows of his mind and toss out all that is worrying him; that he can push open the doors of his heart and sweep out all that is hurting him or causing him to doubt; that he can lift the lid on his music box and let it play hymns of thanksgiving to "the God of peace," who happens to be His heavenly Father; that he can encourage his Philippian congregation members to follow in his footsteps, laying before God their *prayer books* (their intercessions and supplications), always placing beside those prayer books their well-worn *hymnbooks* (their songs of praise and thanksgiving).

How can Paul, imprisoned, even think about speaking of hymnbooks, of songs of praise, of thanksgiving? Peering into his past, he sees the many, many prayers which he prayed—and which God answered. For these he can praise the Lord! Facing the future, he can know that, if God answered the prayers which he prayed in his yesterdays, that same God will most assuredly answer in his tomorrows the prayers which he is praying now. So he can thank God for those answers—even before they are made! He can bless God for His helping hand—even before it is extended! Thinking about his past, Paul is able to pray *joyously*. Wondering about his future, Paul is able to pray *confidently*.

Too often, when we think about our past, we recall the dark clouds and completely forget about the silver linings. A thousand prayers God answers; one in His love He refuses to grant; and we, ignoring the thousand prayers which He answered, complain before His throne about the one which He could not grant.

A story, in which I seem to spot myself, comes to mind. A doting grandmother, against her daughter's better judgment or wishes, took her daughter's little boy to the beach one day. She would take good care of him—yes, she would! But in one of those unguarded moments the lad waded into the ocean's waters; and the tide, going out, carried him to certain death. For a miracle the grandmother prayed! God would have to understand her dilemma and bring the grandson back to her! He did. A wave, greater than any she had ever seen, splashed across the sands, broke in front of her, and deposited the little one, safe and sound, at her feet. A cry of thanks from the lips of the fortunate grandmother? No! Lifting her angry eyes toward heaven, she screamed: "OK, God! You brought my grandson back to me! But where is the cap that the child was wearing?"

A beautiful boy restored! For that she had no song of praise. An insignificant cap lost! For that she had a tirade of curses. Have we ever blamed God for the caps that were lost—and failed to thank God for the boys who were saved? If we can focus our eyes on the boys who were saved (on the many prayers which God answered), if we keep our minds off the caps which were lost (off the prayers which God in His wisdom could not grant), we will be able to pray *joyfully*—and couple to those prayers a splendid Thanksgiving hymn.

If we know God well, if we have measured His immeasurable power and weighed His unweighable love and fathomed His unfathomable faithfulness, we can pray *confidently*—and thank Him for answers which have not yet been given.

You see, if you cut the smaller word THANKS out of the larger word THANKSGIVING and hang that smaller word on the hands which you fold in prayer, any day can become a Thanksgiving Day—and November 26 can become a *genuine* one.

II. Tag Those Calendars!

Move, if you will, from the praying hands which are on your wrists to the yearly calendars which hang on your walls. Paul ransacks the everyday lives which we live.

In the corners of those lives he finds things which are "true"— real, functional, actual events. Good news came to our ears in some of our yesterdays, and we checked the good news, and it turned out to be true. A blessing from God's great hand!

Things which are "honorable" Paul finds in our lives. We have friends, relatives, and associates who are precisely that way. A blessing from God's great hand!

Look again! Here in our lives are things that are "just." We have had to transact business with many people, and in most cases those people were as just and as fair as we had hoped they would be. A blessing from God's great heart!

And here! Things which are "pure"—like the water which we drink, or like the gold which we wear! Things which are "lovely"—like the roses which we pluck or like the lilies which we plant! Men and women who are extremely "gracious" to us! Artists and scientists, musicians and physicians, psychologists and psychiatrists, educators and counselors, clergymen and theologians, lawyers and laborers, and hosts of others who are tops—"excellent"—in their fields! Folks all around us, small and great, who are "worthy of praise"! Blessings from God's great heart!

Come! Ransack the drawer of your life once more! Find it in the greatest blessing of all—the Gospel!

Jesus, who by thirty-three years of perfect living and by six dread hours of substitutionary dying manufactured the Gospel for us and made God's Good News possible, is "real"! He is not a dream, a bubble, a figment of the imagination, a fairytale fantasy! He belongs on the non-fiction shelf! He was! He is! He happened! He makes it happen!

The ransom which He paid to rescue us from our three horrible kidnappers—sin and death and the power of the devil—was His holy, precious blood and His innocent suffering and death. That ransom is "honorable," deserving of God's respect and acceptance; and that respect and acceptance it received! The Divine Judge called the ransom "just"—fair—more than sufficient to effect our release. This He could do because that ransom and He who paid it were "pure," without the smear of a single sin, without flaw, without error.

By that ransom we were not only rescued from the kidnappers who held us, but were brought to the Savior's cross where we were cleansed and washed and made "lovely" and "gracious," where by God's grace we became people of "excellence," children of God who—because of Christ's righteousness—are found by our Father to be "worthy of praise!"

There it is—the Good News; and it is in *your* drawer, on *your* table, in *your* mind and heart and life!

"Think about these things," says Paul. "Then *do* something about them! Sing songs which will bless the Lord who has worked these great wonders! Then lead lives which will bless that same Lord as much as your sweet songs do! What you have learned and received and heard and seen in me, practice; and the God of peace will be with you!"

Some thirty-six years ago a pastor quoted this poem in his sermon:

> God be in my head
> And in my understanding;
> God be in my eyes
> And in my looking;

> God be in my mouth
>   And in my speaking;
> God be in my heart
>   And in my thinking;
> God be at mine end
>   And at my departing!

To that I would like to add:

> And God be on my calendars
>   And in my everyday living!

For to *hear* a Thanksgiving Day sermon from a Christian pulpit is wonderful, but to *see* a Thanksgiving Day sermon in a Christian life is magnificent. So get busy! Take that little word—THANKS—and pin it to those lives of yours!

I want to do that, too—so that I, as your pastor, can say to you what Paul of old said to his Philippian parishioners: "What you have learned and received and heard *and seen in me,* practice! Together, you see, we can make November 26 and all of the days which follow it real, genuine, honest-to-goodness Thanksgiving Days!

III. Tag Those Cornucopias

Cornucopias and Thanksgiving Days seem to be Siamese twins, undetachable. It is hard to think of the one without recalling the other.

Well, Paul's Philippian friends didn't have too much cash in their cornucopias. Only a consuming concern for imprisoned Paul, a love which had budded in the past but was now bursting into beautiful bloom! A concern and a love which made Paul quite uncomfortable! Poor as church mice they were; yet by the hands of Epaphroditus they had sent Paul a gift which they really couldn't afford. It was beyond their means.

"It might be beyond our means," they said to Paul when he felt pressed to decline their gift. "But we can't afford *not* to give it! It is our way of saying thanks to God for the salvation message which He brought to us through your ministry! You cannot deny us this privilege!"

Paul thought of his own horn-of-plenty. Sometimes it was filled with prosperity. At other times it was filled with want. He knew how to adjust. He could accept the prosperity without letting his head get too big for his shoulders. He could accept the want without letting his heart get too depressed or bitter. He could do all things through Christ who strengthened him. Though very reluctant to do so, even now—through the Christ who was strengthening him—he could receive from his friends their more-than-generous offering. He was not worried about his Philippians. His God would supply every need of theirs according to His riches in glory in Christ Jesus.

His God would graciously repay them for what they had done. It was their way of thanking God.

How about us?

We, like ancient Israel, live in a good land. We have only 6% of the world's population; but we occupy 7% of its land surface, own 71% of its autos, use 56% of its telephones, listen to 50% of its radios, ride 29% of its railroads, and enjoy 83% of its television sets. Our cornucopias are overflowing. But how much of the overflow is used as a way of saying thank-you to God, the Giver of all these things?

Our contributions to the Lord are *delightful thank-you notes* which we can send to God to praise Him for making us, for redeeming us, for sanctifying us. Some of us see them as Paul did: a fragrant offering, a sacrifice acceptable and pleasing to God.

Conclusion

Very well! Do we really wish to make November 26 an honest-to-goodness Thanksgiving Day? Do we wish to make the remaining days of 1981—and all of the days of 1982—and every one of the days of the years which follow—honest-to-goodness Thanksgiving Days?

Then the Holy Spirit must move us to take the word THANKS, underscore it three times, and fasten it to our praying hands, to our everyday lives, and to our physical bounties—to our prayer-books, to our calendars, and to our cornucopias.

To our God and Father—whose Spirit longs to do that for us—be glory forever and ever! So said Paul. So say we. So be it.

Faith—a Study in Contrast

CONFIRMATION DAY
LUKE 16:19-31

Ronald H. Goodsman

Two men were talking about the Bible. The one man said: "Why do you get so concerned about how people use the Bible?" The second man looked at him a bit and responded, "I could answer you in many ways, but what are you really asking?" "I guess what I am saying is, the Bible was written so long ago, why get so 'hung-up' on it?" The second man smiled and confessed: "To me it could have been written this morning."

As you read the text, you have to say, "It could have been written this morning." It's so real, so now! The contrasts in it are all around in life today. Look at the comparisons—a man who's rich, a man who's poor; a sick man who's well, and a well man who's sick; a man who has, and a man who has not; a man in heaven, a man in hell.

Today is your confirmation day. Today you are making a promise of faithfulness at the Lord's altar. Today you are publicly declaring that you are choosing the life with Jesus, rather than a life without Him. We praise the Holy Spirit who works this faith in you. Yes, there are two paths in this life—one leads to heaven and the other destruction. We see this so clearly in our text.

Life on Earth

"There was a certain rich man who was clothed in purple and fine linen and who feasted sumptuously every day. And at his gate lay a poor man named Lazarus, full of sores, who desired to be fed with whatever fell from the rich man's table; moreover, the dogs came and licked his sores" (Luke 16:19-21). This is quite a contrast. As a person looks at these verses and then looks around in life, a question mark usually pops in front of his eyes. "Why does God allow these differences to exist?" "How come some people have so much, and some people can barely make ends meet?" "How come I am always the one who is sick, and my brothers and sisters never have anything wrong with them?" "Why does God allow these things to happen?" "How come?" "Why?" "Why?"

We look at Dives, the rich man, and Lazarus—studies in contrast—and we ask, why? Why did Dives have so much and Lazarus so little? Look at some of the descriptions of Dives in various Scriptural accounts: "There was once a rich man who dressed in the most expensive clothes and lived in great luxury every day" (*Good News For Modern Man*). "There was a rich man, who was clothed in purple and fine linen, and who feasted sumptuously every day" (*Revised Standard Version*).

Now look at the description of Lazarus: "There was also a poor man, named Lazarus, full of sores, who used to be brought to the rich man's door, hoping to fill himself with the bits of food that fell from the rich man's table. Even the dogs would come and lick his sores" (*Good News for Modern Man*). The thought of a dog licking an open sore is so repulsive to a person that is is almost impossible to imagine! "And at his gate lay a poor man named Lazarus, full of sores, who desired to be fed with whatever fell from the rich man's table; moreover, the dogs came and licked his sores" (*Revised Standard Version*). Here we see Lazarus eating things that fell on the floor, things that we, who are so concerned with hygiene, would throw away, in other words—garbage!

The life of Lazarus was not easy on earth, but he knew whose he was—the Lord's, and that made all the difference. God never promised him an easy life. God has never promised you or me an easy life, and you are all old enough to know that that is true, but He has promised to be with us and to give us enough strength for the day. In the Book of Isaiah we see those beautiful words which must have given much comfort to Lazarus: "Fear not, for I am with you; be not dismayed, for I am your God; I will strengthen you, I will help you, I will uphold you with my victorious right hand" (Is. 41:10).

Life in Hell

Our text goes on and says: "The poor man died and was carried by the angels to Abraham's bosom. The rich man also died and was buried; and in Hades, being in torment, he lifted up his eyes, and saw Abraham far off and Lazarus in his bosom. And he called out, 'Father Abraham, have mercy upon me, and send Lazarus to dip the end of his finger in the water and cool my tongue; for I am in anguish in this flame.' But Abraham said, 'Son, remember that in your lifetime you received good things, and Lazarus in like manner evil things; but now he is comforted, and you are in anguish. And besides all this, between us and you there is a great chasm in order that those who would pass from here to you may not be able, and none may cross from there to us' " (vs. 22-26).

In reading this portion of the text, one is reminded of the Scriptures which speak so clearly, "For what does it profit a man if he gains the whole world and loses or forfeits his soul" (Luke 9:25). Or in reading this text, the Parable of the Rich Fool comes to mind. Here we see a farmer who spent his whole life in "getting ahead," "providing for his family," "planning for his retirement," "trying to give his family the very best," or whatever other phrase you would care to use. In all of this he had no time for God. When everything was all set and the barns were full, he thought that now he could enjoy these things and catch up on all that he had missed. "But God said to him, 'You fool! This night your soul is required of you; and the things you have prepared, whose will they be?' So is he that lays up treasure for himself and is not rich towards God" (Luke 12:15-21).

A great lesson can be learned from the movie, "The Towering Inferno." Here we see a party of the great people in society celebrating the completion of the world's tallest building. This was the building built to show the genius of man, the perfection of age. This was the building that was built to withstand anything. The ribbon is cut. The party begins. The champagne begins to flow as toasts are drunk to the genius of man. In the midst of all this, the building is on fire and is destroyed in a nightmare of suffering. You watched it go up in flames and you wondered. Was this God's way of destroying a heathen temple? Do we really just build buildings, or are they really temples built in our worship of the great god called MONEY?

Newsweek Magazine once had as the cover picture a stack of silver dollars. On them were written the words, "In Oil We Trust."

In 1929 people jumped out of windows for religious reasons their god, "Money," had failed them. They had put all their trust on the altar of this god, and this god had not proven faithful. This was the god that Dives worshiped. He learned too late.

One person said that hell is truth seen too late. Another man has said that we need to be reminded of it more often. Dives would agree here. He said to Abraham, "Then I beg of you, father, to send him (Lazarus) to my father's house, for I have five brothers, so that he may warn them, lest they also come to this place of torment.' But Abraham said, 'They have Moses and the prophets, let them hear them.' And he said, 'No, father Abraham, but if someone goes to them from the dead, they will repent.' He said to him, 'If they do not hear Moses and the prophets, neither will they be convinced if someone should rise from the dead' " (vs. 27-31).

It has been said that "the doctrine of hell should be preached in all its terribleness. It is no kindness to spread a pretty covering of leafy branches over a pit into which many have fallen and broken their necks. That may be the cunning hunter's business, as it is the business of him who hunts the world for souls. But it is not the business of preachers to ruin men's souls in order to spare their feelings."

Where is your trust? In what do you put your trust? Dives put his in money. Lazarus put his in God.

Life in Faith

"The poor man died and was carried by the angels to Abraham's bosom." (v. 22). I'm sure that one of the first things he said as he entered eternity was "Lord, now I see why! Now I know why!" It was Paul who said: "Now we see through a glass darkly, but then face to face" (1 Cor. 13:12).

Lazarus may not have had much of a life as far as the things of this world goes, but he had all that was important—faith and trust in God! He could say with the apostle Paul: "I reckon that the sufferings of this present life are not worthy to be compared with the glory which shall be revealed in us" (Rom. 8:18).

As was said before, hell is seeing truth too late. That's why Lazarus is in heaven. He saw the way of salvation. He knew the way to heaven. Jesus said: "I am the Way, the Truth, and the Life; no one comes to the Father but by Me" (John 14:6). Dives trusted in money and went to hell. Lazarus trusted in the blood of Jesus Christ which was shed for him on the cross and received the crown of life.

What does it mean to have faith? What does it mean to trust? There's a story that illustrates this. A tightrope walker stretched a rope over Niagara Falls. A crowd gathered to watch him walk. He looked at the crowd and then went to a microphone and asked, "How many of you believe that I can walk across this wire and come back?" The crowd hesitated. They looked at the thin wire. They looked at the terrible drop over the mighty rushing falls. They looked at the man. In a hesitating way they said, "You can do it, you're a tightrope walker." He walked across the wire and came back. The crowd cheered and cheered. He came to the microphone again and said, "Now, who believes that I can walk across backwards and come back safely?" Again they looked, and then they yelled, "You can do it, you're a tightrope walker!" He walked across and came back. The crowd cheered more wildly than they did the first time. Again he came to the microphone. When all was quiet, he said: "Now, who believes that I can walk across and come back with this chair tied to my back?" Now they were really screaming. "You can do it, you're a tightrope walker!" He walked across and came back. The audience was wild. The cheering continued for what seemed like forever. Again he went to the microphone. He said: "You have seen me walk across and come back. You've seen me walk across backwards and come back. You've seen me walk across with this chair on my back and come back. You've seen me do things that no one else is able to do. Now for my next feat, who will get in the chair?" That's faith! Who will get in the chair? We totally put our trust in Jesus Christ, trusting that He will not fail us, trusting that He will bring us safely home to Himself in heaven. That's faith!

What was it that enabled Lazarus to bear his cross, the faith that enabled him to say, "Jesus Christ died for me?" "He lives!" What was it that enabled people to bear their cross in the early church, to confess, "He lives!"? What was it that gave people the hope at the turn of the century? Wasn't it in the fact that "He lives!" Where is the same strength to be found today? Is it not in that marvelous fact that "He lives!" Death could not hold on to Jesus Christ. The grave was not able to keep Him. The devil was not able to destroy Him. "He lives!"

You see, Lazarus knew Jesus. He may not have known worldly goods or good health, but He knew his Savior. He knew that God never promised to make us rich. He never promised to make us famous, popular, good-looking, or smart. But He did promise to send us a Savior (Gen. 3:15), and this Savior, Jesus Christ, promised that He would never leave us (Matt. 28:20). God said, "Behold a virgin shall bring forth a son, and they shall call His name Immanuel, which being interpreted is 'God with us.' " (Matt. 1:23).

If God would love us enough to send His only-begotten Son, the "apple of His eye," to suffer the agony that Jesus suffered in order to save our souls, He is not going to forsake us. Jesus bought us with

His holy precious blood. He has forgiven my sins and your sins. He has cleansed the sores on my soul, which are the results of sin, with His own blood. I am alive as a new person in Jesus. Now I am His—forever! He has gone to prepare a place for us and will return for you and me just as certainly as He returned for Lazarus. We also can say with Lazarus and Paul again, "Yes, I reckon that the sufferings of this present life are not worthy to be compared with the glory that will be revealed in us" (Rom. 8:18). These blessings are only in the Lord Jesus Christ. "What must I do to be saved? Believe on the Lord Jesus Christ and you will be saved" (Acts 16:30-31).

This is the faith of your baptism. This is the faith that you are being confirmed in. This is the faith that is centered only in the person and work of Jesus Christ. This is what we are confirming today, and for the rest of us here—renewing. In closing I charge you with the last two verses in the Small Catechism:

> Be thou faithful unto death, and I will give thee a crown of life (Rev. 2:10).
> Hold that fast which thou hast, that no man take thy crown (Rev. 3:11).

Be to Him Commended

ONE HUNDREDTH ANNIVERSARY
ACTS 20:32

Arthur H. Drevlow

One hundred years ago a small congregation was cast upon the rippling waters of time. Christian faith organized a congregation and divine providence watched over it. That little congregation was blessed with pastors who announced God's plans for the salvation of humanity; in it were found men, women, and children who said with young Samuel: "Speak, Lord, for Your servant is listening" (1 Sam. 3:10).

Little by little a family of believers was gathered. The congregation was small enough and so frail that it could have been removed from its place. Yet the divine Founder did not permit this. This anniversary underscores the assertion: "Happy are the eyes that see what you see" (Luke 10:13).

There is a hymn verse directing us both to the past and the future. It says, "With the Lord begin thy task, Jesus will direct it. For His aid and counsel ask, Jesus will perfect it. Every morn with Jesus rise, and when day is ended, In His name then close thine eyes: Be to Him commended!" Let this day express the wish:

Be to Him Commended

I. Appreciate God's Word and Grace

"And now, brethren, I commend you to God, and to the Word of His grace, which is able to build you up." This is Paul's farewell address to the elders at Miletus. Paul's entire ministry had been a testimony to "the Gospel of the grace of God." This Word of grace has been the strength of this congregation the past century. The central activity of congregational life has been the acts of worship in God's house. Family worship, instruction by various agencies of the congregation have all exerted a vital role; yet what has been announced in the house of God has reached the largest percentage of the membership throughout the years. Spiritual fathers of Lutheranism stated this in the Apology of the Augsburg Confession as they said: "Of all the acts of worship that is the greatest, most holy, most necessary, and highest . . . to preach the Word of God." Do you appreciate what God's Word has done for you for one hundred years?

The wonderful means God's Spirit used to build this congregation is called the means of grace. The means of grace are composed of the Good News of salvation, frequently called the Gospel and the Sacraments. For their building up in the faith, St. Paul commended his hearers to "the Word of grace," which he treasured so highly. God is in His Word. When that Word is spoken, the Good News about our Lord Jesus Christ, who is cradled in the Scripture, then the Spirit of God enters human hearts. As that Word takes root, the power of the Spirit becomes apparent. By receiving our Lord Jesus as our Savior from sin, we are lifted out of our lost condition. The means of grace have power to renew people inwardly. Have you noticed that when this takes place you observe a life-style that pleases God and Christian men and women? This is what the Spirit of God has been doing here during the span of one hundred years. Every service has featured the reading and preaching of that Word; from Bible and Catechism its influence has extended to every believing member of this flock. This day, then, is a memorial to God's Word and grace. As we "commend you to God and to the Word of His grace," may yours be a profound gratitude for the heavenly blessings. Cultivate a desire to use that Word each day, for the center of that Word and its message is Christ the Word of Life! Offer an unyielding loyalty to its doctrine and instruction.

II. Submit to the Power of God's Word

As we join the hymnwriter in his prayer, "Be to Him commended," we encourage you to submit to the power of God's Word. Our church often harks back to the Formula of Concord, which observes that "Holy Scripture remains the only judge, rule, and norm according to which as the only touchstone all doctrines should be understood and judged as good or evil, right or wrong." This anniversary day suggests that we submit to this Word constantly as we proclaim Christ the Word as Lord of Life.

In submitting to this Word, one discovers its power. The apostle says it "is able to build you up." The man who uttered these words once tried to build himself up by the bootstraps of his own good works. However, when he uttered the words and phrases before us, his dependence upon his own goodness had been shattered, and he was glad to receive the holiness of Christ as his very own. That selfsame Word has been building up the members of this congregation for the past century. On the foundation of God's work of reconciliation in Christ, the power of divine grace builds its holy superstructure: a new life of faith in obedience to Christ and His gracious will. For a century the love of the Savior has been shining in this congregation, and its light has been reflected in words and actions performed to please and honor Him. For many people this divine power has been reaching deeper into human lives. Has that always been true in your life? Have you followed the advice of the apostle in permitting "the Word of Christ to dwell in you richly" as available from the Word and Sacrament, which this parish extends to all? Should you ask, how deeply shall I eat and drink this spiritual food? Let the Savior's words guide you, "If you are thirsty ... Come ... take the water of life freely" (Rev. 22:17). Is it your constant aim and ambition to grow in faith and daily demonstrate your faith by your actions?

The close of the first century brings this congregation to a bend in the road. Will the second century find you continuing to submit your hearts to our Lord Jesus Christ and His revelation of Himself in the Book of Books? It would be a fatal mistake if this congregation were now to ignore, to set aside, to change, or contradict any part of the unveiling of Jesus in the Book of Books. Yet people often include to do just that. Some pick and choose what they will accept and reject of the Word of life. What seems inconvenient to them, they dispose by some trick of interpretation. Have you noticed such policies at work? Will you not rather continue to submit to the instruction that will direct your lives along God's way?

Thank God that your fathers built a school alongside the church. Support it and all forms of advancing adult instruction. Should some of you ever wonder if the luxury of a parochial school and expenditures for instruction of adults is so necessary, recall Watergate. The president of the University of Minnesota told the graduating class at Notre Dame that nearly every malefactor in Watergate was a graduate of a university such as Harvard. He posed the question: "Where did we go wrong?"

Responding to his own question, the president of the University of Minnesota replied: "The sad fact is that there is no moral guidance anywhere in our public schools from kindergarten up to high school. The fear of contamination by religion is so great that there is no place in our schools for teaching what is right or wrong." This is not to downgrade all public schools but to show they are limited in what they can do. This would suggest that you younger members of the congregation thank God for the wisdom of the pioneer fathers and mothers who sacrificed so much to build and maintain educational institutions side by side with our churches. Does it appear that our church schools are too costly in terms of dollars and cents? Then compare the gigantic cost of the Watergate hearings and the resulting loss of respect for America the world over.

With St. Paul let me commend you to continued devotion and study of that Word which is able *to build you up.* Just how does the Spirit of God build us up in our faith? Our heaven-sent Teacher uses His Word to give us, among other things, what the graduation speaker called "moral guidance." Your pastors and teachers have a guide for moral instruction in the Ten Commandments. They will be saying with Luther: "We have the Ten Commandments, a summary of divine teaching on what we are to do to make our whole life pleasing to God. They are the true fountain from which all good works must spring." Do not, however, restrict this guidance to those in their youthful years. The *St. Cloud Daily Times* stated: "Adult church members need religious education for their own sakes. When the storms of life beat about their heads, they need the kind of spiritual resources—the strength, insight, and understanding—that come ... from reading and pondering the Scriptures and wrestling with the claims and demands of Christian theology." Do you hear at this point an echo of St. Paul, urging submission to the power of the Word which is "able to build you up?"

III. Glory in the Inheritance Through the Word

Once again let it be said, "Be to Him commended." As you do so glory in the inheritance made yours by the Word. "And now, brethren, I commend you to God, and to the Word of His grace, which is able to build you up, and to give you an inheritance among all them which are sanctified." God's Word and grace come to us from another realm. The Spirit of our God has caused this Word to be placed before us through the medium of human language. It is to guide us through this life to the city that has foundations. This explains why the apostle sees our building up in the faith as being blest with "an inheritance among all them that are sanctified." Will you therefore treasure this day as a memorial of praise to God for all who have received the inheritance immortal?

Many in this audience will recall the occasion of the 75th

anniversary of this congregation. While this day has created much holy joy and enthusiasm, there is also a tinge of sadness. So many of those who gave evidence of joy at the previous anniversary no longer live among us or walk on our streets. Those of us who remain bear in our bodies the signs of the fulfillment of our text. However, why should sadness mar the thrill of this holy day? What a joy to know that the believers who are no longer with us are now "with the Lord." Be happy that those who have "known Him whom they have believed" now are enjoying the victory that Christ died to win. As you may read their names on the stones of God's acre, realize again that our Lord Jesus Christ who suffered and died for them and rose again promised them, even as He promises us today, "Because I live you shall live also!" So our real home is above. Then all the energies of pastor and people are to guide people through this vale of tears to the inheritance of those that are sanctified. Having now come to another fork in the road, continue to appreciate God's Word, admit to its power, and may our aims all tend toward the inheritance of the home not built by hands, eternal in the heavens. In spirit we join hearts and hands and say may we "be to Him commended!"

The Finest Song Ever Sung

WEDDING
SONG OF SOLOMON 8:7

David M. Albertin

The Song of Solomon, that Old Testament book of poetry from which your wedding text is taken, is also known as the Song of Songs. Such a high honor has been awarded to it because many consider this song, a love song, to be one of the finest songs ever sung. It is a song, made up of a number of shorter songs, which was dedicated to one of the finest and grandest kings to ever rule over Israel, Solomon. His glorious court provided an appropriate setting for these splendid verses. So splendid are these verses that one of the ancient rabbis of Israel, Akiba, called the the Song of Songs the "Holy of Holies" of the Hebrew Scriptures. Akiba defended his honored claim for this book on the grounds that here is the finest testimony possible to the love that exists on the part of God for His chosen people.

The one verse from chapter 8, which is your wedding text, is a fine example of this love. Listen again as it sings to you about the quality and pricelessness of such love. "Many waters cannot quench love, neither can floods drown it. If a man offered for love all the wealth of his house, it would be utterly scorned" (Song of Solomon 8:7). This love, eternal and without price, is the love of God.

God's Love Is Eternal

God's love is eternal. Nothing can ever put out its flame. No amount of water can ever quench its fire. Water is fire's greatest enemy. Fire, if it is to burn, must be kept away from water. That is the way it is according to the laws of nature. But that is not the way it is when it comes to the fire of God's love.

The inspired poet who wrote your wedding verse knew this well. He knew that the fire of God's love for His people could not be quenched. This he knew from both experience and history. He knew of many unsuccessful attempts to quench it. For example, he knew for a fact that there were times when God's own people intentionally tried to put out the fire of His love. Yes, there actually were times when they didn't want Him as their God any more. Imagine them saying such things as: "Leave us alone. . . . We don't love You any more. . . . We can't stand You anymore." Such words are like cold water being thrown on a hot fire. But the fire of God's love would not go out.

At other times the carelessness and thoughtlessness of His people was like the throwing of cold water in the face of God's love. It was like they were always confronted with the temptation to take His love for granted. You can almost hear them saying: "He'll always be there when we need Him." Consequently at times the people forgot to celebrate the festivals which were anniversaries of some of the great days made possible by God's love for them. Perhaps these anniversaries were not important to them any more, or maybe they thought that they didn't have time for such holidays.

In addition there were also other times when it appeared that God's love was not able to kindle any kind of warmth for Him in the hearts of the people because they didn't understand Him. It seemed as if it was so difficult for them to appreciate how important He really was to them. Therefore, they would go about their own business completely unaware of how miserable it would be for them if God loved them no more. They were blind to the fact that it was God's love that made things fit together in their lives. How cold they became towards Him!

Yes, an awful lot of cold water has been thrown on God's love by the very people He has loved. Yet no matter how much contempt, carelessness, or ignorance they demonstrated, He kept on loving them. All through the Scripture you can hear the same song being sung: God's love cannot be quenched. His Gospel of love and care, of forgiveness and renewal, is without end.

God's Love Is Without Price

God's love is also without price. You cannot buy or trade for what He offers. There is absolutely nothing you can give to get it. Contrary to most everything else in life, it is freely given.

How many times have you heard the expression, "You get what you pay for"? I am sure they are many. From little on we are told, "If you want something, you must work for it." Thus all through life we go about the business of trading: "I'll give you this if you give me that." This is a principle that is not limited to the marketplace or the negotiating table. It is also a motivating principle in the relationships between people at home. Husbands and wives, parents and children, brothers and sisters all practice it to one degree or the other. In fact, so common is this practice that it seems to be the rule by which we must live if we want to get along with each other.

But this is not the way it is with God. Without price, without silver or gold, without negotiating, without striking up a deal or making a trade, without even any merit or worthiness on our part He gives His love. No wonder then that all the wealth a person might possess is not only not enough to buy God's love, it also is not even necessary or wanted. God does not bargain. It is His style to love.

God's Love Is a Model

This style of God is held up as the model for human love. I think that was behind what Shakespeare had in mind when he wrote:

Love is not love which alters when it alteration finds,
Or bends with the remover to remove:
O, no! it is an ever-fixed mark,
That looks on tempests and is never shaken;
It is the star to every wand'ring bark,
Whose worth's unknown, although his height be taken.
Love's not Time's fool, though rosy lips and cheeks
Within his bending sickle's compass come;
Love alters not with his brief hours and weeks,
But bears it out even to the edge of doom.
If this be error and upon me proved,
I never writ, nor no man ever loved. (*Sonnets* CXVI)

Shakespeare sings the praises of never-ending and priceless love.

Joining in this song is another poet, Kahlil Gibran. He too sings of a perfect love and tells us where to find it.

Love gives naught but itself and takes naught but from itself,
Love posseses not nor would it be possessed;
For love is sufficient unto love.
When you love you should not say, "God is in my heart," but
    rather, "I am in the heart of God."
And think not you can direct the course of love, for love,
    if it finds you worthy, directs your course. (*The Prophet* p. 13)

The Key to God's Love: Jesus

Here is the key: "Say not, 'God is in my heart,' but rather, 'I am in the heart of God.'" That's like saying "God is love, and if you are in God, then you are in love; and if you are in love, then you are in God."

Here is the key, for when we say "God is love," when we are talking about the love of God, we are speaking of something far more than a passing human passion, a rousing of the emotions, or even the displaying of noble virtues. When we say "God is love," we are saying more than anything else that this is the love He has shown us through His Son, Jesus Christ. Here then is "your" key, "your" key to love. It is Jesus Christ.

John the Evangelist in his first Epistle is the one who has coined the expression "God is love" (1 John 4:16). However, if we are going to understand what he means by those words, it is important for us to put them into their proper context. Listen, as he writes: "Whoever confesses that Jesus is the Son of God, God abides in him, and he in God. So we know and believe the love God has for us. God is love, and he who abides in love abides in God, and God abides in him" (1 John 4:15-16). To be in real love, to know real love, is to be in Jesus and to know Him as Savior and Redeemer.

That means that He is also the Savior and Redeemer of your marriage. No matter how high your ideals are, the love of which Solomon's patron sings, the love of which Shakespeare and Kahlil Gilbran write, the love of God held us as an example for you, can and will be real for you only in as much as you are in Jesus Christ.

I don't wish to discourage you, but there will be times when the love between the two of you will fall far short of the ideal love the poets write about and the example of God's love held up before us. You are about to make some promises: "I'll love you always.... In sickness and in health, for better or for worse, to the end of time, I will not leave you or forsake you.... I'll go to the end of the earth for you." These words are testimonies of love. But sooner or later they will have cold water poured on them. There will be attempts to quench their flame. Perhaps some of those attempts will be intentional (especially when love turns to anger), perhaps some will be because of carelessness (when two people take each other for granted), or perhaps some will be because of ignorance (when two people just don't see the warning signals).

To make matters worse, there will also often be present the temptation to think that before you are going to give you are going to make sure you first get. Husbands and wives with varying degrees of skill play the game of trading off, bartering and bantering for favors, considerations, and advantages. It is in situations like that when the words of the Song of Songs serve as more than just a model of love. They point to the Christ who was, is, and who shall always be exactly what is meant by the words "God is love."

God's Love Is Redeeming

God is love, and His love is redeeming. That is what John meant when he wrote the most well-known words he ever penned: "For God so loved the world that He gave His only Son" (John 3:16). God's Son died on a cross so that all our sins might be forgiven. All! That also includes every one that comes from the hot bed of family feuds. Husbands and wives often do terrible things to each other. But nothing is so terrible that God through Jesus will not forgive. Time and time again, so often as it is necessary, claim that forgiveness of God. And in the forgiveness of God find forgiveness for each other.

God's Love Is Renewing

The love of God is also renewing. St. Paul tells us that "if any one is in Christ, he is a new creation; the old has passed away, behold, the new has come" (2 Cor. 5:17). Think of the fantastic implications that has for you as husband and wife in Christ. You are a new creation. When your life together falters, when you feel like giving up, remember the new lease on life which is promised to you by Jesus who pledges "I will never fail you nor forsake you" (Heb. 13:5).

Conclusion

After today has gone forever, remember the words from the Song of Songs which have served as your wedding text. Think too of what Shakespeare and Kahlil Gibran have said. But above all think of God's love for you through Jesus Christ. Here is a love which serves as more than just a model for your love. Here is a love which redeems and renews. It is a love which cannot be quenched and which comes without price. Such love in Christ is for you.

God Took Him

FUNERAL
GENESIS 5:24

B. Dale Thomas

Here's almost a complete summary of the entire life of Enoch. "And Enoch walked with God: and he was not; for God took him." (We find him mentioned also in Hebrews and then again in Jude.) But, basically, that tells us a lot. This man was so close to the Lord that God took him home in a very special way. The word in Hebrew that is used for "He took him" is the same word that is used when Elijah was taken up into heaven with the fiery chariot. We believe that both Enoch and Elijah were the only two human beings who were ever translated into heaven without seeing death.

We are using this text today, the last Sunday of the church year, as we have for several years, to reflect on our departed loved ones, especially those that have died during this past year. We are also using this as an opportunity to find strength to endure our loss, to reflect on our approaching death, and to be sure that we are prepared when death comes to us.

I. Death Does Not Respect Our Plans, Wealth, or Age

What the Scriptures do tell us about death is that it really doesn't respect your plans or mine. I don't know how many times I hear our people say, "You know, just two more years and he would have retired. We were planning to go to Florida." "Next year we were going to take a long trip. We'd never done that. We put so much hope into it, and now he's gone." So time and time again, no matter what our plans are, death comes, and it intervenes; it interrupts.

It also is no respecter of money. It comes to the rich and to the poor.

It's not respecter of age. It comes to the little child. It comes to the person in mid-life. It comes to the person in old age.

II. We Face a Mixture of Feelings When Death Invades Our Circle of Loved Ones

When it comes to somebody who is close to us, we have a mixture of feelings. One of the feelings that we get is *guilt*. We remember the last time we saw that individual. We were very unhappy with something he said or did. We weren't too kind to him. Maybe we even left in a huff. Now he is dead, and we have no way of setting that right. We feel guilty. I know there are many families where the husbands, wives, brothers, or sisters are not on speaking terms. One dies, and the survivors have deep guilt feelings. They should have made peace; they should not have let the division go on. I think of the moment when death occurs to a husband or wife. You can think of so many things that you should have done, and could have done, and could have said, but you didn't. And so there are all those guilt feelings.

Sometimes *anger* is there. We get downright angry at God. "Why did You take him, just at this time in our lives? It wasn't fair." We even have some people quit the church at that time, because of their anger against God's justice.

Also, there is real *sorrow*. When we are very close to someone, and he dies, that empty chair jerks at our very heartstrings. I find it so curious that men have difficulty expressing that feeling. They've lost a loved one, and they want to cry. Our society says that's not manlike, and so they didn't. Inside they're churning, and they can't release that sorrow. Yet, I think of my Lord Jesus Christ, and how he wept at the loss of His good friend, Lazarus. I think of Luther, how he wept at the loss of his daughter, Magdalena; and there is certainly nothing wrong with that. I find that, some years after the loss, even women are embarrassed at their tears when the name is mentioned, or memories come back, or a particular song is sung in church. They don't really want anybody to see. There's nothing wrong with those tears, because that's an expression of a very deep hurt and a deep loss.

And yet, at the same time, if our loved ones died believing in Jesus Christ, we should never weep for them as though there were no hope. Because there is *hope*.

There is another feeling that I think the Christian ought to be able to have when we lose a loved one. And that's *joy*. There's honest joy in our heart when they die believing in Jesus Christ. Of course, if they didn't die believing in Jesus, there's nothing to rejoice about. There's no hope, and they're lost. That's what I believe, and I hope you believe that. That's what the Bible teaches. Anyone who dies, not believing in Jesus Christ, is lost eternally in hell. And there is not a thing you and I can do about it. Except one thing—not follow them. We dare not follow them. We dare not be unbelieving too, and thus go to an eternal damnation.

III. Let Me Encourage You to Be Thankful

Let me share a few reasons why, in the midst of your loss, you ought to have thanksgiving in your heart.

Give Thanks to God

The first thing is to give thanks to God. Thank God that your loved ones were baptized; that the Holy Spirit came into their hearts and gave them faith; then kept them in that faith; preserved them in the faith until their dying breath. Sometimes for eighty to ninety years God's Spirit in His grace loved, preserved, and protected your loved ones from Satan's efforts to lead them to hell. And that's certainly something for which we ought to be very thankful.

Heavenly Sounds

I think of some of the sounds. I think of the sounds they heard before they died, and then the next *sounds as they entered into eternal life*. I think of some of our people who were in the hospital, the sounds in that room with the doctors and nurses, and the crying of some of the loved ones. Then the next sounds were those of angels singing beautiful, heavenly songs: Jesus Christ is speaking to them and welcoming them home! What a marvelous sound to hear from our Lord's own lips, "Welcome home, My daughter, My son."

Sights in Heaven

Think of the sights that have changed. You know, the sights of the doctors and nurses, or gathered loved ones in the hospital room, or the sight of an oncoming car, or whatever the last thing was that person saw this side of heaven. And then the next sights are those beautiful angels and all the hosts of martyrs and saints that have gone before, dressed in white robes, washed in the blood of the Lamb. Jesus Christ, the Lamb of God, sitting upon His great, white throne. The city of God, the streets of gold, the gates of pearl, all those wonderful pictures that the Scripture give to tell us heaven is really a beautiful place! And what a beautiful place for our loved ones to be!

I think of the *reunions* that happen, and that is something to be thankful for. Can you just imagine what it would be like to be in heaven, to meet Enoch and Elijah and Moses and Peter and John and Paul and Mary and all the many other saints that have gone before? And then think of the relatives. Think of our parents who have gone before us. Maybe even a child who died before us. Our spouse. And to be able to be united now with them forevermore. I think there are just so many things for which we can be thankful.

Heavenly Home

We really ought not wish them back. Sometimes selfishly we do. We miss them so. We want them to be with us here. And yet, this isn't home. They're home now in heaven. We give thanks that they're home with God where there is no sorrow, and no sickness, no pain, no death, no sin, no devil. How could we ever wish them back into this life, when we have to face all of these kinds of things day in and day out?

They won the victory; praise be to God! That's what St. Paul said in 1 Cor. 15:57: "Thanks be to God, who gives us the victory through our Lord Jesus Christ."

Memories

I think there is one other thing you can be thankful for, and that is *memories*. And, you know, nobody can ever take those memories away from you. I enjoy being with people after the funeral, because it is interesting how they begin to tell all these beautiful stories about their loved one. They laugh, and they rejoice, and I think that is beautiful. Years later those memories are there. Nobody can ever take them away from you. Those are some of the warm moments that are very dear and meaningful to you. And you have them as

long as you are this side of heaven. And when you get there to be
with God, you can rejoice in their presence once more.

IV. What About Us; Are We Ready to Die?

Well, I hope that is comforting to you. But really, what I have to
say has to do with you and me. What is our attitude toward our
death?

We Don't Want to Die

I don't want to ask you, "Do you want to die?" I don't think most
of us do. I imagine if somebody would come up with a gun and stick
it to our temple and say, "Do you want to die now or live?" most of us
would say, "Well, if it's all right with you, I'd kinda like to stay
around a while. I've got some kids. I want to see them grow up. I've
got lots of plans." Most of us don't want to die, unless we are in
intense pain, or things are really going badly in our lives. Then I
hear people say, "I want to die." But if life is fairly smooth and we
are fairly healthy, we really want to live.

But We Will Die

Maybe the better question to ask ourselves is, "Am I ready to die
whenever it might come?" Are we ready? You know the insurance
companies tell us that life expectancy is increasing. So most of us
have, on an average, an expectancy of living here longer than our
parents and grandparents. But, at the same time, the death rate is
still the same. One death per person. Each and everyone of us will
die, and there is not a thing that you and I can do about it. That's
the only sure thing in life. Nothing else is as sure as that. You and I
will die!

One of these days I am going to be in a coffin, and my friends
and relatives will gather around at my funeral. I know that for sure,
and so do you. It is a terribly important question that we ask
ourselves, "Am I ready to die?" What saddens me is that there are a
lot of people who think they're ready—but they really aren't! There
are a lot of people who think they've got it together—but they really
haven't.

Some Falsely Think They are Ready

I think of 910 cults members down there in Georgetown, under
Reverend Jim Jones, who decided to drink cyanide. Obviously, they
were not following the directions of the Lord. That was in direct
opposition to God. They turned their lives over to a cult and its
leader, and ended up being lost eternally. But most of those people, I
believe, probably drank that cyanide believing that everything was
all right; and they weren't afraid to die. And they had everything to
fear that you and I can imagine. Because to die without our hand in

the hand of Jesus Christ is to enter into an eternity of damnation and hell that will never end.

It's sad to me to talk to people who are not church members, and to see how absolutely self-satisfied and indifferent they are to what happens after death. They are not believers in Christ and really don't face death with any fear, and they should. When you try to talk to them about it, it just doesn't seem to compute.

What is even sadder to me is that within the church there can be people who persist in sin, and are not penitent for their sin. Yet, they can say all the right words. "Yes, I believe Jesus died on the cross for my sins." But they persist impenitently in their sinfulness. My Bible says those people will not be saved. My Bible says those people are going to be damned, too. Even though they're clutching a Baptism certificate in one hand and a Confirmation certificate in the other, they're going to be damned if they don't come with a saving faith before their Lord and Savior. That's why it's terribly important to share this with you on this day. Let's not get that indifferent about our death. Let's be sure we are prepared.

Enoch Was Ready

Enoch walked with God. What does that mean? A radio preacher once said it this way: "Every day Enoch was out there at the gate. God would come walking by, and Enoch would run out to greet Him and take His hand, and they'd walk together. During their walk, they'd talk about God and things of heaven, and they'd also talk about the earth and how to serve men better. Then Enoch would say, 'I've got to get back now,' and so he'd go back to his work and to his daily chores. One day when Enoch met God, they got involved in talking about heavenly things and spiritual relationships. Soon God said to him, 'You know, it's almost the end of the day, and we're a long way from your home. It's a lot closer to mine. Why don't you come home with me?' And so God took him."

Now, of course, that's putting a few words into the Scriptures, but I think it is a beautiful way of looking at it. And it certainly emphasizes the kind of faith that you and I need to have.

We, Too, Can Be Ready

Everyday we need to run out there and greet God. We need to take His hand in ours by faith. We need to talk to Him in prayer.

We need to listen to Him talk to us by reading His Word.

Daily we need to penitently kneel before the cross, and say, "God, I have forsaken You again. I've put myself in front of You. I don't think the thoughts that I should. I don't serve others like I should. God, have mercy on me, a sinner." And Jesus reaches down and lifts us up and says, "You know, I knew that all the time. I died on the cross just to pay for that sin. I love you, and I forgive you.

Now let's walk some more together. I promise to take you home with me one day."

Wouldn't that be beautiful, if on your and my tombstones those words could be written: "He walked with God. He is no more, for God took him."

For Jesus' sake God writes these words about your loved ones. As we continue to believe in this same Jesus as our only Savior, He will write these words about us, too!